Yale Repertory Theatre. *An Attempt at Flying.* Photo: Kirsten Beck.

Theatre Profiles 5

The illustrated reference guide to America's nonprofit professional theatres.

Introduction by Alan Schneider
Foreword by Sara O'Connor

Laura Ross, *Editor*
David J. Skal, *Creative Director*

TheatreCommunications
Group, Inc.

Theatre Communications Group, Inc.

Peter Zeisler
Director

Lindy Zesch
Arthur Bartow
Associate Directors

Board of Directors 1981–82

Sara O'Connor
President

Alan Schneider
Vice President

Marjorie Kellogg
Secretary/Treasurer

Lee Breuer
Rene Buch
Peter Culman
Robert Falls
Arden Fingerhut
Edes Gilbert
Adrian Hall
Alison Harris
John Hirsch
James Earl Jones
Bill Ludel
Zuri McKie
Brian Murray
Richard Nelson
Michele Shay
Donald Schoenbaum
Ron Sossi
Patrick Tovatt
M. Burke Walker
Michael Weller
Lanford Wilson
Peter Zeisler

Theatre Profiles Series
ISSN 9361-7947
LC No. 76-641618

Volume 5
Price: $14.95

Theatre Profiles 5
ISBN 0-930452-21-6

Printed in U.S.A.

Acknowledgements

TCG gratefully acknowledges the support of the Alcoa Foundation, American Telephone and Telegraph Company, Robert Sterling Clark Foundation, Equitable Life Assurance Society of the United States, Exxon Corporation, Ford Foundation, William and Flora Hewlett Foundation, Andrew W. Mellon Foundation, National Endowment for the Arts, New York Community Trust, New York State Council on the Arts and Scherman Foundation.

The editors wish to thank the following people for their support, advice and special assistance during the lengthy editorial process: Harvey Brater, Lauren Craig, Glenda Hastings, Nancy Kassak, Gilbert Lesser, Sara O'Connor, Alan Schneider, Laurence Shyer and Marilee Talman.

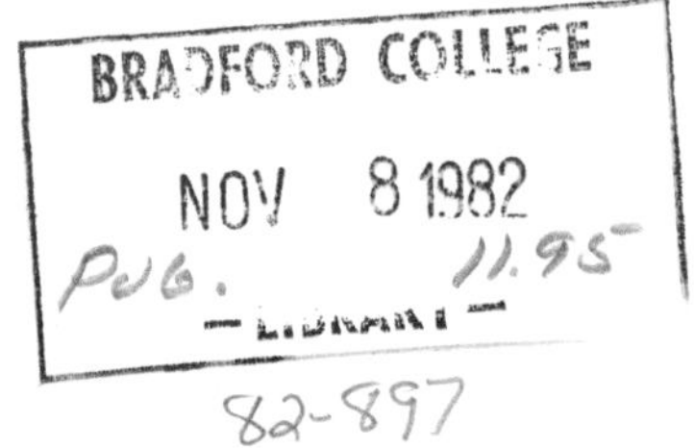

Dedication: W. McNeil Lowry

Photo: Nancy Moran.

This volume, published in TCG's 20th anniversary year, is dedicated with great affection and respect to W. McNeil Lowry. Without his vision and persistence as vice president for the humanities and the arts at The Ford Foundation from 1957 to 1975, theatre in this country today would be entirely different. A visionary with great perseverance and devotion, Mac changed the face of the American theatre because he believed in the importance of the theatre—and, indeed, all the arts—to society. What we know, irrefutably, is that there would not have been a TCG had he not invented it in 1961; what we more than suspect is that this book about America's theatres would have very few pages had he not supported so strenuously their birth, growth and development in a society that had previously known no tradition of noncommercial professional theatre dedicated to creating and preserving dramatic literature in communities all over the United States.

Peter Zeisler
Director
Theatre Communications Group, Inc.

New York Shakespeare Festival. Zvee Scooler and Craig Chang in *The Haggadah.* Photo: Martha Swope.

Contents

The Cleveland Play House. Wayne S. Turney in *A Christmas Carol.* Photo: Michael Edwards.

Introduction: The Whaddaya-call-it Theatre

BY ALAN SCHNEIDER

The theatre, like everyone who works in it, takes 20 years to achieve an overnight success.

As we come in our various ways—including the arrival of a fifth edition of *Theatre Profiles*—to observe the 20th anniversary of Theatre Communications Group's presence in our steadily increasing midst, it is good to be reminded that this anniversary more or less coincides with the "great leap forward" of the American noncommercial or nonprofit theatre (alas, a pithier term still eludes us!), the whaddaya-call-it theatre, as Zelda Fichandler once termed us. For some of us take our present numbers, distribution and status so for granted, that we forget most of us are still minors, if no longer entirely minor in the life of our society.

I shall leave to later historians the task of sorting out exactly what percentage of our development is *propter hoc* or simply *post hoc* TCG. Surely, however, in our current birthday mood, we can agree that today's panorama of theatre—that's a good name for it!—might have turned out considerably differently had not TCG sprung forth fully armed, so to speak, from the head of "Mac" Lowry and his cohorts at The Ford Foundation. Mac, along with his associate Marcia Thompson, was trying to deal with the scattered geographical and psychological disparity of the American theatre, the loneliness of those early long-distance runners in our theatrical wilderness. They were keenly aware of our "inadequacy of communication or the pursuit of common objectives" (to quote somewhat indiscreetly from the Ford Foundation's original "Confidential Memorandum" of February 27, 1961).

It was one month later that the Foundation announced its initial grant of $244,000 for the establishment of a Theatre Communications Group "to improve cooperation among professional, community and university theatres in the United States." Innocents at home, as Mark Twain would have put it, and as I am sure Mac and Marcia must have thought many times since. But then, in Nietzsche's words, the great moments of life "come not with the sound of thunder and lightning, but softly as with the footsteps of doves." The doves had to step lightly in this case; otherwise they would have fallen into a thousand booby-traps.

The changes in the work processes of the nonprofit theatre itself in these 20 intervening years have, however, been tremendous. Apart from our growth in actual numbers, which has been geometric, there has been a significant transformation in the level and even the nature of our work—and therefore in our fundamental relationship to the commercial theatre, to our respective communities, and to our national awareness of what the theatre should really do or be.

All along, it has been TCG which has heckled us, goaded us and encouraged us, pushed and pulled, illuminated the dark corners, and connected and re-connected the far-flung strands. It is TCG which, all through these 20 years has shown us not only the insides of each other's rehearsal rooms, box offices and budgets, but gotten us to sit down and *talk* to each other about

Center Stage. Tania Myren, Anne Pitoniak and Jo Henderson in *Agnes of God.* Photo: Richard Anderson.

what's really going on inside our very vulnerable interiors—inside our individual dilemmas and dreams and uncertainties. It is TCG which has not only helped us cast our seasons, but championed us; given us space, solace and advice (which we too rarely took); made us realize when we most needed to realize it that no theatre is an island, and that the bells of change, as well as of possibility, toll for all of us, usually twice on matinee days. TCG brought us each year to Chicago to listen to actors (until we knew so many we stopped hiring them), to Princeton to listen to scientists (who confused the hell out of us but made us think about ourselves in a different way) and to New York to listen to Peter Zeisler, Lindy Zesch and Arthur Bartow (who usually told us something worth bringing back home with us).

It is the American nonprofit theatre, aided and abetted by TCG in a thousand different ways, that has solidified the idea of theatres as opposed to "shows," long-run quality in place of long runs—the *theatre* instead of show business. It is TCG, aided and abetted by the growing vitality and even the growing middle-aged spread of the nonprofit theatre, which has continually fought for and stressed the commonality and community of the entire American theatre. And it is TCG, more than any other outfit, institution or force, which has continuously made us familiar with each other, aware of each other even though the map tried hard to keep us apart, and which has helped to define the American theatre as a national and nationwide phenomenon. Historians, please note.

Not that the American nonprofit theatre has been or is without problems, contradictions or critics. Our numbers have indeed grown amazingly, and some of our quality; but then the available financial pies don't go around so easily anymore, and we're not entirely sure what to do about that. A few years ago, we were being asked to justify our artistic existences in terms of social good. That seems a long time and place away now when there is the actual and increasingly explicit possibility that the base of federal support, for most of us our very life-providing plasma, is in danger of being taken away, or at least severely curtailed. Here again, we are grateful to TCG (and to the American Arts Alliance) for helping to mount a nationwide campaign of outrage and protest which gives some evidence (at least as of this writing) that it has made the most avid of Washington's budget-cutters at least pause to ponder the consequences, social and political.

Cable television is a-comin' 'round the mountain, and we're all keeping a wary eye on it, not yet really certain whether it will redeem us or ruin us. On our other side, having failed to lick us, the denizens of the Broadway jungles—producers, agents, operators of all kinds—are trying a variety of ways to join us. But as we have sadly discovered, alliances with the commercial theatre marketplace are not entirely unfraught with risk. Along the way, we may have made ourselves grow administratively top-heavy, over-bureaucratized and sometimes desensitized to our original impulses. The indigenously American disease of confusing ends and means is always in danger of infecting us.

Only a year ago, a close British observer of our theatrical goings-on around the country, writing about us in *Theatre Quarterly,* observed that the nonprofit theatre in America was not so much in any way "disgraceful" as it was simply competent, homogenized, "dull." Ours was a "theatre that doesn't matter," and we had to come to terms with that realization. Although I have myself, from time to time, waxed almost as critical in my thinking, such wholesale negativism coming after such a fleeting visit strikes me as unfair and untrue. Back in 1961 or 1962, I wrote in *The New York Times,* "Put bluntly, but with some sadness, the overall achievement of these theatres in acting and production is more typically good second-rate than first-rate. The talent available and the standards adhered to are good but not good enough. Both audiences and managements (if not their critics) tend to be too easily satisfied, too cautious, too concerned with the box office, too apt to follow where they should lead.

"It is not just that many of these theatres produce last year's Broadway success or ape Broadway while sneering at it. It is that they have not—except for a few conspicuous examples—found their own aesthetic purpose or identity. They exist to put on plays. They have initiated no new production styles (with the possible exception of the arena form); they have not evolved any first-rank acting companies; they have produced no new playwrights since the early days when Margo [Jones] nurtured the early Williams and Inge. They have no real influence on the shape or ultimate destiny of today's theatre. They have survived—and that is something—but at the level of the Bristol Old Vic, not of the Berliner Ensemble."

I am happy indeed, two decades later in 1981, to retract most if not quite all of these critical sentiments. For our situation has changed, and changed considerably. Not all of our present-day achievement is yet first-rate, but some of it—more and more of it—is. This past season, for example, Liviu Ciulei moved into the once-sacred halls of the Guthrie Theater and effectively spruced up the mantle old pioneering Sir Tony once threw over that part of the American landscape. John Hirsch is newly ascendant at Stratford, Ontario (American too, remember!). Ed Sherin has pitched his three-ring circuses now at Stamford. Mark Lamos is quietly but persistently digging in at Hartford. Jon Jory in Louisville is bringing in new playwrights and audiences from all over. Pat Brown is picking up from Nina Vance at a rejuvenated Alley. All these as well as other new breaths of artistic leadership and imagination have given us new hope and enthusiasm. Just as the continued presence of such youngish old faithfuls as Joe Papp and Doug Ward in New York, Zelda Fichandler in Washington, Gordon Davidson in Los Angeles, Bob Brustein transplanted to a new Ivy League campus in Cambridge, Adrian Hall in

Providence, Bill Ball in San Francisco, and Lloyd Richards and Arvin Brown in New Haven, give clear evidence of continuity and strength. Plus all the others I left out.

In a year in which Liviu Ciulei directs a *Tempest* that ranks with anything done anywhere in the world and hires Richard Foreman to stage Moliere, Nikos Psacharopoulos puts on *The Greeks* with an all-star cast of non-star actors that could not be matched anywhere else in the American theatre, Joe Papp braves both the Shakespeare and Gilbert and Sullivan buffs—with Lee Breuer's helicopters in Central Park and a totally contemporary *Pirates of Penzance* directed by Will Leach—we are definitely leading and not just following.

Nor do we any longer always just put on last year's Broadway hit; today that hit has, in practically every case, *originated* somewhere with us. In fact, I know of no serious American playwright of the past decade, from Sam Shepard at the Magic Theatre to Lanford Wilson at Circle Rep to Beth Henley at Actors Theatre of Louisville, who has not come from the nonprofit theatre. And few successful American performers, directors or designers who have not served their apprenticeship outside of the commercial theatre.

There is no question that we may not yet have produced a production style the equal of the early Berliner Ensemble (the later one is now in its own doldrums) or Britain's present Royal Shakespeare Company, which can bring over its productions of *Nicholas Nickleby* and charge the customers one hundred bucks for the privilege of seeing it; or even of the Broadway musical at its toe-tapping best. But let us not forget either that when Arena Stage or the American Conservatory Theatre plays before the "Establishment" abroad, or when Ellen Stewart's LaMama or Mabou Mines meets the "Fringe" elsewhere, at both extremes, their work is respected and extolled—and serves to influence those theatres they have visited. The days when the nonprofit theatre had "no real influence on the shape or ultimate destiny of today's theatre" are over and have been long over. Even though some of us are not always aware of that fact, which all those persistent notes and publications from TCG keep trying to tell us.

In what we must keep reminding ourselves is an amazingly short time, we have come a long distance. We have survived. So that our newly established roots can now dig in a bit deeper. So that our growing number of shade trees can spread their branches more fully.

The nay-sayers will always be with us to keep us from getting too carried away. They will continue to tell us that the so-called "regional" theatre doesn't matter; that it has rarely if ever belonged to its region. (Although whenever such a theatre accidentally or deliberately becomes specifically regional, either in its choice of play material or its personnel, they then accuse it of becoming too provincial or folksy.) When we were not doing nearly so many new plays, we were blamed for timidity (when in fact we were as yet simply unable to convince the playwrights and agents to join our cause). When we started to produce new plays in steadily increasing quantity and quality, we got bawled out for being interested only in doing tryouts for New York (which was not always so) and for selling our non-profitable souls. When we were able, before TV got them all, to field companies of actors and have them stick around for a season or two, we were blamed for encouraging mediocrity and for imitating the Europeans so abominably. When most of our theatres had to go back to casting for individual productions only, we were accused of giving in to the Broadway system, which we weren't.

At a time when theatres were doing mostly classics (as the Guthrie is doing now), we were told that we were just playing it safe. When we weren't doing classics, we were blamed for being afraid to tackle the grand themes. And if a theatre failed, as many did and always do for a host of reasons, it was always only because it was made up of fools and knaves—not because the critics or the audiences might have had any limitations of their own. If a theatre happened through some good fortune to survive and prosper, as a few have managed from time to time, that could only be because it was conservative and "dull." Because the nonprofit theatre, after a period of time slightly longer than a generation, had not yet produced international stars or more than a handful of world-class productions, or a new theatrical aesthetic, it was immediately dubbed inferior to Broadway. When it did begin to produce such stars or soon-to-be-stars as Patti Lupone, Kevin Kline, Meryl Streep, James Earl Jones, Ed Herrmann, Jane Alexander and a flock of others, all the gossip columnists soon forgot where they came from.

With all due respect to our critics, within and without, and all thanks to our friends and supporters, TCG prominent among them, that theatre which is TCG's constituency really does matter. It began to matter that morning some 20 years ago when Mac Lowry, with the whole weight of The Ford Foundation at his back and with the strength of his own personal vision, sat a bunch of us down in Canada to ask us what we felt was most needed to make the American theatre tick better. We told him: "Communication!" And he gave us a crack at getting a lot more of that to spread around.

And now, as the Broadway theatre retreats to its ever-shrinking although still glittering beach-heads of boulevard comedy, recycled musicals and pre-tested imports from other climes, it is the nonprofit theatre that is "profiting." In New York, in Los Angeles and San Francisco, and lots of places in between, this theatre is more alive and shining than ever before. It has come increasingly to matter—even to the purveyors of the "Tony" Awards, and soon, they tell me, to the Pulitzer Prize Committee. Who knows what might come next? For whatever the turns in the road ahead, it remains astoundingly clear that this theatre will be going on to new heights of artistic leadership and responsibility. It is now the nonprofit theatre which carries the promise of the future, for those who work in the theatre as well as for those who continue to want to experience it.

The pages of this book, once undreamed of in Horatio's philosophy, seem to me to offer up some revealing and fascinating previews of attractions yet to come.

Alan Schneider has been responsible for more than 100 productions in the American theatre, combining work on Broadway, Off Broadway, Off-Off Broadway and in Regional Theatre. He is known chiefly as a director of new and experimental works and has staged the original American productions of plays by Samuel Beckett, Harold Pinter, Edward Albee, Robert Anderson, Joe Orton and Michael Weller. He has had a long association with Arena Stage in Washington, DC, and currently serves as an artistic director of The Acting Company, a national touring theatre. Mr. Schneider is the former head of the Juilliard School's Theatre Center and currently heads the graduate directing program of the University of California, San Diego. Mr. Schneider first served on the founding board of TCG in 1961 and was re-elected to the board in 1978.

American Place Theatre. Mary McDonnell, John Spencer and Timothy Near in *Still Life.* Photo: Martha Holmes.

Foreword: On Being American . . .

The heart of the great American experiment has been the belief that a nation could be brought into existence whose sense of community would hold firm despite its immense geography, regional differences, and a culture endlessly assaulted, changed and renewed by wave after wave of immigrants from divergent and conflicting cultures. To believe that a nation could be forged out of such material flies almost in the face of reason.

Yet here we are, trying to weld a sense of community out of pieces of everybody else's history and a bare 300 years of our own. We haven't always done well. The majority/minority struggles leave an enduring trail of blood, greed and racism. Still, we *are* a nation, glued precariously together by the idea of community *based* on diversity. A ridiculous, magnificent dream.

Out of and parallel with this dream, a true national theatre has emerged. Not the Comédie Française or the National Theatre on the banks of the Thames, but a peculiarly American fabric of diverse activity blanketing thousands of miles of territory, serving millions of people and representing wildly independent aesthetic viewpoints. Theatre Communications Group today has nearly 200 Constituent and Associate theatres. These theatres, plus many others, have become a "national treasure" through a uniquely American brand of spiky, argumentative, individualistic self-help, cooperation and sense of community. To disagree and yet be together is a peculiarly American mode. Theatre Communications Group is in itself nearly unique in the world. This concept of a theatre community which thrives on the exchange of knowledge across conflicting aesthetics, artistic purposes and kinds of audience is treated with something close to awe in other countries. What's more, this network has the great strength of having grown *naturally,* out of the combined desires of the artists and their audiences.

We are building a unique national network, a treasure made up of hundreds of companies fighting their way toward excellence, and many of them understand "regional" in a positive sense. *One* national theatre company, or even a few companies, cannot serve adequately as the model we need if we are to reflect the American experience. We *have* a national theatre—a multiple and diverse one. What we must build is a national *awareness* of it, a desire to strengthen it and to force it to the highest possible level *wherever* it may be found. And there are no limits to its size or its creativity. In a democratic society, a national theatre is theatre for all the people.

Sara O'Connor
President
Theatre Communications Group, Inc.

Editors' Note

Now in its fifth edition, *Theatre Profiles* has become something of an institution among theatre reference books. First published in 1974, the biennial series is now recognized as the major resource for theatre professionals—actors, playwrights, directors, administrators, journalists and others all rely on *Theatre Profiles* as the most accurate record of the production activity, artistic evolution and financial health of nearly 170 professional companies nationwide.

The format of this year's edition has been streamlined to make the information even more accessible. The inclusion of director and designer listings in the body of each theatre's entry, rather than in an appendix, is intended to improve the book's readability and usefulness. Other new features include separate indexing for names and play titles, bullets indicating new plays and translations, and a new subcategory listing the "media resources" of theatres that have documented their work through radio, video or film.

All theatres included are constituents of Theatre Communications Group, Inc., the national service organization for nonprofit professional theatre. Information was requested in the spring and summer of 1981 from approximately 170 theatres, and the text of this volume is based on the materials they submitted. The following notes are provided as a guide to the use of this book:

Directors
The artistic and administrative directors of each theatre are listed. The information is current as of summer 1981 and does not necessarily reflect the theatres' leadership during the 1979–80 and 1980–81 seasons.

Founding
The founding date represents the beginning of public performances, or in a few cases, the conceptual or legal establishment of the institution.

Season
The months listed indicate the beginning and closing dates of the theatre's major performing season. "Year-round" indicates that the company performs throughout the year, often without formal opening and closing dates. "Variable" indicates a changeable or unstructured season. In such cases, current season information can be obtained directly from the theatre.

Schedule
Evening and matinee performance days are listed for theatres which have established regular performing schedules for the run of each production. Wherever possible, this edition also includes variable performance days (e.g., "Selected Saturdays"). Specific information on variable schedules should be requested directly from the theatre; please note that even regular schedule information is subject to change and should always be verified with the theatre in advance of attendance.

Facilities
Seating capacities and types of stages are included only for those theatres that own, rent or regularly use a specific performing space or spaces. Theatre facility names and addresses are included when they differ from the institutional name and or business mailing address. The information is current as of August 1981 and does not necessarily reflect the two seasons highlighted in the book.

For the sake of clarity, a common terminology for types of stages has been adopted, eliminating idiosyncratic nomenclature in favor of the following general designations:

Proscenium
The traditional, picture-window stage, which the audience views from a single "fourth wall" perspective.

Modified Thrust
Also called a "modified proscenium," it utilizes a jutting or fan-shaped apron on which much of the action can be played. The audience still maintains a basic "fourth wall" relationship to the action.

Thrust
All types of stage arrangements in which the audience sits on three sides of the playing area.

Arena
The audience completely surrounds the playing space.

Flexible
All types of stages and spaces which can be altered or converted from one category to another (e.g., proscenium to thrust, thrust to arena). Also included in this designation are "environmental" spaces or stages created to meet the demands of individual productions.

Cabaret
A simple performance platform.

Finances
Financial figures reflect the fiscal year most recently completed when the information for *Theatre Profiles* was gathered. All figures (operating expenses, earned income and grants/contributions) have been rounded to the nearest thousand dollars. While most are based on precise, audited figures, their purpose in this book is to provide a sense of the *general* relationship between expenses and income and the overall size of the theatre operation.

Audience
The estimated total annual attendance for the most recently completed season is provided, in addition to the number of subscribers for that season.

Touring contact
For the convenience of potential sponsoring organizations, specific names are listed for theatres offering major touring and residency programs.

Booked-in events
Many theatres regularly sponsor arts events or rent their facilities to other performing groups and individual artists. Interests in specific types of events are indicated to assist other companies and performers seeking performance spaces or bookings.

Playwrights Horizons. Christine Baranski, Griffin Dunne and June Gable in *Coming Attractions.* Photo: Susan Cook.

Equity contracts
Information on Actors' Equity Association (AEA) contracts is included for each theatre employing actors under union jurisdiction. Please note that the League of Resident Theatres (LORT) contract has four categories (A, B, C and D), based on the number of seats in the theatre. For more specific information on these and other contracts listed, contact Actors' Equity Association, 165 West 46th St., New York, NY 10036.

Artistic statements
All theatres were invited to submit an artistic statement of any length up to 250 words reflecting their current philosophy and goals, performance activities and community relationship. While most have been edited for style, every attempt has been made by the editors to retain the individuality and unique flavor of these statements. Because of the increasing importance of theatres not only as producing units but also as local cultural resources, descriptions of programs and services outside of regular theatrical production may also be a part of these statements.

Production lists
Productions of the 1979–80 and 1980–81 seasons (1980 and 1981 for theatres with summer operations) are listed with authors, translators, adaptors, composers and lyricists, along with the source of literary adaptations, as provided by the theatres. In the case of revivals, only the title of the production is repeated in the second listing. Bullets (•) appearing before titles indicate new plays or translations.

Media resources
Because of the growing importance of electronic media in research, training and performance, a new section of media resources has been added for theatres that have recorded their work via film, video and radio. Both dramatic and documentary works are listed, along with the names of producers. For information on the availability and distribution of specific film, video or radio productions, contact the theatre directly.

Photographs
Photographs were selected to convey the range and diversity of production activity. In general, individual performers are identified when appearing in groups of five or less. In this edition, special prominence is given to photographs of high technical quality.

Directors/Designers
Directors, as well as scenic, costume and lighting designers are listed alphabetically under each theatre, for both seasons combined. For information on specific production credits, please contact the individual theatres.

Theatre on Tour
A popular feature in the last edition among sponsors wishing to book theatrical events, *Theatre on Tour* provides another handy "at-a-glance" reference guide to theatres available for regional or nationwide touring.

Regional Index
To readily identify theatres located in individual states, a geographical listing is included.

Theatre Chronology
The "time line" history of the nonprofit professional theatres included in this volume is intended to demonstrate the amazing growth and decentralization of the American theatre.

Index of Names
All playwrights, composers, artistic and administrative directors, stage directors, designers and theatre founders appearing in this edition are listed in the Index of Names.

Index of Titles
For the reader's convenience, all titles of dramatic works are listed in a separate index.
As in the past, reader response will help to chart the course of the *Theatre Profiles* series as a fluid, ever-evolving resource. Special thanks are extended to the TCG Board of Directors for its assistance in the shaping of this volume.

—Laura Ross and
David J. Skal

CSC Repertory. Catherine Rust and Eric Tavaris in *Leonce and Lena*. Photo: Gerry Goodstein.

Theatre Profiles

A Contemporary Theatre

Gregory A. Falls
Producing Director

Louise Campion Cummings
Administrative Manager

Phil Schermer
Production Manager

Box 19400
Seattle, WA 98109
(206) 285-3220 (business)
(206) 285-5110 (box office)

Founded 1965
Gregory A. Falls

Season
Mainstage
May–October, December
Family & Children's
January–April

Schedule
Evenings
Tuesday–Sunday
Matinees
First Wednesday, second Saturday, third Sunday

Facilities
100 West Roy St.
Mainstage
Seating capacity: 454
Stage: thrust
Backstage
Seating capacity: 100
Stage: flexible

Finances
January 1, 1980–December 31, 1980
$963,000 operating expenses
$729,000 earned income
$406,000 grants/contributions

Audience
Annual attendance: 150,490
Subscribers: 7,479

Touring contact
Karen Rains

AEA LORT (C) and Theatre for Young Audiences contracts

A Contemporary Theatre has produced more than 100 new or recent plays for Northwest audiences since 1965 and is one of Seattle's six major cultural institutions. Its year-round activities include a six-play mainstage season, a touring children's theatre company, an annual family production and a recently inaugurated Backstage program to develop new scripts.

The ACT mainstage brings the works of important contemporary playwrights to the Northwest. Many mainstage productions are world, American, or West Coast premieres. The ACT Backstage, a "black box" performing space, houses a program for the development of new scripts and encourages emerging playwrights.

The Young ACT Company, which has achieved international recognition, annually presents original scripts on tour. It is the oldest Equity children's theatre company on the West Coast and has appeared at the Kennedy Center and at international children's theatre festivals. In affirming its commitment to theatre for young audiences, ACT expects to inaugurate an annual family production in early 1982. A yearly family-oriented Christmas show has been part of ACT's operations for several seasons.

ACT continues to be a leader in international theatre exchange, hosting individuals and visiting panels of international theatre representatives as well as soliciting local businesses to buy theatre tickets for foreign students in the area. The theatre also maintains a relationship with Australian theatre through exchanges of artists and presentations of Australian performing groups and works. For example, a distinguished Australian actor performed during ACT's 1981 season in a direct exchange with the Playbox Theatre in Melbourne.

ACT's other special activities include informal post-performance discussions of each mainstage play, signed performances for the deaf, free ticket distribution, student and senior citizen rush tickets, administrative and technical/production internships, theatre rentals and an annual humanities dialogue series. Subscribers also enjoy a free Creative Dramatics program for their small children, a Solo Series for one-seat subscribers, as well as newsletters and group sales discounts.

Productions 1980
For Colored Girls who have Considered Suicide/When The Rainbow is Enuf, Ntozake Shange
• *Catholics,* Brian Moore

Artichoke, Joanna Glass
Wings, Arthur Kopit
Buried Child, Sam Shepard
Starting Here, Starting Now, Richard Maltby, Jr. and David Shire
• *A Wrinkle in Time,* adapt: Gregory A. Falls, from Madeleine L'Engle
A Christmas Carol, adapt: Gregory A. Falls, from Charles Dickens

Productions 1981
Custer, Robert E. Ingham
Getting Out, Marsha Norman
Billy Bishop Goes to War, John Gray and Eric Peterson
Night and Day, Tom Stoppard
Loose Ends, Michael Weller
Whose Life Is It Anyway?, Brian Clark
The Pushcart War, adapt: Gregory A. Falls, from Jean Merrill
Seattle Eclectic, Rob Duisberg and Jean Burch Falls

Directors
John Dillon, Richard Edwards, Robert Egan, Gregory A. Falls, Judith Haskell, John Kauffman, Robert Loper, Eileen MacRae Murphy, Tawnya Pettiford, M. Burke Walker

Designers
Sets: William Forrester, Karen Gjelsteen, Bill Raoul, Shelley Henze Schermer, Scott Weldin. *Costumes:* Nanrose Buchman, Laura Crow, Julie James, Sally Richardson, Susan Tsu. *Lights:* Jody Briggs, Paul W. Bryan, Donna Grout, Phil Schermer, Frank Simons.

A Contemporary Theatre. Suzy Hunt, Daniel Daily, Steven Rose and David Hunter Koch in *The Pushcart War.* Photo: Chris Bennion.

Academy Theatre. Rosemary Newcott and Greg Gurley in *Canterbury Tales!* Photo: Charles Rafshoon.

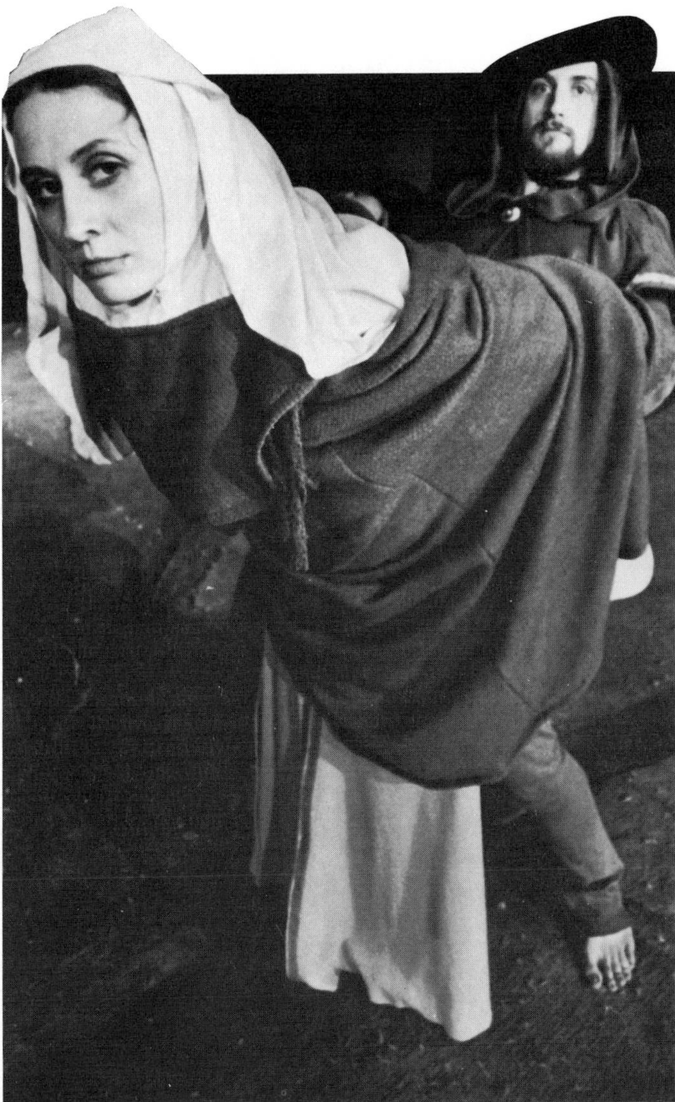

Academy Theatre

Frank Wittow
Producing Director

Nancy Hager
General Manager

Box 77070
Atlanta, GA 30309
(404) 873–2518 (business)
(404) 892–0880 (box office)

Founded 1956
Frank Wittow

Season
October–May

Schedule
Evenings
Wednesday–Saturday
Matinees
Academy Children's Theatre: Monday–Saturday;
Mainstage: Sunday

Facilities
581 Peachtree St., NE
Seating capacity: 450
Stage: thrust

Finances
August 1, 1979–July 31, 1980
$442,000 operating expenses
$184,000 earned income
$258,000 grants/contributions

Audience
Annual attendance: 120,000
Subscribers: 2,000

Touring contact
Nancy Hager

The Academy Theatre is built around a resident company whose annual performing season is concurrent with, and inseparable from, a continuing program of theatre training for professional actors and students. For actors, it provides a versatile company and the opportunity to build careers in Atlanta and the Southeast. For the community, it provides a thoughtful, actor-centered theatre which presents classic, contemporary and new plays, as well as an extensive share in the creative process through workshops and community outreach programs.

The mainstage season for adults includes a subscription series of four plays. Several of these plays remain in the repertoire for touring and other nonsubscription performances. The Theatre for Youth program provides three original plays for children and a regional artists-in-schools residency program of plays and workshops for elementary through high school students and teachers. Each season a new play on a given theme for older students is created around the contributions of students across the state. The Academy is a founding member and active participant in the annual Atlanta New Play Project. Its School of Performing Arts provides professional training, including intensive study in the apprentice and pre-company programs. The school also has its own Lab Theatre which produces 10 to 15 new scripts and lesser-known classics each season. The company plans to create one play for each mainstage season in the style of the unique physical and vocal work of the pre-company and company workshops.

Internships for college students provide credit toward their degrees and a small stipend. Other representative services include the In-Touch program for blind and visually impaired patrons, senior citizen programs, special projects with youthful offenders and adults in prison, and the traditional range of study guides, student discounts, etc.

The Academy is presently conducting a capital fund campaign for the purchase and renovation of a new home in a revitalized area of downtown Atlanta.

Productions 1979–80
The Caretaker, Harold Pinter
• *Mark Twain,* John Stephens
A Moon for the Misbegotten, Eugene O'Neill
• *Brothers and Sisters,* Frank Wittow and company
The Country Wife, William Wycherly; music: John F. Ferguson
Richard III, William Shakespeare
• *Tales of King Arthur,* John Stephens and company; music: John F. Ferguson
• *Doolans's Wake,* John Stephens and company

Productions 1980–81
A Moon for the Misbegotten
• *Families,* Frank Wittow and company
• *Alice in Wonderland,* John Stephens; music: John F. Ferguson and company
A Christmas Carol, adapt: Adrian Hall and Richard Cumming, from Charles Dickens
• *The Dream Nibbler,* company-developed
The Queen and the Rebels, Ugo Betti
Getting Out, Marsha Norman
• *Canterbury Tales!,* adapt: Arnold Wengrow, from Chaucer; music: John F. Ferguson
• *The True Story of Frankenstein,* John Stephens; music: John F. Ferguson
Emigres, Slawomir Mrozek

Directors
Barbara Lebow, Margaret Mosher, Rosemary Newcott, Leo Shapiro, John Stephens, Frank Wittow

Designers
Sets: Fred Fonner, Bryan Hager, Michael Halpern, Leo Shapiro, John Stephens, Ezra Wittner. *Costumes:* Katherine Munroe, Jo Weinstein, Erin Wertenberger, Judy Winograd. *Lights:* Keith Crofford, Fred Fonner.

Media Resources
Film: *Bridge of Hands* (United States Information Agency).

The Acting Company. Richard Iglewski, Keith David, Paul Walker and Richard Howard in *Waiting for Godot.* Photo: Martha Swope.

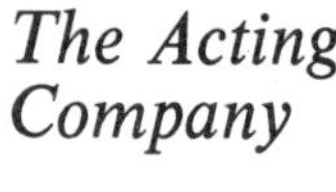

The Acting Company

John Houseman
Producing Artistic Director

Michael Kahn
Alan Schneider
Artistic Directors

Margot Harley
Executive Producer

Mary Beth Carroll
General Manager

Box 898, Times Square Station
New York, NY 10108
(212) 564–3510

Founded 1972
John Houseman, Margot Harley

Season
August–May

Finances
July 1, 1980–June 30, 1981
$1,098,000 operating expenses
$ 524,000 earned income
$ 574,000 grants/contributions

Audience
Annual attendance: 100,000

Touring contact
Rob Hill

AEA LORT (B) and (C) contracts

The touring arm of the Kennedy Center for the Performing Arts, The Acting Company remains the only theatre company in America founded for and dedicated to the development of American actors.

In 1972, John Houseman, then head of the Drama Division of the Juilliard School in New York, saw in his first graduating class a group of actors so talented that he felt they should not disband. Together with Margot Harley, now the company's executive producer, he organized the graduates as a professional company which made its debut as the dramatic wing of the Saratoga Performing Arts Festival in New York State.

The Company now consists of 17 intensively trained actors selected from America's finest professional schools, conservatories and resident theatres. Once chosen, they rehearse in the ensemble tradition of the company, taking on a variety of roles which they perform in repertory on tour throughout the United States. The performers sustain a rigorous schedule over an extended period, playing in vastly differing theatres week after week. This experience allows them further to test and develop themselves into the outstanding professionals for which The Acting Company has become known.

The second and equally important commitment of the company is to tour professional productions of both classical and contemporary plays to theatres across America. To date, The Acting Company has performed a repertoire of 39 plays in 199 cities, in 41 states, before over one million people, and has traveled more than 200,000 miles.

A number of the company's productions have received prestigious awards and nominations, including two Antoinette Perry ("Tony") awards and an Obie Special Citation for Outstanding Achievement. Numerous company members have gone on to successful careers in theatre, films and television.

Productions 1979–80
Broadway, George Abbott and Philip Dunning
The White Devil, John Webster
Elizabeth I, Paul Foster
Domino Courts, William Hauptman
Split, Michael Weller

Productions 1980–81
A Midsummer Night's Dream, William Shakespeare

Waiting for Godot, Samuel Beckett
• *Il Campiello–a Venetian Comedy,* Carlo Goldoni; trans: Richard Nelson

Directors
David Chambers, Liviu Ciulei, Jonathan Furst, Gerald Gutierrez, Richard Hamburger, Michael Kahn, Alan Schneider

Designers
Sets: John Arnone, John Lee Beatty, Radu Boruzescu, Liviu Ciulei, Andrew Jackness, Heidi Landesman. *Costumes:* Miruna Boruzescu, Jane Greenwood, David James, Carol Oditz, Dunya Ramicova, John David Ridge. *Lights:* Jo Mayer, Gregory MacPherson, Dennis Parichy, David F. Segal.

Media resources
Film: *The Time of Your Life* (WNET); *Stages: Houseman Directs Lear* (Amanda C. Pope, documentary). Video: *New Actors for the Classics* (WNET, documentary); *The Acting Company in Residence* (UCLA, documentary).

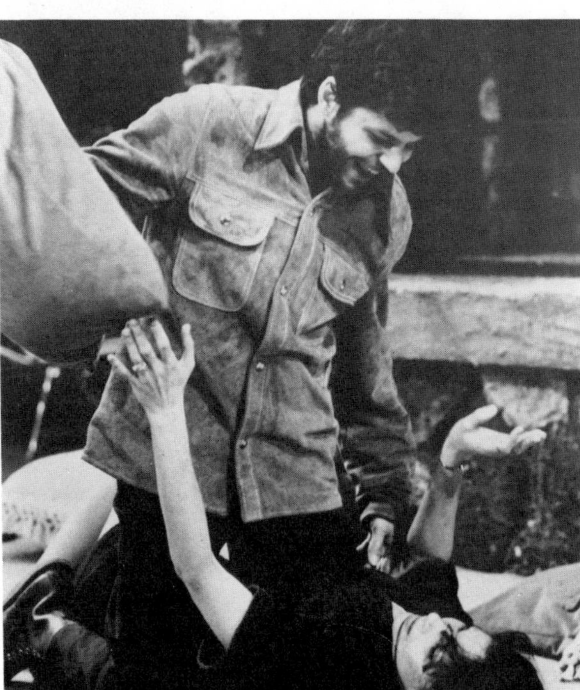

Actors Theatre of Louisville. Danton Stone and Ellen Barber in *Extremities.* Photo: David S. Talbott.

Actors Theatre of Louisville

Jon Jory
Producing Director

Alexander Speer
Administrative Director

316 West Main St.
Louisville, KY 40202
(502) 584–1265 (business)
(502) 584–1205 (box office)

Founded 1964
Richard Block, Ewel Cornett

Season
October–May

Schedule
Evenings
Tuesday–Sunday
Matinees
Wednesday, Saturday

Facilities
Pamela Brown Auditorium
Seating capacity: 637
Stage: thrust
Victor Jory Theatre
Seating capacity: 161
Stage: thrust

Finances
June 1, 1980–May 31, 1981
$2,349,000 operating expenses
$1,537,000 earned income
$ 856,000 grants /contributions

Audience
Annual attendance: 169,366
Subscribers: 16,900

Touring contact
Vaughn McBride

AEA LORT (B) contract

Actors Theatre of Louisville is an important source of new American writing for the stage. Through its wide range of services to the writer, ATL annually produces new work by dozens of playwrights while maintaining a large subscription audience in a city of moderate size.

In addition to producing its two subscription series and a wide range of outreach programs, ATL's schedule includes two major festivals, one in its sixth season and one having begun its second. The Festival of New American Plays is practically a season in itself. In 1981, it included eight evenings of fully produced theatre as well as peripheral events and workshops. The works of 16 playwrights premiered here in 1981. The Festival has become one of the most interesting and significant events in American theatre, and plays produced in the Festival have moved rapidly into the general repertoire.

ATL began the Shorts Festival in December 1980, devoted entirely to new work in the one-act form. The nine new works presented for the theatre's subscription audiences were commissioned under the aegis of the theatre's New Play Program.

In 1981, ATL took its productions on a countrywide tour of Israel and to the B.I.T.E.F. Festival in Belgrade, Yugoslavia; the Dublin Festival; the Toronto International Theatre Festival; and the Baltimore International Theatre Festival.

Actors Theatre has been the recipient of some of the most prestigious awards bestowed upon a resident theatre. In 1978, Jon Jory and ATL were honored with the Margo Jones Award for the encouragement of new American plays. Jory is the only person to have received this award twice. ATL is one of three theatres to receive the James N. Vaughn Memorial Award for its contributions to the development of professional theatre, and by winning the 1980 Antionette Perry ("Tony") Award, ATL became the first theatre in the country to receive all three of these honors.

Productions 1979–80
Mornings at Seven, Paul Osborn
• *The Slab Boys,* John Byrne
Childe Byron, Romulus Linney
Otherwise Engaged, Simon Gray
A Christmas Carol, adapt: Barbara Field, from Charles Dickens
The Time of Your Life, William Saroyan
The Incredible Murder of Cardinal Tosca, Walter Learning and Alden Nowlan
• *Tarantara! Tarantara!,* Ian Taylor
Lone Star, James McLure
• *Louisville Zoo Two,* Peter Ekstrom
Fourth Annual Festival of New Plays:
- • *Today a Little Extra,* Michael Kassin
- • *Power Plays,* Shirley Lauro
- • *Agnes of God,* John Pielmeier
- • *They're Coming to Make It Brighter,* Kent Broadhurst
- • *Sunset/Sunrise,* Adele Edling Shank
- • *Remington,* Ray Aranha
- • *Doctors and Diseases,* Peter Ekstrom
- • *The America Project,* various authors

In Fashion, book: Jon Jory; music: Jerry Blatt; lyrics: Lonnie Burstein

Productions 1980–81
Sea Marks, Gardner McKay
Terra Nova, Ted Tally
Cyrano de Bergerac, Edmond Rostand
Shorts:
- • *Chocolate Cake,* Mary Gallagher
- • *Semi-Precious Things,* Terri Wagener
- • *Final Placement,* Ara Watson
- • *Just Horrible,* Nicholas Kazan
- • *Morning Call,* Alan Gross
- • *Propinquity,* Claudia Johnson

- *Chug,* Ken Jenkins
- *The Most Trusted Man in America,* Stuart Hample
- *Let's Us,* Vaughn McBride

A Christmas Carol
Sly Fox, Larry Gelbart
On Golden Pond, Ernest Thompson
Black Coffee, Agatha Christie
Fifth Annual Festival of New Plays:

- *Future Tense,* David Kranes
- *Autobiography of a Pearl Diver,* Martin Epstein
- *Early Times,* various authors
- *Extremities,* William Mastrosimone
- *My Sister in This House,* Wendy Kesselman
- *A Full-Length Portrait of America,* Paul D'Andrea
- *SWOP,* Ken Jenkins
- *Shorts,* various authors

Getting Out, Marsha Norman
Bus Stop, William Inge

Directors
John Bettenbender, Pamela Burtnett, Larry Deckel, Radha Delamarter, Alan Duke, Ray Fry, Marilyn Hamway, Michael Hankins, Israel Hicks, Elizabeth Ives, Ken Jenkins, Walton Jones, Jon Jory, Victor Jory, Pirie MacDonald, William McNulty, Peter Maloney, Marsha Norman, Adale O'Brien, Amy Saltz, B.J. Whiting

Designers
Sets: David S.S. Davis, David B. Hager, Hugh Landwehr, Grady Larkins, Paul Owen, Karen Schulz, Hal Tine, Joseph A. Varga. *Costumes:* Nancy Flanagan, Katharine Kraft, Paul Owen. *Lights:* Geoffrey T. Cunningham, Thomas B. Dean, Karl Haas, David B. Hager, Jeff Hill, Paul Owen.

Media resources
Radio: *Third and Oak (Earplay).* Video: *In Fashion* (WNET), *Actors Theatre of Louisville's Fifth Annual Festival of New American Plays* (WNET, documentary).

Actors Theatre of St. Paul

Michael Andrew Miner
Artistic Director

Jan Miner
Managing Director

2115 Summit Ave.
St. Paul, MN 55105
(612) 227–0050

Founded 1977
Michael Andrew Miner

Season
October–April

Schedule
Evenings
Wednesday–Sunday
Matinees
Saturday, selected Thursdays

Facilities
Foley Theatre
Seating capacity: 260
Stage: proscenium

Finances
July 1, 1980–June 30, 1981
$301,000 operating expenses
$114,000 earned income
$173,000 grants/contributions

Audience
Annual attendance: 27,500
Subscribers: 2,000

AEA LORT (D) contract

Actors Theatre of St. Paul is committed to developing a cohesive ensemble approach to a stylistically varied repertoire of contemporary and classical plays. At the heart of its aesthetic is a resident professional acting company responsive to the unique demands of ensemble acting. Every aspect of the theatre's program is formulated, organized, measured and modified in light of that goal.

Although the theatre is not organized as a collective, the company participates extensively in script selection, working with the artistic director to identify plays offering growth opportunities for individual artists and stylistic challenges to the company as a whole.

From its inception, ATSP has eagerly embraced the responsibility of developing new writers and new works for the stage. The theatre has consistently assisted writers through both seasonal and production-length residencies, readings, productions, and representation at national playwriting conferences and festivals. In the 1980–81 season ATSP produced two works commissioned by the theatre for its resident company: *Outlanders* by Amlin Gray, and *Gift of the Magi,* book and lyrics by playwright-in-residence John Olive, music by composer Libby Larsen.

Plans for the 1981–82 season include continued emphasis on company development, production of a developmental work in an alternative space, advance work on scripts commissioned for 1982–83, and improvements of a variety of production resources available to scenic and costume designers.

Productions 1979–80
Philadelphia, Here I Come!, Brian Friel
The Lady's Not for Burning, Christopher Fry
The Three Sisters, Anton Chekhov

Actors Theatre of St. Paul. Barbara Kingsley, Mark McGovern, John P. Connolly and Alan Woodward in *Fighting Bob.* Photo: Paul Christenson.

A Touch of the Poet, Eugene O'Neill
The Two Character Play, Tennessee Williams
• *The Pavilion Room: A Victorian Reverie,* Amlin Gray

Productions 1980–81
• *Fighting Bob,* Tom Cole
How the Other Half Loves, Alan Ayckbourn
Gift of the Magi, book and lyrics: John Olive; music: Libby Larsen
• *Spokesong,* book and lyrics: Stewart Parker; music: Mark Bloom
• *Outlanders,* Amlin Gray
Miss Julie, August Strindberg; trans: Michael Meyer
Ring Round the Moon, Jean Anouilh; trans: Christopher Fry
• *Vikings,* Steve Metcalfe

Directors
Michael Brindisi, Michael Andrew Miner, Kristin Overn, Louis Rackoff, Scott M. Rubsam, Jeff Steitzer, George C. White

Designers
Sets: James Guenther, Chris Johnson, Dick Leerhoff, Paul Peloquin, James Michael Waters, Don Yunker. *Costumes:* Tessie Bundick, Michael L. Hansen, Anne Ruben, Nan Zabriskie. *Lights:* Bob Bye, Chris Johnson, Paul Peloquin, Paul Scharfenberger, Michael Vennerstrom.

Alabama Shakespeare Festival

Martin L. Platt
Artistic Director

Michael Maso
Managing Director

Josephine E. Ayers
Executive Producer

Box 141
Anniston, AL 36202
(205) 236–7503 (business)
(205) 237–2332 (box office)

Founded 1972
Martin L. Platt

Season
Mainstage
July–August
Touring
September–November

Schedule
Evenings
Tuesday–Sunday
Matinees
Friday–Sunday

Facilities
Festival Theatre
12th and Woodstock Sts.
Seating capacity: 950
Stage: thrust
ACT Playhouse
1020 Noble St.
Seating capacity: 100
Stage: modified thrust

Finances
January 1, 1980–December 31, 1980
$528,000 operating expenses
$332,000 earned income
$153,000 grants/contributions

Audience
Annual attendance: 75,000
Subscribers: 2,600

Touring contact
Patricia Lavendar

Booked-in events
Music, film

AEA LORT (C) contract

The Alabama Shakespeare Festival celebrated its 10th anniversary in 1981 and continues to produce professional, classical theatre for Alabama and the Southeast. During its first 10 seasons, the Festival produced 29 Shakespearean plays plus works by Ibsen, Wilde, Moliere, Coward, Wycherley, Stoppard and others.

In addition to a five-play repertoire each summer in its two theatres, ASF mounts a three-month fall tour to 10 southeastern states. In 1981 for

Alabama Shakespeare Festival. *Cymbeline.* Photo: Michael Doege.

the first time, ASF originated a production, *Oh, Coward!,* in Atlanta prior to including the play in its summer season in Anniston.

The Conservatory, an actor training program for college students, has grown rapidly since its birth in 1978, and in 1981 three former students were cast in major roles in the company. Other ASF activities include a chamber music series and lecture series offered in the summer, and a classic film series in the winter.

The Festival remains committed to providing a cultural resource for its region. ASF brings Shakespeare's plays to life bearing in mind that he was writing for the common audience, entertaining, exciting, moving and uplifting them and becoming a part of their lives.

The artistic growth of the Festival has been fostered by the development of a resident acting company and by the use of a true rotating repertory system, which allows the actors greater variety in casting and experience than they might receive in many other institutions.

The Festival is a theatre where the classics can live and breathe before an eager and informed audience, a theatre where the masterworks of world theatre live side-by-side with the realities of the modern South.

Productions 1979–80

Romeo and Juliet, William Shakespeare
Cymbeline, William Shakespeare
Two Gentleman of Verona, William Shakespeare
Tartuffe, Moliere; trans: Richard Wilbur
The Importance of Being Earnest, Oscar Wilde

Productions 1980–81

Oh, Coward!, music & lyrics: Noel Coward; adapt: Roderick Cook
Henry IV, Part 1, William Shakespeare
A Midsummer Night's Dream, William Shakespeare
Much Ado About Nothing, William Shakespeare
The Servant of Two Masters, Carlo Goldoni; adapt: Tom Cone
The Marowitz Hamlet, adapt: Charles Marowitz, from William Shakespeare
The Importance of Being Earnest, Oscar Wilde

Directors

Jay Broad, James Donadio, Judith Haskell, Martin L. Platt, Russell Treyz

Designers

Sets: Michael Stauffer. *Costumes:* Susan Cox, Lynne Emmert. *Lighting:* Lauren Miller, Michael Stauffer.

Alaska Repertory Theatre. *A Midsummer Night's Dream.* Photo: Jim Lavrakas.

Alaska Repertory Theatre

Robert J. Farley
Artistic Director

Paul V. Brown
Producing Director

Mark Somers
Managing Director

705 West Sixth Ave.
Suite 201
Anchorage, AK 99501
(907) 276–2327 (business)
(907) 276–5500 (box office)

Founded 1976
Alaska State Council on the Arts

Season
November–June

Schedule
Evenings
Tuesday–Saturday
Matinees
Saturday, Sunday

Facilities
Sydney Laurence Auditorium
Sixth Ave. and F St.
Seating capacity: 626
Stage: proscenium
University of Alaska Fine Arts Theatre
University of Fairbanks
Fairbanks, AK
Seating capacity: 481
Stage: proscenium

Finances
July 1, 1980–June 30, 1981
$1,547,000 operating expenses
$ 485,000 earned income
$1,011,000 grants/contributions

Audience
Annual attendance: 46,600
Subscribers: 7,704

Touring contact
Barbara Spear

Booked-in events
Regional and children's theatre, music, dance

AEA LORT (B) contract

Alaska Repertory Theatre is the state's first professional performing arts institution. Founded in 1976,

Alley Theatre. Ruth Nelson and Eva LeGallienne in *To Grandmother's House We Go.* Photo: Carl Davis.

Alaska Rep strives to provide top quality theatre productions, services and cultural awareness for every Alaskan, from Barrow to Ketchikan.

The theatre consists of a statewide volunteer board of directors and a professional theatre staff. Scores of professional actors and technicians participate in all productions statewide. The staff ranges in size from 20 during the off-season to over 140 at the peak of an average season. Alaska Rep also has a volunteer organization to assist the staff.

The seasons in Anchorage and Fairbanks are complemented by statewide tours of such plays as *Diamond Studs* in 1980 and *Will Rogers' U.S.A.* in 1981. Alaska Rep also serves the community with educational programs, statewide resources and outreach services. The educational programs include student matinees, an internship program, backstage tours and in-school workshops. The theatre provides consultation by Rep staff members, a performing arts library and equipment loans to other performing arts groups in the state. The Rep reaches out to all Alaskans with cultural enrichment programs and special projects.

A future goal is to increase programs designed to reach all Alaskans. The theatre's scope is broadening to include plans for children's theatre performances, increased statewide touring, a resident playwright, an experimental theatre, additional programs for the handicapped and continued cultivation of Alaskan talent.

Productions 1979–80
A Christmas Carol, adapt: Martin L. Platt, from Charles Dickens
Talley's Folly, Lanford Wilson
Something's Afoot, James McDonald, David Vos and Robert Gerlach
Sly Fox, Larry Gelbart
Loose Ends, Michael Weller
Diamond Studs, Jim Wann and Bland Simpson

Productions 1980–81
Will Rogers' U.S.A., adapt: Paul Shyre
On Golden Pond, Ernest Thompson
The Elephant Man, Bernard Pomerance
A Midsummer Night's Dream, William Shakespeare

Directors
Gary D. Anderson, Margaret Booker, Clayton Corzatte, Robert J. Farley, Walton Jones, Russell Treyz

Designers
Sets: Timothy Ames, Kathleen Armstrong, Karen Gjelsteen, Jamie Greenleaf, Robert W. Zentis. *Costumes:* Timothy Ames, Nanrose Buchman, Jamie Greenleaf, William Ivey Long, Michael Olich. *Lights:* Steven Barnes, Hugh Hall, James D. Sale, Michael Stauffer, Robert W. Zentis.

Alley Theatre

Pat Brown
Artistic Director

Iris F. Siff
Managing Director

615 Texas Avenue
Houston, TX 77002
(713) 228–9341 (business)
(713) 228–8421 (box office)

Founded 1947
Nina Vance

Season
October–September

Schedule
Evenings
Tuesday–Sunday
Matinees
Saturday, Sunday

Facilities
Large Stage
Seating capacity: 798
Stage: thrust

Arena Stage
Seating capacity: 296
Stage: arena

Finances
October 1, 1980–September 30, 1981
$2,600,000 operating expenses
$1,800,000 earned income
$ 800,000 grants/contributions

Audience
Annual attendance: 310,000
Subscribers: 21,807

Booked-in events
Theatre

AEA LORT (B) contract

With the death of founding director Nina Vance in February 1980, the Alley Theatre faced the challenge of keeping itself in full production while maintaining the artistic standards established during the more than three decades of her leadership. A team of four directors was assembled and the 1980–81 season maintained continuity, met the challenge, and achieved the goal.

Each of the Alley's two stages offered a subscription series, and 10 plays were produced, including a world premiere and a controversial new work by Thomas Babe. Excitement about the Alley was at a new high on April 1, 1981, when Pat Brown was selected to be its new artistic director. Brown brings 25 years of professional experience back to her native Texas; her association with resident theatres began when she was the first director of Theatre Communications Group.

While the original Alley philosophy will not be ignored, Brown believes bold new directions are in order and early planning portends an adventurous future for the Alley. It will begin with the 1981 Summer Fair, offering summer theatre to Alley patrons for the first time. The 1981–82 season will introduce rotating repertory on both stages; an historic exchange between the Alley and Alan Ayckbourn's Stephen Joseph Theatre in England; at least three premieres; and Lunchtime Theatre. Ongoing programs for apprentices and acting fellows will receive greater emphasis than ever before. An innovative university-affiliated directors' training program will be established, supported by the Nina Vance Memorial Fund. Other important Alley activities will continue, such as the 17-year-old Merry-Go-Round school for young people; Monday Night Live, a program of rehearsed readings of new plays; and children's theatre. The 1981–82 season will offer 12 plays on the two Alley stages between October and July, followed by the second Summer Fair—establishing year-round production.

Productions 1979–80

Indulgences in the Louisville Harem, John Orlock
Black Coffee, Agatha Christie
The Cherry Orchard, Anton Chekhov; trans: Sir Tyrone Guthrie & Leonid Kipnis
• *The Gospel According to St. Matthew,* adapt: Robert Symonds
Oh, Coward!, music and lyrics: Noel Coward; adapt: Roderick Cook
The Goodbye People, Herb Gardner
The Wizard of Oz, adapt: Elizabeth F. Goodspeed, from L. Frank Baum

Productions 1980–81

• *To Grandmother's House We Go,* Joanna Glass
The Threepenny Opera, book and lyrics: Bertolt Brecht; music: Kurt Weill; trans: Marc Blitzstein
Fathers and Sons, Thomas Babe
On Golden Pond, Ernest Thompson
Romeo and Juliet, William Shakespeare
Ten Little Indians, Agatha Christie
The Mousetrap, Agatha Christie
Strider, book: Mark Rozovsky; lyrics: Uri Riashentsev and Steve Brown; adapt: Robert Kalfin and Steve Brown; music: Mark Rosovsky, S. Vetkin and Norman L. Berman
Betrayal, Harold Pinter
Da, Hugh Leonard
The Adventures of Tom Sawyer, adapt: Timothy Mason, from Mark Twain

Directors

B.H. Barry, Pat Brown, Roderick Cook, Louis Criss, Beth Sanford, Robert Symonds, John Vreeke, Clifford Williams

Designers

Sets: John Bos, Matthew Grant, Michael Olich, Jeff Seats, William Trotman, Jerry Williams. *Costumes:* Ariel Ballif, Michael J. Cesario, Jane Greenwood, Tom McKinely, Michael Olich, Ellen Ryba. *Lights:* Jonathan Duff, Matthew Grant, Al Oster, James Stephens.

AMAS Repertory Theatre

Rosetta LeNoire
Artistic Director

Gary Halcott
Administrator/Business Manager

1 East 104th St.
New York, NY 10029
(212) 369-8000

Founded 1969
Rosetta LeNoire, Gerta Grunen, Mara Kim

Season
October–August

Schedule
Evenings
Wednesday–Saturday
Matinees
Sunday

Facilities
Experimental Theatre
Seating capacity: 99
Stage: modified thrust

Finances
July 1, 1980–June 30, 1981
$163,000 operating expenses
$ 39,000 earned income
$101,000 grants/contributions

Audience
Annual attendance: 9,100

Touring contact
Rosetta LeNoire

AEA Showcase code

AMAS Repertory Theatre is a multiracial performing arts organization devoted exclusively to the development of musical theatre. Entering its 15th season under the artistic direction of its founder Rosetta LeNoire, AMAS (which means, "You love") is dedicated to bringing all people, regardless of race, creed, color or religion, together through the creative arts.

AMAS is perhaps best known for its professional showcase theatre program. In creating and developing new musical theatre works, AMAS places emphasis on biographies. Past seasons have included new musicals based on the lives of Bill "Bojangles" Robinson, Langston Hughes, Paul Lawrence Dunbar, Ethel Waters and George Washington Carver. In 1978, AMAS was selected as one of six national recipients of a

AMAS Repertory Theatre. *Before the Flood.* Photo: Cathy Blaivas.

special Kennedy Center Black Playwrights Award; AMAS has received numerous Audience Development Committee "AUDELCO" Awards for excellence in musical theatre. *Bubbling Brown Sugar,* originally developed and produced at AMAS, was successful both on Broadway and in London, and continues national and international touring. In the past two seasons alone, such distinguished theatre artists as Luther Henderson, Maya Angelou, Bernard Johnson, Lalo Schifrin, Billie Allen, Danny Holgate and William Mooney have collaborated on AMAS productions.

AMAS is equally proud of its training and outreach programs. The Eubie Blake Children's Theatre offers comprehensive, professional training in music, dance and drama to children 9 through 16, culminating in a public presentation. Adult workshops in acting and voice offer professional instruction for both the experienced performer and the interested beginner; this program also presents a public revue at the end of the year. The AMAS Summer Tour brings an original musical revue to senior citizen centers, nursing homes, community centers and various public sites throughout the five boroughs of New York City, free of charge.

AMAS has also toured to local schools, performing and conducting workshops sponsored by the Arts Connection and the New York City Department of Cultural Affairs, and provided free tickets for students and disadvantaged groups. In 1981 AMAS inaugurated a free summer instruction program for young people and senior citizens.

Productions 1979–80
- *And Still I Rise,* book and lyrics: Maya Angelou; music: Lalo Schifrin
- *Before the Flood,* book: Rudy Gray; music: Paul Piteo; lyrics: David Blake
- *Dunbar,* adapt: Ayanna and Ron Stacker Thompson; music: Paul Tilman Smith and Quitman Fludd III; lyrics: Lonnie Hewitt and Paul Lawrence Dunbar
- *Jam,* John Gerstad

Productions 1980–81
- *The Peanut Man,* book, music and lyrics: Melvin Hasman
- *Mama, I Want to Sing,* book: Vy Higginsen; music and lyrics: Vy Higginsen, Ken Wydro and Richard Tee
- *Mo' Tea, Miss Ann?,* book and lyrics: Bebe Ross Coker; music: Leander Morris
- *The Crystal Tree,* book and lyrics: Doris Julian; music: Luther Henderson

Directors
Billie Allen, Maya Angelou, Duane L. Jones, Regge Life, William Mooney, Dennis Shearer, Ron Stacker Thompson

Designers
Sets: Lisa Cameron, Felix Cochren, Giles Hogya, Patrick Mann, Vicki Paul, Bob Phillips, William Waithe. *Costumes:* Georgia Collins-Langhorne, Leslie Day, Bernard Johnson, Amanda Klein, Jeffrey Mazor, Vickie McLaughlin. *Lights:* Mark DiQuinzio, William Grant III, Fred Jason Hancock, Sandra Ross, Bob Scheeler, Paul Sullivan.

American Conservatory Theatre

William Ball
General Director

James B. McKenzie
Executive Producer

450 Geary St.
San Francisco, CA 94102
(415) 771–3880 (business)
(415) 673–6440 (box office)

Founded 1965
William Ball

Season
October–May

Schedule
Evenings
Monday–Saturday
Matinees
Wednesday, Saturday

Facilities
Geary Theatre
415 Geary St.
Seating capacity: 1,364
Stage: proscenium
Marines' Memorial Theatre
Sutter and Mason Sts.
Seating capacity: 640
Stage: proscenium
Playroom
450 Geary St.
Seating capacity: 50
Stage: flexible

Finances
June 1, 1980–May 31, 1981
$7,020,000 operating expenses
$5,495,000 earned income
$1,525,000 grants/contributions

Audience
Annual attendance: 600,000
Subscribers: 20,000

Touring contact
Ben Moore

Booked-in events
Theatre, dance

AEA LORT (A) contract

The American Conservatory Theatre is San Francisco's resident

American Conservatory Theatre. *A History of the American Film.* Photo: William Ganslen.

professional theatre, and the nation's largest, most active repertory company. In its 15-year history, ACT has presented more than 175 major productions ranging from the classics of world drama to outstanding contemporary works, attracting a total audience of more than five million.

From its inception, ACT was envisioned as a theatre of national significance with a double purpose: to present a professional repertory season in conjunction with, and inseparable from, a professional theatre training program. The company continues to fulfill those goals today. Each season, 10 plays are presented in the rotating style of continental repertory, enabling audiences to choose in a given week from works by Shakespeare, Shaw, Hellman or Stoppard. At the same time, actors and directors are expanding their artistry to meet the challenges of changing dramatic forms, styles and periods.

The Advanced Training Program, with an annual enrollment of 85, is awaiting accreditation in the state of California, making ACT the first and only professional company empowered to grant an M.F.A. in acting.

In addition to ACT's repertory and training activities, the theatre also sponsors engagements of non-repertory productions at the smaller Marines' Memorial Theatre, and at the Geary Theatre when the resident company is not performing. Now entering its 11th season, the Plays in Progress series presents five previously unproduced American works, with the writers in residence for the entire rehearsal and production period. Regional and national touring, with an annual two-week Hawaii residency, complete ACT's performance activities.

Ancillary programs and services of the company include classes for non-professional adults and children; administrative and technical/production internships; public lecture series and post-performance discussions; signed performances for the hearing-impaired; and discount programs for the handicapped, senior citizens, military personnel and students.

Productions 1979–80
Romeo and Juliet, William Shakespeare
Buried Child, Sam Shepard
Hay Fever, Noel Coward
The Little Foxes, Lillian Hellman
A Christmas Carol, adapt: Dennis Powers and Laird Williamson, from Charles Dickens
The Crucifer of Blood, Paul Giovanni
The Girl of the Golden West, David Belasco
A History of the American Film, Christopher Durang
Pantagleize, Michel de Ghelderode
Ah, Wilderness!, Eugene O'Neill

Productions 1980–81
Much Ado About Nothing, William Shakespeare
Ghosts, Henrik Ibsen; trans: Allen Fletcher
The Trojan War Will Not Take Place, Jean Giraudoux; trans: Christopher Fry
A Christmas Carol
Night and Day, Tom Stoppard
Another Part of the Forest, Lillian Hellman
The Rivals, Richard Brinsley Sheridan
The Three Sisters, Anton Chekhov; trans: Randall Jarrell
The Little Foxes

Directors
Allen Fletcher, Edward Hastings, David Hammond, Elizabeth Huddle, Nagle Jackson, Tom Moore, Jack O'Brien, Jerry Turner, Laird Williamson

Designers
Sets: Robert Blackman, William Bloodgood, Ralph Funicello, Richard Hay, Michael Miller, Karen Schulz, Richard Seger. *Costumes:* Robert Blackman, Martha Burke, Cathy Edwards, Robert Fletcher, Robert Morgan, Michael Olich, Carrie Robbins, Warren Travis. *Lights:* F. Mitchell Dana, Richard Devin, Dirk Epperson, James Sale, Duane Schuler.

Media resources
Video: *Under Milkwood, Cyrano de Bergerac, The Taming of the Shrew* (WNET), *Misalliance, Glory! Hallelujah!* (KQED), *ACT Now* (KQED, documentary).

The American Place Theatre. *The Fuehrer Bunker.* Photo: Martha Holmes.

The American Place Theatre

Wynn Handman
Director

Julia Miles
Associate Director

111 West 46th St.
New York, NY 10036
(212) 246–3730 (business)
(212) 247–0393 (box office)

Founded 1964
Wynn Handman, Michael Tolan, Sidney Lanier, Myrna Loy

Season
September–June

Schedule
Evenings
Tuesday–Saturday
Matinees
variable

Facilities
Mainstage
Seating capacity: 315
Stage: flexible thrust
SubPlot Cabaret
Seating capacity: 74
Stage: flexible

Finances
July 1, 1980–June 30, 1981
$585,000 operating expenses
$270,000 earned income
$385,000 grants/contributions

Audience
Annual attendance: 22,000
Subscribers: 1,580

Touring contact
Julia Miles

Booked-in events
Theatre, dance, music

AEA Special Production contract

The American Place Theatre was founded in 1964 at St. Clement's Church, as a place for developing and producing plays by living American writers. The theatre moved to its present location in 1971 and has continued to maintain a creative environment for new works without commercial pressure. The selection of writers and plays is eclectic, as is reflected in the more than 60 full productions in the theatre's 17-year history. These include William Alfred's *Hogan's Goat* and Robert Lowell's *The Old Glory;* plays by Sam Shepard, Ronald Tavel and Maria Irene Fornes; and the first plays of Ronald Ribman, Steve Tesich and Jonathan Reynolds. Early plays by black playwrights Ed Bullins, Philip Hayes Dean, Elaine Jackson, Ron Milner and Charlie Russell, by Asian-American Frank Chin and by distinguished writers in other media, such as Robert Coover, Anne Sexton, W.D. Snodgrass, Joyce Carol Oates and Bruce Jay Friedman, have also been presented.

A total program provides optimum conditions for the growth and realization of each writer's work. The season includes at least four fully mounted productions, numerous works-in-progress and performances from the ongoing American Humorists Series. The Women's Project, begun in 1978, exists to develop the talents of women playwrights and directors through rehearsed readings and studio productions.

Additional programs and services include professional training for directors, designers, technicians and administrators; artistic, administrative and technical/production internships; study materials, student and senior citizen discounts, post-performance discussions, workshop productions and staged readings, a cabaret, newsletter and theatre rentals.

The aim of the American Place is to cultivate a concerned and knowledgeable audience that will participate in the process of contemporary theatre to the benefit of artists and audience members alike.

Productions 1979–80

- *Letters Home,* adapt: Rose Leiman Goldemberg
- *Paris Lights: The All Star Literary Genius Expatriate Revue,* music: William Russo
- *Killings on the Last Line,* Lavonne Mueller
- *Smart Aleck: Alexander Woollcott at 8:40,* Howard Teichmann
- *Sim: One Night With a Lady Undertaker from Texas,* William Osborn
- *Holy Places,* Gail Kriegel Mallin
- *Milk of Paradise,* Sallie Bingham

Productions 1980–81

- *The Impossible H.L. Mencken,* adapt: John Rothman
- *Memory of Whiteness,* Richard Hamburger

Still Life, Emily Mann

- *The Fuehrer Bunker,* W.D. Snodgrass; music: Richard Peaslee
- *The Amazin' Casey Stengel,* Michael Zettler and Shelly Altman
- *After the Revolution,* Nadja Tesich
- *The Prevaricated Life History of Constance McMalley,* Caroline Kava

Directors
Robert Gainer, Emily Mann, William Osborn, Scott Redman, Dorothy Silver, Joan Micklin Silver, Howard Teichmann, Joan Vail Thorne, Carl Weber

Designers
Sets: William Barclay, Jim Clayburgh, Charles Cosler, Kate Edmunds, Fred Kolouch, Manuel Lutgenhorst, Tom Lynch, Henry Millman, Michael Molly, Tom Schwinn, Bill Stabile. *Costumes:* Whitney Blausen, Susan Denison, K.L. Fredericks, Fred Kolouch, Sally Lesser, William Ivey Long, Mimi Maxmen, Kathleen Smith, David Toser, Christina Weppner. *Lights:* Jim Clayburgh, Charles Cosler, James F. Ingalls, Fred Kolouch, Manuel Lutgenhorst, Robby Monk, Roger Morgan, Laura Rambaldi, Judy Rasmuson, Annie Wrightson.

Media resources
Film: *Five on the Black Hand Side* (United Artists). Video: *Hogan's Goat, The Old Glory, Journey of the Fifth Horse, Brother to Dragons, Ceremony of Innocence, Baba Goya, Year of the Dragon, Father Uxbridge Wants to Marry* (WNET).

American Repertory Theatre

Robert Brustein
Artistic Director

Robert J. Orchard
Managing Director

Loeb Drama Center
64 Brattle St.
Cambridge, MA 02138
(617) 495–2668 (business)
(617) 547–8300 (box office)

Founded 1980
Robert Brustein

Season
Year-round

Schedule
Evenings
Tuesday–Sunday
Matinees
Saturday, Sunday

Facilities
Loeb Drama Center
Seating capacity: 556
Stage: flexible
City Hall Plaza
City Hall
Boston, MA
Seating capacity: 1,500
Stage: outdoors
Wilbur Theatre
Tremont St.
Boston, MA
Seating capacity: 1,100
Stage: proscenium

Finances
July 1, 1980–June 30, 1981
$2,065,000 operating expenses
$1,027,000 earned income
$ 874,000 grants/contributions

Audience
Annual attendance: 140,000
Subscribers: 13,000

Touring contact
Robert J. Orchard

Booked-in events
Theatre, dance

AEA LORT (B) contract

The American Repertory Theatre is a professional company in residence at the Loeb Drama Center. The company is an outgrowth of the original Yale Repertory Theatre, founded by Robert Brustein in 1966, and many of the Rep's productions, staff and personnel have moved with him to Cambridge.

ART's repertoire is generally chosen from three categories: neglected but relevant plays of the past; more familiar classical works reinterpreted for our time; and the most interesting new plays available, preferably (though not exclusively) by American playwrights. Recently, the ART has also rediscovered and staged certain works of musical theatre. Past productions at both Yale Repertory Theatre and in Cambridge have included most of the musical works of the Brecht-Weill canon, often in their American premieres, and the wedding of the scores of Henry Purcell and the plays of Shakespeare in such productions as *A Midsummer Night's Dream* and *The Tempest.*

The ART is located in the heart of Cambridge, near Harvard Square, on the edge of the Harvard campus. It serves a large subscription audience, including many from the greater Boston area and its various university communities. The theatre offers a 40-week season of five to seven productions, most of them performed in rotating repertory.

The company also offers 11 courses in dramatic arts to Harvard undergraduates, as well as six graduate courses in the Harvard Extension School. Performance activities in addition to the regular season include a Monday series of staged readings, debates and lectures; a weekend Loeb Cabaret featuring satiric and comic sketches, one-act plays and musical revues; performances in the city of Boston at Government Center and the Wilbur Theatre; tours of U.S. and European cities; and a non-subscription series of new and experimental plays offered at the Hasty Pudding Theatre.

Productions 1979–80

A Midsummer Night's Dream, William Shakespeare

- *Terry by Terry,* Mark Leib

Happy End, book and lyrics: Bertolt Brecht; music: Kurt Weill; adapt: Michael Feingold

The Inspector General, Nikolai Gogol; trans: Sam Guckenheimer and Peter Sellars

Productions 1980–81

As You Like It, William Shakespeare

- *The Berlin Requiem* and *The Seven Deadly Sins,* book and lyrics: Bertolt Brecht; music: Kurt Weill; trans: Michael Feingold
- *Lulu,* Frank Wedekind; adapt: Michael Feingold
- *Has "Washington" Legs?,* Charles Wood
- *Figaro,* Pierre de Beaumarchais; trans and adapt: Mark Leib
- *Grownups,* Jules Feiffer

Directors

Andrei Belgrader, Lee Breuer, Alvin Epstein, Walton Jones, Michael Kustow, John Madden, Travis Preston, Peter Sellars

Designers

Sets: Kate Edmunds, Andrew Jackness, Adrianne G. Lobel, Tom Lynch, Tony Straiges, Michael H. Yeargan. *Costumes:* Zack Brown, Nan Cibula, Adrianne G. Lobel, William Ivey Long, Nancy Thun, Dunya Ramicova, Rita Ryack. *Lights:* William Armstrong, Paul Gallo, James H. Ingalls.

Media resources

Video: *A Midsummer Night's Dream* (WGBH).

American Repertory Theatre. Frederick Neumann and Catherine Slade in *Lulu.* Photo: Richard Feldman.

American Stage Festival. *Working.* Photo: Tom Bloom.

American Stage Festival

Larry Carpenter
Artistic Director

Will Maitland Weiss
Managing Director

Box 225
Milford, NH 03055
(603) 673–3143 (business)
(603) 673–7515 (box office)

Founded 1975
Terry C. Lorden and local citizens

Season
June–August

Schedule
Evenings
Tuesday–Sunday
Matinees
Wednesday

Facilities
Mont Vernon St. (Rte. 13N)
Seating capacity: 480
Stage: proscenium

Finances
November 1, 1979–October 31, 1980
$295,000 operating expenses
$208,000 earned income
$ 87,000 grants/contributions

Audience
Annual attendance: 40,000
Subscribers: 2,500

Touring contact
Will Maitland Weiss

Booked-in events
Music, dance, children's theatre, arts & crafts

AEA Stock (Z) contract

The American Stage Festival stands on a nine-acre peninsula of woods and fields on New Hampshire's Souhegan River. Its year-round administrative staff produces a summer season of 10 weeks on its 40-foot modern proscenium stage. In its seventh season, the ASF has grown to be New Hampshire's largest professional arts organization, drawing its audience primarily from its home state and northern Massachusetts, and utilizing the best of regional and New York talent.

ASF's season includes five plays and has, over the course of its development, adhered to the format of one classic, two American revivals, one new play and one new musical. New work has included Horovitz's *Alfred Dies,* a new *Dracula* adaptation, the first theatrical adaptation of *The Hunchback of Notre Dame,* Michael Kimberley's *Almost an Eagle* and five new musicals. ASF has produced such established authors as O'Neill, Williams, Miller, Wilder, Kaufman, Steinbeck, Moliere, Chekhov, Shaw and Shakespeare. Productions aim for appropriate, responsible renderings of dramatic literature in striking, well-produced physical mountings.

In addition to presenting plays, ASF maintains a rounded cultural trusteeship for its community by producing a children's workshop series, weekly art gallery exhibits, a special events series including such groups as the New Hampshire Symphony and the Hartford Ballet, play discussion seminars, a twice-weekly farmers' market and an annual arts and crafts fair.

The ASF maintains its commitment to the training of young theatre artists and has adopted a conservatory approach to its apprentice and intern companies. This facilitates the mixing of the good, honest hard work of the theatre with professional seminars and working exposure to acting, singing, dance, improvisation, design, production and administration.

Productions 1979–80
Room Service, John Murray and Allen Boretz
The Bat, Mary Roberts Rinehart and Avery Hopwood
On Golden Pond, Ernest Thompson
The Cherry Orchard, Anton Chekhov
Working, book adapt: Stephen Schwartz, from Studs Terkel; music and lyrics: Stephen Schwartz, et al.

Productions 1980–81
Feathertop, book: Bruce Peyton; music and lyrics: Skip Kennon
Angel Street, Patrick Hamilton
• *Almost an Eagle,* Michael Kimberly
The Comedy of Errors, William Shakespeare
Hobson's Choice, Harold Brighouse

Directors
Craig Belknap, Larry Carpenter, Harold De Felice, Nagle Jackson, Stephen Kanee, Donald Moffat, Brian Murray, Ted Pappas, Austin Pendleton, William Peters

Designers
Sets: Edward Cesaitis, Andrew Jackness, John Kasarda, Hugh Landwehr, Adrianne G. Lobel, Brian Martin, David Potts, Barry Robison, Patricia Woodbridge.
Costumes: Nan Cibula, Elizabeth Covey, John Falabella, Linda Fisher, David Murin, Barry Robison, Rita Ryack, Giva Taylor, Robert Wojewodski.
Lights: Frances Aronson, Paul Gallo, John Gisondi, Todd Lichtenstein, Robby Monk, Dennis Parichy.

American Theatre Arts

Don Eitner
Artistic Director

James Bennett
Nancy Jeris
Managing Directors

6240 Hollywood Blvd.
Hollywood, CA 90028
(213) 466–2462

Founded 1976
Don Eitner

Season
Year-round

Schedule
Evenings
Thursday–Saturday
Matinees
Sunday

Facilities
Thornton Theatre
Seating capacity: 60
Stage: proscenium
Demorest Theatre
Seating capacity: 60–80
Stage: flexible

Finances
January 1, 1981–December 31, 1981
$164,000 operating expenses
$ 73,000 earned income
$ 61,000 grants/contributions

Audience
Annual attendance: 7,380
Subscribers: 264

AEA 99-seat waiver

American Theatre Arts is a conservatory theatre interrelating professional productions and professional training. At the heart of ATA's artistic commitment is the development of an ensemble which epitomizes the life-blood of theatre. To quote Harold Clurman, "It's a group art entirely

American Theatre Arts. John Terry Bell, Rob Donohoe and Chandler Garrison in *Misalliance.* Photo: Dean Larsen.

dependent on team work."

Such a commitment requires intensive study by the developing actors and continuing creative interaction among the professionals, evolving and refining every member of the company, providing new fields of study for ATA artists and much needed "workouts" for voice and body.

Developing new ensemble plays and meeting the challenges of new playwrights' work are also ATA goals that have been realized through the production of several world premieres. Among these is *The Gin Game,* which later won the Pulitzer Prize for drama in 1978, and has been produced throughout the country at nonprofit professional theatres as well as on Broadway and internationally. In conjunction with new works, American Theatre Arts revives little known plays by major playwrights, such as Shaw's *In Good King Charles' Golden Days,* in order to return them to the mainstream of theatrical literature.

Productions 1979
Misalliance, George Bernard Shaw
Time Remembered, Jean Anouilh
The Physicists, Friedrich Durrenmatt
• *Bluewater Cottage,* D.L. Coburn
The Chalk Garden, Enid Bagnold

Productions 1980
• *Days in the Dark Light,* James Kearns
Nude with Violin, Noel Coward
Out of the Crocodile, Giles Cooper
Winesburg, Ohio, adapt: Christopher Sergel, from Sherwood Anderson
Richard's Cork Leg, Brendan Behan

Directors
James J. Agazzi, Don Eitner, Bruce Ewen, Bette Ferber, Diane Haak, Kip Niven, Joseph Ruskin

Designers
Sets: James J. Agazzi, Dale Barnhardt, Nancy J. Shaffer, Daniel Truxaw. *Costumes:* Ed Castro, Timmaree McCormick, Darlene Morgan, Bernadette O'Brien, Lisa Ruocco. *Lights:* Bruce Mathews, Ward Russell, Nancy J. Shaffer, Vance Sorrells, Daniel Truxaw.

American Theatre Company

Jerald D. Pope
Artistic Director

Kitty Roberts
Producing Director

Box 1265
Tulsa, OK 74101
(918) 747–9494 (business)
(918) 581–5271 (box office)

Founded 1970
Kitty Roberts, Jerald Pope, Robert L. Odle, Richard Ellis

Season
October–May

Schedule
Evenings
Tuesday–Saturday
Matinees
Sunday

Facilities
John H. Williams Theatre
Performing Arts Center
Second and Cincinnati Sts.
Seating capacity: 429
Stage: proscenium
Brook Theatre
3403 S. Peoria St.
Seating capacity: 700
Stage: proscenium

Finances
January 1, 1981–December 31, 1981
$479,000 operating expenses
$186,000 earned income
$194,000 grants/contributions

Audience
Annual attendance: 55,000
Subscribers: 3,788

Touring contact
Robert L. Odle

Booked-in events
Theatre, dance, music

American Theatre Company is the only professional stage company in a 300-mile radius of Tulsa, Oklahoma. While Oklahoma achieved statehood in 1907, it remains in many ways, but especially culturally, a frontier state. Tulsa's opera house, built in 1894 and torn down in 1974 had as many seats at the gambling tables as it did on the Golden Horseshoe.

Finding and producing plays which educate and enlarge the audience while remaining satisfying to the company and a small core of sophisticated theatregoers has been the biggest challenge in ATC's 11-year history. The search for those universal chords of feeling and experience that ring through great art, that can cause Shakespeare to move the most rustic heart, has resulted in a tight, hard-working ensemble, composed almost entirely of actors from Oklahoma—a truly "regional" theatre.

ATC's season includes classics and original plays, as well as the work of contemporary playwrights such as Sam Shepard and Lanford Wilson. As the resident company of the Tulsa Performing Arts Center, ATC also maintains a second stage in a converted movie theatre, offering satire, improvisation, musicals, concerts, films and dance. A statewide education program administered by the Department of Education is combined with a growing Youth Theatre Department based in Tulsa to find, encourage and develop future actors and future audiences.

ATC has been under the same artistic management since its founding in 1970. This continuity has helped make American Theatre Company a strong and exciting example of the possibilities for flourishing theatre in the 1980s.

American Theatre Company. Jeannine Haas, Kitty Roberts and Vic Tolman in *The Taming of the Shrew.* Photo: J.R. Jones.

Productions 1979–80
The Mousetrap, Agatha Christie
Da, Hugh Leonard
A Christmas Carol, adapt: Robert L. Odle, from Charles Dickens; lyrics: Richard Averill and Robert L. Odle; music: Richard Averill
The Taming of the Shrew, William Shakespeare
Ah, Wilderness!, Eugene O'Neill
5th of July, Lanford Wilson

Productions 1980–81
Crucifer of Blood, Paul Giovanni
Buried Child, Sam Shepard
• *Treasure Island,* book adapt: Robert L. Odle, from Robert Louis Stevenson; lyrics: Richard Averill and Robert L. Odle; music: Richard Averill
The Alchemist, Ben Jonson
Talley's Folly, Lanford Wilson
The Tavern, George M. Cohan

Directors
Harold W. Barrows, Kerry L. Hanger, Jerald D. Pope, James E. Runyan

Designers
Sets: Jeff Darby, Richard Ellis, Eduardo Sicangco, Ed Taylor. *Costumes:* Gene Barnhart, Kerry Hanger, Jo McClelland. *Lights:* Jeff Darby, David Morong, Robert Shafer, Ed Taylor, Richard Wilson.

Arena Stage

Zelda Fichandler
Producing Director

Thomas C. Fichandler
Executive Director

Sixth & Maine Ave., SW
Washington, D.C. 20024
(202) 554–9066 (business)
(202) 488–3300 (box office)

Founded 1950
Zelda Fichandler, Thomas C. Fichandler, Edward Mangum

Season
September–June

Schedule
Evenings
Tuesday–Sunday
Matinees
Saturday, Sunday

Facilities
The Arena
Seating capacity: 827
Stage: arena
The Kreeger Theater
Seating capacity: 514
Stage: modified thrust
The Old Vat Room
Seating capacity: 180
Stage: cabaret

Finances
July 1, 1980–June 30, 1981
$3,275,000 operating expenses
$2,127,000 earned income
$1,148,000 grants/contributions

Audience
Annual attendance: 240,000
Subscribers: 14,400

Booked-in events
Theatre, music, variety acts

AEA LORT (B) contract

The 1980–81 season marked the 30th anniversary of Arena Stage, one of the longest standing acting ensembles in the country. Since its beginnings in 1950, Arena's artistic and philosophical viewpoint has been molded by its co-founder and producing director, Zelda Fichandler, a resident theatre pioneer.

New American plays, premieres of important European plays, classics reborn in vivid new interpretations, new musical works, recent plays that proved unsuccessful that can be given new life all are presented in Arena's triplex of modern, intimate playhouses. The resident acting company is supplemented by actors engaged for one or more plays each season.

Arena Stage began in the Hippodrome, an old Washington movie house. After five seasons, the company moved into an old brewery dubbed the Old Vat. When the Old Vat was slated for demolition, a new theatre was designed based on the direct experience of an existing theatre company. It is the only playhouse in the country built as a total arena. The new Arena opened in 1960, and a second stage, the contrasting fan-shaped Kreeger followed in 1971. Five years later, a 180-seat cabaret dubbed the Old Vat Room after Arena's previous home was opened in the Kreeger's basement.

In 1973, Arena Stage was selected by the U.S. Department of State to be the first American company to tour the Soviet Union, presenting *Our Town* and *Inherit the Wind.* Arena became the first theatre outside New York to receive an Antoinette Perry ("Tony") Award for theatrical excellence. Recently, the company was the first from America to participate in the Hong Kong Arts Festival. Since 1965, Arena Stage has also housed and supported The Living Stage, an improvisational community outreach company (see separate entry).

The 1979–80 season was produced by David Chambers while Zelda Fichandler took a leave of absence. The 30th anniversary season was produced by Zelda Fichandler.

Arena Stage. Robert Prosky and Stanley Anderson in *Galileo.* Photo: Joe B. Mann.

Productions 1979–80
The Winter's Tale, William Shakespeare
Teibele and Her Demon, Isaac Bashevis Singer and Eve Friedman
Design for Living, Noel Coward
You Can't Take It with You, George S. Kaufman and Moss Hart
After the Fall, Arthur Miller
Plenty, David Hare
Emigrés, Slawomir Mrozek; trans: Maciej and Theresa Wrona, Robert Holman

- *An American Tragedy,* adapt: Anthony Giardina, from Theodore Dreiser

Productions 1980–81

Galileo, Bertolt Brecht; adapt: Charles Laughton
One Mo' Time, Vernel Bagneris; music adapt: Lars Edegran and Orange Kellin
The Man Who Came to Dinner, Moss Hart and George S. Kaufman
The Suicide, Nikolai Erdman; trans: Xenia Youhn; adapt: Richard Nelson
Kean, Jean-Paul Sartre; trans and adapt: Frank Hauser
- *Disability: A Comedy,* Ron Whyte
- *The Child,* Anthony Giardina
Cold Storage, Ronald Ribman
- *Pantomime,* Derek Walcott
God Bless You, Mr. Rosewater, book and lyrics: Howard Ashman, from Kurt Vonnegut; music: Alan Menken; additional lyrics: Dennis Green
American Buffalo, David Mamet

Directors

Howard Ashman, Vernel Bagneris, David Chambers, Liviu Ciulei, Zelda Fichandler, Martin Fried, Stephen Kanee, Michael Lessac, Gene Lesser, Ron Lagomarsino, Gary Pearle, Robert Prosky, Richard Russell Ramos, Douglas C. Wager

Designers

Sets: Karl Eigsti, Desmond Heeley, Marjorie Kellogg, Ming Cho Lee, Adrianne G. Lobel, Santo Loquasto, Tom Lynch, Lance Pennington, Tony Straiges. *Costumes:* Nan Cibula, JoAnn Clevenger, Sandra Yen Fong, Desmond Heeley, Carol Oditz, Mary Ann Powell, Marjorie Slaiman. *Lights:* Arden Fingerhut, Allen Lee Hughes, Hugh Lester, Roger Milliken, William Mintzer, Nancy Schertler, Duane Schuler.

Media resources

Video: *Zalmen or the Madness of God* (WNET).

Arizona Theatre Company

Gary Gisselman
Artistic Director

David Hawkanson
Managing Director

120 West Broadway
Tucson, AZ 85701
(602) 884-8210 (business)
(602) 622-2823 (box office)
(602) 253-1014 (Phoenix business)
(602) 258-0812 (Phoenix box office)

Founded 1966
Sandy Rosenthal

Season
October–June

Schedule
Evenings
Tuesday–Sunday
Matinees
Wednesday, Sunday

Facilities
Tucson Community Center Little Theatre
Seating capacity: 526
Stage: proscenium
Phoenix Little Theatre
25 East Coronado Road
Seating capacity: 450
Stage: proscenium

Finances
July 1, 1980–June 30, 1981
$988,000 operating expenses
$602,000 earned income
$386,000 grants/contributions

Audience
Annual attendance: 81,168
Subscribers: 5,634

Touring contact
David Hawkanson

AEA LORT (C) contract

The Arizona Theatre Company opened its 14th season in 1981, under the new leadership of Gary Gisselman. Situated in the rapidly growing city of Tucson, the ATC maintains the state's largest subscription audience serving over 80,000 patrons statewide.

Originally named the Arizona Civic Theatre, the ATC was founded in 1966 by Sandy Rosenthal as a community theatre employing professional guest artists. In 1977, the company evolved into a fully professional theatre operating on an Equity contract. Since then the company's budget has increased five-fold and the audience has tripled.

ATC strives to present quality professional theatre on a continuing basis to the people of Arizona. The mainstage season in Tucson consists of six plays over 22 weeks, and the Phoenix facility houses an eight-week four-play season. In 1981, the company opened the Flagstaff Festival of the Arts. ATC's repertoire is a blend of classics, contemporary works and musical theatre. The prime focus is on ensemble excellence, and for the past four seasons the theatre has operated with a resident acting company ranging in size from 15 to 20 members.

Arizona Theatre Company. Jane Murray, Richard Allison and Benjamin Stewart in *The Rivals.* Photo: Tim Fuller.

Arkansas Repertory Theatre.
Robert Boles in *Waiting for Lefty.*
Photo: Ken Klingenmeier.

In recent years the company has developed numerous educational and cultural programs. Its theatre training program Encompass is a cultural resource for all age groups. Since the school's inception in 1977, its annual enrollment has exceeded 700 in the company-taught classes. Operating from its own facility in Tucson's historic downtown district, Encompass provides an outlet for innovative programming. In the fall of 1981, a similar program will be started in Phoenix. ATC's other activities include a speakers bureau, seminars, career guidance sessions, teacher workshops and special performances for students and for the hearing-impaired.

Productions 1979–80
A Flea in Her Ear, Georges Feydeau; trans: John Mortimer
Twelfth Night, William Shakespeare
The Glass Menagerie, Tennessee Williams
Father's Day, Oliver Hailey
The Seagull, Anton Chekhov; trans: Ann Jellicoe and Ariadne Nicolaeff
The Threepenny Opera, book and lyrics: Bertolt Brecht; music: Kurt Weill

Productions 1980–81
The Rivals, Richard Brinsley Sheridan
Custer, Robert Ingham
Indulgences in the Louisville Harem, John Orlock
The Elephant Man, Bernard Pomerance
A Little Night Music, book: Hugh Wheeler; lyrics & music: Stephen Sondheim
Talley's Folly, Lanford Wilson

Directors
Gary Gisselman, George Keathley, Phil Killian, Mark Lamos, Harris Laskawy, Michael Maggio, Richard Russell Ramos

Designers
Sets: Jack Barkla, Tom Butsch, Gene Davis Buck, Christina Haatainen, John Kavelin, Michael Merritt, Jim Newton, Ruth A. Wells. *Costumes:* Jared Aswegan, Christopher Beesley, Gene Davis Buck, Jack Edwards, Christina Haatainen, Anna Belle Kaufman, Ruth A. Wells. *Lights:* John B. Forbes, Dan T. Willoughby.

Arkansas Repertory Theatre

Cliff F. Baker
Director

Steven J. Caffery
General Manager

712 East 11th St.
Little Rock, AR 72202
(501) 378–0405

Founded 1976
Cliff F. Baker

Season
September–June

Schedule
Evenings
Wednesday–Sunday
Matinees
Sunday

Facilities
Seating capacity: 150
Stage: flexible

Finances
July 1, 1980–June 30, 1981
$300,000 operating expenses
$175,000 earned income
$125,000 grants/contributions

Audience
Annual attendance: 50,000
Subscribers: 800

Touring contact
Beverly Stang

Booked-in events
Theatre, music

The Arkansas Repertory Theatre is committed to creative performance and innovative programming. Now in its fifth season, ART exemplifies the phenomenal growth of a resident theatre with a responsive public, sound management and an emphasis on artistic quality. There is a six-production mainstage season balancing contemporary works, classics, experimental and original pieces. Each year, two productions are selected for statewide and regional touring through the Mid-America Arts Alliance. A workshop theatre series called ACT II offers two experimental or original productions each season.

Both ART and its founding director Cliff F. Baker, are committed to serving people not traditionally considered "culture consumers." The artists-in-schools program yearly provides hundreds of performances and workshops to Arkansas students and teachers. Three productions selected to complement school curriculum are specially staged for student audiences. An innovative workshop program involves gifted high school students on a semester-long basis.

The 10 actors who compose the resident company bring a variety of talents and experience to ART, and have been drawn from across the nation. In order to increase the opportunities for professional training in Arkansas, an internship/apprentice program will be established in 1981–82. ART's primary goals during the coming year are audience development and the establishment of this intern/apprentice program. Education and touring programs reflect the theatre's statewide commitment to provide important cultural opportunities for thousands of Arkansans.

The underlying concept of

"ensemble" is very important and affects all facets of the organization. ART looks for works that challenge the company and the audiences. A varied season, growing outreach programs and a versatile company have made ART a major state arts institution.

Productions 1979–80
Dracula, Lord of the Undead, Joyce Stroud and Charles Dee Mitchell; concept: Christopher P. Nichols
Dames at Sea, book and lyrics: George Haimsohn and Robin Miller; music: Jim Wise
Waiting for Lefty, Clifford Odets
The House of Blue Leaves, John Guare
The Prime of Miss Jean Brodie, adapt: Jay Presson Allen, from Muriel Spark
Slow Dance on the Killing Ground, William Hanley
Something's Afoot, book, music and lyrics: James McDonald, David Vos and Robert Gerlach; additional music: Ed Linderman

Productions 1980–81
Blithe Spirit, Noel Coward
Hedda Gabler, Henrik Ibsen
Side by Side by Sondheim, music and lyrics: Stephen Sondheim, et al; adapt: Ned Sherrin
Getting Out, Marsha Norman
Merton of the Movies, George S. Kaufman and Marc Connelly
The Merry Wives of Windsor, William Shakespeare
• *Peanuts and Cracker Jack,* Jerry Slaff
Chicago, book: Fred Ebb and Bob Fosse; music: John Kander; lyrics: Fred Ebb

Directors
Cliff F. Baker, Pat Brown, Vanya Franck, Monte Kuklenski

Designers
Sets: Kathy Gray, Scot Shapiro, Bob Simpson, Micheal Smith. *Costumes:* Cyndy Campbell, Donia Crafton, Robin Kelly Cywinski, Kathy Gray, Gwen Odom. *Lights:* Scott Clevenger, Kathy Gray, Byl Harriell, Scot Shapiro, Bob Simpson.

Media resources
Video: *Waiting for Lefty* (Union National Bank); *The Making of a Musical* (Jones Television Productions, documentary).

Asolo State Theater. Clockwise: Monique Morgan, Clark Niederjohn, Bradford Wallace and Robert Elliott in *The Tempest.* Photo: Gary W. Sweetman.

Attic Theatre. Glen Allen Pruett and Paul Hopper in *Bent.* Photo: Eric Smith.

Asolo State Theater

Richard G. Fallon
Executive Director

David S. Levenson
Managing Director

Stuart Vaughan
Artistic Advisor

Drawer E
Sarasota FL 33578
(813) 355–7115 (business)
(813) 355–2771 (box office)

Founded 1960
Arthur Dorlang, Richard G. Fallon, Eberle Thomas, Robert Strane

Season
February–September

Schedule
Evenings
Tuesday–Sunday
Matinees
Wednesday–Sunday

Facilities
Ringling Museums
Court Playhouse
5401 Bayshore Road
Seating capacity: 320
Stage: proscenium

Finances
October 1, 1979–September 30, 1980
$1,292,000 operating expenses
$ 712,000 earned income
$ 603,000 grants/contributions

Audience
Annual attendance: 196,883
Subscribers: 3,500

Touring contact
Linda M. DiGabriele

AEA LORT (C) contract

Firmly committed to the challenges and rewards of European-style rotating repertory, the Asolo State Theater remains first and foremost an actor's theatre. Here the actor's presence, scope and versatility can flourish in a wide variety of classic and contemporary roles. Casting exigencies are primary in the choice of repertoire: shows must be cast with productive use of the company in mind, and within budgetary means. Rehearsals begin in mid-January and the season closes Labor Day weekend. The season is divided into three sections: three plays run in rotating repertory, followed by the straight run of a musical, and then three more plays in repertory.

Since tourism is a major industry, the schedule is planned so that Asolo audiences may see as many as three plays during a short stay in Sarasota. Every effort is made to ensure diversity in the season lineup, including the use of guest directors and designers. Consequently, the typical Asolo season is quite eclectic.

The Asolo Conservatory of Professional Actor Training offers a two-year M.F.A. program in association with Florida State University, with classes in dance, movement, speech, voice, musical theatre, acting and mime. Students are associate members of the professional company, performing roles and acting as understudies. Internships are available in stage management, technical production, directing and arts management.

The Asolo Touring Theater travels throughout Florida from October to May, giving over 300 performances for 120,000 students from kindergarten through high school. An educational director provides study materials and workshops for students and teachers. A second touring company will be initiated in 1981 to tour the southeastern United States.

Asolo's others activities include staged readings, a newsletter and a volunteer auxiliary.

Productions 1979–80
Ah, Wilderness!, Eugene O'Neill
The Tempest, William Shakespeare
Da, Hugh Leonard
Tintypes, music and lyrics: various; adapt: Mary Kyte, Mel Marvin and Gary Pearle
Man and Superman, George Bernard Shaw
Idiot's Delight, Robert E. Sherwood
The Warrens of Virginia, William C. deMille
• *Transcendental Love,* Daryl Boylan
Stand-Off at Beaver and Pine, Sally Netzel

Productions 1980–81
On Golden Pond, Ernest Thompson
The Beggar's Opera, John Gay
Terra Nova, Ted Tally
The Song is Kern!, Neal Kenyon
• *The Three Musketeers,* adapt: Eberle Thomas, from Alexandre Dumas
Picnic, William Inge
Once in a Lifetime, Moss Hart and George S. Kaufman

Directors
Bernerd Engel, Jim Hoskins, Neal Kenyon, Gene Lesser, Howard J. Millman, John Reich, Robert Strane, Eberle Thomas, Isa Thomas, William Woodman

Designers
Sets: Bennet Averyt, William Barclay, Robert C. Barnes, Franco Colavecchia, Robert Darling, Holmes Easley, David Emmons, John Ezell, Sandro La Ferla. *Costumes:* Vicki S. Holden, Flozanne John, Catherine King, Sally A. Kos, Paige Southard. *Lights:* Martin Petlock.

Media resources
Video: *The Patriots, End of Summer* (WNET).

Attic Theatre

Lavinia Moyer
Artistic Director

Herbert Ferrer
Managing Director

525 Lafayette St.
Detroit, MI 48226
(313) 963–7750 (business)
(313) 963–7789 (box office)

Founded 1976
Lavinia Moyer, Divina Cook, Nancy Shaynes, Herbert Ferrer, James Moran

Season
Year-round

Schedule
Evenings
Thursday–Sunday

Facilities
Seating capacity: 175–200
Stage: flexible

Finances
July 1, 1980–June 30, 1981
$234,000 operating expenses
$135,000 earned income
$ 98,000 grants/contributions

Audience
Annual attendance: 20,000
Subscribers: 550

Touring contact
Kathryn Millar or Lavinia Moyer

AEA Chicago Off Loop Theatre contract

The Attic Theatre is now in its fifth year of producing innovative, professional productions for Detroit audiences. Located in the Greektown district, the theatre has showcased the work of several hundred local artists, has garnered firm support from the artistic and business communities, and has captured the imaginations of people committed to the emergence of a strong arts community in Detroit.

Starting on a shoestring budget

and using local talent, the Attic has become a year-round, resident professional theatre. To the dozen Michigan artists who started the theatre, the past few years have been a constant challenge. Their purpose has been to create a theatre that will become a resource for the development of artistic opportunities for Michigan residents.

In addition to the year-round mainstage season, the Attic conducts a number of support projects: the Attic Actor Training Program; *Detroupe,* a traveling mime company; the Oldsters, a senior citizens' mime troupe; the New Playwrights Forum; and experimental midnight theatre on weekends. In the face of a worsening economic climate for the arts, the Attic is developing new methods to expand programming and raise revenues to provide artists with a living wage.

In May 1981, The Attic joined the Music Hall Center for the Performing Arts to produce *Wings* by Arthur Kopit. For this and other innovative efforts, the Attic received a certificate of merit from the Business Committee for the Arts for its outstanding contribution to the cultural life of Southeastern Michigan.

Productions 1979–80
Buried Child, Sam Shepard
A Midsummer Night's Dream, William Shakespeare
Bloody Bess: A Tale of Piracy and Revenge, William J. Norris, John Ostrander, Stuart Gordon and Organic Theater Company
• *The Motherlode,* John Beem
The Sea Horse, Edward J. Moore

Productions 1980–81
Getting Out, Marsha Norman
The Robber Bridegroom, book and lyrics: Alfred Uhry; music: Robert Waldman
Time Steps, Gus Kaikkonen
Bent, Martin Sherman
Bleacher Bums, Organic Theater Company
Steambath, Bruce Jay Friedman

Directors
Sam Ellis, Robert Grossman, Martin LaPlatney, Ron Martell, James Moran, Lavinia Moyer, Sam Pollak, Edward Townley, Robert Wright, Daniel Yurgaitis

Designers
Sets: Michael Fitzgerald, Lavinia Moyer, Bill Moore, Samuel Pollak, Eve Pruden, Joseph Zubrick. *Costumes:* Donna DiSante, Michael Fitzgerald, Helen King, Kathryn Millar, Lavinia Moyer, Barbara Oleszuck, Samuel Pollak, Eve Pruden, Joseph Zubrick. *Lights:* Brad Butler, Michael Fitzgerald, Lavinia Moyer, Bill Moore, Eve Pruden, Joseph Zubrick.

BAM Theater Company. *A Midsummer Night's Dream.* Photo: Ken Howard.

BAM Theater Company

David Jones
Artistic Director

Arthur Penn
Associate Director

Charles Dillingham
Managing Director

Brooklyn Academy of Music
30 Lafayette Ave.
Brooklyn, NY 11217
(212) 636–4100

Founded 1976
Frank Dunlop, Harvey Lichtenstein

Season
January–June

Schedule
Evenings
Tuesday–Sunday
Matinees
Saturday, Sunday

Facilities
Helen Owen Carey Playhouse
Seating capacity: 1,078
Stage: proscenium
Lepercq Space
Seating capacity: 300–450
Stage: flexible
Opera House
Seating capacity: 2,102
Stage: proscenium

Finances
July 1, 1979–June 30, 1980
$1,769,000 operating expenses
$ 461,000 earned income
$ 540,000 grants/contributions

Audience
Annual attendance: 74,424
Subscribers: 10,500

Booked-in events
Theatre, dance, music

AEA LORT (A) contract

During its first two years, the aim of the BAM Theater Company was to provide New York with a major classical repertory theatre. Playing in the winter and spring, a company of 32 actors presented 10 productions covering the spectrum of world drama.

Play selection for the first season (1979–80) was exploratory and adventurous, earning the company an Obie Award for innovative programming. Shakespeare's fantasy *The Winter's Tale* was produced along with two neglected American plays by Charles MacArthur and Rachel Crothers, the English language premiere of Gorky's *Barbarians,* and an unusual double-bill of farces by Brecht and Feydeau.

In its second season, the company presented more familiar and demanding classics such as *Oedipus* and *A Midsummer Night's Dream.* Associate director Arthur Penn's production of *The Wild Duck* provoked lively controversy, and *The Recruiting Officer* and *Jungle of Cities* continued the policy of mounting works rarely available to American audiences.

In its presentation of European classics, the company emphasized the need for vigorous new American versions of these plays.

BAM Theater's belief has been in a company approach to the classics. Actors were engaged for a full season and 50 percent of the founding group returned for the second year, stressing continuity, shared objectives and a sustained experience. Daily voice and movement classes were provided during the initial rehearsal periods, and productions were performed in rotating repertory to insure variety and freshness in the company's work. Many of America's leading designers contributed to the high standard of visual presentation, and here, too, continuity was encouraged.

The BAM Theater Company will not be in operation during 1981–82 because of insufficient funding to support its planned third season. The futu.e direction of the company is undergoing extensive evaluation. Disappointed to have to suspend the company's operations, the Brooklyn Academy of Music nevertheless maintains a commitment to theatre in New York City.

Productions 1979–80

The Winter's Tale, William Shakespeare
Johnny on a Spot, Charles MacArthur
Barbarians, Maxim Gorky; trans: Kitty Hunter Blair, Jeremy Brooks and Michael Weller
He and She, Rachel Crothers
The Marriage Dance (two one-acts):
The Wedding, Bertolt Brecht; trans: Richard Nelson and Helga Ciulei
The Purging, Georges Feydeau; adapt: Peter Barnes

Productions 1980–81

A Midsummer Night's Dream, William Shakespeare
The Recruiting Officer, George Farquhar
The Wild Duck, Henrik Ibsen; trans: Erik J. Friis; adapt: Thomas Babe
Jungle of Cities, Bertolt Brecht; adapt: Richard Nelson
Oedipus the King, Sophocles; adapt: Stephen Berg and Diskin Clay

Directors

Edward Cornell, Andre Ernotte, David Jones, Emily Mann, Arthur Penn, Laird Williamson

Designers

Sets: John Lee Beatty, Robert Blackman, David Gropman, Andrew Jackness, John Jensen, Heidi Landesman, Ming Cho Lee, Santo Loquasto. *Costumes:* Susan Hilferty, William Ivey Long, Santo Loquasto, Jennifer von Mayrhauser, Carol Oditz, Dunya Ramicova, John David Ridge, Julie Weiss. *Lights:* F. Mitchell Dana, Arden Fingerhut, William Mintzer.

Barter Theatre

Rex Partington
Producing Director

Abingdon, VA 24210
(703) 628–2281 (business)
(703) 628–3991 (box office)

Founded 1933
Robert Porterfield

Season
April–October

Schedule
Evenings
Tuesday–Sunday
Matinees
Wednesday, Saturday

Facilities
Theatre
Seating capacity: 380
Stage: proscenium
Playhouse
Seating capacity: 160
Stage: thrust

Finances
November 1, 1979–October 31, 1980
$715,000 operating expenses
$342,000 earned income
$158,000 grants/contributions

Audience
Annual attendance: 78,000
Subscribers: 2,670

Touring contact
Pearl Hayter

AEA LORT (C) contract

The Barter Theatre was founded in 1933 by Robert Porterfield, at a time when plays could be seen for "30 cents or the equivalent in produce." Except for three years during World War II, Barter has been in continual operation. It is a true regional theatre, serving the five-state area of Virginia, Tennessee, North Carolina, West Virginia and Kentucky.

In 1946, Barter became the first theatre in the country to receive a direct appropriation from its state legislature. Three years later, the Barter production of *Hamlet* was chosen to represent the United States at Kronborg Castle in Elsinore, Denmark.

The company performs in Abingdon from April through October, producing 10 plays in its two performance spaces. In late winter and early spring, the Barter Players tour the southeastern states with a major production, while a second company tours high schools and communities of Virginia with a Theatre-in-Schools program. During the Abingdon season, Barter operates an apprentice program which emphasizes on-the-job training, and in the summer, high school English and drama teachers may attend a week-long workshop.

Following Robert Porterfield's death in 1972, Rex Partington was selected as artistic director and producer. Placing a primary emphasis on artistic achievement, he guides Barter's growth as an ensemble repertory company, producing plays in a wide variety of styles.

Productions 1980

Misalliance, George Bernard Shaw
The Odyssey, adapt: Gregory A. Falls and Kurt Beattie, from Homer
The Importance of Being Earnest, Oscar Wilde
The Royal Family, George S. Kaufman and Edna Ferber
Ah, Wilderness!, Eugene O'Neill

Barter Theatre. *Home of the Brave.* Photo: John Cornelius.

The Desperate Hours, Joseph Hayes
The Heiress, Ruth and Augustus Goetz
Blithe Spirit, Noel Coward
Berlin to Broadway with Kurt Weill, music: Kurt Weill; lyrics: various; adapt: Gene Lerner
Riverwind, book, music and lyrics: John Jennings
Starting Here, Starting Now, music: David Shire; lyrics: Richard Maltby, Jr.

Productions 1981
The Fantasticks, book and lyrics: Tom Jones; music: Harvey Schmidt
The Odyssey
Home of the Brave, Arthur Laurents
Dulcy, George S. Kaufman and Marc Connelly
On Golden Pond, Ernest Thompson
Gallows Humor, Jack Richardson
Arms and the Man, George Bernard Shaw
Two by Five, music: John Kander; lyrics: Fred Ebb
Deathtrap, Ira Levin
Talley's Folly, Lanford Wilson
Oh, Coward!, music and lyrics: Noel Coward; adapt: Roderick Cook

Directors
Patricia Carmichael, Fred Chappell, John Going, Byron Grant, Pamela Hunt, James Kirkland, Ada Brown Mather, Jeff Meredith, John Olon, Rex Partington, Allen Schoer, Mark Sumner, George Touliatos

Designers
Sets: Bennet Averyt, C.L. Hundley, John C. Larrance, Galen M. Logsdon, Rex Partington, Lynn Pecktal. *Costumes:* Nancy Atkinson, Carol Blevins, C.L. Hundley, Sigrid Insull, Rachel Kurland, Galen M. Logsdon, Mary Jane McCarty. *Lights:* Bennet Averyt, Tony Partington, Christopher Shaw, Karen Wenderoff.

Berkeley Repertory Theatre

Michael Leibert
Producing Director

Mitzi Sales
General Manager

2025 Addison St.
Berkeley, CA 94704
(415) 841-6108 (business)
(415) 845-4700 (box office)

Founded 1968
Michael Leibert

Season
Year-round

Schedule
Evenings
Tuesday–Sunday
Matinees
Thursday, Sunday

Facilities
Mainstage
Seating capacity: 400
Stage: thrust
Second Stage
Seating capacity: 70
Stage: flexible

Finances
September 1, 1980–August 31, 1981
\$893,000 operating expenses
\$742,000 earned income
\$182,000 grants/contributions

Audience
Annual attendance: 108,000
Subscribers: 11,043

AEA LORT (C) contract

Berkeley Repertory Theatre. Charles Dean and Don West in *Galileo.* Photo: Hank Kranzler.

Berkeley Repertory Theatre is committed to nurturing the acting, directing and design talent flourishing on the West Coast.

Founded in 1968 by Michael Leibert, the Rep began its life in an 85-seat converted storefront theatre. The intimacy of the old theatre was, this past year, successfully translated into the design of the Rep's new 400-seat theatre. The company mounts a seven-play subscription series in the new space, with each play running for four weeks plus five previews. A full summer season allows Berkeley Rep to employ its production staff year-round.

In its 13 seasons, the Rep's resident ensemble has appeared in a wide range of plays, including some world premieres. The repertoire is currently founded upon several classic playwrights with whom the Rep has become associated: Shakespeare, Shaw and Coward. The season is rounded out with works by such 20th Century masters as Brecht and Williams, and with new plays, many receiving their northern California premieres.

For Berkeley Rep, 1980 was a watershed year. The new theatre was inaugurated and the size of the company grew to 50. The number of subscribers exceeded 11,000 which, combined with single-ticket sales, nearly filled the new house for the entire 1980–81 season. The Rep initiated a production intern program and a subscriber newsletter. The Second Stage opened, with performances of in-house projects. When fully equipped, this "black box" space will be used for such programs as a new play series and small touring shows from other theatres.

At age 14, Berkeley Repertory Theatre is in its adolescence; an exciting period of transition and growth.

Productions 1979–80
A Delicate Balance, Edward Albee
Children of Darkness, adapt: Jeffrey Hirsch, from Edwin Justus Mayer
Waltz of the Toreadors, Jean Anouilh; trans: Lucienne Hill
Hedda Gabler, Henrik Ibsen; adapt: Don West
What the Butler Saw, Joe Orton

Productions 1980–81
Galileo, Bertolt Brecht; trans: Ralph Manheim and Wolfgang Sauerlander
Fallen Angels, Noel Coward
My Heart's in the Highlands, William Saroyan

Pygmalion, George Bernard Shaw
Measure for Measure, William Shakespeare
The Shadow Box, Michael Cristofer
A Life in the Theatre, David Mamet
The Norman Conquests, Alan Ayckbourn

Directors
Dennis Bigelow, Peter Layton, Michael W. Leibert, William I. Oliver, Albert Takazauckas, Don West

Designers
Sets: George Barcos, William Bloodgood, Andrew DeShong, Ralph Funicello, Richard L. Hay, Jesse Hollis, Warren Travis, Noel Uzemack. *Costumes:* Deborah Dryden, Cathleen Edwards, Sarajane Milligan, Merrily Ann Murray, Diana L. Smith, Warren Travis. *Lights:* S. Leonard Auerbach, George Barcos, John Chapot, Dirk Epperson, Lynn Koolish, Robert Peterson, Betty Schneider, Greg Sullivan.

Berkeley Stage Company

Angela Paton
Artistic Director

Robert W. Goldsby
Executive Director

Box 2327
1111 Addison St.
Berkeley, CA 94702
(415) 548–4728

Founded 1974
Angela Paton, Robert W. Goldsby, Drury Pifer

Season
October–July

Schedule
Evenings
Monday–Sunday
Matinees
Sunday

Facilities
Seating capacity: 99
Stage: flexible

Finances
October 1, 1979–September 30, 1980
$143,000 operating expenses
$ 53,000 earned income
$141,000 grants/contributions

Audience
Annual attendance: 18,038
Subscribers: 1,260

AEA 99-seat waiver

Berkeley Stage Company is a theatre company where the future is the focus: a training ground where talents are found and nurtured, and a springboard in the research and development of drama. New forms, new voices, and, in these precarious times, new means of expression emerge on its flexible stage. The visual artist and composer join the dramatist in a theatrical and passionate presentation of the ideas, questions and problems that engage and baffle the contemporary mind. The artistic emphasis is on a truly *living* theatre.

A script development committee prepares free play readings for public presentation and discussion, and a pilot audience education outreach program incorporates the considerable resources of the University of California at Berkeley.

Productions 1979–80
- *Jacob's Ladder,* Barbara Graham
- *Wisdom Amok,* Albert Innaurato

Bosoms and Neglect, John Guare
Bonjour, la, Bonjour, Michel Tremblay; trans: John Van Burek and Bill Glassco
- *The Derby,* book and lyrics: Michael McClure; music: Robert MacDougall

The Great God Brown, Eugene O'Neill

Productions 1980–81
- *Three,* Crispin Larangeira
- *A Memory for Saturday,* Thomas W. Stephens
- *An Evening in Our Century,* Drury Pifer
- *Tingeltangel,* Karl Valentin; trans: Sue-Ellen Case and Roswitha Mueller
- *Loves Labours Wonne,* Don Nigro

Directors
Sue-Ellen Case, Robert W. Goldsby, Jan Lewis, Robert MacDougall, David Ostwald, Angela Paton, Ed Weingold, Richard E.T. White, Leigh Woods

Designers
Sets: Patricia Amlin, Gene Angell, Ariel, William Eddelman, Ewald Hackler, Dennis Howes, Ron Pratt, Warren Travis, Noel Uzemack. *Costumes:* Lani Abbott, Patricia Amlin, Ariel, Barbara Bush, William Eddelman, Mary Gould, Ewald Hackler, Shan Otey, Warren Travis. *Lights:* Peter Clark, Dennis Howes, Kurt Landisman, Wilbur Obata, Jeff Schuenke, Thomas Stocker.

Media resources
Film: *Black Girl, Chile Pequin, Sister of the Bride, Catch a Falling Star* (company produced), *Poetry Playhouse* (KQED), *Dial-a-Lawyer* (KQED, documentary), *The Actor's Eye,* (University of California, documentary). Video: *The People vs. Inez Garcia* (KQED).

Berkeley Stage Company. Jack Shearer, Loretta Sheridan, Bob Kip and Susan Dills in *The Derby.* Photo: Jerald Morse.

The BoarsHead Theater. John Peakes and Carmen Decker in *Clara's Play.* Photo: Rick Brown.

BoarsHead Theater

Richard Thomsen
John Peakes
Artistic Directors

Carol Conn
Managing Director

425 South Grand Ave.
Lansing, MI 48933
(517) 484–7800 (business)
(517) 484–7805 (box office)

Founded 1970
Richard Thomsen, John Peakes

Season
October–September

Schedule
Evenings
Thursday–Sunday
Matinees
Saturday

Facilities
Center for the Arts
Seating capacity: 250
Stage: thrust
Ledges Playhouse
Fitzgerald Park
Grand Ledge, MI 48837
Seating capacity: 350
Stage: thrust

Finances
October 1, 1979–September 30, 1980
$316,000 operating expenses
$204,000 earned income
$104,000 grants/contributions

Audience
Annual attendance: 50,100
Subscribers: 1,517

AEA letter of agreement

The BoarsHead Theater is committed to American plays and the development of American playwrights, and dedicated to the idea that a vital theatre must grow from within in order to become the voice of the community which it serves. At least half of each season is devoted to new works, preferably plays of a distinctly theatrical nature.

A resident core of actors provides the BoarsHead with artistic continuity. Young actors remain with the company an average of three years, and some acting interns are accepted from area universities. The BoarsHead's resident design and technical staffs are augmented by qualified interns accepted on a limited basis. Its summer theatre conducts an apprentice program through Lansing Community College.

The theatre works with playwrights in a reading program that places particular emphasis on plays of midwestern origins or themes. The BoarsHead also seeks to encourage the development of young directors.

Productions 1979–80
The Passion of Dracula, Bob Hall and David Richmond
• *Brontosaurus Tales,* Gus Kaikkonen
Sly Fox, Larry Gelbart
A Christmas Carol, adapt: Richard Thomsen, from Charles Dickens
The Glass Menagerie, Tennessee Williams
• *Back in the Race,* Milan Stitt
The Collected Works of Billy the Kid, Michael Ondaatje
Sizwe Bansi Is Dead, Athol Fugard, John Kani and Winston Ntshona
• *Minnesota Moon,* John Olive
• *A Blue Note Memory of Harvey and Ricky,* Doug Clark
California Suite, Neil Simon
Hello, Dolly!, book: Michael Stewart; music and lyrics: Jerry Herman
Broadway Spirit, various authors
Twigs, George Furth

Productions 1980–81
Waltz of the Toreadors, Jean Anouilh
Gemini, Albert Innaurato
The Palace of Amateurs, John Faro PiRoman
A Christmas Carol
• *Letters from Bernice,* Jeanne Michels and Phyllis Murphy
Ah, Wilderness!, Eugene O'Neill
• *Clara's Play,* John Olive
Oh, Coward!, music and lyrics: Noel Coward; adapt: Roderick Cook
• *Total Abandon,* Larry Atlas
• *Uncle King Arthur,* Milburn Smith
You're a Good Man, Charlie Brown, Charles Schultz; music and lyrics: Clark Gesner
Godspell, book: John Michael Tebelak; music and lyrics: Stephen Schwartz
Deathtrap, Ira Levin

Directors
Charles S. Burr, Barbara Carlisle, Bob Hall, Gus Kaikkonen, B. Rodney Marriott, Andrew Mendelson, Marcia Milgrom, John Peakes, Leonard Peters, Nina A. Simons, Richard Thomsen

Designers
Sets: Peter P. Allburn, Bil Mikulewicz, Gordon Phetteplace, Tim Stapleton. *Costumes:* Sea Daniel, Kerry Shanklin, Patricia K. Smith. *Lights:* David Arnold, Joseph P. Grigaitas, Kim Hartshorn, Arthur Meister, A.J. Rocchio.

The Body Politic Theatre. Barrie Mason and Brendan Phillips in *Macbeth.* Photo: Stuart Markson.

The Body Politic Theatre

James D. O'Reilly
Artistic Director

Sharon Phillips
Managing Director

2261 North Lincoln Ave.
Chicago, IL 60614
(312) 348–7901 (business)
(312) 871–3000 (box office)

Founded 1969
Community Arts Foundation

Season
January–December

Schedule
Evenings
Wednesday–Sunday
Matinees
Sunday

Facilities
Seating capacity: 190
Stage: thrust

Finances
January 1, 1980–December 31, 1980
$272,000 operating expenses
$131,000 earned income
$ 68,000 grants/contributions

Audience
Annual attendance: 23,340
Subscribers: 240

Booked-in events
Theatre, music, dance, poetry readings

AEA Chicago Off Loop Theatre contract

The 1981 season is one of new beginnings for The Body Politic, Chicago's oldest Off-Loop theatre. New artistic director James D. O'Reilly and managing director Sharon Phillips have recruited a new advisory board and restructured the season on a calendar-year schedule. The artistic emphasis is on Chicago artists (actors, directors and designers, as well as playwrights) coupled with a variety of subscription offerings. For example, the 1981 season consisted of one Shakespeare play, two plays by Chicagoans (one of them a world premiere) and a revival of a classic American play, as well as another play by two local playwrights held over from the previous season. The casts, design staffs and directors were exclusively Chicago artists.

The Body Politic is one of five Chicago theatres participating in a two-year program to further strengthen its artistic, management and board teamwork. The theatre is also launching its first major audience development program in some time, as it moves to a broader citywide subscription base. The building itself is experiencing a rebirth, as performance space and seating capacity have both been enlarged, and the building is now co-owned and used by The Body Politic and Victory Gardens Theater. While the two companies will maintain distinct identities, they will cooperate on various educational and administrative programs.

The Body Politic continues to develop its community-oriented outreach programs, including a Bible Story Theatre, signed performances for the hearing-impaired, student and senior citizen discounts, and an annual street festival of performing and visual arts and crafts. The theatre is beginning to develop a magnet program with a local performing arts high school, as well as a professional internship program with production students from the Goodman School of Drama at DePaul University. The Body Politic offers professional training in acting and directing, and houses a gallery for works by local artists, provides workspace for the Chicago Actors Workshop, and rents its theatres to outside groups.

Productions 1979–80
The Ruffian on the Stair and *Funeral Games,* Joe Orton
• *The King's Clown,* David Vando
The Decline and Fall of the Entire World As Seen through the Eyes of Cole Porter, adapt: Ben Bagley
• *Parsifal,* company-developed
Macbeth, William Shakespeare
• *Rhyming Couplets,* Kevin Grattan
• *Coming Attractions,* Shelly Goldstein and Jerry Haislmaier

Productions 1980–81
Twelfth Night, William Shakespeare
The Sea Horse, Edward J. Moore
The Petrified Forest, Robert Sherwood

Directors
Kate Benton, Pauline Brailsford, Bruce Burgun, Dean Button, Susan Dafoe, Dale McFadden, Tom Mula, James D. O'Reilly, Carol Yeckel

Designers
Sets: Nels Anderson, Thomas Beall, Sara Berg, Frances M. Maggio, Luis Ramirez, John Rodriguez, Lynn Ziehe. *Costumes:* Maggie Bodwell, Kerry Fleming, Carl Forsberg, Julie A. Nagel, Elizabeth Passman, Sherry Ravitz, Paul Shoun, Nan Zabriskie. *Lights:* Thomas Beall, Sara Berg, G. Paul Davis, Geri Kelly, Gary Heitz, Luis Ramirez, John Rodriguez.

Boston Shakespeare Company

William P. Cain
Artistic Director

B.J. Krintzman
Managing Director

300 Massachusetts Ave.
Boston, MA 02115
(617) 267–5630 (business)
(617) 267–5600 (box office)

Founded 1975
William P. Cain, Janet Buchwald, Norman Frisch

Season
September–June

Schedule
Evenings
Wednesday–Saturday
Matinees
Sunday

Boston Shakespeare Company. Rishi Puntes and Henry Woronicz in *The Winter's Tale.* Photo: Dan Coven.

Facilities
Seating capacity: 320
Stage: modified thrust
New England Life Hall
Clarendon St.
Seating capacity: 685
Stage: proscenium

Finances
July 1, 1980–June 30, 1981
$342,000 operating expenses
$250,000 earned income
$ 72,000 grants/contributions

Audience
Annual attendance: 120,000
Subscribers: 1,800

Touring contact
Charles Marz

Boston Shakespeare Company has two basic and enduring commitments: to bring exciting, lively and moving productions of the world's greatest plays to the broadest based audience possible, and to serve as a cultural and educational resource to area students and educators. The company performs a full September to June season of Shakespeare and other classical works in rolling repertory. Recently, more contemporary works have been added—particularly on BSC's experimental Secondstage.

The company mounts two new touring productions for schools annually: *An Invitation to Theatre!* (a potpourri of theatre from around the world) and *Shakespeare's World* (a sampler of scenes and playlets drawn from the full range of Shakespeare's work). BSC also conducts student workshops and schedules special student matinees and evening performances of its mainstage productions throughout the year. Additionally, the company operates a year-round school offering courses in acting, mime, circus, stage combat, voice, theatre for the hearing-impaired and arts management.

A growing concern of Boston Shakespeare Company has been community outreach programs. These programs include signed performances for the hearing-impaired; teacher seminars on the problems of teaching Shakespeare at the secondary level; special touring productions at centers for handicapped children; special senior citizen discounts and matinees; and student discounts and subscription series. Current plans call for fully mounted touring productions of mainstage works.

Under the leadership of artistic director Bill Cain and with a dedicated resident acting ensemble, BSC continues to explore new production concepts and new directions for its repertoire. During 1981–82 BSC will have its first playwright-in-residence.

Productions 1979–80
King Lear, William Shakespeare
The Time of Your Life, William Saroyan
The Comedy of Errors, William Shakespeare
The Taming of the Shrew, William Shakespeare
The Winter's Tale, William Shakespeare

Productions 1980–81
Macbeth, William Shakespeare
The Tempest, William Shakespeare
All's Well That Ends Well, William Shakespeare
Tartuffe, Moliere; trans: Richard Wilbur
Richard III, William Shakespeare
The Island, Athol Fugard, John Kani and Winston Ntshona
The Private Life of the Master Race, Bertolt Brecht

Directors
William P. Cain, Grey Cattell Johnson, Richard McElvain, Susan McGinley, Vincent Murphy, Henry Woronicz

Designers
Sets: Dru Minton Clark, Elizabeth Delp, William Groener, Pamela Knauert, Lauren Kurki, Donald Meuse, Kevin J. Roach, Laurence K. Sammons. *Costumes:* Dru Minton Clark, Kay Haskell, Elaine Nicholson, Craig Sonnenberg, Marjorie Tucker. *Lights:* Steven G. Friedlander, Michael Murphy, Kevin J. Roach, Steven Schwartzbert, Patricia Tampone.

Center Stage

Stan Wojewodski, Jr.
Artistic Director

Peter W. Culman
Managing Director

700 North Calvert St.
Baltimore, MD 21202
(301) 685–3200 (business)
(301) 332–0033 (box office)

Founded 1963
Community Arts Committee

Season
September–June

Schedule
Evenings
Tuesday–Sunday
Matinees
Wednesday, Saturday, Sunday

Facilities
Seating capacity: 541
Stage: modified thrust

Center Stage.
Frederick Coffin, Peggy Cosgrave, Paul McCrane and Talia Balsam in *Sally's Gone, She Left Her Name.* Photo: Richard Anderson.

Finances
July 1, 1980–June 30, 1981
$1,670,000 operating expenses
$1,047,000 earned income
$ 720,000 grants/contributions

Audience
Annual attendance: 177,955
Subscribers: 15,696

Touring contact
Jean Reyes

Booked-in events
Summer film series

AEA LORT (B) contract

Center Stage structures its seasons to include masterworks (both classic and contemporary) and the recent work of both American and foreign playwrights. Scripts, both proven and unproven, are chosen to challenge the theatre's artists and audiences alike.

The subscription series includes six mainstage productions performed by a small group of resident actors supplemented by others especially suited to particular productions. Two or three guest directors, in addition to those working in the theatre's developmental program, are engaged each season. Close association with a small pool of designers stimulates full and varied use of the modified thrust stage.

1980 marked the inauguration of the First Stage series, designed to provide workshops for new scripts, a means for testing new conceptual approaches to proven texts, and the discovery (or rediscovery) of appropriate performance styles for them. The First Stage series develops full-scale projects for mainstage presentations outside the subscription series: work not constricted by the traditional four-week rehearsal process, whose evolution might extend over an 18- to 24-month period. Of the 13 First Stage projects initiated thus far, three have gone on to full productions: David Berry's *The Whales of August* at Trinity Square Repertory Company in Providence, and both Lance Mulcahy's adaption of *The Duenna* and Russell Davis' *Sally's Gone, She Left Her Name,* at Center Stage.

Center Stage views its work as integral to the life of its community. By supporting mature artists and encouraging fledgling talent, the theatre insures its long-range development.

Productions 1979–80
Mother Courage and Her Children, Bertolt Brecht; trans: Eric Bentley
Lone Star and *Pvt. Wars,* James McLure
• *A Christmas Carol: Scrooge and Marley,* adapt: Israel Horovitz, from Charles Dickens
Watch on the Rhine, Lillian Hellman
A Day in the Death of Joe Egg, Peter Nichols
Crimes of the Heart, Beth Henley
Cyrano de Bergerac, Edmond Rostand; trans and adapt: Anthony Burgess

Productions 1980–81
The Front Page, Ben Hecht and Charles MacArthur
Agnes of God, John Pielmeier
• *The Duenna,* Richard Brinsley Sheridan; music and adapt: Lance Mulcahy
A Man for All Seasons, Robert Bolt
• *Sally's Gone, She Left Her Name,* Russell Davis
Inherit The Wind, Jerome Lawrence and Robert E. Lee

Directors
Irene Lewis, Jackson Phippin, J Ranelli, Geoffrey Sherman, Stan Wojewodski, Jr., Garland Wright

Designers
Sets: Richard Goodwin, Desmond Heeley, John Kasarda, Hugh Landwehr, Henry Millman, Barry Robison, Paul Wonsek. *Costumes:* Melissa Binder, Linda Fisher, Dona Granata, Desmond Heeley, Tiny Ossman, Barry Robison, Carrie Robbins, Lesley Skannal, Fred Voelpel, Robert Wojewodski. *Lights:* Frances Aronson, Bonnie Ann Brown, Arden Fingerhut, Paul Gallo, John Gleason, Spencer Mosse, Judy Rasmuson, Annie Wrightson.

The Changing Scene

Alfred Brooks
President

1527½ Champa St.
Denver, CO 80202
(303) 893–5775

Founded 1968
Alfred Brooks, Maxine Munt

Season
Year-round

Schedule
Evenings
Thursday–Saturday
Matinees
Sunday

Facilities
Seating capacity: 76
Stage: flexible

Finances
January 1, 1981–December 31, 1981
$80,000 operating expenses
$74,000 earned income
$20,000 grants/contributions

Audience
Annual attendance: 25,000

The basic premises of The Changing Scene are that theatre is an ideal place to combine a diversity of art forms, and that successful theatre can be accomplished by young, unknown artists as well as those more mature and widely recognized. All Changing Scene productions are of new works, and they may embrace sculpture, music, dance, architecture, poetry, mime, film and video. The result is the discovery of new talent and a theatre that has been called "a cross between a kaleidoscope and a merry-go-round."

Three special projects are designed to explore both the experimental and participatory aspects of theatre. The playwright-in-residence works with The Changing Scene actors on the development of a new production over a six-week period. The ongoing environmental theatre workshop, which welcomes free of charge all those who want to work creatively in the theatre, develops two new productions each season. A third project provides scholarships to minority teenagers in the form of three dance classes a week.

Productions 1979
• *Coke Dreams* and *Bride Doll,* Teresa Marffie-Evangelista
• *The Man Who Knew John Dillinger,* Janet McReynolds
• *Transformations,* Alfred Brooks
• *Spit,* Robert Breuler
• *Parade of Arms,* Don Katzman
• *The Sand Rats,* William Lang
L'Anglais Tel Qu'on le Parle, Tristan Bernard
Le Mot de Cambronne, Sacha Guitry
• *Signs of Life,* Joan Schenkar

The Changing Scene. Jack Henri and Ralph Palasek in *Gone for Good.* Photo: Larry Laszlo.

Productions 1980

- *Gone for Good,* John Paul Cannon
- *American Autograph,* John Kaplan
- *Late Sunday Afternoon, Early Sunday Evening,* Jean Lenox Toddie
- *The Masquerade,* Arunas Radvila
- *Kali's Children,* Robert Breuler
- *The Reader,* Joe Getz
- *Our Lady of the Depot,* Terry Stafford
- *Still Life,* Susan Yankowitz

Directors
Robert Breuler, Alfred Brooks, John Paul Cannon, J. H. Crouch, Melanie Donovan, Joe Getz, Mark Herko, Teresa Marffie-Evangelista, Maxine Munt, Michel Reynders

Designers
Sets: Denis Horvath, Dennis Lockhart, Allan McMullen, Jr., Russ Stevenson, Rod Thompson. *Costumes:* Alfred Brooks, Janette Keene, Colette Reynders, Deborah Watson. *Lights:* Mark Gitlis, Ed Intemann, Dennis Lockhart, Gary Miller, Peter Nielson.

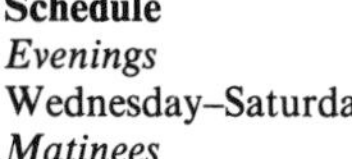

The Children's Theatre Company

Sarah Lawless
Executive Director

John Clark Donahue
Artistic Director

2400 Third Ave. South
Minneapolis, MN 55404
(612) 874-0500 (business)
(612) 874-0400 (box office)

Founded 1961
Beth Linnerson

Season
September–July

Schedule
Evenings
Wednesday–Saturday
Matinees
Tuesday–Sunday

Facilities
Mainstage
Seating capacity: 746
Stage: proscenium
Studio Theatre
Seating capacity: 50–90
Stage: flexible

Finances
July 1, 1980–June 30, 1981
$1,913,000 operating expenses
$1,153,000 earned income
$ 736,000 grants/contributions

Audience
Annual attendance: 216,814
Subscribers: 8,048

Touring contact
Mark Jacobs, Tony Steblay

Booked-in events
Theatre, dance, music, lecture/symposiums

"This children's theatre can and has been training audiences . . . to expect from the theatre somewhat higher, more involved standards . . . accepting that which is truly the magic of theatre: that which is adventuresome, novel, difficult, wild and fanciful . . . " observed Edward Albee upon presenting to John Clark Donahue, artistic director of The Children's Theatre Company and School, the American Theatre Critics Association's 1980 Margo Jones Award (in recognition of achievement in the production and development of new plays and playwrights). Since its beginning in the early 1960s, the company has been committed to the growth of artists and audiences through participation in performing arts classes for young people and adults, and attendance at live productions. CTC has become the nation's largest professional theatre organization of its kind.

More than 270 performances of up to eight productions are offered annually to a diverse audience of children, adults and families. The company presents weekday matinees for school groups with study materials and post-performance discussions and demonstrations enhancing the experience. During the past two seasons, the company and its patrons had the unique opportunity to participate in the first authorized dramatizations of works by Theodor Geisel (Dr. Seuss) and Tomie de Paola. Both pieces were created in collaboration with the authors, and seminars accompanied the projects.

The company's scope is enlarged through studio theatre productions and touring, and indirect exposure to CTC's work continues to expand through script rental to other companies (over 300,000 people viewed CTC's plays in 1980–81). Video productions also reach a vast,

The Children's Theatre Company. *The Story of Babar, the Little Elephant.* Photo: George Heinrich

potentially international audience.
The accredited Theatre School provides some 80 teenagers with daily afternoon coursework in all aspects of performance and production, while a five-week Summer Theatre Institute offers 90 international students-in-residence a more intense curriculum coupled with the performance of three student-developed productions. Internships are offered in every department; a community school and an outreach/residency program respond to the varied needs of the local and national theatre and education communities.

Productions 1979-80

Treasure Island, adapt: Timothy Mason, from Robert Louis Stevenson; music: Hiram Titus
• *The Emperor's New Clothes,* adapt and lyrics: Timothy Mason, from Hans Christian Andersen; music: Libby Larsen
• *The Sleeping Beauty,* adapt: John Clark Donahue and Thomas W. Olson, from The Brothers Grimm; music: Steven M. Rydberg
• *The Hound of the Baskervilles,* adapt: Frederick Gaines, from Arthur Conan Doyle; music: Hiram Titus
• *Falling Moons,* book: Kirk Ristau; music: Ted Unseth
• *The 500 Hats of Bartholomew Cubbins,* adapt and lyrics: Timothy Mason, from Theodor Geisel (Dr. Seuss); music: Hiram Titus
• *Moon over Rio,* book and lyrics: Gene Davis Buck; music: Roberta Carlson
The Festival of Our Lord of the Ships, Luigi Pirandello; music: Steven M. Rydberg; trans: Josephine Mangano

Productions 1980–81

• *The Adventures of Huckleberry Finn,* adapt: Timothy Mason, from Mark Twain; music: Roberta Carlson
• *The Story of Babar, the Little Elephant,* adapt: Thomas W. Olson, from Jean de Brunhoff; music: Steven M. Rydberg; trans: George Muschamp
• *The Virgin Unmasked,* book and lyrics: Sharon Holland; music: Hiram Titus
Cinderella, adapt: John Davidson, from Charles Perrault; music: Ted Gillen, Diane Cina Sherman, John Gessner and Hiram Titus
• *The Three Musketeers,* adapt: Frederick Gaines, from Alexandre Dumas; music: Hiram Titus
• *The Clown of God,* adapt: Tomie De Paola and Thomas W. Olson, from Tomie de Paola; music: Steven M. Rydberg; lyrics: Thomas W. Olson
• *The Marvelous Land of Oz,* adapt: Thomas W. Olson, from L. Frank Baum; lyrics: Gary Briggle; music: Richard A. Dworsky

Directors
Bain Boehlke, Gene Davis Buck, Jon Cranney, John Clark Donahue, Warren Frost, Israel Hicks, Myron Johnson, Vern Sutton, Hiram Titus

Designers
Sets: Jack Barkla, Robert Braun, Gene Davis Buck, Tom Butsch, Dahl Delu, Tomie de Paola, John Clark Donahue, Kristine Haugan, Edward Haynes, Scott Martin, Steven Rydberg, James Waters, Don Yunker. *Costumes:* Gene Davis Buck, Judith Cooper, Jeannie Davidson, Tomie de Paola, Kristine Haugan, Rae Marie Pekas, Barry Robison, Steven Rydberg. *Lights:* Jon Baker, Patrick Thomas Boemer, Robert S. Hutchings, Jr., Scott Martin, Karlis Ozols, Michael Scott, Andrew Sullivan.

Media resources
Film: *A Children's Theatre* (D.A. Pennebaker, documentary). Video: *The Marvelous Land of Oz* (company-developed).

Cincinnati Playhouse in the Park

Michael Murray
Producing Director

Baylor Landrum
Managing Director

Box 6537
Cincinnati, OH 45206
(513) 421-5440 (business)
(513) 421-3888 (box office)

Founded 1960
Community members

Season
October–June

Schedule
Evenings
Tuesday–Sunday
Matinees
Saturday, Sunday

Facilities
962 Mt. Adams Circle
Robert S. Marx Theatre

Seating capacity: 627
Stage: thrust
Thompson Shelterhouse
Seating capacity: 219
Stage: thrust

Finances
September 1, 1980–August 31, 1981
$1,500,000 operating expenses
$ 965,000 earned income
$ 535,000 grants/contributions

Audience
Annual attendance: 200,000
Subscribers: 15,020

Touring contact
Michael Murray

AEA LORT (B) and (D) contracts

The professional theatre for a three-state region of the Ohio River Valley, Cincinnati Playhouse in the Park was founded in 1960 in a 100-year-old shelterhouse, a

Cincinnati Playhouse in the Park. *Compulsion.* Photo: Sandy Underwood.

Circle in the Square. Irene Papas and chorus in *The Bacchae.* Photo: Martha Swope.

Victorian fieldstone structure in a hilltop park overlooking downtown Cincinnati and, across the river, Kentucky. The innovative 627-seat Robert S. Marx Theatre was built in 1968 to complement the refurbished Thompson Shelterhouse. In the fall of 1980, work was completed on the Vontz Theatre Center which encompasses both theatre structures, new offices and an atrium containing a bar and restaurant.

The Playhouse schedule includes two subscription series as well as the seasonal transformation of the Marx stage into a summer cabaret and the site of occasional concerts and special productions. Each season's schedule is designed for variety, challenge and high quality entertainment. Plays are drawn from the entire spectrum of dramatic literature with special emphasis on those works whose human values create a bond between the performers and the audience. At least one musical is presented each year.

Productions are cast individually, and directors and designers engaged are among the finest freelance artists in the country. Four mainstage productions each season are given a week of student preview performances, with study guides prepared for teachers. Regular post-performance seminars feature guest critics discussing the production with audience and cast members. Subscribers receive *Prologue,* a journal of background information, interviews and theatre news. The Playhouse Prompters, a vigorous volunteer organization, provides assistance in a wide range of activities from actor-support services to fund-raising. A recently inaugurated program gives a dozen young theatre workers professional training and experience over the course of each season.

Productions 1979–80

The Diary of Anne Frank, adapt: Frances Goodrich and Albert Hackett
Twelfth Night, William Shakespeare
Ashes, David Rudkin
• *The Cherry Orchard,* Anton Chekhov; trans: Michael Henry Heim
• *The Downstairs Boys,* Murray Schisgal
The Baker's Wife, book: Joseph Stein; music and lyrics: Stephen Schwartz

Productions 1980–81

Compulsion, Meyer Levin
Buried Child, Sam Shepard
The Man Who Came to Dinner, George S. Kaufman and Moss Hart
Loose Ends, Michael Weller
Serenading Louie, Lanford Wilson
The School for Scandal, Richard Brinsley Sheridan
A View from the Bridge, Arthur Miller
The Gin Game, D. L. Coburn
Tintypes, music and lyrics: various; adapt: Mary Kyte, Mel Marvin and Gary Pearle
I Love My Wife, book and lyrics: Michael Stewart; music: Cy Coleman

Directors

Edward Berkeley, Jacques Cartier, Martin Fried, Worth Gardner, John Going, Michael Hankins, Emily Mann, Michael Murray, Amy Saltz

Designers

Sets: Jonathan Arkin, Ursula Belden, Karl Eigsti, Neil Peter Jampolis, David Jenkins, William Schroder, Karen Schulz, Paul Shortt, Joseph A. Varga, Patricia Woodbridge. *Costumes:* Ursula Belden, Jeanne Button, Ann Firestone, Jess Goldstein, Elizabeth Palmer, William Schroder, Rebecca Senske, Caley Summers, Jennifer von Mayrhauser. *Lights:* Pat Collins, F. Mitchell Dana, Jay Depenbrock, Neil Peter Jampolis, Amy Merrill, Spencer Mosse, Marc B. Weiss.

Circle in the Square

Theodore Mann
Artistic Director

Paul Libin
Managing Director

1633 Broadway
New York, NY 10019
(212) 581-3270 (business)
(212) 581-0720 (box office)

Founded 1951
Theodore Mann, Aileen Cramer, Edward Mann, Jose Quintero, Emily Stevens, Jason Wingreen

Season
Year-round

Schedule
Evenings
Tuesday–Saturday
Matinees
Wednesday, Saturday, Sunday

Facilities
Circle in the Square Uptown
Seating capacity: 681
Stage: arena

Finances
July 1, 1979–June 30, 1980
$2,538,000 operating expenses
$2,178,000 earned income
$ 436,000 grants/contributions

Audience
Annual attendance: 189,375
Subscribers: 13,500

AEA Production and LORT (B) contracts

In 1951, Circle in the Square, New York's oldest theatre company, sparked the beginning of the Off Broadway theatre movement. Now celebrating its 30th anniversary and operating year-round *on* Broadway, the theatre presents important new works and established classics, preserving the heritage of the world's great drama and providing leading American stage artists with challenges. In the past three decades, Circle in the Square has presented over 125 productions and has reached nearly two million audience members since

1972. Circle's four-sided, 681-seat arena theatre creates intimacy between actor and audience.

The Circle in the Square Theatre School is 20 years old, with an annual enrollment peaking at 250 students. The school provides rigorous, highly personalized training in acting, singing, voice production and dance, and it draws upon the finest acting and directing talents in New York for its faculty. The school also offers a four-year B.A. program in conjunction with New York University.

The theatre's commitment to the future includes development of new plays and playwrights as well. Each year the artistic staff reviews more than 750 new plays, and promising works are given readings by professional actors at the Monday Night Readings series. The free-of-charge readings are attended by the public, the playwright, artistic director Theodore Mann and his staff, all of whom participate in a discussion afterwards.

Circle-and-the-Schools is an outreach program designed to develop future audiences by enriching the theatre-going experiences of high school and college students. The program offers study guides, half-price tickets and pre- as well as post-performance discussions conducted by the company's staff and actors. This year, Circle-and-the-Schools will attract 9,000 students to the theatre. Circle in the Square also offers free ticket distribution and ticket discounts to disadvantaged groups, senior citizens and the handicapped; an administrative internship program which provides training and experience in various management areas; and a newsletter.

Productions 1979–80

- *Loose Ends,* Michael Weller
  Major Barbara, George Bernard Shaw
- *Past Tense,* Jack Zeman
  The Man Who Came to Dinner, George S. Kaufman and Moss Hart

Productions 1980–81

- *The Bacchae,* Euripides; trans: Michael Cacoyannis
- *John Gabriel Borkman,* Henrik Ibsen; trans: Rolf Fjelde
  The Father, August Strindberg; trans: Harry G. Carlson
- *Scenes and Revelations,* Elan Garonzik

Directors
Michael Cacoyannis, Liviu Ciulei, Sheldon Epps, Goran Graffman, Theodore Mann, Austin Pendleton, Stephen Porter, Alan Schneider

Designers
Sets: Zack Brown, John Conklin, Andrew Jackness, Marjorie Kellogg, Jane Thurn, Nancy Winters. *Costumes:* Zack Brown, John Conklin, Oleksa, Vel Riberto, Jennifer von Mayrhauser, Kristina Watson. *Lights:* William Armstrong, Betsy Adams, Pat Collins, Jeff Davis, Arden Fingerhut, Paul Gallo, John McLain, David F. Segal.

Circle Repertory Company. *Innocent Thoughts, Harmless Intentions.* Photo: Gerry Goodstein.

Circle Repertory Company

Marshall W. Mason
Artistic Director

Porter Van Zandt, Jr.
Producing Director

161 Avenue of the Americas
New York, NY 10013
(212) 691-3210 (business)
(212) 924-7100 (box office)

Founded 1969
Marshall W. Mason, Lanford Wilson, Tanya Berezin, Robert Thirkield

Season
October–August

Schedule
Evenings
Tuesday–Sunday
Matinees
Sunday

Facilities
Sheridan Square Playhouse
99 Seventh Avenue South
Seating capacity: 160
Stage: flexible

Finances
October 1, 1980–September 30, 1981
$850,000 operating expenses
$395,000 earned income
$455,000 grants/contributions

Audience
Annual attendance: 60,000
Subscribers: 4,216

Booked-in events
Music

AEA Off Broadway contract

Circle Repertory Company, a permanent ensemble of actors, playwrights and designers, was founded in 1969 in a loft on upper Broadway by directors Marshall W. Mason and Rob Thirkield, playwright Lanford Wilson and actress Tanya Berezin. Today, Circle Rep has the distinction of being the only theatre in America which has major playwrights in residence creating roles for specific actors. Circle Rep is a national resource: plays born in the company's developmental programs have been presented in 67 professional productions at 34 major regional theatres, and in some 743 amateur productions in all 50 states and eight foreign countries.

For a decade, Circle Rep has led in the rediscovery of lyric realism as the native voice of the American theatre. The company has been honored with 73 major awards, including the Pulitzer Prize, the Antoinette Perry Award ("Tony") and the Margo Jones Award. Circle Rep produces one or two classics each season in addition to new American plays. Among its 75 world premieres are such landmark productions as the 1980 Pulitzer prize-winning *Talley's Folly* as well as *Fifth of July, Gertrude Stein Gertrude Stein Gertrude Stein, The Hot l Baltimore, Knock, Knock, When You Comin' Back Red Ryder?* and *The Sea Horse.* It has produced New York premieres of Sam Shepard's *Suicide in Bb,* David Storey's *The Farm* and Tennessee Williams' *Battle of Angels.* The company's production of *Gemini* is currently the longest running play on Broadway.

In 1974, Circle Rep moved to its present location on Sheridan Square, where it offers a mainstage subscription season and a Projects-in-Progress series. The company also operates the Circle Lab, where projects can develop free of commercial and critical pressure. The Lab holds play readings, playwright and director's units, actors' training workshops and an annual one-act play festival.

Through the interaction of its artistic family—a resident ensemble of actors, designers and directors—Circle Rep strives to bring the scripts of its resident writers to life, so that the action of the play becomes the experience of the audience.

Productions 1979-80

Reunion, David Mamet
Hamlet, William Shakespeare
Mary Stuart, Friedrich von Schiller
• *Innocent Thoughts, Harmless Intentions,* John Heuer
• *Back in the Race,* Milan Stitt
• *The Woolgatherer,* William Mastrosimone
Macready, Frank Barrie

Productions 1980–81

• *The Diviners,* Jim Leonard
Twelfth Night, William Shakespeare
The Beaver Coat, Gerhart Hauptman; trans: Michael Feingold
Childe Byron, Romulus Linney
• *In Connecticut,* Roy London
• *A Tale Told,* Lanford Wilson

Directors

John Bettenbender, John Bishop, Tom Evans, Daniel Irvine, Donald MacKechnie, David Mamet, B. Rodney Marriott, Marshall W. Mason, Leonard Peters

Designers

Sets: John Lee Beatty, Karl Eigsti, David Jenkins, Fred Koluch, Tom Lynch, Bil Mikulewicz, David Potts. *Costumes:* Clifford Capone, Laura Crow, James Berton Harris, Michael Warren Powell, Jennifer von Mayrhauser, Joan E. Weiss. *Lights:* Arden Fingerhut, John Gisondi, Dennis Parichy.

Media resources

Film: *Sextet* (Yes). Video: *The Mound Builders* (WNET).

Cleveland Play House

Richard Oberlin
Director

Janet Wade
General Manager

Box 1989
Cleveland, OH 44106
(216) 795-7000

Founded 1915
Raymond O'Neil

Season
October–April

Schedule
Evenings
Wednesday–Saturday
Matinees
Thursday, Saturday, Sunday

Facilities
2040 East 86th St.
Francis E. Drury Theatre
Seating Capacity: 515
Stage: proscenium
Charles S. Brooks Theatre

Seating capacity: 160
Stage: proscenium
Euclid-77th St. Theatre
7710 Euclid Ave.
Seating capacity: 560
Stage: thrust

Finances
July 1, 1980–June 30, 1981
$1,811,000 operating expenses
$1,064,000 earned income
$ 747,000 grants/contributions

Audience
Annual attendance: 138,000
Subscribers: 11,000

Touring contact
Janet Wade, Richard Oberlin

Booked-in events
Theatre

AEA LORT (C) contract

The Cleveland Play House, America's oldest resident professional theatre, regards artistic growth as its first priority. The company's basic goal is to provide quality productions of the classics, well-crafted plays relevant to the times and new works, all presented by a skilled resident company supplemented by visiting directors and performing artists.

Begun in 1915 with just three full-time employees and productions that attracted only a handful of spectators, the Play House now employs nearly 100 full-time staff members and plays to more than 150,000 people each year. In 1927, the Play House moved into a new building with two theatres, and at present a new theatre complex, designed by architect Philip Johnson, is scheduled for completion in the early 1980s. It will be located adjacent to the existing Drury and Brooks Theatres.

Audiences and staff alike benefit from the range as well as the variety of theatrical challenges offered at the Play House. Among some 73 American and world premieres staged by the theatre are Tennessee Williams and Donald Windham's *You Touched Me,* Donald Freed's *The United States vs. Julius and Ethel Rosenberg (Inquest),* Paul Zindel's *The Effect of Gamma Rays on Man-in-the-Moon Marigolds* and Lawrence and Lee's *First Monday in October.*

The Play House provides Cleveland area students with a number of educational services including programs-in-schools and, since 1933, a Youtheatre, as well as student matinees of all productions, frequent symposia and theatre enrichment programs. Other programs include professional training in acting and administration, classes for children, administrative and technical production fellowships, study materials, student and senior-citizen ticket discounts, free ticket distribution, regional touring, post-performance discussions, workshop productions and staged readings, guest lecturers, a speakers bureau, volunteer auxiliary, theatre rentals, a newsletter and a restaurant.

The Cleveland Play House. William Rhys in *Strider: The Story of a Horse.* Photo: Michael Edwards.

Productions 1979–80
A History of the American Film, Christopher Durang; music: Mel Marvin
Catsplay, Istvan Orkeny; trans: Clara Gyorgyey
A Midsummer Night's Dream, William Shakespeare
Side by Side by Sondheim, music and lyrics: Stephen Sondheim, et al.; adapt: Ned Sherrin
A Lovely Sunday for Creve Coeur, Tennessee Williams
Da, Hugh Leonard
Custer, Robert Ingham
Wings, Arthur Kopit
Wuthering Heights, adapt: Paul Lee, from Emily Bronte
Present Laughter, Noel Coward
Peanuts and Cracker Jack, Jerry Slaff

Productions 1980–81
Watch on the Rhine, Lillian Hellman
Indulgences in the Louisville Harem, John Orlock
Filumena, Eduardo de Filippo; trans: Keith Waterhouse and Willis Hall
A Christmas Carol, adapt: Doris Baizley, from Charles Dickens
Bedroom Farce, Alan Ayckbourn
Emigrants, Slawomir Mrozek; trans: Peter Sander
Strider: The Story of a Horse, book: Mark Rozovsky, lyrics: Uri Riashentsev and Steve Brown; adapt: Robert Kalfin and Steve Brown
Children of Darkness, Edwin Justus Mayer
On Golden Pond, Ernest Thompson
A Funny Thing Happened on the Way to the Forum, book: Larry Gelbart and Burt Shevelove; music: Stephen Sondheim
How I Got That Story, Amlin Gray

Directors
Kenneth Albers, Lynn Gannaway, Joseph J. Garry, Jr., Judith Haskell, Paul Lee, Evie McElroy, Richard Halverson, Richard Oberlin, Michael Maggio, William Rhys, Peter Sander, Larry Tarrant

Designers
Sets: Charles Berliner, Gary C. Eckhart, Richard Gould, James Irwin, William Martin Jean, Wayne Merritt, Paul Rodgers. *Costumes:* Larry Bauman, Charles Berliner, Mary H. Carey, Diane B. Dalton, Richard Gould, Estelle Painter. *Lights:* Richard Gould, James Irwin, David Langston.

The Cricket Theatre. Set for *Blues,* designed by Vera Polovko—Mednikov. Photo: Patrick Boemer.

The Cricket Theatre

Lou Salerni
Artistic Director

Cynthia Mayeda
Managing Director

Hennepin Center for the Arts
528 Hennepin Ave.
Minneapolis, MN 55403
(612) 333-5241 (business)
(612) 333-2401 (box office)

Founded 1971
William H. Semans

Season
October–June

Schedule
Evenings
Wednesday–Sunday
Matinees
Sunday

Facilities
Seating capacity: 384
Stage: modified thrust

Finances
July 1, 1980–June 30, 1981
$676,000 operating expenses
$215,000 earned income
$439,000 grants/contributions

Crossroads Theatre Company.
Purlie. Photo: Rick Khan.

Audience
Annual attendance: 29,714
Subscribers: 1,777

AEA LORT (C) contract

The Cricket Theatre is dedicated primarily to the production of plays by living American writers, in the belief that the future of American theatre depends greatly upon the discovery and encouragement of talented new playwrights.

Since the theatre's first full season in 1971, it has produced a total of 72 plays of which 16 have been world premieres and 46 have been area premieres. In 1977, The Cricket established a program entitled Works-In-Progress, designed to further the production of new works. This program provides promising playwrights the opportunity to work with actors, directors and other theatre artists preparing new plays for professional production. To date, four works developed through the Works-In-Progress program have been produced on the the Cricket's mainstage.

In addition, a unique outreach program was instituted in 1980 to encourage Minnesota colleges to mount new works by American playwrights. Through this program, the Cricket offers plays already done in workshop to area colleges for full production with the promise of guidance from the Cricket's staff.

In September 1979, the theatre moved from an old movie house in northeast Minneapolis to the new Hennepin Center for the Arts in downtown Minneapolis. The 384-seat theatre was specially designed to meet the Cricket's needs and is now its permanent home. Listed as a landmark building in the National Historic Register, it has been restored as a cultural center housing the Cricket along with the Minnesota Dance Theatre and several smaller arts organizations.

Along with its world and area premieres, the Cricket periodically produces fresh interpretations of contemporary classics with the intent of bringing to its audience a complete picture of American theatre including its history and major influences.

Productions 1979–80
Gossip, George F. Walker
Buried Child, Sam Shepard
Starting Here, Starting Now, music: David Shire; lyrics: Richard Maltby, Jr.
Wings, Arthur Kopit
• *Revolution of the Heavenly Orbs,* John Orlock
• *The Paranormal Review,* Erik Brogger
A Streetcar Named Desire, Tennessee Williams

Productions 1980–81
• *Blues,* Kirk Ristau
• *Sightlines,* Mark Eisman
• *Tactics for Non-Military Bodies,* John Orlock
• *Northern Lights,* Erik Brogger
The Dark at the Top of the Stairs, William Inge
Side by Side by Sondheim, music and lyrics: Stephen Sondheim, et. al; adapt: Ned Sherrin

Directors
Howard Dallin, Sean Michael Dowse, Robert Engels, Lou Salerni

Designers
Sets: James Guenther, Dick Leerhoff, Vera Polovko-Mednikov, Thom Roberts. *Costumes:* Christopher Beesley, Vera Polovko-Mednikov, Gregory Lee Robbins, Cynthia Savage. *Lights:* Phillip Billey, Lisa Johnson, Michael Vennerstrom.

Media resources
Video: *A Beginning, a Middle and End* (KTCA, documentary).

Crossroads Theatre Company

L. Kenneth Richardson
Artistic Director

Rick Khan
Producer

320 Memorial Parkway
New Brunswick, NJ 08901
(201) 249–5561
(201) 249–5560

Founded 1978
Rick Khan, L. Kenneth Richardson

Season
September–June

Schedule
Evenings
Wednesday–Sunday
Matinees
Saturday

Facilities
Seating capacity: 150
Stage: flexible

Finances
July 1, 1979–June 30, 1980
$175,000 operating expenses
$ 21,000 earned income
$164,000 grants/contributions

Audience
Annual attendance: 14,000
Subscribers: 1,100

Touring contact
Rick Khan

Booked-in events
Community arts groups

AEA letter of agreement

Crossroads Theatre Company was created to provide a forum for black theatre artists and to educate audiences of all races as to the significance of black theatre in American culture. As a black theatre company, Crossroads faces an image problem: the public is not quite sure what to expect. Are the plays relevant exclusively to black people? Does black theatre include interracial plays? Are white artists involved in black theatre? Will the plays be anti-white? Until these questions are clarified, Crossroads and theatres like it will not successfully tap the widest possible audience.

Crossroads focuses on the work of black (African, Afro-American and West Indian) playwrights, in an attempt to portray the truth, complexity and aesthetic of black culture. Through the presentation of quality plays that project a positive image of the black experience, Crossroads attempts to identify the universal nature of black drama.

Crossroads serves as a black regional theatre and provides a working environment that is free of commercial pressure, where black theatre artists can work on scripts and plays not traditionally performed by black casts. The theatre is located in New Brunswick, a small community that is quickly becoming a major business and cultural center in New Jersey. Since its inception Crossroads has been developing audiences from a large minority population that has little or no theatre-going tradition. Outreach programs include in-class performance workshops, technical and creative training for young people interested in theatre, free performances for students and senior citizens and consultant work with community organizations.

Productions 1979–80
The Zoo Story, Edward Albee
Snowangel, Louis Carlino
Slow Dance on the Killing Ground, William Hanley
Eden, Steve Carter
For Colored Girls who have Considered Suicide/When The Rainbow is Enuf, Ntozake Shange
• *On the Corner,* company-developed
Lovers and Other Strangers, Renee Taylor and Joseph Bologna

Productions 1980–81
• *One Monkey Don't Stop No Show,* Don Evans
My Sweet Charlie, David Westheimer
Purlie, book: Ossie Davis, Phillip Rose and Peter Udell; music: Gary Geld; lyrics: Peter Udell
Ceremonies in Dark Old Men, Lonnie Elder III
Medal of Honor Rag, Tom Cole
The Owl and the Pussycat, Bill Manhoff

Directors
Maureen Heffernan, Daniel Irvin, Rick Khan, L. Kenneth Richardson

Designers
Sets: Lloyd Harris, Craig Martin, Bill Motyka, Daniel Proett. *Costumes:* Valerie Charles, Judith Hart, Brenda Jones, Linda Reynolds. *Lights:* Greg Chabay, Daniel Stratman.

CSC Repertory

Christopher Martin
Artistic Director

Stephen J. Holland
Managing Director

136 East 13th St.
New York, NY 10003
(212) 677-5808 (business)
(212) 677-4210 (box office)

Founded 1967
Christopher Martin

Season
September–May

Schedule
Evenings
Tuesday–Saturday
Matinees
Saturday, Sunday

Facilities
Seating capacity: 200
Stage: thrust

Finances
July 1, 1980–June 30, 1981
$350,000 operating expenses
$189,000 earned income
$158,000 grants/contributions

Audience
Annual attendance: 30,000
Subscribers: 2,000

AEA Off Broadway contract

"Classics in the present tense" is the artistic imperative of Christopher Martin, CSC's founder and artistic director. Influenced by the European collective ensembles—and by the work of Roger Planchon and Peter Stein in particular—CSC sets about breaking down the literary barrier in the theatre, forcing a confrontation between the audience and the text.

In bridging the playwright's world and our own Western socio-political environment, CSC is committed to carefully researched productions,

CSC Repertory. Robert Stattel and Karen Sunde in *Oedipus at Colonus.* Photo: Gerry Goodstein.

Dallas Theater Center. Eleanor Lindsay, Pamela Hurst and Nancy Wilkins in *Ladybug, Ladybug, Fly Away Home.* Photo: Linda Blase.

exploratory design and a permanent ensemble dedicated to the immediacy of the text. In order to create more rehearsal time for each production, the company recently has chosen to mount interlocking plays such as Shakespeare's *Richard II* and *Henry IV Parts I and II,* Yeats' complete Cuchulain Cycle, Buchner's *Woyzeck* and *Leonce and Lena,* and the complete Oedipus cycle of Sophocles. In the fall of 1981, CSC will mount an uncut *Peer Gynt* spanning two evenings. In addition, the company rescues forgotten plays like Wedekind's *Marquis of Keith* (1979) and Lermontov's *Maskerade,* scheduled for the spring of 1982.

To maintain a dialogue with CSC's European counterparts, Christopher Martin and dramaturg Karen Sunde spend the off-season observing such theatres as Stein's Schaubuhne am Halleschen Ufer and Planchon's Theatre National Populaire and the major international festivals. Planchon's collaboration on his own *Gilles de Rais* at CSC was a direct result of such interactions, and future projects are under discussion with other key theatres.

During the next few seasons, CSC plans to expand beyond its five-play repertory season, including remountings of past productions. A second space for new works, a larger ensemble, and year-round production including touring and international exchange, are also planned.

Productions 1979–80
The Cuchulain Plays, William Butler Yeats; music: Noble Shropshire:
At the Hawk's Well
The Green Helmet
On Baile's Strand
The Only Jealousy of Emer
The Death of Cuchulain
The Cavern, Jean Anouilh; trans: Lucienne Hill and Christopher Martin
Doctor Faustus, Christopher Marlowe
Don Juan, Moliere; trans: Christopher Martin
The Merchant of Venice, William Shakespeare

Productions 1980–81
The Oedipus Cycle, Sophocles; trans: Paul Roche:
Oedipus Rex
Oedipus at Colonus
Antigone
• *Gilles de Rais,* Roger Planchon; trans: John Burgess
Woyzeck, Georg Buchner; trans: Christopher Martin
Leonce and Lena, Georg Buchner; trans: Christopher Martin

Directors
Christopher Martin, Karen Sunde

Designers
Sets: Terry A. Bennett, Pamela Howard, Christopher Martin. *Costumes:* Terry A. Bennett, Pamela Howard. *Sets:* Christopher Martin, Seth Price.

Dallas Theater Center

Paul Baker
Artistic Director

Al Milano
Managing Director

3636 Turtle Creek Blvd.
Dallas, TX 75219
(214) 526–8210 (business)
(214) 526–8857 (box office)

Founded 1959
Robert D. Stecker, Sr., Beatrice Handel, Paul Baker, Dallas citizens

Season
October–August

Schedule
Evenings
Tuesday–Saturday
Matinees
Wednesday, Saturday

Facilities
Kalita Humphreys Theater
Seating capacity: 516
Stage: thrust
Down Center Stage
Seating capacity: 56
Stage: proscenium

Finances
September 1, 1979–August 31, 1980
$1,472,000 operating expenses
$ 853,000 earned income
$ 728,000 grants/contributions

Audience
Annual attendance: 175,000
Subscribers: 13,484

Touring contact
Timothy H. Haynes

Booked-in events
Theatre

AEA Actor–Teacher contract

Led by founding artistic director Paul Baker, the Dallas Theater Center is firmly committed to professional and educational excellence and strong community involvement. Since the theatre complex, Frank Lloyd Wright's last great building, opened in 1959, over 7,000 performances have been staged there and on tour.

The continuing development of the acting company is of primary importance, and during the 1980–81 season, four guest directors were imported: English actor/director Anton Rodgers, New York director Joan Vail Thorne, international director Derek Goldby and playwright Mark Medoff, who directed his *Children of a Lesser God.* An intensive annual workshop in acting, movement and voice is held for the company.

Seeking to appeal to varied audiences, DTC presents a balanced selection of classics, contemporary plays and premieres in the Kalita Humphreys Theater, while promising new plays are produced at Down Center Stage. The Saturday Magic Turtle is a season for young people, presenting such plays as *Androcles and the Lion, Beauty and the Beast* and *Winnie-the-Pooh.* Works in progress are given professional readings as part of the Eugene McKinney New Play Series.

DTC is one of the nation's leading supporters of playwrights and new works, having produced more than 100 world or American premieres by its own playwrights and such prominent writers as Preston Jones, Mark Medoff and Robert Anderson. The Theater Center has sponsored three Playmarkets of new plays staged for invited agents, critics, directors and writers from across the country.

Dallas Theater Center operates a graduate program offering an MFA degree in theatre through Trinity University, San Antonio. It also has a Teen-Children's Theater for ages four through 18, devoted to helping young people discover their creative abilities. Sponsored by the Texas Commission on the Arts and the National Endowment for the Arts, DTC toured schools and communities throughout Texas in the spring of 1981. During the summer, MimeAct, in association with the City Arts Program division of the Dallas Park and Recreation Department, presents free performances in city parks.

Productions 1979–80
A Man for All Seasons, Robert Bolt
A Christmas Carol, adapt: Sally Netzel and John Filgmiller, from Charles Dickens

The Dell'Arte Players Company. Jael Weisman and Donald Forrest in *Whiteman Meets Bigfoot.* Photo: Peter Canclini.

• *The Illusion,* book, music and lyrics: Randolph Tallman, Steven Mackenroth, John Henson and John Logan
Ladybug, Ladybug, Fly Away Home, Mary Rohde
Sly Fox, Larry Gelbart
Holiday, Philip Barry
Da, Hugh Leonard
• *The Darning Tree,* Trey Hall
• *Angel's Crossing,* Allen Hibbard
• *Cheese Garden,* Sam Havens
Dr. Jekyll and Mr. Hyde, adapt: Jim Marvin, from Robert Louis Stevenson
Village Wooing, George Bernard Shaw

Productions 1980–81
Cyrano De Bergerac, Edmond Rostand; trans: Brian Hooker
On Golden Pond, Ernest Thompson
A Christmas Carol
• *The French Have a Word for It,* Georges Feydeau; trans: Barnett Shaw
The Incredible Murder of Cardinal Tosca, Alden Nowlan and Walter Learning
Children of a Lesser God, Mark Medoff
Deathtrap, Ira Levin
• *Land of Fire,* Glenn Allen Smith
Goya, Henry Beissel
• *Stagg and Stella,* Fred Getchell
Grandma Duck Is Dead, Larry Shue
The Chronicle of Queen Jane, Florence Stevenson

Directors
Hanna Cusick, Judith Kelly Davis, Robyn Flatt, Andrew Gaupp, Derek Goldby, Martha Goodman, Tim Haynes, C.P. Hendrie, John Henson, Mary Lou Hoyle, Pamela Hurst, Mary Sue Jones, Jeffrey Kinghorn, Eleanor Lindsay, John Logan, Peter Lynch, Mark Medoff, Ryland Merkey, Michael Mullen, Paul Munger, Bryant J. Reynolds, Anton Rodgers, Michael Scudday, Campbell Thomas, Joan Vail Thorne, Dennis Vincent

Designers
Sets: Yoichi Aoki, Virgil Beavers, Randy Bonifay, Cheryl Denson, Robert Duffy, James Eddy, Joe Ficocolla, Raynard Harper, John Henson, Jak Herring, Allen Hibbard, Doug Jackson, Michael Krueger, Peter Lynch, Stella McCord, Barbara Sanderson, Cliff Smith. *Costumes:* Deborah Allen, Yoichi Aoki, Sally Askins, Sally Dorothy Bailey, H. Byron Ballard, Irene Corey, Cheryl Denson, Scott L. Hammar, Tim Haynes, Russell Henderson, John Henson, Mary Lou Hoyle, Doug Jackson, Jeffrey Kinghorn, Renee Le Cuyer, Peter Lynch, Stella McCord, Carol Miles, Gregory Schwab, Cliff Smith, Jeff Storer, Nancy Wilkins. *Lights:* Linda Blase, Robert Duffy, Joe Fioccola, Scott L. Hammar, Raynard Harper, Jak Herring, Allen Hibbard, Ken Hudson, Wayne Lambert, Stella McCord, Carol Miles, Randy Moore, Bill Nufer, Martin L. Sachs, Gregory Schwab, Michael Scudday, Don Thomas, Brent Williams.

Media resources
Film: *Stages of Preston Jones* (KERA-TV, documentary); *The Theater At Work, In Production, Opening Night* (Institutional Television Center, Dallas County Community College District, documentaries). Radio: *Ladybug, Ladybug, Fly Away Home (Earplay).*

Dell'Arte Players Company

Joan Schirle
Managing Director

Box 98
Arcata, CA 95521
(707) 668–5782

Founded 1971
Carlo and Jane Mazzone-Clementi

Season
Year-round touring

Finances
October 1, 1979–September 30, 1980
$136,000 operating expenses
$ 62,000 earned income
$ 73,000 grants/contributions

Audience
Annual attendance: 15,000

Touring contact
Michael Fields

The Dell'Arte Players Company is an ensemble of professional actors and musicians inspired by commedia dell'arte, combining traditional acting values with highly developed skills in mask, acrobatics, juggling, etc. Based in rural Blue Lake, California, they have dramatized such subjects as herbicide spraying and the search for "Bigfoot;" their newest work, commissioned by a local clinic, promotes male involvement in birth control and family planning.

Themes derived from a rural lifestyle achieve universality in the hands of this touring company, and when combined with high performing standards (all company members are fulltime, salaried professionals), a unique and exciting style results. In February 1980, the Players were guests of the Italian government, the only American company to perform at the 1980 Venice Biennale.

The company creates only one or two major works each year, after a long process of creation and investigation. Works are toured, rewritten and toured again, with continuous refinement of style, idea and execution. Each play is meant to be both entertaining and relevant to the lives of the company and their community. *Intrigue at Ah-Pah,* a mystery-comedy about the future of California's ecology, used the movie-detective genre with a private eye heroine; the legendary Bigfoot came to life from the pages of an R. Crumb comic book adapted for the stage with music.

Residencies and workshops are a major part of each touring itinerary, which includes rural towns, colleges, community centers and extended runs in major West Coast cities. A European tour is planned for the summer of 1982. The company is associated with the Dell'Arte School of Mime and Comedy in Blue Lake, a professional training school emphasizing physical performance skills in a year-long program. The company has presented two intensive summer workshops: Cabaret Peformance Style in 1980, and The Mask: Techniques and Performance in 1981. Programs-in-schools, outreach through community service agencies and children's theatre are additional services of Dell'Arte.

Productions 1979–80

- • *Intrigue at Ah-Pah,* book: company-developed; music and lyrics: Joan Schirle and Lisa Garcia
- *Birds of a Feather,* Stan Laurel
- *The Loon's Rage,* Joan Holden, Steve Most and Jael Weisman
- • *Alice in "I Really Wonderland",* Jon Paul Cook

Productions 1980–81

- • *Whiteman Meets Bigfoot,* book: company-developed; music and lyrics: Joan Schirle
- *Intrigue at Ah-Pah*
- • *Colonel Pottie's Bigfoot Revue,* company-developed
- • *Once upon a Box,* developed by students of the Dell'Arte School of Mime and Comedy
- • *The Crooked Mirror, a Cabaret Revue,* various authors

Directors
Jon Paul Cook, Alain Schons, Jael Weisman, Sam Woodhouse

Designers
Sets: Alain Schons. *Costumes:* Cindy Claymore, Laura Hussey, Antonia Reis. *Lights:* Alain Schons, Ted Vukovich.

Media resources
Video: *Whiteman Meets Bigfoot, Intrigue at Ah-Pah* (Demystavision).

Denver Center Theatre Company

Edward Payson Call
Artistic Director

Gully Stanford
Managing Director

1050 13th St.
Denver, CO 80204
(303) 893–4200 (business)
(303) 893–4100 (box office)

Founded 1980
Denver Center for the Performing Arts

Season
November–April

Schedule
Evenings
Monday–Saturday
Matinees
Saturday

Facilities
The Stage
Seating capacity: 650
Stage: thrust
The Space
Seating capacity: 400
Stage: flexible
The Lab
Seating capacity: 100
Stage: flexible

Finances
July 1, 1980–June 30, 1981
$2,387,000 operating expenses
$ 832,000 earned income
$1,555,000 grants/contributions

Audience
Annual attendance: 99,063
Subscribers; 6,655

Booked-in events
Theatre, music, dance, lectures, fashion shows

AEA LORT (B) contract

The Denver Center Theatre Company, the only major repertory theatre between Minneapolis and the West Coast, strives to be a regional theatre in the best sense of the word. Since its inception three years ago, the company has concentrated on producing the classics of dramatic literature, in order to make these great works available to audiences of the Rocky Mountain West. Along with this commitment on the part of the company and its directors is the desire to explore and refine their classical acting styles.

Using Colorado history to generate theatre works is another way in which the company maintains its regional focus, and several new plays of this kind will be commissioned in 1981.

The Denver Center Theatre Company performs its seven-play season in rotating repertory, using two theatres: a 650-seat thrust stage called The Stage and a 400-seat environmental theatre called The Space. A third playhouse, The Lab, seats 100 and houses experimental works.

Other company activities include an innovative assistant director's program, local touring, a high school usher's workshop and artists-in-the-schools programs.

Denver Center Theatre Company. Tandy Cronyn, Teddy Denious, James Lawless and Tyne Daly in *The Caucasian Chalk Circle.* Photo: Christopher Kirkland.

Productions 1979–80
The Caucasian Chalk Circle, Bertolt Brecht; trans: Eric Bentley
The Learned Ladies, Moliere; trans: Richard Wilbur
Moby Dick—Rehearsed, Orson Welles
A Midsummer Night's Dream, William Shakespeare
• *Passing Game,* Steve Tesich

Productions 1980–81
Henry IV, Part I, William Shakespeare
Under Milk Wood, Dylan Thomas
Misalliance, George Bernard Shaw
Loot, Joe Orton
Medea, Euripides; adapt: Robinson Jeffers
Wings, Arthur Kopit
How to Succeed in Business Without Really Trying, book: Abe Burrows, Jack Weinstock and Willie Gilbert; music and lyrics: Frank Loesser

Directors
Edward Payson Call, Jerome Kilty, Gene Lesser, Kenneth Welsh, Laird Williamson, William Woodman, Stuart Vaughn

Designers
Sets: Robert Blackman, Peter Davis, Robert Ellsworth, Ralph Funicello, Marjorie Kellogg, Robert Mitchell, Bob Schmidt. *Costumes:* Nanzi Adzima, Deborah Bays, Robert Blackman, Lowell Detweiler, Sam Fleming, Merrily Ann Murray, Kristina Watson. *Lights:* Pamela Cooper, Donald Darnutzer, Dirk Epperson, Danny Ionazzi, Robert Jared, Duane Schuler.

Media resources
Radio: *Misalliance* (KCFR-FM).

Detroit Repertory Theatre. Ruth Palmer, Roberta Rutherford, Dennis Moore, Dee Andrus and Robert Skrok in *Decision at Valley Forge.* Photo: Bruce E. Millan.

Detroit Repertory Theatre

Bruce E. Millan
Artistic Director

Robert Williams
Executive Director

13103 Woodrow Wilson Ave.
Detroit, MI 48238
(313) 868–1347

Founded 1965
Bruce E. Millan

Season
September–June

Schedule
Evenings
Thursday–Sunday
Matinees
Saturday

Facilities
Seating capacity: 196
Stage: proscenium

Finances
January 1, 1980–December 31, 1980
$156,000 operating expenses
$101,000 earned income
$ 26,000 grants/contributions

Audience
Annual attendance: 18,884
Subscribers: 637

AEA letter of agreement

The Detroit Repertory Theatre, located in the heart of Michigan's largest city, is a self-contained creative system operating out of three buildings and producing a professional theatre alternative for southeastern Michigan. The company produces new plays, well known works in new ways and revives worthwhile forgotten plays. It has been a vital cultural resource to the immediate neighborhood, the city and the region for over 15 years.

The company produces at least four major plays each season for a total of up to 160 performances, with each play running approximately eight weeks. In addition, the Repertory produces numerous workshops and children's plays. It is the theatre's policy to cast without regard to race or gender, unless these distinctions are crucial to the meaning of the play. This policy allows minority and women actors to play roles previously denied them, and challenges the audience to see characters rather than colors or genders.

The theatre houses a fully equipped proscenium stage with intimate seating for 196. Works of local artists are displayed in the lobby, and the unique and comfortable setting encourages conversation before and after the performances.

The Detroit Repertory Theatre has instituted a variety of work-development and feedback programs designed to meet the needs of local artists, audiences and the community. These programs include the Cultural Fellowship Program, Free Acting Workshop Program, Michigan Playwrights Program, Poster Program, Living History Program and the "Own the Repertory" Charitable Fund Raising Program. The depth of the Repertory's commitment to the community, the quality of the work produced by skilled indigenous artists, the nature of the programs, the casting policy, the choice of plays, the intimate theatre and the pleasant lobby combine to enhance the cultural experience provided by the Detroit Repertory Theatre.

Productions 1979–80
A Delicate Balance, Edward Albee
• *Decision at Valley Forge,* Muriel Andrew
Desire Under the Elms, Eugene O'Neill
Design for Living, Noel Coward

Productions 1980–81
Catsplay, Istvan Orkeny; trans: Clara Gyorgyey
American Buffalo, David Mamet
Puntila and Matti, His Hired Man, Bertolt Brecht; music: Kelly Smith
Bosoms and Neglect, John Guare

Directors
Dee Andrus, Barbara Busby, Bruce E. Millan

Designers
Sets: Marylynn Kacir, Bruce E. Millan, Dick Smith. *Costumes:* Marianna Hoad, Bernadine Vida Darrell. *Lights:* Marylynn Kacir, Dick Smith.

East West Players

Mako
Artistic Director

Janet Mitsui
Administrator

4424 Santa Monica Blvd.
Los Angeles, CA 90029
(213) 660–0366 (business)
(213) 666–0867 (box office)

Founded 1965
Mako, James Hong, June Kim, Guy Lee, Pat Li, Yet Lock, Beulah Quo

Season
October–September

Schedule
Evenings
Thursday–Sunday

Facilities
Seating capacity: 99
Stage: flexible

Finances
July 1, 1980–June 30, 1981
$178,000 operating expenses
$100,000 earned income
$ 77,000 grants/contributions

Audience
Annual attendance: 60,000
Subscribers: 460

Touring contact
Janet Mitsui

AEA Theatre for Young Audiences and 99-seat waiver contracts

The goal of East West Players is to preserve and express a language, a literature and a "sound" of its own by developing an Asian-American theatre that is vital, truthful and alive. Responding to the frustration that Asian/Pacific Americans have faced because they are different in a country where "belonging" is paramount, East West Players celebrates what these Americans have contributed to society over the past several generations. Through its productions, East West is opening the door to a culture, to reveal a tapestry rich in sensitivity and creativity.

In addition to its resident season, East West Players tours, celebrating the Asian/Pacific American experience in much the same way that their ancestors celebrated the harvest: a theatrical troupe comes into the village and performs amidst a supportive air of friendship and recreation. In this way, East West aims to refocus the self-image of its people, to look at their past and deal with the present.

Productions 1979–80
- *Stories with Sticks and Shadows,* adapt: Michiko Tagawa
- *Hawaii No Ka Oi,* Ed Sakamoto
- *What the Enemy Looks Like,* Perry Miyake
- *Da Kine,* Leigh Kim

Happy End, book and lyrics: Bertolt Brecht; music: Kurt Weill, adapt: Michael Feingold

Productions 1980–81
F.O.B., David Henry Hwang
- *Oofty Goofty,* Frank Chin

Hokusai Sketchbooks, Seiichi Yashiro; trans: Ted T. Takaya
Godspell, book: John-Michael Tebelak; music and lyrics: Stephen Schwartz
- *Life of the Land,* Ed Sakamoto

Directors
Shizuko Hoshi, Alberto Isaac, Mako, Sam Shimono

Designers
Sets: Rae Creevey, Jay Koiwai, Woodward Romaine, Jr., Ellen Wakamatsu. *Costumes:* Rodney Kageyama, Terence Tam Soon, J. Maseras Pepito, Ellen Wakamatsu. *Lights:* Rae Creevey, Emily Kuroda, Bill Schaffner.

Media resources
Film: *Faces of Change* (KNXT, documentary). Video: *And the Soul Shall Dance* (KCET *Hollywood Television Theatre),* *Total Theatre Ensemble* (KNBC).

East West Players. Clyde Kusatsu, Soon-Teck Oh, Saachiko and J. Maseras Pepito in *Hokusai Sketchbooks.*

El Teatro Campesino. Don J. Boughton and W. Dennis Hunt in *Rose of the Rancho.*

El Teatro Campesino

Luis Valdez
Artistic Director

Andres V. Gutierrez
General Manager

Box 1278
San Juan Bautista, CA 95045
(408) 623–4505 (business)
(408) 623–2444 (box office)

Founded 1965
Luis Valdez

Season
Year-round

Schedule
Evenings
Thursday–Sunday
Matiness
Saturday, Sunday

Facilities
705 Fourth St.
Seating capacity: 250
Stage: flexible

Finances
January 1, 1980–December 31, 1980
$418,000 operating expenses
$262,000 earned income
$145,000 grants/contributions

Audience
Annual attendance: 50,000

Touring contact
Jose Delgado

Booked-in events
Dance, theatre

El Teatro Campesino looks back on 15 years of growth and accomplishment in the Chicano cultural, sociological and political renaissance. Today, the theatre continues to be a progressive, reasoned voice for the Chicano movement.

The Campesino aesthetic is rooted in the indigenous culture of Mexican farmworkers, and it now encompasses a vision of the world that combines urban and rural realities of the Chicano today. Increasingly, the theatre serves as a bridge between Chicanos and the other ethnic and cultural groups that form the fabric of American society.

El Teatro Campesino strives to create and produce in its home theatre "popular" works with broad audience appeal, integrating music, drama and dance, and then to tour these productions nationally and internationally.

The theatre provides a unique institution in a rural setting for gifted aspiring artists—from large urban areas, small towns or farm labor camps—to train together and develop professional skills in the performing arts.

Productions 1979–80
Virgen del Tepeyac, adapt: Luis Valdez
Fin del Mundo, Luis Valdez

Productions 1980–81
La Pastorela, adapt: Luis Valdez; music: Frank Gonzalez
Mundo, Luis Valdez; music: Frank Gonzales
Rose of the Rancho, David Belasco; music: Frank Gonzales

Directors
Frank Condon, Luis Valdez

Designers
Sets: Robert Morales, Russell Pyle. *Costumes:* Diane Rodriguez, Francis Romero, Kim Simons. *Lights:* Robert Morales, Russell Pyle, Gregory Ridenour.

Media resources
Film: Los Vendidos (KNBC), *El Corrido* (KCET), *I Am Joaquin* (company-produced), *NET Playhouse: El Teatro Campesino* (WNET, documentary).

Empty Space Theatre

M. Burke Walker
Artistic Director

Daniel Caine
Managing Director

919 East Pike St.
Seattle, WA 98122
(206) 325–4444 (business)
(206) 325–4443 (box office)

Founded 1970
M. Burke Walker, Charles Younger, Julian Schembri, James Royce

Season
October–June

Schedule
Evenings
Tuesday–Sunday
Matinees
Sunday

Facilities
Seating capacity: 99
Stage: flexible

Finances
September 1, 1980–June 30, 1981
$328,000 operating expenses
$197,000 earned income
$140,000 grants/contributions

Audience
Annual attendance: 44,000
Subscribers: 3,300

Touring contact
James Royce

AEA letter of agreement

Since 1970, Seattle's Empty Space Theatre has been a home for new plays and playwrights in the Pacific Northwest. Employing a professional staff of artists and administrators, the Space produces a nine-play, year-round season in its small, flexible theatre.

Empty Space's programming philosophy has remained consistent: the heart of the repertoire, its passion and its obligation, has always been new plays by new authors. These works are supplemented by classic and modern plays and excursions

Empty Space Theatre. David Colacci. Bob Wright and Dan Daily in *The Paranormal Review.* Photo: Nick Gunderson.

into the uncharted worlds of low comedy. In the first two seasons, 18 productions were presented ranging from the first Seattle productions of Sam Shepard, Lanford Wilson and Peter Handke, to *The Tempest, Happy Days* and Fielding's *Tom Thumb.*

From 1970 to 1977, playwrights such as Bond, Mamet and Babe premiered at the Space, along with commissioned world premieres from Seattle writers. With the inception of the New Playwrights Forum in 1978, play development began in a formal way, through staged readings, workshops and more world premieres on the mainstage. Spring of 1981 saw the first Northwest Playwrights Conference, a week-long program of play development, staged readings and symposia. Future plans at the Space include more play commissioning and playwright residencies.

The classics included in the season are welcome complements to the new works, as are the eccentric Midnight Theatre productions and annual Summer Park Shows, which tend toward burlesque, melodrama, vaudeville, musical comedy, improvisation and slapstick.

Other Empty Space programs include administrative and technical production internships, statewide touring, guest lectures, a newsletter and a volunteer auxiliary.

Productions 1979–80

5th of July, Lanford Wilson
• *Heads and Tails,* Janet Thomas
Comedians, Trevor Griffiths
Room Service, John Murray and Allen Boretz
Dusa, Fish, Stas and Vi, Pam Gems
The Woods, David Mamet
Pvt. Wars, James McLure
• *Deadwood Dick,* John Kauffman and company

Productions 1980–81

Agnes of God, John Pielmeier
The Workroom, Jean-Claude Grumberg; trans: Sara O'Connor and Dan Stein
Twelfth Night, William Shakespeare
Still Life, Emily Mann
We Won't Pay! We Won't Pay!, Dario Fo; adapt: R.G. Davis
Paranormal Review, Eric Brogger
• *Midnight Snack,* company-developed
• *Back to Back,* Al Brown
• *The Day They Came from Way Out There,* John Engerman, Rex McDowell, Phil Shallat and Robert Wright

Directors

Richard Edwards, Robert Egan, Jouh Kauffman, Lori Larsen, William Partlan, Morgan Sloane, Jeff Steitzer, M. Burke Walker, R. Hamilton Wright

Designers

Sets: W. James Brown, William Forrester, Karen Gjelsteen, Jeff Robbins, Scott Weldin. *Costumes:* Celeste Cleveland, Laura Crow, Julianne Dechaine, Julie James, Susan Min, Michael Murphy, Sally Richardson, Scott Weldin. *Lights:* Tina Charney, Michael Davidson, Anne Kallenbach, Gary Mintz, Jeff Robbins, Jim Royce, Phil Schermer, Frank Simons.

Media resources

Video: *Deadwood Dick* (company-produced).

Ensemble Studio Theatre

Curt Dempster
Artistic Director

Deborah Dahl
Managing Director

549 West 52nd St.
New York, NY 10019
(212) 247–4982

Founded 1971
Curt Dempster

Season
October–June

Schedule
Evenings
Wednesday–Sunday
Matinees
Saturday, Sunday

Facilities
Mainstage
Seating capacity: 99
Stage: flexible
Workshop
Seating capacity: 50
Stage: flexible

Finances
July 1, 1980–June 30, 1981
$300,000 operating expenses
$ 50,000 earned income
$250,000 grants/contributions

Audience
Annual attendance: 10,000
Subscribers: 200

AEA Nonprofit Theatre code

The Ensemble Studio Theatre was founded in 1971 as a membership organization of theatre professionals, and today it is composed of more than 400 playwrights, actors, directors, designers and technicians. The theatre, located on two floors of a city-owned warehouse, has two flexible performing spaces as well as offices, dressing rooms and rehearsal areas.

Dedicated to nurturing the resources of professional theatre, EST develops new works for the stage and provides artistic and financial support for the individual artist. A permanent home base is provided for artists, who can work among their peers without commercial pressures.

Principal programs of the Ensemble Studio include: the Major Production Series of five new American plays; the Workshop and Experimental Projects Series of 10 to 15 workshop productions and 40 to 50 play readings; the Playwrights' Unit, in which 25 writers meet regularly to present works-in-progress and discuss craft problems; the Theatre Bank, providing stipends to playwrights, directors and actors for production-related expenses, commissions, emergency grants and loans; the Summer Conference in Amenia, New York; the Ensemble Studio Theatre Institute for Professional Training; and the administrative and technical production internship program. During the past two seasons, EST has addressed its concern for the one-act form by hosting a spring Marathon of one-acts by both new and established writers.

Productions 1979–80

The Invitational I:
- *The Pushcart Peddlers,* Murray Schisgal
- *Tennessee,* Romulus Linney

The Invitational II:
- *Life Boat Drill,* Tennessee Williams
- *Sister Mary Ignatius Explains It All to You,* Christopher Durang
- *The Laundromat,* Marsha Norman
- *Shoeshine,* David Mamet

• *The Perfect Stranger,* Neil Cuthbert
• *What's So Beautiful About a Sunset over Prairie Avenue?,* Edward Allan Baker

Marathon '80:
- *On the Fritz,* Lewis Black
- *Two Part Harmony,* Katherine Long
- *Landscape with Waitress,* Robert Pine
- *An Arrangement of Convenience,* Rosemary Fresino
- *Sittin,* Christopher Ceraso
- *Bella Figura,* Brother Jonathon Ringkamp
- *The Store,* Marcia Haufrecht
- *Asylum,* Onaway Schange

Ensemble Studio Theatre. Kristin Griffith and Delphi Harrington in *American Garage.* Photo: Stephanie Saia.

Productions 1980–81

Three from the Marathon:
- *El Hermano,* Romulus Linney
- *Landscape with Waitress*
- *Two Part Harmony*

• *Father Dreams,* Mary Gallagher
• *The Scented Garden,* Tim Kelly
Geography of a Horse Dreamer, Sam Shepard

Marathon '81:
- *A Public Street Marriage,* Edward Allan Baker
- *Stuck in the Pictures on a Sunday Afternoon,* Bill Bozzone
- *The Sermon,* David Mamet
- *The Lady or the Tiger,* Shel Silverstein
- *April Offering,* Elizabeth Karp
- *Down the Tubes,* Brian McConnachie
- *In Cahoots,* James Ryan
- *The Smash,* Neil Cuthbert
- *Dumping Ground,* Elizabeth Diggs
- *The Rodeo Stays in Town for at Least a Week,* Jerry Stubblefield
- *Good Help Is Hard to Find,* Arthur Kopit
- *Open Admissions,* Shirley Lauro
- *American Garage,* Peter Maloney

Directors

Pamela Berlin, Risa Bramon, Jack Caputo, Bill Cwikowski, Curt Dempster, Ken Frankel, Walton Jones, Charles I. Karchmer, Kent Lantaff, Lloyd Lynford, Pirie MacDonald, W.H. Macy, Peter Maloney, Rodney Marriott, Anthony McKay, Jim Pasternak, John Schwab, David Shookoff, Art Wolff, Jerry Zaks, Stephen Zuckerman

Designers

Sets: Stephen Edelstein, Dana Hasson, Dale Jordon, Brian Martin, Leslie Taylor. *Costumes:* Madeleine Cohen, Gayle Everhart, Sigrid Insull, Brian Martin, Karen Miller, Robert Musco, Elena Pellicciaro, Chip Schoonmaker, Jeffery Ullman, Marcia Whitney. *Lights:* Frances Aronson, Rick Lund, Marie Louise Moreto, Cal Vornberger.

Fairmount Theatre of the Deaf

Robert Tolaro
Artistic Director

Betty Kravitz
Administrative Director

11234 Bellflower Road
Cleveland, OH 44106
(216) 795–7000 (box office)
(216) 421–0122 (business)

Founded 1975
Brian Kilpatrick, Charles St. Clair

Season
September–May

Schedule
Evenings
Wednesday–Saturday
Matinees
Saturday, Sunday

Facilities
Brooks Theatre
2040 East 86th St.
Seating capacity: 160
Stage: proscenium

Finances
July 1, 1980–June 30, 1981
\$244,000 operating expenses
\$ 44,000 earned income
\$204,000 grants/contributions

Audience
Annual attendance: 10,000
Subscribers: 252

Touring contact
Peggy Shumate

Fairmount Theatre of the Deaf is the first and only resident professional sign language theatre in America. Since its incorporation as a nonprofit theatre in 1979, FTD has developed a company of 10 actors, five hearing and five deaf. FTD is dedicated to the creative development and production of scripts translated into American Sign Language (ASL), to entertain both deaf and hearing audiences. The theatre's two-fold objective is to enhance the quality of life for hearing-impaired persons by providing live theatre in ASL, and to introduce hearing audiences to the beauty and theatricality of sign language.

FTD offers a subscription season of four productions, many of which are original adaptations; its 1981 western version of *The Miser* was chosen for production on public television. The company offers outreach programs, including artists-in-the-schools performances throughout northeastern Ohio. A touring program, workshops and one-act plays are available for run-outs and residencies periodically throughout the year.

The goal for this unique theatre is to provide a training ground for deaf actors and for hearing actors with sign language skills. Beginning in September 1981, FTD will be performing at the Brooks Theatre of the Cleveland Play House, under the artistic direction of Robert Tolaro.

Productions 1979–80
Gaslight, Patrick Hamilton
Waiting for Godot, Samuel Beckett
• *The Half-Baked Bride,* Jonathan Bank and Richard Jaris
The Good Doctor, Neil Simon
• *Silence, Please,* Gregory Koppel

Productions 1980–81
The Four Poster, Jan de Hartog
A Holiday Package, various authors
La Ronde, Arthur Schnitzler
• *The Miser,* Moliere; adapt: Don Bangs
Seascape, Edward Albee

Directors
Ken Albers, Robert Blumenstein, Gregory Koppel, William Rhys, Charles Rosenow, Robert Tolaro

Designers
Sets: Richard Jaris, Don McBride. *Costumes:* Jackie Kilpatrick, Mark Passerell. *Lights:* Richard Jaris, Bruce Keller, Don McBride, Robert Tolaro.

Media resources
Video: *Beauty and the Beast, The Miser* (WVIZ), *With These Hands* (WKYC). In-house videotapes are available for all 1980–81 productions.

Fairmount Theatre of the Deaf. Brian Kilpatrick, Tom Vegh and Juliet Johnson in *The Miser.* Photo: Herbert Ascherman, Jr.

The First All Children's Theatre

Meridee Stein
Producer/Artistic Director

Thomas Fordham
Business Manager

37 West 65th St.
New York, NY 10023
(212) 873-6400

Founded 1969
Meridee Stein

Season
October–June

Schedule
Evenings
Variable
Matinees
Saturday, Sunday

Facilities
Seating capacity: 125
Stage: thrust

Finances
September 1, 1979–August 31, 1980
$280,000 operating expenses
$ 49,000 earned income
$239,000 grants/contributions

Audience
Annual attendance: 17,704

Touring contact
Tom Fordham

The First All Children's Theatre is a repertory company composed of New York City young people ages 7 to 19, and a professional staff. First ACT serves as a catalyst for writers, composers and lyricists in the development of musical works for family audiences, as well as being a training center for young performers. First ACT's productions help to inspire and cultivate a youthful audience's awareness of the excitement and challenge of theatre.

Each season the company produces four original musicals, one of which is a world premiere developed over a two to three year period. First ACT has produced 18 of these scripts in its 12 years of operation. The company has performed at the New York Shakespeare Festival, Ontario Summer Festival of the Arts, O'Neill Theater Center, Berkshire Theatre Festival, Annenberg Center, Beacon Theatre and in annual benefits on Broadway, as well as appearing on all three major television networks and in a film about teamwork in America entitled *Nobody Does It Better Than You, America.*

Over the past several years, the company has emerged as a national resource for child arts. In this capacity, First ACT was chosen to represent the United States on the satellite telecast officially launching the United Nations International Year of the Child. First ACT was also one of the American sponsors of *Belgium Today,* performing with the Flemish Children's Theatre of Ghent at the Smithsonian Institution in Washington, D.C., and at Lincoln Center in New York.

Artistry has been and shall remain First ACT's primary

The First All Children's Theatre. *Clever Jack and the Magic Beanstalk.* Photo: Anthony Stein.

objective, but its commitment to the growth of young people has brought about a host of community outreach programs. These include performing arts workshops, teacher training seminars, free and discounted tickets for handicapped and disadvantaged youngsters and Education through the Performing Arts programs in inner-city classrooms, in conjunction with the Fordham University Learning Center.

Productions 1979–80

- *Grownups!,* book: John Forster and Vicky Blumenthal; music and lyrics: John Forster

Incredible Feeling Show, book and lyrics: Elizabeth Swados
Alice Through the Looking Glass, book: Meridee Stein and Susan Dias; music: Philip Namanworth; lyrics: Susan Dias
Clever Jack and the Magic Beanstalk, book: Ian Eliot and Meridee Stein; music: Judie Thomas; lyrics: John Forster

Productions 1980–81

- *The Children's Crusade,* book and lyrics: Kenneth Cavander; music: Richard Peaslee

Grownups!
Incredible Feeling Show
Guess Again, book and lyrics: Benjamin Goldstein; music: Philip Namanworth

Directors
Vicky Blumenthal, Linda Reiff, Meridee Stein

Designers
Sets: Eric Bass, Marjorie Kellogg, Kathy Kunkle, Dennis Moyes, Mavis Smith. *Costumes:* Christine Andrews, Cheryl Blalock, Annie J, Eloise Lowry. *Lights:* Lee De Weerdt, Victor En Yu Tan, Jonathan Townley

Media resources
Film: *Nobody Does It better Than You America* (Connecticut Mutual Life Insurance and Corporation for Entertainment and Learning, documentary). Video: *Clever Jack and the Magic Beanstalk* (Corporation for Entertainment and Learning and WCBS), *Clown Who Lost His Smile* (WABC).

Florida Studio Theatre

Richard Hopkins
Artistic Director

Jim Waechter
Managing Director

1241 North Palm Ave.
Sarasota, FL 33577
(813) 355-4096

Founded 1973
Jon Spelman

Season
January–May

Schedule
Evenings
Wednesday–Saturday
Matinees
Saturday

Facilities
Seating capacity: 75
Stage: flexible

Finances
July 1, 1980–June 30, 1981
$119,000 operating expenses
$ 17,000 earned income
$112,000 grants/contributions

Audience
Annual attendance: 35,000
Subscribers: 450

Touring contact
Jim Waechter

Booked-in events
Theatre, dance, music, mime, comedy, variety acts

AEA Guest Artist contract

Florida Studio Theatre, having recently undergone a change in artistic leadership, is striking out in a bold new direction. Although the extensive touring program will be maintained as in the past, greater emphasis is now being placed on the resident theatre season in Sarasota.

FST is headquartered in an historic building in downtown Sarasota, one block from the bay. The building contains offices, shops and a flexible 75-seat theatre presently under expansion to 115

Florida Studio Theatre.
Patricia Ficke and Curry Worsham in *Dear Liar.* Photo: Chuck Koelsch.

seats. Each season, the company presents five plays in rotating repertory and a mini-festival of new plays by new playwrights.

A second company performs in colleges, schools, prisons, community centers and churches throughout the state, often for audiences lacking access to live theatre and usually at no charge to the host organization.

FST bills itself as Sarasota's Off Broadway theatre. The company is dedicated to presenting the best new plays available, both tried and untried, as well as new adaptations and exciting new approaches to selected classics.

The Studio has produced plays by Handke, Beckett, Pinter, Orton, Albee and Simon. It has commissioned original plays and worked with playwrights in residence. Currently, attention is being focused on a new play mini-festival whereby playwrights can see staged readings of their unproduced works and get feedback from a highly appreciative, discerning subscription audience.

In the off-season, FST rents its facilities to selected dance, music, mime and theatre groups.

Productions 1979–80
- • *Getting On,* Carol Flynt
- • *Sometimes Rhymes and Other Rhythms,* Carol Flynt

What the Butler Saw, Joe Orton
The Doctor in Spite of Himself, Moliere
The Dumb Waiter, Harold Pinter

Productions 1980–81
The Good Doctor, Neil Simon
The Gingerman, J.P. Donleavy
A Phoenix Too Frequent, Christopher Fry
Seascape, Edward Albee
Dear Liar, Jerome Kilty
Sea Marks, Gardner McKay

Directors
Lach Adair, Jon Bennett, Richard Hopkins, Jim Hoskins, Robert Miller, Jon Spelman

Designers
Sets: Angelyn Page. *Costumes:* Angelyn Page. *Lights:* David Belcher, Allen Hardacre.

Folger Theatre Group

John Neville-Andrews
Acting Artistic Producer

Mary Ann de Barbieri
General Manager

201 East Capitol St., SE
Washington, D.C. 20003
(202) 547–3230 (business)
(202) 546–4000 (box office)

Founded 1970
O.B. Hardison, Richmond Crinkley

Season
September–August

Schedule
Evenings
Tuesday–Sunday
Matinees
Variable, twice weekly

Facilities
Folger Theatre
Seating capacity: 214
Stage: thrust
Terrace Theatre
John F. Kennedy Center for the Performing Arts
Seating capacity: 513
Stage: proscenium

Finances
July 1, 1980–June 30, 1981
$1,475,000 operating expenses
$ 897,000 earned income
$ 578,000 grants/contributions

Audience
Annual Attendance: 100,000
Subscribers: 5,963

Touring contact
Mary Ann de Barbieri

AEA LORT (B) and (D) contracts

The Folger Theatre Group is a division of the internationally known Folger Shakespeare Library. In accord with the institution's mandate, the theatre stages Shakespeare on a beautiful evocation of an Elizabethan stage. In its 11 seasons, the last eight of which have been under the artistic direction of Louis W. Scheeder, the Folger has developed a distinctly American approach to Shakespeare with a reliance on the text itself, rather than an arbitrary imposition of time, place or style. As the theatre nears completion of the canon, it has begun to produce other related classics such as John O'Keeffe's *Wild Oats* and Sheridan's *The Rivals.*

From the first season, the production of new plays has been integral to the Folger's work and spirit. Concommitant work on the old and new creates a constructive cross-fertilization of style and sensibility. Among its premieres, Folger lists such plays as Brian Clark's *Whose Life Is It Anyway?,* Tom Cole's *Medal of Honor Rag,* David Freeman's *Creeps* and Alonso Alegria's *Crossing Niagara,* as well as American premieres by Edward Bond, David Hare and David Storey.

In 1979, the Group began using the Terrace Theatre of the John F. Kennedy Center for the Performing Arts as its "second stage." It has since produced four new works there as theatre company in residence. In the past two years, the Folger Theatre Group has produced a national tour and moved two productions to other major cities. One of them, Arnold Wesker's *Love Letters on Blue Paper,* was named by Philadelphia critics Best Play of the season after its run at the Annenberg Center; and the American premiere of the musical *Charlie and Algernon* moved to Broadway.

Among its outreach accomplishments, the Folger was the first American professional theatre regularly to schedule signed performances for the hearing-impaired. This program became a model for theatres nationwide.

Productions 1979–80
Macbeth, William Shakespeare; music: William Penn
Wild Oats, John O'Keeffe; music: William Penn
Custer, Robert E. Ingham
Love Letters on Blue Paper, Arnold Wesker
The Taming of the Shrew, William Shakespeare; music: Lori Laitman
- • *Charlie and Algernon,* book and lyrics: David Rogers; music: Charles Strouse

Folger Theatre Group. David Cromwell and Leonard Cimino in *Twelfth Night.* Photo: Joan Marcus.

Twelfth Night, William Shakespeare; music: William Penn

Productions 1980–81

Measure for Measure, William Shakespeare; music: William Penn
Museum, Tina Howe
The Rivals, Richard Brinsley Sheridan; music: William Penn
• *Crossing Niagara,* Alonso Alegria
Love's Labour's Lost, William Shakespeare; music: William Penn
How I Got That Story, Amlin Gray
Romeo and Juliet, William Shakespeare; music: William Penn

Directors
Kenneth Frankel, Mikel Lambert, Leonard Peters, Carole Rothman, Louis W. Scheeder, Roger Hendricks Simon, Michael Tolaydo

Designers
Sets: Ursula Belden, Kate Edmunds, John Hodges, Hugh Lester, Russell Metheny, Patricia Woodbridge. *costumes:* Susan Denison, Jess Goldstein, Rosemary Ingham, Bary Allen Odom, Hilary A. Sherred, Julie Weiss. *Lights:* Allen Lee Hughes, Hugh Lester, Richard Winkler.

George Street Playhouse

Eric Krebs
Artistic Director

John Herochik
Managing Director

414 George St.
New Brunswick, NJ 08901
(201) 846–2895 (business)
(201) 246–7717 (box office)

Founded 1974
John Herochik, Eric Krebs

Season
September–May

Schedule
Evenings
Tuesday–Sunday
Matinees
Wednesday, Saturday, Sunday

Facilities
Seating capacity: 260
Stage: thrust

Finances
July 1, 1980–June 30, 1981
$436,000 operating expenses
$239,000 earned income
$189,000 grants/contributions

Audience
Annual attendance: 44,236
Subscribers: 3,773

AEA LORT (D) contract

The George Street Playhouse produces new scripts, classics and popular contemporary works. Each season includes two premieres developed by the artistic director in collaboration with commissioned writers and musicians. These new productions often focus on current social and moral issues.

Because of the theatre's proximity to New York City and its resources, no attempt has been made to form a permanent company, but a pool of actors dedicated to working at the Playhouse constitutes an unofficial company. In addition to a subscription season, the Playhouse produces children's theatre and has been instrumental in the creation of Crossroads, New Jersey's first black Equity theatre. The Playhouse offers apprenticeships with small stipends, and internships for college credit to those interested in working with a professional company.

George Street Playhouse. Bill Cwikowski, Richard Shepard and Edmond Genest in *Death of a Salesman.* Photo: Robert Faulkner.

Productions 1979–80
Tobacco Road, Jack Kirkland
• *Toast & Jelly,* P.J. Barry
Jacques Brel Is Alive and Well and Living in Paris, music and lyrics: Jacques Brel; adapt: Eric Blau and Mort Shuman
Victim, Mario Fratti
Hedda Gabler, Henrik Ibsen
Private Lives, Noel Coward

Productions 1980–81
Death of a Salesman, Arthur Miller
• *Parlay,* David Richmond
Purlie, book: Ossie Davis, Philip Rose and Peter Udell; lyrics: Peter Udell; music: Gary Geld
• *Viaduct,* Aleen Malcolm
Candida, George Bernard Shaw
Two for the Seesaw, William Gibson

Directors
Paul Austin, Peter Bennett, Miriam Fond, Bob Hall, Maureen Heffernan, Rick Khan, David Kitchen, Samuel Maupin, Dino Narizzano

Designers
Sets: Jonathan Arkin, Allen Cornell, Gary Fassler, Harry Feiner, Bob Moeller, Bob Phillips, Daniel Proett, Daniel Stratman. *Costumes:* Vickie McLaughlin, Linda Reynolds, Jane Tschetter, Sandra Wallace. *Lights:* Susan Dandridge, Gary Fassler, Harry Feiner, Cynthia J. Hawkins, Natasha Katz, Gary Kechely, Bob Moeller, Dan Stratman.

Germinal Stage Denver

Edward R. Baierlein
Director/Manager

1820 Market St.
Denver, CO 80202
(303) 572–0944

Founded 1974
Edward R. Baierlein, Sallie Diamond, Ginger Valone, Jack McKnight

Season
October–July

Schedule
Evenings
Thursday–Sunday

Facilities
Seating capacity: 170
Stage: thrust

Finances
August 1, 1980–July 31, 1981
$67,000 operating expenses
$54,000 earned income
$13,000 grants/contributions

Audience
Annual attendance: 12,000
Subscribers: 925

Germinal Stage Denver is composed of theatre professionals committed to living and working in Denver, Colorado. The theatre is located in a converted warehouse in the lower downtown area and has been part of a dramatic upgrading of this former skid-row district. However, the company is now seeking a new location because of increased property values and the planned razing of its building. GSD is operated as a nonprofit small business and takes active steps toward avoiding institutional goals and outlook.

In seven full seasons, GSD has never missed a scheduled performance, has operated on 85 percent earned income and has increased its subscription rolls by 400 percent. The choice of material has been eclectic, ranging from Shaw to Williams to Pinter to de Ghelderode to Handke, and the performance techniques have been many and varied. Sometimes a resident company is utilized, sometimes not.

While the theatre has been basically "traditional" in structure, in the 1981–82 season, major changes are being instituted based on a need for redefinition. What is anticipated is a series of productions employing techniques borrowed from the Greek, Elizabethan and Japanese forms and applied to contemporary dramatic and non-dramatic literature. The company hopes that out of these explorations will develop a *popular* non-representational form.

Productions 1979–80
Inadmissible Evidence, John Osborne
The Comedy of a Lie Laid Bare, Luigi Pirandello
The Night of the Tribades, Per Olov Enquist; trans: Ross Shideler
Candida, George Bernard Shaw
No Exit, Jean-Paul Sartre; trans: Paul Bowles

Productions 1980–81
Spoon River Anthology, adapt: Charles Aidman, from Edgar Lee Masters
Present Laughter, Noel Coward
A Streetcar Named Desire, Tennessee Williams
Jokes for Springtime, Anton Chekhov; trans: Theodore Hoffman and Eric Bentley
A Marriage Proposal
The Celebration
The Brute
A Moon for the Misbegotten, Eugene O'Neill

Director
Edward R. Baierlein

Designers
Sets: Edward R. Baierlein, Rod Thompson. *Costumes:* Penny Stames. *Lights:* Edward R. Baierlein, Karen Collins.

Germinal Stage Denver. David Kristin, Ginger Valone and Jeannie Marlin in *No Exit.* Photo: Jim Valone.

GeVa Theatre. *Keystone.* Photo: Steve Levinson

GeVa Theatre

Gideon Y. Schein
Producing Director

Timothy C. Norland
General Manager

168 Clinton Ave. South
Rochester, NY 14604
(716) 232–1366 (business)
(716) 232–1363 (box office)

Founded 1972
William and Cynthia Selden

Season
October–April

Schedule
Evenings
Tuesday–Sunday
Matinees
Saturday, Sunday

Facilities
Seating capacity: 230
Stage: thrust

Finances
July 1, 1980–June 30, 1981
$518,000 operating expenses
$195,000 earned income
$323,000 grants/contributions

Audience
Annual attendance: 31,000
Subscribers: 3,666

AEA LORT (D) contract

Founded in 1972 as the Genessee Valley Arts Foundation, GeVa Theatre is located in the heart of downtown Rochester, allowing it to serve the outlying communities while contributing to the revitalization of the inner city. GeVa was created as a resident repertory company, and its artistic philosophy has evolved in response to new leadership and changing audience needs.

As the only professional theatre serving the Rochester area, GeVa strives to provide its subscription audience with a variety of experiences. Along with occasional reinterpretations of classics, GeVa relies on the intimacy and flexibility of its newly renovated thrust-stage theatre to produce primarily contemporary works. The theatre develops new plays and musicals, produces works that have not yet achieved commercial success and occasionally mounts a play whose recent success elsewhere should be shared with the Rochester audience. In all cases, the play selection is partially dependent upon the production team available. While always searching for new talent, GeVa believes in providing a home base to which its artists can return whenever possible.

In addition to its mainstage subscription series, GeVa is committed to outreach programs and education. Classes for adults and children, administrative and technical internships for high school and college students and access for the handicapped are among the theatre's services. GeVa has also been participating in the curriculum development of a regional aesthetic institute modeled on the Lincoln Center Institute in New York City.

Productions 1979–80
Who's Afraid of Virginia Woolf?, Edward Albee
Buried Child, Sam Shepard
Waltz of the Toreadors, Jean Anouilh; trans: Lucienne Hill
• *Flight to the Fatherland,* Michael Moriarty
Side by Side by Sondheim, music and lyrics: Stephen Sondheim, et al; adapt: Ned Sherrin
Twelfth Night, William Shakespeare

Productions 1980–81
Terra Nova, Ted Tally
Hay Fever, Noel Coward
Sea Marks, Gardner McKay
Agnes of God, John Pielmeier
• *Keystone,* book: John McKellar; music: Lance Mulcahy; lyrics: John McKellar and Dion McGregor
• *In Connecticut,* Roy London

Directors
Laurence Carr, Beth Dixon, Mark Harrison, Richard Humphrey, Ben Levit, Marshall W. Mason, Gideon Y. Schein

Designers
Sets: Daniel P. Boylen, John Gisondi, Michael Louis Grube, Desmond Heeley, Susan Hilferty, Richard M. Isackes, Philipp Jung. *Costumes:* Henry Davis, Lewis Rampino, Pamela Scofield, Kristina Watson, Joan Weiss, Linda Joan Vigdor. *Lights:* Frances Aronson, Lee Delorme, John Gisondi, Richard M. Isackes, Robert Jared, Dennis Parichy, Annie Wrightson.

Goodman Theatre. Audrie J. Neenan, Seth Allen and Margaret Hilton in *The Suicide.* Photo: Lisa Ebright.

Goodman Theatre

Gregory Mosher
Artistic Director

Roche Schulfer
Managing Director

200 South Columbus Drive
Chicago, IL 60603
(312) 443–3811 (business)
(312) 443–3800 (box office)

Founded 1925
Art Institute of Chicago

Season
September–June

Schedule
Evenings
Tuesday–Sunday
Matinees
Thursday, Sunday

Facilities
Goodman Mainstage
Seating capacity: 683
Stage: proscenium
Goodman Theatre Studio
Seating capacity: 135
Stage: proscenium

Finances
July 1, 1980–June 30, 1981
$2,537,000 operating expenses
$1,566,000 earned income
$ 603,000 grants/contributions

Audience
Annual attendance: 170,200
Subscribers: 17,882

Touring contact
Roche Schulfer

Booked-in events
Theatre, dance, music, lectures, special events

AEA LORT (B) contract

The 1980–81 season marks the fourth year for the Chicago Theatre Group as the independent producing organization at the Goodman Theatre. During this period, the Goodman, Chicago's oldest regional theatre and second oldest in the nation, has presented numerous award-winning productions and premieres. Goodman productions have traveled to Broadway, the Kennedy Center in Washington, Philadelphia's Annenberg Center, Princeton's McCarter Theatre, the American Shakespeare Theatre in Stratford, Connecticut, the Westwood Playhouse in Los Angeles, and have made statewide tours of Illinois. Goodman's 1981 production of Samuel Beckett's *Krapp's Last Tape* was directed by Beckett himself, and has since appeared in Dublin, Edinburgh, London and reopened at Goodman on a bill with *Endgame,* which was staged by Beckett for the first time.

The theatre offers a five-play subscription series on its mainstage, emphasizing new works or translations, and occasionally including classics. The Goodman Theatre Studio produces new plays, works-in-progress and special events. A Writers In Performance series has featured such authors as Tennessee Williams, Studs Terkel and Derek Walcott, and the Chicago Playwrights Project develops the work of a local playwrights through staged readings.

Realizing its responsibility to the community, Goodman reaches out, educates and develops new and future audiences through its Education and Community Service Program. During its first year of operation, more than 7,000 persons became involved in its activities: a young people's drama workshop, internships, apprenticeships, special student matinees, volunteer programs and adult education classes. A renovation program has made the theatre completely accessible to the handicapped, and braille programs and signed performances are available.

Productions 1979–80
- *Death and the King's Horseman,* Wole Soyinka

A Christmas Carol, adapt: Barbara Field, from Charles Dickens
An Enemy of the People, Henrik Ibsen; adapt: Arthur Miller
- *Bal,* Richard Nelson

Talley's Folly, Lanford Wilson
Cyrano de Bergerac, Edmond Rostand; trans: Brian Hooker
A Life in the Theatre, David Mamet
Krapp's Last Tape, Samuel Beckett

Productions 1980–81
- *The Suicide,* Nikolai Erdman; adapt: Richard Nelson

A Christmas Carol
Betrayal, Harold Pinter
Plenty, David Hare
- *Play Mas,* Mustapha Matura
- *Dwarfman, Master of a Million Shapes,* Michael Weller

Krapp's Last Tape and *Endgame,* Samuel Beckett
- *Still Life,* Emily Mann
- *Tennessee Laughs,* three one-acts, Tennessee Williams:
  A Perfect Analysis Given by a Parrot
  The Frosted Glass Coffin
  Some Problems for the Moose Lodge
- *A House Not Meant to Stand,* Tennessee Williams

Directors
Samuel Beckett, Andre Ernotte, Michael Maggio, Emily Mann, Marshall Mason, Tony Mockus, Gregory Mosher, Wole Soyinka, Gary Tucker, Derek Walcott

Designers
Sets: John Lee Beatty, David Gropman, Marjorie Kellogg, Adrianne Lobel, Tom Lynch, Michael Merritt, Joseph Nieminski. *Costumes:* James Edmund Brady, Jessica Hahn, Virgil Johnson, Marsha Kowal, Adrianne Lobel, Tom Lynch, Dunya Ramicova, Rita Ryack, Ellen Ryba, Christa Scholtz, Teresita Garcia Suro, Jennifer von Mayrhauser. *Lights:* Robert Christen, Pat Collins, Arden Fingerhut, Paul Gallo, Dennis Parichy, Rita Pietraszek, Duane Schuler, Bud Thorpe, Jennifer Tipton.

The Great-American Children's Theatre Company

Teri Solomon Mitze
Executive Producer

Box 92123
Milwaukee, WI 53202
(414) 276–4230

Founded 1976
Thomas C. Mitze, Teri Solomon Mitze

Season
October–May

Schedule
Matinees
Monday–Friday,
selected Saturdays and Sundays

Facilities
Pabst Theatre
144 East Wells St.
Seating capacity: 1,432
Stage: proscenium
Oscar Meyer Theatre
211 State St.
Madison, WI 53703
Seating capacity: 2,215
Stage: proscenium

Finances
July 1, 1980–June 30, 1981
$230,000 operating expenses
$209,000 earned income
$ 21,000 grants/contributions

Audience
Annual attendance: 175,000

Booked-in events
Children's theatre

The Great-American Children's Theatre Company was founded to produce large-scale productions for young audiences throughout Wisconsin and northern Illinois. Each year, approximately 100,000 youngsters and adults attend performances at the company's two theatres, and another 75,000 experience its programs in the schools.

In 1977, Milwaukee's historic Pabst Theatre became the company's home base, and with the 1980 opening of the Madison Civic Center, the season has expanded to include performances of all productions in its 2,200-seat Oscar Meyer Theatre. The Great-American Children's Theatre Company holds the house records in both the Pabst Theatre and the Madison Civic Center.

Each year, the company is commissioned by Gimbel's to produce a "breakfast theatre" production where young audiences enjoy an original holiday musical following bacon, eggs and hot chocolate. In addition to their own productions, the company sponsors touring companies which perform children's theatre around Milwaukee and Madison.

To augment the season, the company offers "A Peek Behind the Scenes" to all schools attending performances at the theatres. This in-school program is designed to teach young people about the theatre and its history, and to relate the artistic experience to that of the classroom. A souvenir full-color educational poster is given to each audience member at all performances.

The Children's Theatre's own productions include original plays and musicals, and adaptations. The combination of in-school programming and attendance at full productions rounds out the formative theatrical experience of its audience.

Productions 1979–80
- *Turn on the Lights,* book: Bill Solly and Donald Ward; music and lyrics: Bill Solly

The Legend of Sleepy Hollow, adapt: Frederick Gaines, from Washington Irving

Productions 1980–81
- *Trouble in Toyland,* book: Bill Solly and Donald Ward; music and lyrics: Bill Solly

Treasure Island, adapt: Timothy Mason, from Robert Louis Stevenson

Directors
Montgomery Davis, Edmund Assaly

Designers
Sets: D. Albert Tucci. *Costumes:* Edmond Boerner, Ellen Kozak, D. Albert Tucci. *Lights:* Carl Schmidt.

Media resources
Video: *Ali Baba and the Forty Thieves, It Must Be Magic* (WITI); *The Legend of Sleepy Hollow, Treasure Island, Turn on the Lights, Trouble in Toyland* (company-produced).

The Great-American Children's Theatre Company. *Treasure Island.* Photo: Bob Smith.

Great Lakes Shakespeare Festival. Emery Battis and Peter Robinson in *Titus Andronicus*. Photo: Joseph Karabinus.

Great Lakes Shakespeare Festival

Vincent Dowling
Artistic Director

Mary Bill
General Manager

Box 598
Edgewater
Cleveland, OH 44107
(216) 228–1225 (business)
(216) 521–0090 (box office)

Founded 1962
Community members

Season
July–September
Touring
October

Schedule
Evenings
Tuesday-Sunday
Matinees
Sunday

Facilities
Lakewood Civic Auditorium
14100 Franklin Blvd.
Seating capacity: 781
Stage: modified thrust

Finances
November 1, 1979–October 31, 1980
$781,200 operating expenses
$286,400 earned income
$765,500 grants/contributions

Audience
Annual attendance: 52,470
Subscribers: 2,144

Touring contact
Mary Bill

Booked-in events
Theatre

AEA LORT (B) contract

The Great Lakes Shakespeare Festival's acting company is comprised largely of artists who have been working together frequently over the past decade, under the artistic direction of Vincent Dowling. This is increasingly true of the designers, directors and technicians as well, making the Festival a truly company-oriented theatre striving to create its own classical acting tradition.

In 1980, the Festival engaged a part-time voice and text coach (Robert Williams) to work intensively with the acting company. The presence of the coach has been so beneficial that beginning in 1982, the company will expand the position to a full-time one.

Recently, the Great Lakes Festival created a "teaching group," which enables younger actors associated with the company to go into high schools to teach Shakespeare, mainly by acting in the plays along with students in the classroom. The Festival views the program as an augmentation of training for both actors and audiences.

The 1982 season, the Festival's 21st, will take place in the renovated Ohio Theatre, part of a three-theatre restoration of Playhouse Square in downtown Cleveland.

Productions 1980
Henry IV, Part I, William Shakespeare
Charley's Aunt, Brandon Thomas
• *My Lady Luck,* James A. Brown
Hughie, Eugene O'Neill
The Boor, Anton Chekhov; trans: Eric Bentley
The Comedy of Errors, William Shakespeare
Titus Andronicus, William Shakespeare

Productions 1981
The Matchmaker, Thornton Wilder
King Lear, William Shakespeare
A Doll's House, Henrik Ibsen
Much Ado About Nothing, William Shakespeare

Directors
Vincent Dowling, Michael Egan, Robert Ellenstein, Donald MacKechnie, Dorothy Silver, Edward Stern

Designers
Sets: John Ezell, Robert Schmidt. *Costumes:* Mary-Anne Aston, Richard Donnelly, Estelle Painter, Lew Rampino, Linda Vigdor, Kurt Wilhelm. *Lights:* Kirk Bookman, Jonathan Duff.

The Guthrie Theater

Liviu Ciulei
Artistic Director

Donald Schoenbaum
Managing Director

725 Vineland Place
Minneapolis, MN 55403
(612) 377–2824 (business)
(612) 377–2224 (box office)

Founded 1963
Tyrone Guthrie, Oliver Rea, Peter Zeisler

Season
June–March

Schedule
Evenings
Monday–Saturday
Matinees
Wednesday, Saturday

Facilities
Seating capacity: 1,441
Stage: thrust

Finances
April 1, 1980–March 31, 1981
$5,159,000 operating expenses
$3,841,000 earned income
$1,320,000 grants/contributions

Audience
Annual attendance: 739,115
Subscribers: 15,353

Touring contact
Chris Tschida

Booked-in events
Theatre, dance, music, mime, opera

AEA LORT (A) contract

Since its founding in 1963, The Guthrie Theater has been dedicated to the classics as they grapple with the questions of our time. Its new artistic director, Liviu Ciulei, joined by Garland Wright and dramaturg Arthur Ballet, form a new artistic "team" which promises to respect those classical traditions while expanding the physical space and repertoire of the Guthrie.

In Ciulei's words, "It will not be an overnight job, and it

The Guthrie Theater. John Seitz and Roy Brocksmith in *Don Juan.* Photo: Bruce Goldstein.

requires less wizardry than hard work, for this theatre will need to prepare to answer the problems of the future . . . while it deals with the issues of our time."

For Ciulei, theatre is a forum in which the human spirit, the human condition, is explored, refreshed and examined by artists and audience together. This is a particularly daring posture because the Guthrie is one of the largest nonprofit companies in America, playing in rotating repertory for nine months each year. The artistic team will reflect a probing curiosity in searching for new plays, both from America and abroad, that will provide audiences with new perspectives, visions and questions.

The Guthrie is dedicated to leadership and adventure, not merely to be different for its own sake, but because this is the only way any theatre can remain vibrant in today's world. Beyond the mainstage season, the theatre produces plays designed specifically for touring, and also takes some of its major productions on tour. Workshop productions and staged readings; interpreted performances for the hearing-impaired; post-performance discussions; educational materials; classes for nonprofessionals; and literary, administrative and technical internships are all part of the Guthrie's community services.

Productions 1979–80

A Christmas Carol, adapt: Barbara Field, from Charles Dickens
Endgame, Samuel Beckett
• *Even as the Sun: A Shakespearean Entertainment,* Warren G. Green
• *I Remember,* Stephen Willems
Monsieur de Moliere, Mikhail Bulgakov; trans: Barbara Field
Right of Way, Richard Lees
Romeo and Juliet, William Shakespeare
The Glass Menagerie, Tennessee Williams
The Rivals, Richard Brinsley Sheridan
You Can't Take It with You, George S. Kaufman and Moss Hart

Productions 1980–81

Christmas Carol
A Midsummer Night's Dream, William Shakespeare
Arms and the Man, George Bernard Shaw
• *Camille,* Alexandre Dumas *fils;* adapt: Barbara Field
Desire Under the Elms, Eugene O'Neill
Macbeth, William Shakespeare
Mary Stuart, Friedrich von Schiller; trans: Joseph Mellish
• *Soldiering,* Stephen Willems
The Tavern, George M. Cohan
Wild Oats, John O'Keeffe

Directors

Rae Allen, Jon Cranney, Ron Daniels, Anatoly Efros, Alvin Epstein, Kenneth Frankel, Edward Gilbert, Edward Hastings, Stephen Kanee, George Keathley, Michael Langham, Emily Mann, Tony Mockus, Richard Russell Ramos, Steven Robman, Stephen Willems, Garland Wright

Designers

Sets: Jack Barkla, Dahl Delu, James Guenther, Desmond Heeley, Marjorie Kellogg, Sam Kirkpatrick, Ming Cho Lee, Valerie Leventhal, Dunya Ramicova. *Costumes:* Jared Aswegan, Lewis Brown, Jack Edwards, Robert Fletcher, Jane Greenwood, Desmond Heeley, Virgil Johnson, Valery Leventhal, Mary Rhopa la Ciera, Jennifer von Mayrhauser. *Lights:* Ronald M. Bundt, Gilbert Hemsley, John McLain, Neil McLeod, Craig Miller, Paul Scharfenberger, Duane Schuler.

Media resources

Video: *A School for Scandal* (WNET), *Camille* (Theater Vision International), *She Stoops to Conquer* (Lincoln Center Research Collection), *Flashbacks: A Scrapbook of Personal Portraits* (company-produced, documentary).

The Harry Chapin Theatre Center

(formerly PAF Playhouse)

Bill Thompson
Producer

John Chicherio
Manager

185 Second St.
Huntington Station, NY 11746
(516) 271-8319 (business)
(516) 271-8282 (box office)

Founded 1966
Clint Marantz

Season
October–May

Schedule
Evenings
Tuesday–Sunday
Matinees
Thursday, Saturday, Sunday

Facilities
Seating capacity: 258
Stage: proscenium

Finances
July 1, 1980–June 30, 1981
$825,000 operating expenses
$403,000 earned income
$470,000 grants/contributions

Audience
Annual attendance: 42,229
Subscribers: 8,435

Touring contact
Lynette Bianchi

AEA LORT (B) contract

To commemorate a man who contributed unrelenting time, energy and enthusiasm to nonprofit theatre, PAF Playhouse has officially changed its name to The Harry Chapin Theatre Center. The late entertainer and Long Island resident assumed chairmanship of the PAF Board in 1975 and was instrumental in leading the company toward national recognition. According to producer Bill Thompson, "Harry was a man of dreams. He took leaps into the future and impatiently looked back to see why we lagged behind. He put not only his money and his voice

The Harry Chapin Theatre Center. Felix Pitre, Ray Virta and Marc Powers in *Androcles and the Lion.* Photo: Joan James.

behind what he believed, he also put his spiritual force behind it, creating a tidal wave of energy that enveloped and reshaped us all. He was a man of vision and we who followed him inherit the task of transforming that vision into reality."

The Center, (which has been known by a total of three other names in its 16-year history) is Long Island's premiere professional theatre, located only one hour by train from Manhattan and operating out of its original space, an intimate proscenium theatre in a converted warehouse.

In April of 1980, Bill Thompson became the Center's new producer and immediately modified its policy of doing only new plays. The repertoire now includes classics and modern plays as well as new works, and the Center will continue its tradition of collaborating with other nonprofit theatres. The longest-running play on Broadway, *Gemini,* and one of the most frequently produced plays in America, *Vanities,* received earlier productions at the Center, in collaboration with Playwrights Horizons and Circle Repertory Company. Each production at the Center is cast independently, with rehearsals held in New York City.

During the past several years, the theatre has undergone severe financial difficulties, causing it to shorten its 1980–81 season. The Center now plans to return to a more traditional and popular repertoire. "Theatre is entertainment," according to producer Thompson, "and we will seek to touch upon and illuminate the human experience in ways that combine strong scripts with fresh, imaginative, entertaining productions."

The theatre's Arts-in-Education Theatre Center, with its own resident professional company, has an extensive touring program to Long Island and other New York State schools. The Arts-in-Education company operates out of a downtown Huntington studio and presents a varied repertoire of predominantly company-developed plays, which over the past five years have played to more than a million children and have toured to Denver and to the John F. Kennedy Center in Washington.

In the past three years, the Theatre Institute, another facet of the Arts-in-Education Theatre Center, has grown dramatically to include over 600 students per year. The adult and teen programs are under the artistic leadership of master teacher George Carabin, a well-known Rumanian actor and director.

Productions 1979–80

• *Good Evening Ladies and Gentlemen,* Michael Barrie and Jim Mulholland
A Conflict of Interest, Jay Broad
• *Damien,* Aldyth Morris
The Tenth Man, Paddy Chayefsky
Ashes, David Rudkin
To Kill a Mockingbird, adapt: Jay Broad, from Harper Lee
Biography, S.N. Behrman
Dear Liar, Jerome Kilty

Productions 1980–81

The Happy Hunter, Georges Feydeau
The Burnt Flowerbed, Ugo Betti
Sizwe Bansi Is Dead, Athol Fugard, John Kani and Winston Ntshona
The Goodbye People, Herb Gardner
Androcles and the Lion, Aurand Harris

Directors

Ann Bowen, Jay Broad, George Carabin, Jose Ferrer, Jerome Kilty, John Reich, Kurt Reis, Steven Robman, Ed Stern

Designers

Sets: Charles Cosler, Neil Peter Jampolis, James Leonard Joy, Marjorie Kellogg, William Ivey Long, Roger Mooney, David Potts. *Costumes:* Annette Beck, John Boyt, Liz Covey, Jess Goldstein, William Ivey Long, Roger Mooney, Ann Morrell, Jennifer von Mayrhauser. *Lights:* Jeff Davis, George Lindsay, Jr., Gary A. Mintz, David F. Segal.

Hartford Stage Company

Mark Lamos
Artistic Director

William Stewart
Managing Director

50 Church St.
Hartford, CT 06103
(203) 525–5601 (business)
(203) 527–5151 (box office)

Founded 1964
Jacques Cartier

Season
September–June

Schedule
Evenings
Tuesday–Sunday
Matinees
Wednesday, Sunday

Facilities
John W. Huntington Theatre
Seating capacity: 489
Stage: thrust
The Old Place
65 Kinsley St.
Seating capacity: 225
Stage: thrust

Finances
July 1, 1980–June 30, 1981
$1,628,000 operating expenses
$1,176,000 earned income
$ 465,000 grants/contributions

Audience
Annual attendance: 127,500
Subscribers: 13,000

Booked-in events
Theatre, music, children's theatre, speaker series

AEA LORT (C) contract

Innovation, theatricality, daring and visual exuberance characterize the aims of the Hartford Stage Company in its annual six-play season. Under the new artistic direction of Mark Lamos, the theatre is committed to original explorations of large-scale classical works, and world premieres investigating contemporary values in unusual and entertaining ways. The company strives to serve the community by encouraging and supporting writers, actors, directors and designers in the realization of their artistic goals.

Since 1977, the Hartford Stage Company has been housed in a $2.5 million thrust-stage theatre at the hub of a major urban renewal project. Its former home, now called The Old Place, will be reopened in the near future under the leadership of associate director Mary B. Robinson. In an attempt to develop a training ground for new artists in the American theatre, the company will undertake alternative projects such as commissioning children's theatre works, presenting a lunch-time series of one-acts and giving staged readings of new plays. The theatre publishes *On the Scene,* a subscriber magazine with original theatre articles, and a study guide mailed to schools participating in the student matinee series. Both are published six times per year.

Each summer, the stage sponsors a Youth Theatre for inner-city teenagers which produces a full-scale musical under professional direction. In 1980, this program received national recognition on CBS television. In this way, the Hartford Stage continues to contribute to the revitalization of the inner city.

The company is actively guided by a governing board of directors who set policies, raise funds and select the producing and managing leadership. An administrative and production staff of 52 works year-round and seasonally, while a company of actors and artists are hired for each production, many of them returning throughout the season.

Productions 1979–80
Old World, Aleksei Arbuzov; trans: Ariadne Nicolaeff
Damn Yankees, book: George Abbott and Douglass Wallop; music and lyrics: Richard Adler and Jerry Ross
The Cocktail Party, T.S. Eliot
Ardele, Jean Anouilh; trans: Lucienne Hill
The Member of the Wedding, Carson McCullers
The Lady from Dubuque, Edward Albee

Productions 1980–81
The Beaux' Stratagem, George Farquhar
Einstein and the Polar Bear, Tom Griffin
Cymbeline, William Shakespeare
Undiscovered Country, Arthur Schnitzler; adapt: Tom Stoppard
• *Is There Life after High School?,* book: Jeffrey Kindley; music and lyrics: Craig Carnelia
• *I, James McNeill Whistler,* Lawrence and Maggie Williams

Directors
Melvin Bernhardt, Jerome Kilty, Mark Lamos, Irene Lewis, Ron Lagomarsino, J Ranelli, Paul Weidner

Designers
Sets: John Lee Beatty, John Conklin, Lowell Detweiler, David Gropman, David Jenkins, John Jensen, Adrianne Lobel, Santo Loquasto, Fred Voelpel. *Costumes:* John Conklin, Lowell Detweiler, Linda Fisher, Jess Goldstein, David Gropman, Adrianne Lobel, Karen D. Miller, Fred Voelpel. *Lights:* William Armstrong, Pat Collins, Arden Fingerhut, Paul Gallo, Peter Hunt, Spencer Mosse, Curt Ostermann, Stephen Ross, Steve Woodring.

Media resources
Video: *All Over* (WNET).

Hartford Stage Company.
Cymbeline. Photo: Lanny Nagler.

Hartman Theatre Company

Edwin Sherin
Producing Artistic Director

Harris Goldman
Executive Director

Box 521
Stamford, CT 06904
(203) 324–6781 (business)
(203) 323–2131 (box office)
(212) 581–0177 (NY direct line)

Founded 1974
Del and Margot Tenney

Season
September–May

Schedule
Evenings
Tuesday–Sunday
Matinees
Wednesday, Thursday, Saturday, Sunday

Facilities
307 Atlantic St.
Seating capacity: 1,034
Stage: proscenium

Finances
July 1, 1980–June 30, 1981
$1,807,000 operating expenses
$1,210,000 earned income
$ 440,000 grants/contributions

Audience
Annual attendance: 49,577
Subscribers: 10,000

Booked-in events
Opera

AEA LORT (A) contract

The Hartman Theatre Company, founded in 1975 by Del and Margot Tenney, is now under the artistic direction of Edwin Sherin. The theatre is located in Stamford, Connecticut, the second largest corporate headquarters in the country–45 minutes from New York–and serves the counties of Fairfield, Connecticut, and Westchester, New York.

The 1,000-seat proscenium theatre was built in 1914, and has hosted such luminaries as Jane Cowl, Lillian Gish, Walter Hampden and the Lunts. The extraordinary acoustics and decor of the Old Stamford Theatre will remain intact as the core of the proposed Stamford Center for the Arts.

In its inaugural season under Sherin's direction, the Hartman presented a variety of plays ranging from premieres of new works to inventive productions of American classics.

Negotiations with Boston University have been completed, instituting a policy of opening each Hartman production at the Boston University Theatre for a two-week run before its regularly scheduled opening in Stamford. It is hoped that this affiliation will enhance the contributions of both the Hartman and Boston University to American theatre and theatrical education.

Productions 1979–80

- *Monsieur Ribadier's System,* Georges Feydeau; trans: Elizabeth Swain

A View from the Bridge, Arthur Miller
Custer, Robert Ingham
Private Lives, Noel Coward
Unexpected Guest, Agatha Christie
Uncle Vanya, Anton Chekhov

Productions 1980–81

- *Showdown at the Adobe Motel,* Lanny Flaherty

Moliere in Spite of Himself, adapt: David Morgan and Michael Lessac, from Mikhail Bulgakov
Merton of the Movies, George S. Kaufman and Marc Connelly
Semmelweiss, Howard Sackler

Directors
Louis Beachner, James Hammerstein, Michael Lessac, Austin Pendleton, Terry Schreiber, Louis Scheeder, Edwin Sherin, Del Tenney, George White

Designers
Sets: Lowell Detweiller, John Falabella, Marjorie Kellogg, Santo Loquasto, David Lovelace, Robert U. Taylor, James Tilton, Robin Watner. *Costumes:* Kathleen Egan, John Falabella, Linda Fisher, Dona Granata, Jane Greenwood, David Lovelace, David Murin, Walter Pickette, Ann Roth. *Lights:* Frances Aronson, Rik Butler, Marcia Madiera, John McLean, Roger Morgan, Andy Phillips, Jeffrey Schiffler, James Tilton.

Hartman Theatre Company. Cecilia Hart and Henry Fonda in *Showdown at the Adobe Motel.* Photo: Gerry Goodstein.

Hippodrome Theatre

Gregory Hausch
Kerry McKenney
Mary Hausch
Marshall New
Artistic Directors

Daniel L. Schay
Executive Director

25 Southeast Second Place
Gainesville, FL 32601
(904) 373-5968 (business)
(904) 375-4477 (box office)

Founded 1973
Bruce Cornwell, Mary Hausch, Gregory Hausch, Kerry McKenney, Marshall New

Season
June–May

Schedule
Evenings
Tuesday–Sunday
Matinees
Sunday

Facilities
Main Stage
Seating capacity: 266
Stage: thrust
Second Stage
Seating capacity: 120
Stage: thrust

Finances
June 1, 1980–May 31, 1981
$389,000 operating expenses
$240,000 earned income
$152,000 grants/contributions

Audience
Annual attendance: 70,000
Subscribers: 3,500

Touring contact
Mary Hausch

Booked-in events
Theatre, dance, music, television shows, art shows

AEA LORT (D) contract

The Hippodrome Theatre was founded in 1973 to provide the best in contemporary theatre to Gainesville, Florida, a community unique in its creative vitality and

Hippodrome Theatre. Louis Tyrrell, Kerry McKenney and Reva Carney in *The Elephant Man.* Photo: Gary S. Wolfson.

resources. Since its inception, the Hippodrome has presented 11 world premieres and 39 southeastern premieres, as well as new interpretations of classic works. The subscription audience has grown to more than 3,500 in a community of only 100,000.

Over its history, the Hippodrome has developed strong bonds with its audience and its region. In 1979, the theatre was chosen as the first state touring theatre, and has reached audiences throughout Florida, while the Theatre-in-Education program presents original plays to over 45,000 students each year. The Hippodrome's 1981 season featured the first Florida Festival of New Plays and a Florida Storytellers series demonstrating the theatre's commitment to new and regional works.

In 1980, with the aid of a National Endowment for the Arts Challenge Grant and the enthusiastic support of the community, the Hippodrome moved to a historic and architecturally distinguished former federal court house, now its permanent home. The newly renovated complex includes two stages, a gallery, offices and production shops. It is home to year-round subscription series offerings, workshop productions, intern and artist-in-the-schools programs, a film series and engagements by visiting artists.

The Hippodrome's interest in visual arts has led to the creation of theatre posters by internationally recognized artists. New and promising relationships with National Public Radio and local video production companies are also developing. The Hippodrome's theatre training program is being expanded with the initiation of a professional acting and production conservatory in conjunction with the University of Florida.

Productions 1979–80

Same Time, Next Year, Bernard Slade
Sleuth, Anthony Shaffer
• *Waking Up,* Margaret Bachus and Louis Tyrrell
Sly Fox, Larry Gelbart
Tiger Tail, Tennessee Williams
A Christmas Carol, adapt: Gregory Hausch, from Charles Dickens
Next Stop, Greenwich Village, adapt: Gregory Hausch, from Paul Mazursky
• *Game Play,* Margaret Bachus, Sarah Safford and Louis Tyrrell
Talley's Folly, Lanford Wilson
Loose Ends, Michael Weller
The Belle of Amherst, William Luce
Candide, adapt: Kerry McKenney, from Voltaire

Productions 1980–81

Bedroom Farce, Alan Ayckbourn
Deathtrap, Ira Levin
• *Tree Tide,* Margaret Bachus, Dan Leonard and Louis Tyrrell
As You Like It, William Shakespeare
The Elephant Man, Bernard Pomerance
Clarence Darrow, David Rintell
Betrayal, Harold Pinter
For Colored Girls who have Considered Suicide/When The Rainbow is Enuf, Ntozake Shange
• *Sign Posts,* Margaret Bachus and Rena Carney
• *Ernie Pyle: This Is My War,* Dan Leonard
Revenge of the Space Pandas, book: David Mamet; music: Eddie Gwaltney; lyrics: Eddie Gwaltney and Gregory Hausch; adapt: Gregory Hausch

Directors

Bruce Cornwell, Gregory Hausch, Mary Hausch, Kerry McKenney, Marshall New, Marilyn Wall Asse

Designers

Sets: Carlos F. Asse, Milan Palec. *Costumes:* Joy A. Arron, Marilyn Wall Asse, Mary Hausch, Tricia Gerent, Lisa Martin. *Lights:* Carlos F. Asse, Bruce Cornwell, Kerry McKenney, Brackley Frayer, Gregory Hausch.

Media resources

Video: *Waking Up, Game Play, Tree Tide* (company-produced).

Honolulu Theatre for Youth

Kathleen Collins
Artistic Director

Jane Campbell
Managing Director

Box 3257
Honolulu, HI 96801
(808) 521–3487

Founded 1955
Nancy Corbett

Season
July–May

Schedule
Evenings
Friday–Sunday
Matinees
Monday–Sunday

Facilities
Leeward Community College Theatre
Pearl City
Seating capacity: 635
Stage: proscenium
Kaimuki High School Theatre
2705 Kaimuki Ave.
Seating capacity: 670
Stage: proscenium
Castle High School Theatre
45–386 Kaneohe Bay Drive
Seating capacity: 670
Stage: proscenium

Finances
June 1, 1980–May 31, 1981
$447,000 operating expenses
$266,000 earned income
$175,000 grants/contributions

Audience
Annual attendance: 126,397
Subscribers: 216

Touring contact
Jane Campbell

Honolulu Theatre for Youth was founded in 1955 in what was then a small Pacific community, to enrich the lives of children who had little contact with the world outside Hawaii. It has grown with Honolulu to become the leading theatre presence in a major American city and has shifted its emphasis from illustrating a world

Honolulu Theatre for Youth. Gerald Kawaoka, Karen Yamamoto and Jerry Tracy in *Ama and the White Crane.* Photo: Debra Rigas Clark.

far away to interpreting a world now very immediate.

HTY's audience began with children, extended first to the family, and now embraces a large portion of the state's population. While the theatre is based in Honolulu and plays most of its season on the island of Oahu, grants from the state legislature, the state arts agency and the National Endowment for the Arts have made possible a five-to-six-week annual tour of the five major neighbor islands of the state.

HTY's challenge is twofold: to celebrate its multi-ethnic community, and to forge a theatre tradition in a community where every member or his forebearer was an immigrant, two-thirds from Asia or the South Pacific. Development of original material has been important to the repertoire since the early 1960s, and in recent years new work has drawn heavily on the myths, history and reality of its unique land.

The HTY acting company reflects Hawaii's ethnic diversity and, for the most part, is drawn from the local community. First paid with federal funds from the Comprehensive Education and Training Act (CETA) in 1977, actors are now part of HTY's regular professional staff.

Works of social significance on subjects of current interest are the emphasis for the 1980s. Inherent in all HTY work is respect for the child and young adult as intelligent, discerning audience members. Education programs are important: HTY provides workshops for teachers and students and encourages the teaching of drama in secondary schools. A young adult apprentice program is also in the works.

After long years of seeking a central home, HTY has adopted for the present the image of theatre on the move, producing each play in a different population center of Oahu.

Productions 1979–80
- *The Nine Dragons,* George Herman
  Halloween Tree, adapt: Wallace Chappell, from Ray Bradbury
- *Snow White,* adapt: Kathleen Collins
  Step on a Crack, Suzan Zeder
  Hansel and Gretel, Moses Goldberg

Productions 1980–81
- *Mark Twain in the Sandwich Islands,* Michael Cowell
  The Miracle Worker, William Gibson
- *Ozma of Oz,* Suzan Zeder
  The Overcoat, adapt: Tom Lanter and Frank Torok, from Nikolai Gogol
  Ama and the White Crane, Maureen O'Toole

Directors
Kathleen Collins, Jim Nakamoto, Dale Ream

Designers
Sets: Joseph D. Dodd. *Costumes:* Joseph D. Dodd, Grace Ligi. *Lights:* Colin J. Fraser, Jr., Gerald Kawaoka, Lloyd S. Riford, III.

Media resources
Video: *Folktales of the Philippines, Momotaro and Other Japanese Folktales* (KHET).

Horse Cave Theatre

Warren Hammack
Artistic Director

Pamela White
Administrative Director

Box 215
Horse Cave, KY 42749
(502) 786–1200 (business)
(502) 786–2177 (box office)

Founded 1977

Season
June–September

Schedule
Evenings
Tuesday–Saturday
Matinees
Saturday

Facilities
107–109 Main St.
Seating capacity: 355
Stage: thrust

Finances
October 1, 1979–September 30, 1980
$184,000 operating expenses
$ 64,000 earned income
$124,000 grants/contributions

Audience
Annual attendance: 14,631
Subscribers: 1,000

Booked-in events
Theatre, music

AEA LORT (D) contract

Horse Cave Theatre is dedicated to presenting outstanding professional theatre to its steadily growing audiences, producing a mixture of contemporary plays, new scripts and popular classics. By selecting its repertoire from the best of our dramatic heritage, Horse Cave hopes to expose its audiences to art that enlightens, excites and challenges. In this way, the theatre can serve the community, the artist and technician, and the art form itself.

In order to present a variety of theatrical and creative statements, talented guest directors and designers supplement the resident staff, and the plays are selected to present a broad and balanced repertoire. Diversity and versatility are requisites for the acting company as well, and many of its professional members return to Horse Cave for several of its rotating repertory seasons, thereby creating an ensemble spirit.

Attracting audiences from surrounding communities as well as the regional and national tourists that flock to the state's spectacular cave country each summer, the theatre plays an important role in the cultural, educational and economic growth of southern Kentucky's primarily rural area.

Enthusiastic community support has been instrumental in the expansion of Horse Cave's services and programs. The Educational Outreach Program presents special school matinees of such classics as *Uncle Vanya, As You Like It* and *Of Mice and Men.* Children have a chance to perform in the Children's Theatre Workshops, and, in 1981, *Time and the Rock* was created, based on a tragic event that occurred in the area in 1925. Other services include an apprentice program; ticket discounts to groups, students and senior citizens; and the hosting of major arts events and touring productions.

Productions 1980

Table Manners, Alan Ayckbourn
The Passion of Dracula, Bob Hall and David Richmond
Tobacco Road, Jack Kirkland
Uncle Vanya, Anton Chekhov
Merely a Madness: A Distillation from the Works of William Shakespeare, adapt: Warren Hammack and Pamela White, from William Shakespeare

Productions 1981

The Last Meeting of the Knights of the White Magnolia, Preston Jones
The Birthday Party, Harold Pinter
Peg o' My Heart, J. Hartley Manners
• *Time and the Rock,* Warren Hammack and Beverley Pevitts
As You Like It, William Shakespeare
Village Wooing, George Bernard Shaw

Directors

John Berry, Warren Hammack, Jim Niessen, David Shookhoff, Pamela White

Designers

Sets: John Bos, Robert Pevitts, James Taylor. *Costumes:* Thomas Crawley, Allene Kilgore. *Lights:* Garry Brown, James Taylor

Horse Cave Theatre. *Tobacco Road.* Photo: C. Hall Park.

Hudson Guild Theatre

David Kerry Heefner
Producing Director

Daniel Swee
General Manager

441 West 26th St.
New York, NY 10001
(212) 760–9836 (business)
(212) 760–9810 (box office)

Founded 1968
Phillip Barry

Season
September–June

Schedule
Evenings
Wednesday–Sunday
Matinees
Saturday, Sunda'

Facilities
Arthur Strasser Auditorium
Seating capacity: 135
Stage: proscenium

Finances
October 1, 1980–September 30, 1981
$203,000 operating expenses
$151,000 earned income
$ 45,000 grants/contributions

Audience
Annual attendance: 22,000
Subscribers: 2,200

Booked-in events
Children's theatre and workshops

AEA letter of agreement

Hudson Guild Theatre produces plays which have never been seen in New York City. Many are world or American premieres, but all are new to New York audiences. They are also unified by a humanistic point of view. Frequently, playwrights remain in residence for the entire rehearsal and performance period, and script revisions are often made right through the final performance.

Located in a Neighborhood House, HGT started as a community Shakespeare Club in 1896, one year after the founding of its parent organization. In recent years the theatre has developed into a completely professional company, winning an international reputation and many awards.

In addition to its five-play subscription season, HGT offers staged readings of new works and workshops or work-in-progress productions. Classes in theatre, music and dance are also provided to community residents at a nominal fee.

Productions 1979–80

• *The Banana Box,* Eric Chappell
• *My Sister's Keeper,* Ted Allan
• *Snapshot,* music: Herbert Kaplan; lyrics: Mitchell Bernard
• *Come Back to the 5 and Dime, Jimmy Dean, Jimmy Dean,* Ed Graczyk
Hughie, Eugene O'Neill
• *Cacciatore,* Joseph Pintauro
• *The Penultimate Problem of Sherlock Holmes,* John Nassivera

Productions 1980–81

• *Summer,* Hugh Leonard
• *The Slab Boys,* John Bryne
• *Waiting for the Parade,* John Murrell
Knuckle, David Hare
• *Ned and Jack,* Sheldon Rosen

Directors
Colleen Dewhurst, Thomas Gruenwald, David Kerry Heefner, Randy Hoey, Barbara Loden, Peter Maloney, Brian Murray, Geoffrey Sherman, Mary Robinson

Designers
Sets: John Falabella, James Leonard Joy, Philip Jung, Steven Rubin, Christina Weppner, Paul Wonsek. *Costumes:* Elizabeth Covey, Jane Greenwood, David Murin, Denise Romano, Pamela Scofield, Christina Weppner. *Lights:* Pat Collins, Jeff Davis, Patricia Moeser, Robby Monk, Dennis Parichy, Paul Wonsek.

Hudson Guild Theatre. Roxanne Hart, Marge Redmond, Marti Maraden and Mia Dillon in *Waiting for the Parade.* Photo: Ken Howard.

The Independent Eye

Conrad Bishop
Artistic Director

Linda Bishop
Administrative Director

115 North Arch St.
Lancaster, PA 17603
(717) 393-9088

Founded 1974
Conrad and Linda Bishop

Season
September–May

Schedule
Evenings
variable

Facilities
J.F. Steinman Theatre
725 Hamilton Road
Seating capacity: 150
Stage: thrust

Finances
July 1, 1980–June 30, 1981
$61,000 operating expenses
$29,000 earned income
$25,000 grants/contributions

Audience
Annual attendance: 22,000
Subscribers: 59

Touring contact
Linda Bishop

The Independent Eye is a national touring ensemble using various storytelling forms to examine deeply felt and commonly shared experience. Founded in 1974, the Eye has presented more than 1,500 performances and workshops in 33 states for theatres and festivals, colleges, high schools, churches, conferences, prisons, social agencies and community groups. Performance sites have ranged from Off-Off Broadway to an Air Force assembly hall, from Jerusalem to a South Georgia church.

The Eye's approach is comic, focusing on human incongruities and incorporating the radical shifts of mood common to real experience. A broad range of styles fuses communication with entertainment: horror melodrama in *Goners;* cabaret in *Sunshine Blue, Black Dog* and *Families;* fragmentary naturalism in *Dessie* and *Lifesaver;* and a mask/puppet dream expressionism in *Macbeth* and *Marvels.* In each piece, the performers' personal commitment to the content and the shared response of the audience are primary.

In 1977, the Eye moved from Chicago to Lancaster, Pennsylvania, expanded and began a variety of local programs to supplement its national touring. Work now centers in four areas: Theatre for Human Values, a repertoire of plays and workshops related to social needs and concerns (which now seeks new sponsors and arenas); the Mask/Mannekin Lab, an ongoing exploration of mask and puppetry techniques; the Audiovisual Project, involving production of videotapes for national distribution and a public radio series; and the Eye Theatre Club, a local season designed as a laboratory for the company, with full-scale premieres, staged readings and open experimental workshops. Most recently, the Eye has begun developing artistic interchange projects with other theatres, the first such being a joint production, with Milwaukee's Theatre X, of Ibsen's *Hedda Gabler.*

Productions 1979–80
• *Lifesaver,* Conrad Bishop
• *Families,* Conrad Bishop
Macbeth, William Shakespeare
Black Dog, Conrad Bishop; music: Elizabeth Fuller
Dessie, Conrad and Linda Bishop

Productions 1980–81
• *Marvels,* Conrad Bishop and Elizabeth Fuller
• *Dreambelly,* Conrad Bishop
Hedda Gabler, Henrik Ibsen
Families
Lifesaver
Dessie

Directors
Conrad Bishop

Designers
Sets: Conrad Bishop, Camilla Schade. *Costumes:* Conrad Bishop, Camilla Schade. *Lights:* Conrad Bishop.

Media resources
Radio: *Families* (WUHY).
Video: *Dessie* (WHA).

The Independent Eye. Linda Bishop in *Medea Sacrament.* Photo: Conrad Bishop.

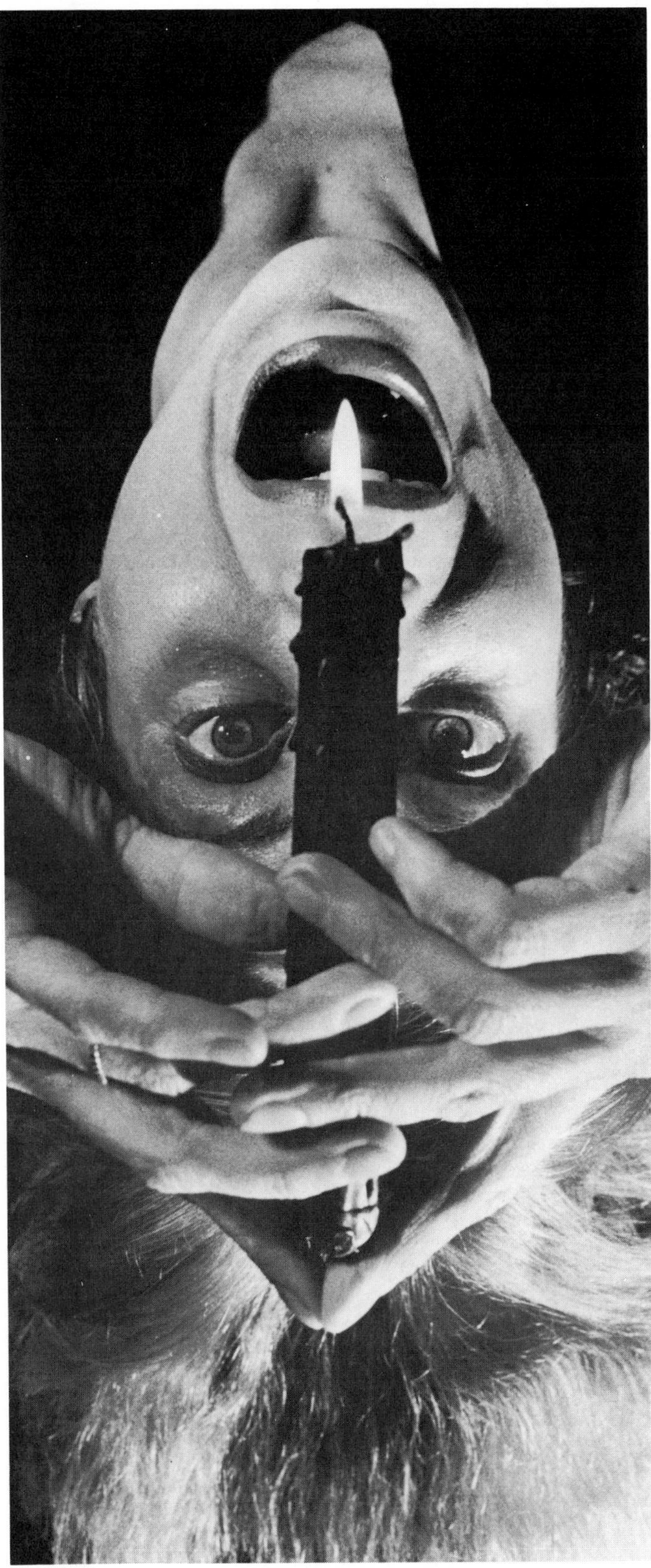

Indiana Repertory Theatre

Tom Haas
Artistic Director

Benjamin Mordecai
Producing Director

140 West Washington St.
Indianapolis, IN 46204
(317) 635–5277 (business)
(317) 635–5252 (box office)

Founded 1972
Gregory Poggi, Benjamin Mordecai, Edward Stern

Season
October–June

Schedule
Evenings
Tuesday–Sunday
Matinees
Saturday, Sunday

Facilities
Mainstage
Seating capacity: 583
Stage: modified thrust
Upperstage
Seating capacity: 250
Stage: proscenium
Theatre 3
Seating capacity: 136
Stage: flexible

Finances
July 1, 1980–June 30, 1981
$1,466,000 operating expenses
$ 890,000 earned income
$ 575,000 grants/contributions

Audience
Annual attendance: 165,525
Subscribers: 14,000

Booked-in events
Dance, theatre, music

AEA LORT (B) contract

On October 24, 1980, the Indiana Repertory Theatre opened its new facility, the historic Indiana Theatre, which provides three full playing spaces: the 600-seat Mainstage, the 250-seat Upperstage and a Cabaret. The complete renovation of the Indiana has enabled the IRT to expand its operations and become a leader in the revival of downtown Indianapolis. Under the auspices of artistic director Tom Haas and producing director Benjamin Mordecai, the IRT looks forward to being a significant voice in American theatre in the 1980s.

The Mainstage presents a traditional repertory with an American point of view. Plays are chosen from classics with contemporary relevance, neglected American works deserving of re-examination, and new material of interest to midwestern audiences. The Upperstage primarily presents new work in a provocative and poetic voice, while the Cabaret provides a forum, strongly musical in format, for new writers working in a satiric, political and comic vein with material that is unashamedly theatrical and entertaining.

In its 10th season and in its marvelous new home, the IRT is able to expand its programming through statewide touring and student matinees. In addition, the theatre hosts professional dance companies such as Dance Kaleidoscope, concerts including the International Violin Competition, and a summer film festival.

Productions 1979–80
Cold Storage, Ronald Ribman
• *Descendants,* Jack Gilhooley
Absurd Person Singular, Alan Ayckbourn
Toys in the Attic, Lillian Hellman
Twelfth Night, William Shakespeare
Born Yesterday, Garson Kanin
• *Musical Mirage Express '80,* John Abajian

Productions 1980–81
• *Hoagy, Bix and Wolfgang Beethoven Bunkhaus,* Adrian Mitchell
A Christmas Carol, adapt: Tom Haas, from Charles Dickens
Rocket to the Moon, Clifford Odets
Treats, Christopher Hampton
• *The Failure to Zigzag,* J.B. Ferzacca
Ah, Wilderness!, Eugene O'Neill
• *Oedipus at the Holy Place,* Robert Montgomery
• *Live Tonight: Emma Goldman,* Michael Dixon
• *Coming of Age,* Barbara Field
• *Murder in the Cabaret,* Tom Haas
• *Musical Mirage Express '81,* John Abajian

Directors
John Abajian, John Going, Thomas Gruenwald, Lynne Gould-Guerra, Tom Haas, Leonard Peters, William Peters, David Rotenberg, Harold Scott, Eric Steiner, Edward Stern

Designers
Sets: John Arnone, Bob Barnett, Ursula Belden, Virginia Dancy, Kate Edmunds, James Leonard Joy, Heidi Landesman, Russell Metheny, David Potts, Steven Rubin, Karen Schultz, Elmon Webb. *Costumes:* Leon Brauner, Nan Cibula, Elizabeth Covey, James Berton Harris, Susan Hilferty, Skip Gindhart, Sigrid Insull, Shelley Steffens Joyce, Rachel Kurland, Carol Oditz, Steven Rubin, Rita Ryack, Dana Harnish Tinsley, Kenneth M. Yount. *Lights:* William Armstrong, Rachel Budin, Geoffrey T. Cunningham, Jeff Davis, Paul Gallo, Joel Grynheim, Steven D. Machlin, Spencer Mosse.

INTAR
International Arts Relations

Max Ferrá
Artistic Director

Janet L. Murphy
General Administrator

Box 788
Times Square Station
New York, NY 10108
(212) 695-6134

Founded 1966
Max Ferrá, Leonor Datil, Elsa and Frank Robles

Season
October–June

Schedule
Evenings
Thursday–Saturday
Matinees
Sunday

Facilities
420 West 42nd St.
Seating capacity: 107
Stage: proscenium
508 West 53rd St.
Seating capacity: 110
Stage: proscenium

Finances
July 1, 1980–June 30, 1981
$198,870 operating expenses
$ 26,500 earned income
$162,370 grants/contributions

Audience
Annual attendance: 15,000

Booked-in events
Theatre

AEA Showcase code and Mini contract

INTAR (International Arts Relations) believes that the future of Hispanic theatre in the United States depends upon the development of local playwrights and new plays which reflect the variety and complexity of the Hispanic experience. This "new" Hispanic theatre which speaks to the needs and experiences of Spanish-American communities, is necessary for the attraction of new audiences. Through the development of this new repertoire, Hispanic theatre, as other ethnic theatres before it, will have an impact upon American theatre as a whole.

This commitment is exemplified by INTAR's frequent production of new works, by the resources the theatre allocates to new playwrights, and by the funding INTAR has received for the commissioning, development and production of new plays. A further goal is to provide a bridge between the Hispanic community and the community at large through bilingual production of classical, modern Spanish and Spanish-American works.

INTAR's January 1978 move to the new Theatre Row on 42nd Street has strengthened its impact by providing a better location for its mainstage. INTAR also maintains INTAR Stage 2, the home of its Playwrights-in-Residence Laboratory. This intensive 25-week playwriting program, begun in 1980, has subsequently expanded into a three-year program which has become an outlet for the vital and vibrant plays of its living Hispanic-American writers.

Productions 1979–80
Rice and Beans, Hector Quintero; trans: Luis Avalos
• *Swallows,* book and lyrics: Manuel Martin, Jr.; music: Paul Radelat, Jr.
Blood Wedding, Federico Garcia Lorca; adapt: Maria Irene Fornes; music: Francisco Zumaque

Productions 1980–81
La Vida Es Sueno, Pedro Calderon de la Barca; adapt: Maria Irene Fornes; music: George Quincy
Life is a Dream, Pedro Calderon de la Barca; adapt: Maria Irene Fornes; music: George Quincy
• *Bodybags,* Tee Saralegui

Directors
Max Ferrá, Maria Irene Fornes, Manuel Martin, Jr., Melvin Van Peebles

Designers
Sets: Randy Barcelo, Donald Eastman, Ken Holamon, Christina Weppner. *Costumes:* Karen Barbano, Randy Barcelo, Ken Holamon, Molly Maginnis. *Lights:* Larry Crimmins, Dennis Dugan, Joe Ray, Larry Steckman.

Indiana Repertory Theatre. Joel Swetow, David Little, Arthur Hanket and Linda Selman in *Oedipus at the Holy Place.* Photo: Dan Francis.

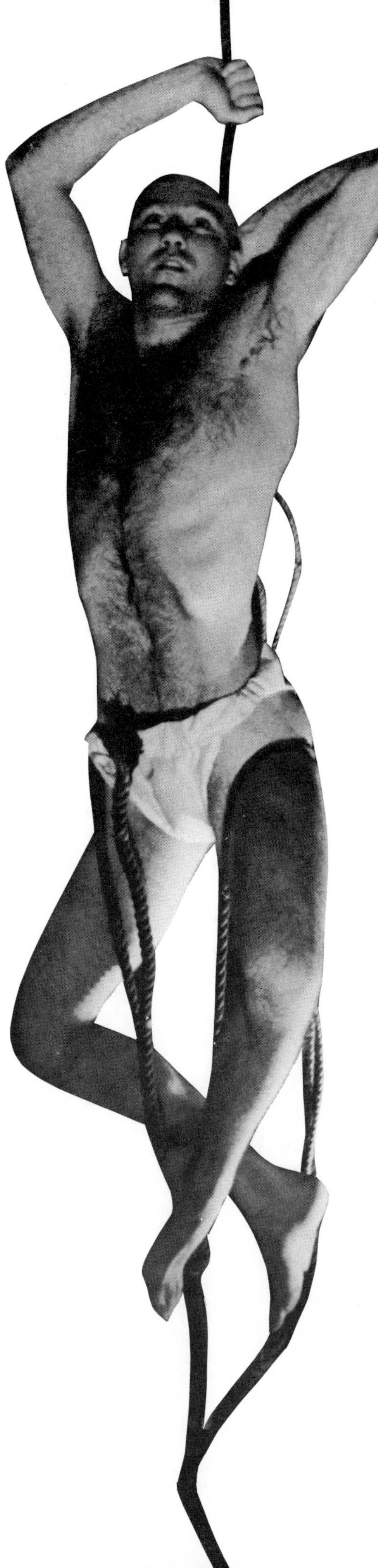

INTAR. Dain Chandler in *Life is a Dream.* Photo: Rafael Llerena.

Interart Theatre

Margot Lewitin
Artistic Director

Abigail Franklin
Managing Director

549 West 52nd St.
New York, NY 10019
(212) 246–1050 (business)
(212) 279–4200 (box office)

Founded 1970
Marjorie De Fazio, Margot Lewitin, Alice Rubenstein, Jane Chambers

Season
October–June

Schedule
Evenings
Wednesday–Sunday
Matinees
Sunday

Facilities
Interart Theatre
Seating capacity: 40–90
Stage: flexible
Interart Theatre Annex
552 West 53rd St.
Seating capacity: 40–75
Stage: flexible

Finances
July 1, 1980–June 30, 1981
$144,000 operating expenses
$ 32,000 earned income
$ 69,000 grants/contributions

Audience
Annual attendance: 7,300

AEA Mini contract

To understand the intent and direction of the Interart Theatre, one must view it within the context of its parent organization, the Women's Interart Center, Inc. The Center is a nonprofit, multi-arts organization which brings to its audience the breadth and quality of work by contemporary women artists in varying disciplines. At the same time, the center provides space and facilities for artists to explore different media including film, video, theatre and writing, through training and workshops. The first production of the Interart Theatre in its newly constructed space opened in 1973, two years after the Center itself was formed.

The concept of "interart"–the interactive process that occurs through working in proximity to other art forms and sharing ideas and responses–is intrinsic to the

Interart Theatre. Joan McIntosh in *Request Concert.* Photo: Peter Krupenye.

total organization. The dedication to interart as a way of approaching the creative process, of expanding one's talent and vision, fosters a sharing experience with the audience as well.

The Interart Theatre is committed to exploring all areas of theatrical expression. While emphasizing the presentation of new plays and playwrights, Interart also undertakes projects designed to encourage the development of directors whose work might revolve around already established texts or more experimental material. All mainstage productions are fully mounted with the design elements realized as completely as possible.

The Interart Theatre does not identify itself as a "feminist" theatre. Artists tend to work from their own lives, bringing their personal views to bear upon the world through their craft. Because historically most established artists have been men, a male sensibility has been primarily communicated. By bringing the work of women to the public, the Interart opens up new perspectives to its audience, enabling then. ‹o share in the discovery of a female sensibility.

Productions 1979–80
- • *Ballad of Brooklyn,* Myrna Lamb
- • *Electra Speaks,* Clare Coss, Sondra Segal and Roberta Sklar
- *The Daughters Cycle: Trilogy,* Clare Coss, Sondra Segal and Roberta Sklar
- *In the Summer House,* Jane Bowles
- • *Yesterday Is Over,* Mady Christian; music: Bill Roscoe
- • *Separate Ceremonies,* Phyllis Purscell

Productions 1980–81
- *Electra Speaks*
- *Request Concert,* Franz Xaver Kroetz
- • *Food,* Sondra Segal and Roberta Sklar

Directors
JoAnne Akalaitis, Francoise Kourilsky, Margot Lewitin, Ann Scofield, Sondra Segal, Roberta Sklar

Designers
Sets: Douglas Ball, Beth Kuhn, Manuel Lutgenhorst, Whitney Quesenbery, Christina Weppner. *Costumes:* Douglas Ball, Jean Steinlein, Whitney Quesenbery, Deborah Van Wetering, Laura Vogel. *Lights:* Frances Aronson, Toni Goldin, Manuel Lutgenhorst, Annie Wrightson.

Media resources
Video: *Request Concert* (Lincoln Center Research Collection), *Savage/Love* (company-produced).

Intiman Theatre Company

Margaret Booker
Artistic Director

Simon Siegl
General Manager

801 Pike St.
Seattle, WA 98101
(206) 624–4541 (business)
(206) 624–2992 (box office)

Founded 1972
Margaret Booker

Season
May–October

Schedule
Evenings
Tuesday–Sunday
Matinees
Saturday

Facilities
2nd Stage Theatre
1419 Eighth Ave.
Seating capacity: 388
Stage: thrust

Finances
January 1, 1980–December 31, 1980
$470,000 operating expenses
$306,000 earned income
$130,000 grants/contributions

Audience
Annual attendance: 50,000
Subscribers: 5,300

Touring contact
Simon Siegl

AEA LORT (C) contract

Named after August Strindberg's intimate theatre in Stockholm, the Intiman Theatre Company was founded by artistic director Margaret Booker in 1972. Intiman is committed to the development of the resident theatre artist, and, to that end, employs a resident company of actors and technicians for its six-play season. The company engages guest directors and designers who offer diverse artistic viewpoints and enrich the season's work. In addition, specialized training is offered for the professional actors, further enhancing their performances.

The company's design aesthetic supports both the text and the living artist. Intiman believes that an optimum actor-audience relationship is vital to the theatre experience, and its plays are performed in an intimate 342-seat facility that places the actors in close proximity to the audience.

Intiman Theatre Company. Amy Beth Williams, Michael Santo, and Peter Silbert in *The Cherry Orchard.* Photo: Chris Bennion.

Intiman draws its repertoire largely from the classics, with emphasis placed on a finely tuned performing ensemble, well defined style and faithfulness to the playwright's intentions. The classical emphasis of the mainstage repertoire is complemented by the New Plays Onstage series, staged readings of new works on nights when the theatre would ordinarily be dark. The company tours *A Holiday Sampler,* an original program of songs and readings, to retirement homes, organization meetings and private parties each December.

Additional programs include educational touring and internships in the artistic, administrative and technical areas. Intiman Theatre Company has been selected as a major participant in *Scandinavia Today,* an international symposium planned for 1982.

Productions 1980
Othello, William Shakespeare
The Lady's Not for Burning, Christopher Fry
Leonce and Lena, Georg Buchner; trans: Henry Schmidt
Mirandolina, Carlo Goldoni; trans: Lady Gregory
The Cherry Orchard, Anton Chekhov; trans: Karl Kramer and Margaret Booker

Productions 1981
Pygmalion, George Bernard Shaw
The Rose Tattoo, Tennessee Williams
Antigone, Sophocles; trans: E.F. Watling
School for Wives, Moliere; trans: Richard Wilbur
A Touch of the Poet, Eugene O'Neill
Damien, Aldyth Morris

Directors
Margaret Booker, Robert J. Farley, William Glover, Elizabeth Huddle, George Kovach, Pat Patton

Designers
Sets: William Bloodgood, Martyn Bookwalter, Robert A. Dahlstrom, Karen Gjelsteen, John Kavelin, Michael Miller. *Costumes:* Laura Crow, Ron Erickson, Michael Olich, Susan Tsu, Andrew Yelusich. *Lights:* Michael Davidson, Richard Devin, Robert Peterson, Robert Scales.

Invisible Theatre

Collective Leadership
Contact: Susan Claassen

1400 North First Ave.
Tucson, AZ 85719
(602) 884–0672 (business)
(602) 882–9721 (box office)

Founded 1971
Dennis Hackin

Season
September–June

Schedule
Evenings
Wednesday–Sunday
Matinees
Sunday

Facilities
Seating capacity: 70–90
Stage: flexible

Finances
July 1, 1980–June 30, 1981
$79,000 operating expenses
$34,000 earned income
$45,000 grants/contributions

Audience
Annual attendance: 18,000
Subscribers: 200

Touring contact
Susan Claassen

Booked-in events
Music, plays, variety

AEA Guest Artist contract

The Invisible Theatre of Tucson takes its name from the invisible energy that flows between performer and audience, creating the magic of theatre. Started as an arena for local playwrights, the Invisible has expanded its programs over its 10-year history to include adaptations of classics, recent Off Broadway plays, a Shakespeare Festival, children's theatre and workshops, while continuing to encourage new playwrights through both full productions and staged readings.

The theatre's main activities take place in a converted laundry building: a flexible "black box" which seats from 75 to 100 for the season's major productions. In early summer, Shakespeare under the Stars is performed in a downtown park with bleacher seating.

The Invisible is strongly committed to community service and outreach programs. The company's 1980–81 touring season included both adult and children's plays, and four residencies in Arizona towns. In addition, workshops were presented throughout the year for elementary schools, senior citizens, prisons and mental health organizations. The theatre supports allied arts by hosting local art shows and concerts, and by collaborating with visual and performing artists in its productions.

The theatre is administered by a collective, each member sharing in the decision-making, and the six-member staff is augmented by approximately 40 theatre artists throughout the year. The Invisible Theatre is Arizona's Off-Off Broadway, drawing actors, directors, designers and audiences who dare to risk the new and believe in the necessity of experimentation.

Productions 1979–80
- *Major Smack's Nuclear Disaster,* company-developed

He Who Gets Slapped, Leonid Andreyev
- *Medea and Jason,* company-developed
- *Dust Summer,* Jacob Clark

Taming of the Shrew, William Shakespeare
- *Pecos Bill and His Singing Sidekicks,* Joan Van Dyke

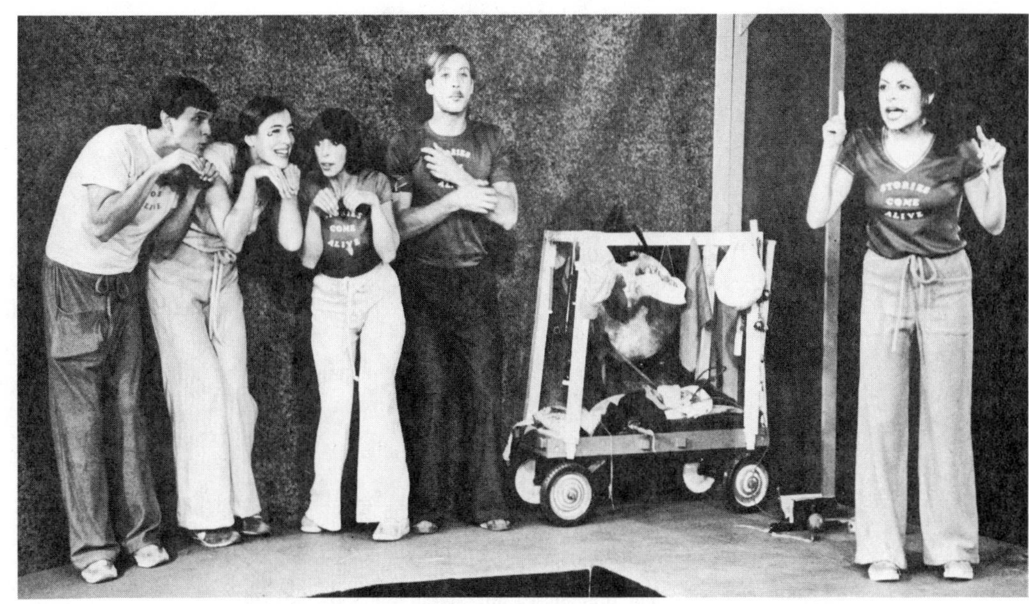

Invisible Theatre. *Stories Come Alive.* Photo: Wyatt Anthony.

Productions 1980–81
Uncommon Women and Others, Wendy Wasserstein
La Ronde, Arthur Schnitzler
• *Sideshow II,* company-developed
• *TaxiDancers,* Molly McKasson
Romeo and Juliet, William Shakespeare
The Belle of Amherst, William Luce
• *Stories Come Alive,* company-developed

Directors Vera Marie Badertscher, Susan Claassen, Glorianne Engel, Gail Fitzhugh, Johanna Lisa Jones, William Lewis, Molly McKasson, Rebecca Peters, Bonnie Popp, Joan Van Dyke

Designers
Sets: Glorianne Engel, Eric Jabloner, Alex McDonald, Jack Schwanke, David Snyder, Mary Wyant. *Costumes:* Coleen Fitzmorris, Regina Gagliano, Nik Krevitsky, Terry Liepman, Deb McGuire, Bonnie Popp. *Lights:* Gail Fitzhugh, Meg Fox, Eric Jabloner, Richard Morgan, John Murphy, Gail Reich, Russell Stagg.

The Iron Clad Agreement. Larry John Meyer and Wilson Hutton in *Art/Work.* Photo: Norman Beck.

The Iron Clad Agreement

Julia R. Swoyer
Producer

Tom Hearn
General Manager

12 Wakeman Rd.
Fairfield, CT 06430
(412) 731–2445

Founded 1976
Julia R. Swoyer, Wilson Hutton

Season
Year-round

Schedule
Evenings
Thursday–Sunday
Matinees
Sunday

Finances
September 1, 1980–August 31, 1981
$90,000 operating expenses
$52,000 earned income
$45,000 grants/contributions

Audience
Annual attendance: 30,000

Touring contact
Tom Hearn

Since its inception, The Iron Clad Agreement has sought to explore the age of America's Industrial Revolution–its inventors, industrialists, workers, feminists and labor leaders. Using historical events, statistical data and often a character's own words, the company presents its productions in diverse locations: theatres, classrooms, union halls, factories, churches, barges and parks, in the East, South and Midwest.

ICA has taken "regional theatre" seriously, creating an original concept and touring extensively among the urban and rural settings of western Pennsylvania with stories of steel, mines, mills and machines. Characters such as Edison, Grimke and Father Kazincy have entertained audiences at Spoleto U.S.A., Pittsburgh's Three Rivers Arts Festival and the Edinburgh International Festival in Scotland. ICA has performed in Edison's West Orange, New Jersey, Laboratory, in the Henry Ford Museum and in Eli Whitney's barn; the company has toured to New York, New Haven, Boston, Chicago and Washington.

The theatre's aim is to communicate clearly, to let history speak for itself, to bring the past to the present. ICA continues to explore the theme of work in America and its historical and contemporary contexts. What men, women and machines have influenced the way we work? The way we view our work?

ICA forgoes scenery, period costumes and theatrical lighting in favor of an environment in which spectators and performers share a space as well as a story. The minimalist style, literally a "platform for ideas," invites participants to interact in ways not often afforded by traditional theatre. For five years, ICA has kept its idea pure and its format simple, whether at Lincoln Center or at Local 1219 in Braddock, Pennsylvania, carving out a company identity which is professional in approach, populist in appeal and original in style. ICA asks its audiences to imagine, to laugh and to think.

Besides performances, the company's services and programs include post-performance discussions; artistic and administrative internships; national and international touring; and workshops in acting, directing, movement, speech and voice.

Productions 1979–80
• *Thomas A. Edison,* Scott Cummings; music: Robert Nesius
• *Father K,* Charlie Peters
• *My Dear Sisters,* James Rosenberg
• *57 by Two,* Chris Blaetz; music: Wilson Hutton, Mark Harlow and Jack Rowley
• *Shiver Me Timbers,* company-developed

Productions 1980–81
• *Interchangeable Parts,* company-developed; music: Robert Nesius
• *Toymakers,* Chris Blaetz; music: Angel Tucciarone
• *Under the Stars and Bars,* adapt: Mary Boykin
• *Ourselves Alone,* adapt: Wilson Hutton
• *Art/Work,* Chris Blaetz, music:

Robert Nesius
- *Gift to America,* David P. Demarest, Jr.
- *Search for Haven,* Bob Henry

Directors
Susan Chapek, Tom Hearn, Geoffrey Hitch, Marc Masterson

Designers
Sets: Jeffrey Quinn

Media resources
Film: *Mr. Edison's Amazing Invention Factories* (Smithsonian Institution). Video: *Interchangeable Parts* (South Carolina Humanities Committee); *The Iron Clad Agreement's Program* (Allegheny Intermediate Unit in Schools, documentary).

Jean Cocteau Repertory

Eve Adamson
Artistic Director

Andrew Cohn
Managing Director

330 Bowery
New York, NY 10012
(212) 677-0060

Founded 1971
Eve Adamson

Season
August–May

Jean Cocteau Repertory. Coral S. Potter and Phyllis Deitschel in *The Tempest.* Photo: Gerry Goodstein.

Schedule
Evenings
Thursday–Saturday
Matinees
Sunday

Facilities
Bouwerie Lane Theatre
Seating capacity: 140
Stage: modified thrust

Finances
July 1, 1980–June 30, 1981
$138,000 operating expenses
$ 67,000 earned income
$ 71,000 grants/contributions

Audience
Annual attendance: 13,800
Subscribers: 811

Booked-in events
Theatre, dance, music

Founded in 1971 in a storefront on Manhattan's lower east side, the Jean Cocteau Repertory moved in 1974 to the landmark Bouwerie Lane Theatre. The company is strongly involved in the promotion of the Bowery-NoHo area as a revitalized commercial and artistic community.

The Cocteau, one of the few rotating repertory companies in the country, presents unusual classics, old and new. Whether the work is a masterpiece once frequently revived but not recently produced in this country, such as Calderon's *Life Is a Dream;* a drama by a writer famous in another field, as in Shelley's *The Cenci;* or a new, experimental work by a contemporary playwright, such as *Kirche, Kutchen und Kinder* by Tennessee Williams, the audience's experience is strong and immediate, with emphasis placed on the relationship between the play, the actors and the audience.

All plays in the repertoire are performed by members of a resident acting company chosen for the whole season by audition at the beginning of the year. To reach the Cocteau's goal of creating a highly trained, sensitive and flexible ensemble, the company participates in weekly workshops in dance, speech and stage dueling.

In addition to its regular season, the Cocteau presents a student matinee series of Shakespearean plays for high school students. These performances take place at the theatre during school hours and are followed by discussions with the acting company.

Productions 1979–80
Exit the King, Eugene Ionesco; trans: Donald Watson
Kirche, Kutchen und Kinder, Tennessee Williams
He Who Gets Slapped, Leonid Andreyev
Ruy Blas, Victor Hugo; trans: Brian Hooker
The Tempest, William Shakespeare
Hamlet, William Shakespeare
In the Bar of a Tokyo Hotel, Tennessee Williams
The Roman Actor, Phillip Massinger

Productions 1980–81
The Roman Actor
The Witch of Edmonton, Thomas Dekker, William Rowley and John Ford
The Dybbuk, S. Ansky; trans: Henry G. Alsberg and Winifred Katzin
The Tempest
Pericles, William Shakespeare
The Alchemist, Ben Jonson
Life Is a Dream, Pedro Calderon de la Barca
The Confession, Sarah Bernhardt

Directors
Eve Adamson, Douglas McKeown, Martin Reymert, Toby Robertson, Karen Sunde

Designers
Sets: G. Brunner, Charles Elliott, Giles Hogya, Tom Keever, Douglas McKeown, James Nichols, Martin Reymert. Costumes: Charles Elliott, Douglas McKeown, James Nichols, Martin Reymert, D. Robinson, Karen Sunde, Tina Watson. *Lights:* Giles Hogya, Edward Matthews, James Payne, Martin Reymert, Toby Robertson, Craig Smith, Karen Sunde.

The Julian Theatre

Richard Reineccius
Artistic/General Director

Nancy Lovejoy
Administrator

953 DeHaro St.
San Francisco, CA 94107
(415) 647-5525 (business)
(415) 647-8098 (box office)

Founded 1965
Douglas Giebel, Richard Reineccius, Brenda Berlin

Season
October–July

Schedule
Evenings
Wednesday–Sunday
Matinees
Sunday

Facilities
Potrero Hill Neighborhood House
Seating capacity: 100–175
Stage: flexible

Finances
July 1, 1980–June 30, 1981
$186,000 operating expenses
$ 64,000 earned income
$122,000 grants/contributions

Audience
Annual attendance: 17,000
Subscribers: 260

Touring contact
Michael Dingle

Booked-in events
Experimental, ethnic and children's dance and theatre

AEA Guest Artist and Bay Area Theatre contracts

The Julian Theatre began as an intimate setting for neglected classics and recent plays, and has now earned a strong reputation on the West Coast for producing new plays, social and historical works, and translations of important foreign writers.

The theatre is considered provocative in its play selection, interpretation and direction. Most of the new works presented are by West Coast writers, often in residence at the theatre, with whom the company works extensively through all stages of script development. Four Julian premieres have subsequently been published by *West Coast Plays.* Many of the works have been by non-white writers, and casting is ethnically mixed whenever possible.

Statewide touring has been a regular activity since the first California tour in 1974 of Enrique Buenaventura's *Documents from Hell.* Plays toured under the California Arts Council's Theatre Tour Program have included Pinter's *No Man's Land* and Tom Cole's *Medal of Honor Rag.* Run-out tours are made regularly to nearby communities, colleges and prisons.

Beginning with the 1980–81 season, Actors' Equity members have been employed under Guest Artist or Bay Area Theatre contracts for most productions, while other shows are done with non-Equity professionals. The Julian also maintains intern programs with area colleges.

Productions 1979–80
- *The Liberation of J.M.L.,* George Crowe
- *Sugar-Mouth Sam Don't Dance No More,* Don Evans

Macbeth, William Shakespeare
- *Penelope's House,* Susan Rivers
- *Sideshow,* Hans Steinkellner
- *Jo: A Lesbian History Play,* Sue-Ellen Case
- *Coyote in Chains,* Michael McClure
- *Last Acts,* Marijane Datson

No Man's Land, Harold Pinter

Productions 1980–81
- *Three Acts of Recognition,* Botho Strauss; trans: Robert Goss

Getting Out, Marsha Norman
- *Justice!,* Rick Foster
- *Mobile Homes,* Elizabeth Wray
- *Jo Anne!,* Ed Bullins

Directors
Brenda Berlin, Cab Covay, John H. Doyle, Suresa Dundes, Dieter Giesing, Robert Mooney, David Parr, Richard Reineccius, Robert Soler, Fred Van Pattnen

Designers
Sets: Gene Angell, David Brune, Donald Cate, Alan Curreri, Al Dulay, William Eddelman, Jeremy Hamm, Peter Maslan, Peggy McDonald, Ron Pratt, John Yarrington. *Costumes:* Marian Berges, Deborah Capen, Regina Cate, Al Dulay, Linda Hauswirth, Pamela Mason, Pam Miner. *Lights:* Dale Altvater, George Gilsbach, Bill Gorgensen, Richard Lund, Susan Paigen, Steven Rehn, Richard Reineccius, Thomas Stocker.

Media resources
Video: *The Autopsy, Rumpelstiltskin and the Magic Eye, The Mild Bunch* (KQED), *Theatre Alive* (KQED, documentary). Most works since 1975 have been taped by DeMystavision of San Francisco for their archive.

The Julian Theatre. *Three Acts of Recognition.* Photo: Allen Nomura.

L.A. Public Theatre

Peg Yorkin
Producing Director

6253 Hollywood Blvd. #222
Los Angeles, CA 90028
(213) 469–3974 (business)
(213) 469–3978 (box office)

Founded 1973
Community members

Season
Year-round

Schedule
Evenings
Tuesday–Sunday
Matinees
Saturday

Facilities
Gallery Theatre, Barnsdall
4800 Hollywood Blvd.
Seating capacity: 285
Stage: proscenium

Finances
November 1, 1980–October 31, 1981
$301,000 operating expenses
$211,000 earned income
$ 95,000 grants/contributions

Audience
Annual attendance: 60,000

Touring contact
Jan Steadman

AEA LORT (B) and (D) contracts

The L.A. Public Theatre (formerly the Free Public Theatre Festival) was founded in 1973 to produce free Shakespearean productions in the parks of Los Angeles and at the outdoor Pilgrimage Theatre. In the intervening years, the repertoire has moved away from Shakespeare in favor of more contemporary offerings.

In 1977, thanks to federal funding from the Comprehensive Education and Training Act (CETA), the theatre began year-round operation, offering elementary school residencies, including performances and workshops, during the winter. With the demise of CETA funds for artists, this program was terminated in March 1981, but the company is seeking new funding to resume it in the future.

L.A. Public Theatre. Lew Horn and George McDaniel in *The Miser.* Photo: Susan Duling.

In 1980, the theatre's repertoire included a modern play, a classic and a new play dealing with upper-middle class California family life. Beginning in January 1982, the company will take up residence at L.A.'s Coronet Theatre, where they will offer a season of contemporary and new plays under a LORT contract. This move will allow expanded programming and continued artistic growth.

Productions 1979–80
- *Ollie's Star,* Dan Duling
- *The Time Piece,* John William See
- *Improvisational Show,* company-developed
- *Fear of Acting,* John William See

Sunset/Sunrise, Adele Edling Shank
The Miser, Moliere; adapt: David Schweizer

Productions 1980–81
- *The Quest for Viracocha,* Roger Holzberg
- *Story Theatre Improvisation,* adapt: Don Malmgren

The Woolgatherer, William Mastrosimone
- *The Rag Show,* book and lyrics: Ralph Steadman and Hugh Monahan; music: Hugh Monahan

Directors
Sam Anderson, Celeste Anlauf, Norman Cohen, Matthew Faison, Roger Holzberg, Don Malmgren, David Schweizer, Patrick Torrelle

Designers
Sets: Jim Carroccio, Jim Doyle, Keith Gonzales, Steve Jezewski, John Kavelin, Terri Katz, Robert Yodice. *Costumes:* Phyllis Corcoran, AnnaBelle Kaufman, Susan Lilly, Jeannie Traina. *Lights:* Karen Katz, Frans Klinkenberg, Greg Sullivan.

Media resources
Video: *Children's Theatre Festival* (company-produced).

L.A. Theatre Works

Susan Albert Loewenberg
Producing Director

Sara Maultsby
Managing Director

Box 49605
Los Angeles, CA 90049
(213) 827–0808

Founded 1974
Jeremy Blahnik, Robert Greenwald

Season
October–May

Schedule
Evenings
Monday–Sunday
Matinees
Saturday, Sunday

Finances
October 1, 1980–September 30, 1981
$193,000 operating expenses
$ 43,000 earned income
$187,000 grants/contributions

Audience
Annual attendance: 4,210
Subscribers: 48

Touring contact
Sara Maultsby

AEA LORT (D) and 99-seat waiver

L.A. Theatre Works voices the social and artistic concerns of its community and its culture in a number of ways. Theatre, music, writing and dance workshops are offered in various social institutions; new and experimental plays are developed and then produced from these and other community-based workshops with special constituencies, such as minorities, the elderly and youth groups. A series of workshops has also been developed for the community at large, as well as professional workshops for directors, designers, playwrights, performing artists and technicians, to promote creative interchange and encourage experimentation.

The theatre has initiated special interdisciplinary projects such as a poets-in-performance series and a film about art in social institutions. Plans are being made for the acquisition of a permanent theatre facility on the west side of Los Angeles which will accommodate rehearsals and performances, as well as these projects and workshops.

The L.A. Theatre Works seeks to become a vital and permanent part of the social and cultural fabric of southern California by reaching an audience often overlooked by mainstream theatres in the United States. The theatre hopes eventually to reach national and international audiences, expanding its community as well as its sources for new material.

Productions 1979–80
- *Catholic Girls,* Doris Baizley; music: Richard Weinstock
- *Pop 31!,* Doris Baizley, Bonnie Banfield and California Institution for Women Theatre Workshop
- *Made in U.S.A.,* James Devney and Terminal Island Theatre Workshop
- *Latina,* Milcha Scott with Jeremy Blahnik

Productions 1980–81
- *Hearts on Fire,* Doris Baizley
- *Not as Sleepwalkers,* Deena Metzger with Jeremy Blahnik

Poets in Performance

Directors
Tony Abatemarco, Bonnie Banfield, Jeremy Blahnik, Norman Cohen, James Devney, Mari Gorman, Dianne Haak

Designers
Sets: David Carpenter, Barbara Ling. Costumes: Louise Hayter, Victoria de Kay, Ingrid Thomas. *Lights:* Stacia Degles, Barbara Ling.

Media resources
Film: *Jump Street* (company-produced, documentary).

L.A. Theatre Works. Lisa Persky and Mark Haining in *Hearts on Fire.* Photo: Christopher Casler.

The Living Stage Theatre Company

Robert Alexander
Director

Susan H. Samuels
Managing Director

Sixth and Maine Aves., SW
Washington, DC 20024
(202) 554–9066

Founded 1966
Robert Alexander

Season
September–June

Facilities
Seating capacity: 75
Stage: proscenium

Finances
July 1, 1980–June 30, 1981
$335,000 operating expenses
$ 52,000 earned income
$284,000 grants/contributions

Audience
Annual attendance: 10,000

Touring contact
Robert Alexander

AEA LORT (B) contract

For more than 15 years, The Living Stage Theatre Company, the community outreach branch of Arena Stage, has drawn its material directly from its audiences the world over. The company makes spectators into participants and artistic collaborators in the performance process, arousing the creative energies of adults and children alike.

The small, multiracial company of improvisational actors and musicians specializes in using serious theatre to help "forgotten" and "invisible" people: the disabled, poor, incarcerated, elderly and helpless. Through artistic dialogue between the actors and audience, the performance pieces explore the shape and meaning of common experiences and celebrate individual discovery. Audience collaborators have ranged from deaf youngsters in Arizona to inmates of the Lorton (Virginia) prison and the D.C. Women's Jail. In 1981, the company spent a week in Milwaukee working with mentally retarded adults and incarcerated teens as part of a training program for theatre and dance artists, psychologists, community organizers and counselors.

On a national level, The Living Stage Theatre Company performs and conducts workshops for universities and resident theatres. Since 1972, the troupe has continued to develop "rituals," sequences of movement and sound that reveal the deeper feelings and subtleties of the improvised characters. A "language" of nonverbal sounds has grown out of this discipline, creating a wide range of expressive possibilities. Both "rituals" and "language"

The Living Stage Theatre Company. Jennifer Nelson and Ron Littman. Photo: Fletcher Drake.

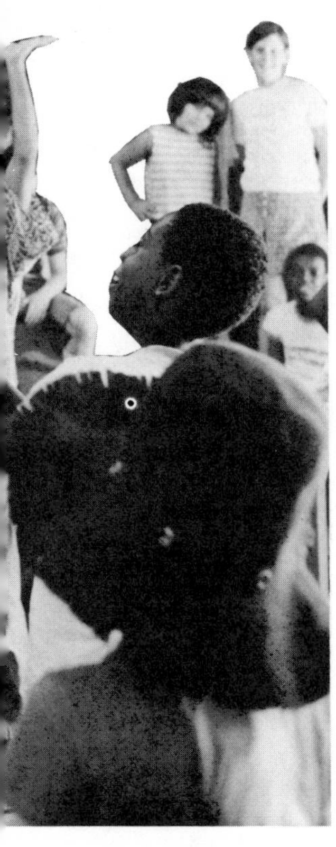

have become vital components of the company's repertoire.

The company provides actor training for professional, nonprofessional and children's groups; student and prison performance/workshops; programs-in-schools; improvisational workshops for all ages; national touring; support groups and newsletters.

Productions 1979–81
All performances are created from improvisations by The Living Stage Theatre Company.

Media resources
Video: *Dream Deferred* (CPTV); *Violence and the Public Response* (WNET); *And Always There's a Rainbow* (NBC, documentary); *Theatre of the Heart* (WETA, documentary).

Long Wharf Theatre

Arvin Brown
Artistic Director

M. Edgar Rosenblum
Executive Director

222 Sargent Drive
New Haven, CT 06511
(203) 787–4284 (business)
(203) 787–4282 (box office)

Founded 1965
Jon Jory, Harlan Kleiman

Season
October–June

Schedule
Evenings
Tuesday–Sunday
Matinees
Wednesday, Saturday, Sunday

Facilities
Main Stage
Seating capacity: 484
Stage: thrust
Stage II
Seating capacity: 199
Stage: flexible

Finances
July 1, 1980–June 30, 1981
$3,080,000 operating expenses
$2,349,000 earned income
$ 635,000 grants/contributions

Audience
Annual attendance: 283,000
Subscribers: 14,004

Booked-in events
Dance, music, theatre

AEA LORT (B) and (D) contracts

Now in its 17th season, Long Wharf Theatre continues its emphasis on new and established, home-grown and foreign works that explore human relationships and suit the company's long-standing reputation as an actor's theatre. The intimacy of LWT's two performance spaces–the Main Stage, which showcases major productions, and the four-year-old Stage II, created to highlight works-in-progress–has greatly enhanced audience involvement.

Many of the world's leading theatrical craftsmen have brought their skills to the unique environment of New Haven, with its proximity to New York yet its total independence of big city commercial pressures. For all its success at home, much of Long Wharf's renown comes from the extended life its productions have experienced on Broadway, Off Broadway and on television. Moving to New York stages, virtually intact, such productions as *American Buffalo, Spokesong, The Gin Game, Streamers, The Shadow Box, Sizwe Banzi Is Dead* and *The Island,* has quite naturally shed luster on their source. Millions of television viewers nationwide have seen the PBS *Theater in America* presentations of *The Widowing of Mrs. Holroyd, Forget-Me-Not Lane* and *Ah, Wilderness!* The awards and acclaim arising from such transfers are rewarding but, to the exasperation of many an ardent young playwright or actor, a Broadway run is far from being LWT's first priority: the potential of transfer does not enter into script selection or casting.

Long Wharf could support a facility twice its current size, perhaps a season twice as full as it now presents. But the LWT philosophy demands concentration on the best possible presentation of the single play in progress. A continuity of leadership underlies and reinforces that guideline–an artistic director and a chairman of the board who have been part of LWT since its inception, and an executive director of only slightly shorter tenure. For Long Wharf, internal growth comes before external expansion.

Productions 1979–80
Watch on the Rhine, Lillian Hellman
Jitters, David French
• *Double Feature,* book, music and lyrics: Jeffrey Moss
• *The Beach House,* Nancy Donohue
The Caretaker, Harold Pinter
Mary Barnes, David Edgar
Who's Afraid of Virginia Woolf?, Edward Albee
Cyrano de Bergerac, Edmond Rostand

Productions 1980–81
American Buffalo, David Mamet
• *Solomon's Child,* Tom Dulack
Waiting for Godot, Samuel Beckett
The Admirable Crichton, James M. Barrie
• *Close Ties,* Elizabeth Diggs
Romeo and Juliet, William Shakespeare
Bodies, James Saunders
A Life, Hugh Leonard
The Lion in Winter, James Goldman
Private Lives, Noel Coward

Long Wharf Theatre. John Kani and Winston Ntshona in *Waiting for Godot.* Photo: Gerry Goodstein.

Directors
Arvin Brown, Barry Davis, Kenneth Frankel, Edward Gilbert, Bill Glassco, Donald Howarth, Bill Ludel, Mike Nichols, John Pasquin, Austin Pendleton, John Tillinger

Designers
Sets: John Conklin, Karl Eigsti, Eldon Elder, David Gropman, Donald Howarth, David Jenkins, John Jensen, Marjorie Kellogg, Hugh Landwehr, Steven Rubin, Tony Walton. *Costumes:* Whitney Blausen, John Conklin, Linda Fisher, Dona Granata, J. Allen Highfill, Rachel Kurland, Michel Stuart, Bill Walker. *Lights:* Jamie Gallagher, Judy Rasmuson, Jennifer Tipton, Ron Wallace.

Media resources
Video: *The Widowing of Mrs. Holroyd, Forget-Me-Not Lane, Ah, Wilderness!* (WNET).

Looking Glass Theatre

Pamela Messore
Producing Director

Box 2853
The Casino, Roger Williams Park
Providence, RI 02907
(401) 781-1567

Founded 1965
Elaine Ostroff, Arthur Torg

Season
October–June

Finances
July 1, 1980–June 30, 1981
$90,000 operating expenses
$41,000 earned income
$41,000 grants/contributions

Audience
Annual attendance: 65,000

Touring contact
Ruby Shalansky

Creativity needs support and challenge, curiosity and order, caution and inquisitiveness, intuition and logic, an open mind and a lot of skepticism. It is the unique combination of all these ingredients that encourages investigation and research, and ultimately inspires invention and discovery. Keeping this "spirit of invention" alive is the most important concern of children's theatre today.

Since children spend most of their time in school, it seems logical to target creative programming toward this "captive" audience, which creates a problem. The child audience, unlike its adult counterpart, has no real access to or choice in this programming, so it must rely on the adults to serve as agents, advisors and liaisons. This situation has been a great benefit to the artist, but what does it do for the children? And what does it do to the art?

For 16 years, Looking Glass Theatre has performed almost exclusively in schools. In recognizing the need for creative programming that could reach outside the school and into the home, Looking Glass has initiated a "Family Series" of its productions, which is designed to complement its traditional in-school tour. Public performances for the Family Series are presented in a forum where children and adults can enjoy the same involvement in the productions, without the restraints that a school performance demands. Now the family can enjoy the creative process together–discovering ordinary things for the first time. The commonplace becomes uncommon, and assumptions are challenged as optimism, courage, commitment, fear, skepticism, curiosity, order, mischief, foolishness and fancy–the elements of creativity–collide in new ways to spark the spirit of invention in all of us.

Productions 1979–80
- *Metricks!.* Peter R. Miller
- *A Look at the Law,* Peter R. Miller
- *Great Shakes,* adapt: Peter R. Miller

Productions 1980–81
Metricks!
A Look at the Law
Great Shakes
Imaginations, company-developed

Directors
Patti L. Booth, Peter R. Miller

Designers
Sets: Gary Delp, Michael Locklair, Julie Trager. *Costumes:* Janna Lynn Cole, Andrea Melville.

Media resources
Video: *Sorcerer, Stranger, and the Great Bird* (International Communications Agency).

Looking Glass Theatre. *Inside Dr. Specks.*

Los Angeles Actors' Theatre. Patricia Mattick, Charles Parks and Frank McCarthy in *The Widow's Blind Date.* Photo: Jim Farber.

Los Angeles Actors' Theatre

William Bushnell, Jr.
President/Producing Director

Alan Mandell
Managing Director

1089 North Oxford Ave.
Los Angeles, CA 90029
(213) 464–5603 (business)
(213) 464–5500 (box office)

Founded 1975
Ralph Waite

Season
September–August

Schedule
Evenings
Wednesday–Sunday
Matinees
Sunday

Facilities
Mainstage
Seating capacity: 174
Stage: thrust
1st Stage
Seating capacity: 40
Stage: flexible
Caminito Theatre
Los Angeles City College
855 North Vermont Ave.
Seating capacity: 99
Stage: thrust

Finances
May 1, 1980–April 30, 1981
$250,000 operating expenses
$ 97,000 earned income
$168,000 grants/contributions

Audience
Annual attendance: 24,249
Subscribers: 1,621

Touring contact
Richard Bailey

AEA Hollywood Area Theatre contract and 99-seat waiver

The Los Angeles Actors' Theatre is a multicultural, multi-ethnic, trilingual, professional performance laboratory dedicated to producing new American plays and exploring established plays in new ways. At the heart of LAAT's artistic philosophy is the development of new material that reflects contemporary life, and the presentation of that work with excellence, beauty and power at the lowest possible price to its diverse audience.

In addition to its active production schedule in three theatres, the LAAT offers workshops run by highly experienced professionals, including an open one-act playwrights workshop and an invitational workshop for advanced playwrights, which culminate in the annual Festival of Premieres. Other workshops include El Teatro de la Unidad, with its own ensemble presenting an alternative season in English and Spanish, the Signed-Spoken Project, training deaf and hearing actors, and a variety of shorter process workshops.

LAAT maintains active administrative/production internship programs with Los Angeles City College, the University of California/Los Angeles, the University of Southern California and other area universities, and its own employees are actively involved in workshops and seminars as students and teachers. Foremost among the theatre's community services are discounted tickets for senior citizens, students and the unemployed; signed matinees for the deaf and hearing impaired; free or low-priced ticket distribution to service organizations; and free admissions to portions of the Festival of Premieres and the Playwrights' Festival of One-Acts.

Augmenting LAAT's five-play subscription season is a full schedule of special events, including LAAT Midnight (an eclectic music, poetry, dance, alternative theatre series), El Teatro de la Unidad productions, the Signed-Spoken Project and alternative theatre pieces presented on the 1st Stage.

In 1980, the LAAT was Los Angeles' most honored theatre, receiving more than 50 awards for distinguished achievement in production, playwriting, directing, acting and design. Most noteworthy of these were the Los Angeles Drama Critics Circle's "Margaret Harford Award," the DramaLogue "Publisher's Award" and the *L.A. Weekly*'s award for "Best Season–1980."

Productions 1979–80
Buried Child, Sam Shepard
La Noche de los Asesinos (The Night of the Assassins), Jose Triana
• *Drop Hammer,* Emanuel Fried
The Trojan Women, Euripides; adapt: Rena Down; American Sign Language adapt: Lou Fant
• *Wild Air,* Tom Huey
• *The Al Chemist Show,* book: James Booth; music: Steve Allen; lyrics: James Booth and Steve Allen
• *The Totem Pole,* Paul Smith
• *The Lady of the House,* Melody Johnson
• *4th Festival of One-Acts,* various authors
• *An Evening with Georgia Brown and Her Friends,* Georgia Brown; music: various composers

Productions 1980–81
• *The Widow's Blind Date,* Israel Horovitz
• *The Midnight Illusions of Carlos Anne Phelps,* Robert Zentis; music: various composers
Eden, Steven Carter
• *Throne of Straw,* Harold Lieberman; music: Arthur Rubinstein; lyrics: John B. Kuntz
Federico, company-adapt, from Federico Garcia Lorca
Macbeth, William Shakespeare
Deus ex Machina, Richard Bailey
2 by South, Frank South:
  • *Precious Blood*
  • *Rattlesnake in a Cooler*
• *5th Festival of One-Acts,* various authors

Directors
Robert Altman, G.W. Bailey, Stephen Book, Ann Bowen, William Bushnell, Jr., Edmund Cambridge, Stanley Dorfman, Rena Down, Jaime Jaimes, Gennaro Montanino, Al Rossi

Designers
Sets: Paul Appel, D. Martyn Bookwalter, Keith Hein, Stephen Howell, John Kavlin, Steve Lavino, Barbara Ling, Robert Zentis. *Costumes:* Naila Aladdin, Joy Barrett-Densmore, Christina Haatainen, Violette Jones, Jeanine Lambeth, Barbara Ling, Sylvia Moss. *Lights:* D. Martyn Bookwalter, Paulie Jenkins, Steve Lavino, Barbara Ling, Ilya Mindlin, Carol Rubinstein, Robert Zentis.

Media resources
Video: *Waiting for Godot* (WNET), *LAAT, The House on Oxford Street* (KCET, documentary).

Lovelace Theatre. *Jack and the Beanstalk.* Photo: Leonard Schugar.

Lovelace Theatre

Margo Lovelace
Artistic Director

Helen Gundlach
Managing Director

5888½ Ellsworth Ave.
Pittsburgh, PA 15232
(412) 361–4835

Founded 1964
Margo Lovelace

Season
October–July

Schedule
Matinees
Saturday, Sunday

Facilities
Carnegie Institute Museum of Art Theatre
4400 Forbes Ave.
Seating capacity: 188
Stage: proscenium

Finances
October 1, 1980–September 30, 1981
$165,000 operating expenses
$102,000 earned income
$ 63,000 grants/contributions

Audience
Annual attendance: 80,000
Subscribers: 3,000

Touring contact
Helen Gundlach

Booked-in events
Puppet theatre

Established in 1964 in a 100-seat studio in Pittsburgh, the Lovelace Theatre is one of the nation's oldest puppet theatres. Under the leadership of founder/director Margo Lovelace, the company has evolved from a traditional marionette troupe into a resident professional company working with a variety of puppets and performance techniques. Lovelace, who won the 1981 Governor's Award for Excellence in Theatre, has led the company into innovative forms of puppet theatre utilizing body puppets, Bunraku figures and live actors in masks alongside the puppets. The Lovelace has gained international recognition for its original pieces and its imaginative stagings of Ghelderode, Giraudoux, Cocteau and Moliere for adult audiences.

The theatre's award-winning film *The Puppet Proposition,* a CINE Golden Eagle Award recipient, represented the United States at the Canadian International Year of the Child Festival and has been an entry in several international festivals. Originally produced as an educational tool, the film has introduced thousands of people worldwide to the work of the Lovelace Theatre.

Since 1976, the theatre has been in residence at the Carnegie Institute Museum of Art in Pittsburgh, and during this five-year period the *Lovelace Theatre and Friends* season has become an important cultural activity for thousands of area families. A comprehensive residency program provides weekend performances for children and their parents and an extensive mid-week series for area schools. Equally important to the theatre is its touring program, which annually brings 200 performances to schools, libraries, colleges and performing arts centers throughout the state and beyond. Past residencies have included the Performing Arts Center in Milwaukee and the Smithsonian Institution in Washington, D.C.

The greatest challenge in puppet theatre is to understand the medium's unique capabilities while finding the most expressive way to present the story. The emphasis is on the creation of *theatre* with puppets, using a diversity of puppets and styles. Why use puppets? How should this puppet move? These are the questions most often asked by Margo Lovelace when designing a new production. Using the combined talents of young designers, directors and puppeteers, the means are found to create a rich, exciting form of theatre for American audiences.

Productions 1979–80

The Puppet Proposition, David Visser
- *Jack and the Beanstalk,* David Visser
- *Ragtime and All That Jazz,* David Visser and Margo Lovelace
- *Incredible Holiday Machine,* Margo Lovelace
- *Tales Told 'Round the Fire,* Margo Lovelace

Productions 1980–81
- *Peter Pan,* adapt: David Visser, from James M. Barrie
- *Top Notch-Hopscotch,* company-developed
- *Crackerjack Clowns,* Margo Lovelace

Jack and the Beanstalk
Incredible Holiday Machine

Directors
Jorge Guerra, Margo Lovelace, Marc Masterson, Margaret Raphael, David Visser

Designers
Sets: Margo Lovelace. *Costumes:* Margo Lovelace. *Lights:* Norman Beck, Les Hartman, Charles Holden, Marc Masterson, Fred Michael.

Media resources
Film: *Museum Piece, The Puppet Proposition* (company-produced).

Mabou Mines. William Raymond in *Wrong Guys.* Photo: Carol Rosegg.

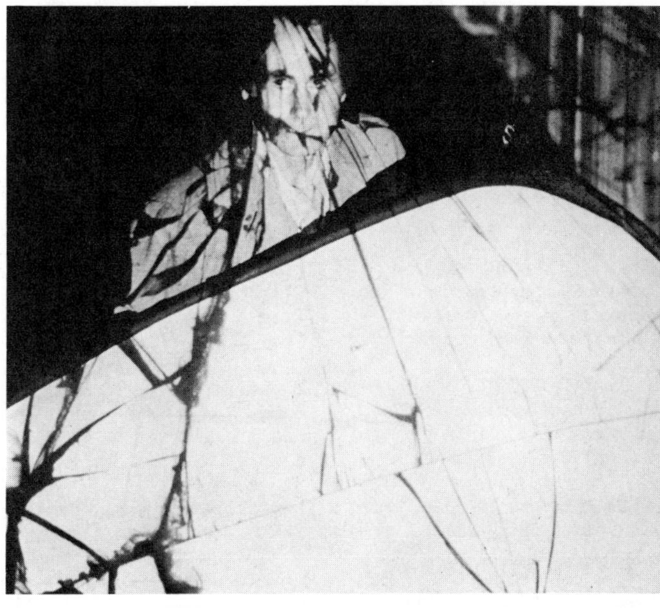

Mabou Mines

JoAnne Akalaitis, Lee Breuer, L.B. Dallas, Ruth Maleczech, Frederick Neumann, Terry O'Reilly, William Raymond
Company Members

c/o Performing Artservices
325 Spring St.
New York, NY 10013
(212) 243–6153 (business)
(212) 598–7150 (box office)

Founded 1970
JoAnne Akalaitis, Lee Breuer, Philip Glass, Ruth Maleczech, David Warrilow

Season
Year-round

Schedule
Evenings
Tuesday–Sunday

Finances
July 1, 1980–June 30, 1981
$333,000 operating expenses
$145,000 earned income
$200,000 grants/contributions

Audience
Annual attendance: 21,000

Touring contact
Jedediah Wheeler

Mabou Mines is a collaborative theatre company formally founded in 1969, following years of shared work by its founding members JoAnne Akalaitis, Lee Breuer and Ruth Maleczech in San Francisco and later in Europe with Philip Glass and David Warrilow. The company spent three early years in residence at LaMama E.T.C., and has performed at the New York Shakespeare Festival's Public Theater since 1975. The company's work is directed primarily toward the creation of original theatre pieces—from the *Animations (Red Horse, B. Beaver* and *Shaggy Dog)* through *A Prelude to Death in Venice,* to 1980–81's *Dead End Kids* and *Wrong Guys.* Mabou Mines is also considered among the theatre's foremost interpreters of Samuel Beckett.

The company has developed a formal yet accessible performance style, synthesizing motivational acting, narrative acting and mixed media performance. Mabou Mines has continually sought collaborations with artists from other disciplines: painters, sculptors, filmmakers and video artists have effected a unique form of theatre design. Musicians with whom the company has developed a rich relationship include Philip Glass and Bob Telson.

Concerns with acting style and space have not diminished a commitment to language as the basic ingredient of theatre, language which varies from the American colloquialism of the *Animations* to the arch and romantic style of Collette to the terse prose of Beckett.

Mabou Mines has most recently extended its explorations to other media: a radio drama program has yielded two series, *Keeper* and *The Joey Schmerda Story;* and company members have begun to create new works for film, video and opera. The company also continues its extensive program of residencies and touring, both in the United States and internationally.

Productions 1979–80
- *Mercier and Camier,* adapt: Frederick Neumann, from Samuel Beckett; music: Philip Glass
- *A Prelude to Death in Venice,* Lee Breuer; music: Bob Telson
- *Vanishing Pictures,* adapt: Beverly Brown, from Edgar Allan Poe and Baudelaire

Dressed Like an Egg, JoAnne Akalaitis; music: Philip Glass

Productions 1980–81
A Prelude to Death in Venice
- *Dead End Kids,* JoAnne Akalaitis; music: Philip Glass

Vanishing Pictures
- *Wrong Guys,* James Strahs

Directors
JoAnne Akalaitis, Lee Breuer, Ruth Maleczech, Frederick Neumann

Designers
Sets: JoAnne Akalaitis, Julie Archer, L.B. Dallas, Robert Israel, Michael Kuhling, Ruth Maleczech, Alison Yerxa. *Costumes:* Dru-ann Chukram, Ann Farrington, Greg Mehrten, Sally Rosen. *Lights:* Julie Archer, Beverly Emmons, Michael Kuhling, Stephanie Rudolph, B. St. John Schofield, Robin Thomas. *Sound:* Craig Jones. *Film/projections:* Mark Daniels, David Hardy, Bill Longcore, Stephanie Rudolph.

Media resources
Radio: *Keeper: Easy Daisy, The Comfort Cage, Laughingstock, Tiger Heaven, The Joey Schmerda Story, Parts I, II and III* (company-produced). Video: *B. Beaver Animation* (Young Filmmakers Cooperative), *Lies* (Doris Chase).

Magic Theatre

John Lion
General Director

Rossi Snipper
Administrative Director

Building D, Fort Mason Center
San Francisco, CA 94123
(415) 441–8001 (business)
(415) 441–8822 (box office)

Founded 1967
John Lion

Season
October–August

Schedule
Evenings
Thursday–Sunday
Matinees
Sunday

Facilities
Magic Theatre Northside
Seating capacity: 99
Stage: thrust
Magic Theatre Southside
Seating capacity: 99
Stage: proscenium

Finances
July 1, 1980–June 30, 1981
$370,000 operating expenses
$135,000 earned income
$267,000 grants/contributions

Audience
Annual attendance: 18,500
Subscribers: 1,000

AEA 99-seat waiver

San Francisco's Magic Theatre, now in its 14th season, has established an outstanding record in the research and discovery of new works for the American theatre. The Magic focuses on the playwright, aiming to generate new and substantial works by established and emerging authors. Since its founding in 1967, the theatre has presented over 100 original productions by such noted writers as Sam Shepard, Michael McClure, Israel Horowitz, Martin Epstein, Adele Edling Shank and Wolfgang Bauer, all while they were in residence at the theatre.

With the added services of dramaturg Martin Esslin, who brings international authors to the attention of the Magic, the theatre has achieved worldwide recognition and its playwrights have been the recipients of distinguished critical awards including the Pulitzer Prize, numerous Obie awards, Bay Area Critic Awards and Dramalogue Awards. Many plays first produced at the Magic have gone on to further productions at distinguished theatres across the country.

During production, it is the policy of the theatre that playwrights be in residence, allowing them to interact with directors, designers, actors and crew. The success of this ensemble approach has been demonstrated by Sam Shepard's two plays, *Buried Child* and *True West:* on the basis of a subsequent New York production, Shepard won the 1979 Pulitzer Prize for *Buried Child,* and his most recent play *True West* has received high acclaim in two separate Magic Theatre productions.

As one of the country's leading producers of contemporary theatre, Magic reads some 700 new scripts per year, and actively participates in various conferences such as the O'Neill Theater Center's National Playwrights Conference and workshops featuring new writers. In addition, the Magic reaches out to the community through various special projects, and during 1980, participated in benefits for organizations such as the Cambodia Relief Fund. The Magic also hosts local showcases of national and international performance groups. Free post-performance discussions are held twice during the run of each production, and audience appreciation is promoted through a quarterly newsletter.

For the 1980–81 season, an expanded season of eight productions was made possible in part by the award of a National Endowment for the Arts challenge grant. Magic's promotional department is now in-house, the development department has assumed full-time status and the production shop is fully operational.

Productions 1979–80

Josephine the Mousesinger, Michael McClure
• *Skywheels,* John Robinson
• *Nightfall,* Lewis Black
• *Emperor Norton,* James Schevill
Perfidia, Studio Scarabee
All Night Long, John O'Keefe
• *Charles the Irrelevant,* Martin Epstein
• *Taxes,* Murray Mednick
• *True West,* Sam Shepard
A Prelude to Death in Venice, Lee Breuer
Sister Suzie Cinema, Lee Breuer

Productions 1980–81

• *Winterplay,* Adele Edling Shank
• *Frankie and Johnnie,* Winston Tong and Bruce Geduldig
The Man Who Killed the Buddha, Martin Epstein
• *Mr. Smith Is Dying,* Martine Getty
• *The Story,* Carol Lashof
• *Europa,* Georg Kaiser
The Feeding, Pat Pfeiffer
• *Memory Hotel,* Wolfgang Bauer
• *Seduced,* Sam Shepard

Directors

Adri Boon, Lee Breuer, Ralph Cook, Andy Doe, Allan Duke, Suresa Dundes, Martin Epstein, Bruce Geduldig, Ken Grantham, John Lion, John O'Keefe, David Ostwald, Theodore Shank, Michelle Perry Swanson, Albert Takazaukas, Robert Woodruff

Designers

Sets: Gene Angell, John Ammirati, L. B. Dallas, William Eddelman, Bruce Geduldig, Jesse Hollis, John Pynchon Holmes, Bernard Lubell, John O'Keefe, Ron Pratt, John Redman, Norvid Roos, Andy Stacklin, Winston Tong, W.M. Watson, John B. Wilson. *Costumes:* Lani Abbott, Ernst-Jan Beeuwkes, Deborah Capen, Regina Cate, William Eddelman, Nancy Faw, Phyllis Kress, Irene Rosen, Rita Ryack, Rita Yovino. *Lights:* Julie Archer, John Chapot, Patty Ann Farrell, Bruce Geduldig, Kurt Landisman, Thomas Mourant, John O'Keefe, Novella Smith, Thomas Stocker, Winston Tong.

Media resources

Video: *Theatre Alive! San Francisco on Stage* (KQED, documentary).

Manhattan Theatre Club

Lynne Meadow
Artistic Director

Barry Grove
Managing Director

321 East 73rd St.
New York, NY 10021
(212) 288-2500 (business)
(212) 472-0600 (box office)

Founded 1970
A.E. Jeffcoat, Peregrine Whittlesey, Margaret Kennedy, Victor Germack, Joseph Tandet

Season
October–June

Schedule
Evenings
Tuesday–Sunday
Matinees
Saturday, Sunday

Facilities
DownStage
Seating capacity: 155

Magic Theatre. Howard Swain and Jack Shearer in *Europa.* Photo: Allen Nomura.

Manhattan Theatre Club. Michael Gross and the late Daniel Seltzer in *Endgame.* Photo: Nathaniel Tileston.

Stage: proscenium
UpStage
Seating capacity: 100
Stage: thrust
Cabaret
Seating capacity: 55
Stage: cabaret

Finances
July 1, 1980–June 30, 1981
$1,290,000 operating expenses
$ 636,000 earned income
$ 540,000 grants/contributions

Audience
Annual attendance: 58,969
Subscribers: 4,857

AEA Off Broadway and Mini contracts

Founded in 1970 by a group of private citizens as an alternative to the commercial theatre, the Manhattan Theatre Club, under the leadership of Lynne Meadow and Barry Grove, has grown from a showcase theatre to one of the most dynamic producing organizations in the country. Many plays originating at MTC become staples of the regional repertoire or move on to extended Broadway or Off Broadway runs, but the theatre's mission remains constant: to provide a professional forum for new plays and musicals regardless of their commercial potential.

Over the nine years of Meadow's artistic leadership, MTC has been committed to demonstrating the infinite variety of theatrical expression, without stylistic bias. The theatre seeks to present new works that illuminate some aspect of our lives and society, with quality as its only criterion, and diversity of programming its primary goal.

The work is presented in a variety of spaces: the DownStage Theatre houses a series of five fully produced American or international plays; the slightly smaller UpStage is the theatre's center for the careful development of new plays and musicals, for finding an "urgent voice rather than a finished form." Both spaces are used by MTC's unique Writers-in-Performance series, for play readings and for an ad hoc series of special events.

The theatre's artistic goals and programs are supported by a committed audience of close to 5,000 subscribers. MTC also reaches out to the community via student and senior citizen discounts, group discounts, free ticket distribution, post-performance discussions and a "Friends of the Manhattan Theatre Club" volunteer program. Also, while it by no means constitutes a conservatory, the theatre does run a thriving administrative and production internship program.

Productions 1979–1980
Losing Time, John Hopkins
The Jail Diary of Albie Sachs, adapt: David Edgar
Endgame, Samuel Beckett
Biography, S.N. Behrman
• *Mass Appeal,* Bill C. Davis
Ice, Michael Cristofer
One Wedding, Two Rooms, Three Friends, John Gwylym Jones
Dusa, Fish, Stas and Vi, Pam Gems
• *Sidewalkin',* Jake Holmes
• *Styne After Styne,* book: Jonathan Reynolds; music: Jule Styne

Productions 1980–1981
• *Vikings,* Steve Metcalfe
American Days, Stephen Poliakoff
Close of Play, Simon Gray
Translations, Brian Friel
Hunting Scenes from Lower Bavaria, Martin Sperr
One Tiger to a Hill, Sharon Pollack
Crimes of the Heart, Beth Henley
• *Real Life Funnies,* adapt: Howard Ashman, from Stan Mack; music and lyrics: Alan Menken
In-the-Works:
  • *After All,* Vincent Canby
  • *The Chisholm Trail Went through Here,* Brady Sewell
  • *A Call from the East,* Ruth Prawer Jhabvala
  • *Scenes from La Vie de Boheme,* Anthony Giardina
Harry Ruby's Songs My Mother Never Sang, Paul Lazarus and Michael S. Roth

Directors
Howard Ashman, Melvin Bernhardt, Patricia Birch, Thomas Bullard, Joseph Chaikin, Joe Dowling, Geraldine Fitzgerald, Ulrich Heising, Fritz Holt, Douglas Hughes, Paul Lazarus, Jacques Levy, Lynne Meadow, Nancy Meckler, Stephen Schacter, Edwin Sherin, John Tillinger, Robert Woodruff

Designers
Sets: John Lee Beatty, Kate Edmunds, Karl Eigsti, David Emmons, Kenneth Foy, David Gropman, Andrew Jackness, Sally Jacobs, David Potts, Barry Robison, Douglas W. Schmidt, Karen Schulz, Paul Steinberg, Tony Straiges, Jane Thurn. *Costumes:* Mary Brecht, Judy Dearing, Linda Fisher, Jess Goldstein, Calista Hendrickson, William Ivey Long, Patricia McGourty, David Murin, Carrie Robbins, Christa Scholtz, Jennifer von Mayrhauser, Kenneth M. Yount. *Lights:* Frances Aronson, Ken Billington, Pat Collins, F. Mitchell Dana, Beverly Emmons, John Gleason, Roger Morgan, Dennis Parichy, David F. Segal, Jennifer Tipton, Tony Tucci, Marc B. Weiss.

Media resources
Video: *Sea Marks* (WNET), *Ashes, Endgame Losing Time, Mass Appeal* (Lincoln Center Research Collection).

Mark Taper Forum. Judd Hirsch and Trish Hawkins in *Talley's Folly.* Photo: Jay Thompson.

Mark Taper Forum

Gordon Davidson
Artistic Director

William P. Wingate
Managing Director

Los Angeles Music Center
135 North Grand Ave.
Los Angeles, CA 90012
(213) 972–7353 (business)
(213) 972–7392 (box office)
(213) 972–7651 (Forum Laboratory box office)
(213) 466–2161 (Aquarius box office)

Founded 1967
Gordon Davidson

Season
July–June

Schedule
Evenings
Tuesday–Sunday
Matinees
Saturday, Sunday

Facilities
Mark Taper Forum
Seating capacity: 742
Stage: thrust
Forum Laboratory
2580 Cahuenga Blvd., Hollywood
Seating capacity: 99
Stage: flexible
Aquarius Theatre
6230 Sunset Blvd., Hollywood
Seating capacity: 1,199
Stage: modified thrust

Finances
July 1, 1980–June 30, 1981
$4,654,000 operating expenses
$3,175,000 earned income
$2,055,000 grants/contributions

Audience
Annual attendance: 321,897
Subscribers: 34,000

Touring contact
Stephen J. Albert

Booked-in events
Theatre

AEA LORT (A) and (B) contracts

The Mark Taper Forum's artistic program, under the direction of Gordon Davidson, comprises five interrelated parts: the major subscription season, New Theatre for Now, Forum Laboratory projects, Aquarius Theatre events and affiliated community programs.

The mainstage season offers a wide range of productions, including classical works, but with an emphasis on new plays and American or West Coast premieres. In addition, the Taper is making a major commitment to the establishment of a permanent repertory company.

Pioneering in the development of new plays, playwrights and directors, New Theatre for Now explores unusual dramatic subjects and innovative staging concepts. The company's commitment to developing new theatre pieces also finds expression through the Forum Laboratory, a program of workshops and readings performed for invited audiences. At the Lab, actors, writers, directors, composers and designers collaborate on projects which explore new modes of dramatic expression, free from critical and box office pressures.

Aquarius Theatre events include transferred Taper mainstage productions that can sustain longer runs, as well as productions specifically designed for performance there. The theatre is also available for lease to commercial producers and other performing arts organizations.

Related community programs include the Improvisational Theatre Project (ITP) and Project DATE (Deaf Audience Theatre Experience). ITP offers innovative experiences to children and adults, calling upon them to develop their imaginations and creativity. The troupe tours locally and statewide, performing and holding workshops in schools and at the Taper. Project DATE offers special performances of subscription season plays for the hearing-impaired.

Productions 1979–80
Talley's Folly, Lanford Wilson
• *5th of July,* Lanford Wilson
• *Children of a Lesser God,* Mark Medoff
Says I, Says He, Ron Hutchinson
• *I Ought to Be in Pictures,* Neil Simon
• *Division Street,* Steve Tesich
A Christmas Carol, adapt: Doris Baizley, from Charles Dickens

Productions 1980–81
• *The Lady and the Clarinet,* book: Michael Cristofer; music: Leonard Rosenman; lyrics: Alan and Marilyn Bergman
Billy Bishop Goes to War, John Gray and Eric Peterson
A Christmas Carol
• *Hoagy, Bix and Wolfgang Beethoven Bunkhaus,* Adrian Mitchell
Tintypes, music and lyrics: various; adapt: Mary Kyte, Mel Marvin and Gary Pearle
• *Chekhov in Yalta,* John Driver and Jeffrey Haddow
Twelfth Night, William Shakespeare

Directors
Frank Condon, Gordon Davidson, John Dennis, John Gray, Diana Maddox, Marshall W. Mason, Tom Moore, Gary Pearle, Ellis Rabb, Steven Robman, Herbert Ross

Designers
Sets: John Lee Beatty, Charles Berliner, Ralph Funicello, David Gropman, David Jenkins, Tom Lynch, Douglas W. Schmidt, Tony Walton, Thomas A. Walsh. *Costumes:* Robert Blackman, Charles Berliner, John Conklin, Laura Crow, Lilly Fenichel, Jess Goldstein, Dona Granata, Nancy Potts, Carrie F. Robbins, Julie Weiss. *Lights:* Martin Aronstein, Paul Gallo, John Gleason, Tharon Musser, Darryl Palagi, Dennis Parichy, Tom Rusika, Jennifer Tipton.

Media resources
Film: *The Trial of the Catonsville Nine* (Gregory Peck) *Zoot Suit* (Universal Studios). Radio: *In Camera* (Earplay). Video: *Who's Happy Now?* (WNET), *Guns, Before You Forget, The Games* (KCET).

McCarter Theatre Company

Nagle Jackson
Artistic Director

Alison Harris
Managing Director

91 University Place
Princeton, NJ 08540
(609) 452–3616 (business)
(609) 921–8700 (box office)

Founded 1972
Daniel Seltzer

Season
September–April

Schedule
Evenings
Wednesday–Sunday
Matinees
Sunday

Facilities
Seating capacity: 1,077
Stage: proscenium

Finances
July 1, 1980–June 30, 1981
$2,115,000 operating expenses
$1,174,000 earned income
$ 855,000 grants/contributions

Audience
Annual attendance: 162,000
Subscribers: 9,000

Touring contact
Thomas Holm

Booked-in events
Dance, film, music, children's theatre

AEA LORT (B) contract

Under the artistic leadership of Nagle Jackson, the McCarter Theatre Company is first and foremost a company of theatre artists, striving to build its own personality *as* a company and aiming to share with its audiences the growth of that personality and artistic expertise.

In addition to its core company, McCarter invites distinguished guest artists to appear in its five subscription productions each year, and in the annual holiday revival of *A Christmas Carol.* Plays are presented in the elegant proscenium auditorium which has served the community and Princeton University as a performing arts center since 1929. Many McCarter productions play in Philadelphia's Annenberg Center as well.

Besides its regular series, McCarter is building a Stage II program and continues its Playwrights-At-McCarter series of formal public readings of new scripts by world-famous authors, seasoned professionals and gifted novices. The McCarter regularly tours a four-state area and provides outreach services to local schools, clubs and prison audiences.

In its development of new works for the American theatre, and in its dedication to the maintenance of a first-ranking theatre company, the McCarter has achieved a reputation as a theatre of excellence on the East Coast.

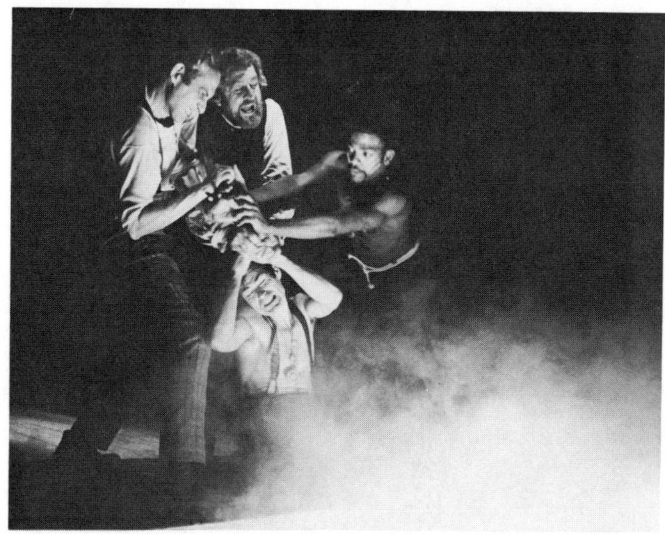

McCarter Theatre Company. Robert Lanchester, Richard Risso, Hubert Kelly and Bruce Somerville in *Moby Dick Rehearsed.* Photo: Cliff Moore.

Productions 1979–80
The Visions of Simone Machard, Bertolt Brecht and Lion Feuchtwanger; trans: Carl Richard Mueller
All the Way Home, Tad Mosel
Jumpers, Tom Stoppard
The Miser, Moliere; adapt: Miles Malleson
• *1959 Pink Thunderbird,* James McLure
Hay Fever, Noel Coward

Productions 1980–81
The Taming of the Shrew, William Shakespeare
Moby Dick Rehearsed, adapt: Orson Welles, from Herman Melville
A Christmas Carol, adapt: Nagle Jackson, from Charles Dickens
• *Eminent Domain,* Percy Granger
Custer, Robert Ingham
The Play's the Thing, Ferenc Molnar; adapt: P.G. Wodehouse
• *Putting on the Dog,* Deloss Brown

Directors
Paul Austin, Barry Boys, Kenneth Frankel, Nagle Jackson, Robert Lanchester, William Woodman

Designers
Sets: Daniel Boylen, Karen Eisler, Ralph Funicello, John Jensen, Brian Martin, Michael Miller.
Costumes: Michael J. Cesario, Elizabeth Covey, Robin Hirsch, Rosemary Ingham, Jennifer von Mayrhauser, Robert Morgan.
Lights: Lowell Achziger, Frances Aronson, Don Ehman, John McLain, Sean Murphy, Marc B. Weiss.

Medicine Show Theatre Ensemble

Barbara Vann
James Barbosa
Artistic Directors

6 West 18th St.
New York, NY 10011
(212) 255–4991

Founded 1970
Barbara Vann, James Barbosa

Season
September–June

Schedule
Evenings
Wednesday–Saturday

Facilities
Newfoundland Theatre
Seating capacity: 74
Stage: arena

Finances
August 1, 1980–July 31, 1981
$58,000 operating expenses
$34,000 earned income
$20,000 grants/comtributions

Audience
Annual attendance: 8,000

Touring contact
James Barbosa

Booked-in events
Theatre, dance, poetry, music

Medicine Show is passionately interested in life. Not the dulling mechanics of living, but the prickly, funny, delirious, mysterious, only-relatively-knowable material it builds its pieces with and around. An informal association of eccentric theatre artists creating and lavishly performing their complex comedic visions, Medicine Show removes any taint of the predictable, comfortable or absolute from its works and keeps them as unlike "artistic taxidermy" as is humanly possible.

The works are expressive and evocative rather than descriptive, with language used as noise, music and for its poetic value. Bodies and ideas move fast; movement and speech stretch their limits. Theories about the works follow the creation of the works themselves. The company, having no tradition or position to maintain, is free to be as adventuresome and changeable as it likes. For example, *Classy Comics (ART Takes a Holiday),* a wild-eyed appreciation of "American Dada," is followed by a musical-theatrical investigation into the funny and horrific works and lives of Edgar Allan Poe.

Then a scripted work joins the repertoire: Shakespeare or Shaw or Brecht or perhaps someone brand-new and just as good.

The company plays for the quick-witted and far-seeing, annoying the critics and delighting the children. Its audience, imagination undimmed by civilization, makes its way loyally to Medicine Show's storefront Newfoundland Theatre. The company is frequently invited to play in universities, prisons, schools, hospitals and festivals, nationwide and abroad, playing in all weather to new audiences whose terrifying freshness of perception is invigorating and educational. Medicine Show is committed to learning and questioning, and attempts to teach others the techniques toward these ends. In its dozen years of continuous artistic and economic struggle, the theatre has outlived several critics, many grants officers, legions of pedants and three presidents. Preposterous.

Medicine Show Theatre Ensemble. *Classy Comics.* Photo: Robert Gould.

Productions 1979–80

Frogs, company-developed with Carl Morse; music: Yenoin Guibbory

The Tragedy of Tragedies, or The Life and Death of Tom Thumb the Great, Henry Fielding; music: Carol Henry

Shipping Out, company-developed with Stephen P. Policoff; music: Carol Henry

• *The Mummers' Play,* adapt: Stephen P. Policoff; music: Carol Henry

Tenth Anniversary Retrospective, various authors

Productions 1980–81

Frogs

Medicine Show, company-developed with Richard Schotter; music: Robert Dennis

The Mummers' Play

• *Classy Comics,* Ring Lardner, George S. Kaufman, Gertrude Stein; music: Michael Rice

Don Juan in Hell, George Bernard Shaw

Directors

James Barbosa, Catherine Mandas, Barbara Vann

Designers

Sets: Joel Handorff, Antony Miralda, Robert Pucci, D. Schweppe, R. Patrick Sullivan. *Costumes:* Martha Bard, Cecilia Fratelli, Joel Handorff, Patricia McGourty, Antony Miralda. *Lights:* Robert Pucci, D. Schweppe, Robin Smith.

Media resources

Film: *Glowworm* (RAI, Italy, documentary). Radio: *Frogs* (WBAI). Video: *Frogs* (University of South Carolina).

Merrimack Regional Theatre

Mark Kaufman
Artistic Director

Patricia Littrell-Wayne
Managing Director

Box 228
Lowell, MA 01853
(617) 454–6324 (business)
(617) 454–3926 (box office)

Founded 1979
Mark Kaufman, John R. Briggs

Season
October–May

Schedule
Evenings
Tuesday–Saturday
Matinees
Wednesday, Sunday

Facilities
Mahoney Hall
Broadway and Wilder Sts.
Seating capacity: 420
Stage: proscenium
Shattuck Street Theatre
Seating capacity: 1,000
Stage: flexible

Finances
July 1, 1980–June 30, 1981
$301,000 operating expenses
$143,000 earned income
$158,000 grants/contributions

Audience
Annual attendance: 30,000
Subscribers: 2,200

AEA LORT (D) contract

The Merrimack Regional Theatre was founded in 1979 to bring high quality professional theatre to the Merrimack Valley region of Massachusetts, while providing artists with an environment conducive to artistic growth.

The theatre is located in historic Lowell, the birthplace of the American Industrial Revolution and the nation's first urban National Park. The city has undergone massive urban renewal within the past five years, and MRT has been called the cornerstone of the cultural renaissance of Lowell.

Merrimack Regional Theatre. Michael Rothaar and Richard Lupino in *Sleuth.* Photo: Fotene Jean.

Now in its third year, MRT produces a regular season of six plays, each running from three to four weeks in a proscenium theatre located on the campus of the University of Lowell. The seasons have primarily focused on traditional American playwrights, with the 1980–81 season bringing forth MRT's first premiere, Bill C. Davis's *Gentle Catapults.*

MRT also offers a summer season, the first of which included two musicals in repertory, performed at an outdoor facility in downtown Lowell. These plays were sponsored by the Lowell Historic Preservation Commission, the City of Lowell and the United States Department of the Interior. In its second summer, the Merrimack produced the world premiere of an historical script by David Riley based on Lowell history, also sponsored by the City and the Preservation Commission. Both summer seasons were offered free to the public. Artistic director Mark Kaufman also conducts workshops in the community during the theatre's regular season.

Productions 1979–80
The Passion of Dracula, David Richmond and Bob Hall
A Christmas Carol, adapt: Timothy Near and Rae Allen, from Charles Dickens
Romeo and Juliet, William Shakespeare
Same Time, Next Year, Bernard Slade
The Glass Menagerie, Tennessee Williams
Vanities, Jack Heifner
The Fantasticks, book and lyrics: Tom Jones; music: Harvey Schmidt
A Funny Thing Happened on the Way to the Forum, book: Burt Shevelove and Larry Gelbart; music and lyrics: Stephen Sondheim

Productions 1980–81
Sleuth, Anthony Shaffer
Side by Side by Sondheim, music and lyrics: Stephen Sondheim, et al; adapt: Ned Sherrin
The Sea Horse, Edward J. Moore
The Gingerbread Lady, Neil Simon
• *Gentle Catapults,* Bill C. Davis
On Golden Pond, Ernest Thompson
If the Falls Could Speak, David Riley

Directors
John R. Briggs, Bick Goss, Sandra C. Hastie, D.J. Maloney, Mark Kaufman, Stephen Zuckerman

Designers
Sets: Ed Cesaitis, Charles Cosler, David Dorwart, John Kleis, Robert McBroom, Stephen Pater, Larry von Werrssowetz, Larry Willette, Patricia Woodbridge. *Costumes:* Barbara Forbes, Larry Willette, Karl Wendelin. *Lights:* Paul Everett, Charles Cosler, David Lockner, Stephen Pater.

Milwaukee Repertory Theater

John Dillon
Artistic Director

Sara O'Connor
Managing Director

Performing Arts Center
929 North Water St.
Milwaukee, WI 53202
(414) 273-7121 (business)
(414) 273-7206 (box office)

Founded 1954
Mary John

Season
September–May

Schedule
Evenings
Tuesday–Sunday
Matinees
Wednesday, Sunday

Facilities
Todd Wehr Theater
Seating capacity: 504
Stage: thrust
Pabst Theater
144 East Wells St.
Seating capacity: 1,388
Stage: proscenium
Court Street Theater
315 West Court St.
Seating capacity: 99
Stage: flexible

Finances
July 1, 1980–June 30, 1981
$1,693,000 operating expenses
$1,130,000 earned income
$ 579,000 grants/contributions

Audience
Annual attendance: 193,600
Subscribers: 19,000

Touring contact
Susan Medak

AEA LORT (C) contract

The Milwaukee Repertory Theater views its activities as a collaboration between a company of artists and its audience in both the development of new works and the development of an acting and production style capable of creatively interpreting the full range of world drama.

The MRT maintains a relationship with a group of playwrights, some in full-time residence, some part-time affiliates. The Court Street Theater is a developmental arena for works which often move to the mainstage. The collaboration of artistic director John Dillon and resident director Sharon Ott has resulted in an unusual approach to major projects: a regional sensibility is reflected in commissioned works based on the history and literature of the Upper Midwest, as well as in a state and regional touring program.

At the heart of the MRT is a strong resident acting company able to make distinctive stylistic statements, augmented by a sizable number of guest actors. In addition to productions on the thrust stage of the intimate Todd Wehr Theater, scenic opportunities are extended by the use of the 19th century proscenium stage of the Pabst Theater.

Internationalism permeates the philosophy of the theatre. In 1980 the MRT introduced Jean-Claude Grumberg's *L'Atelier (The Workroom)* to the United States; in 1981 *A Streetcar Named Desire* toured Japan as part of an ongoing exchange with Japanese theatre artists, and an exchange of directors and actors is currently underway with the Royal Exchange Theatre, Manchester, England.

After 27 years of activity, the MRT's stability and flexibility are rooted in the solid support of the Milwaukee audience and the community's financial support through the local United Performing Arts Fund.

Productions 1979–80
The Recruiting Officer, George Farquhar
The Dance of Death, August Strindberg; trans: Michael Meyer
• *On the Road to Babylon,* book: Richard Wesley; music and lyrics: Peter Link
• *Dead Souls,* Nikolai Gogol; adapt: Mikhail Bulgakov; trans: Tom Cole
• *The Workroom,* Jean-Claude Grumberg; adapt: Daniel A. Stein and Sara O'Connor
Of Mice and Men, John Steinbeck
A Christmas Carol, adapt: Nagle Jackson, from Charles Dickens

Productions 1980–81
Cyrano de Bergerac, Edmond Rostand; trans: Brian Hooker
Mother Courage and Her Children, Bertolt Brecht; trans: Ralph Manheim
Children of a Lesser God, Mark Medoff
Julius Caesar, William Shakespeare
A Streetcar Named Desire, Tennessee Williams
• *The Nerd,* Larry Shue
A Christmas Carol
• *Six Toes,* Amlin Gray
• *Stark Mad in White Satin,* Daniel A. Stein
• *Lakeboat,* David Mamet
The Taming of the Shrew, William Shakespeare; adapt: Amlin Gray, John Dillon and Jonathan Abarbanel
Fighting Bob, Tom Cole
An Independent Woman, Daniel A. Stein

Directors
Richard Cottrell, John Dillon, Bill Ludel, Sharon Ott, Sanford Robbins, Garland Wright

Designers
Sets: William Eckart, Karl Eigsti, David Emmons, Hugh Landwehr, Laura Maurer, Michael Merritt, Joseph Nieminski, Stuart Wurtzel. *Costumes:* Patricia McGourty, Colleen Muscha, Carol Oditz, Jo Peters, Susan Tsu. *Lights:* Rachel Budin, Dawn Chiang, Arden Fingerhut, Toni Goldin, Spencer Mosse.

Media resources
Radio: *Grandma Duck Is Dead* (Earplay). Video: *The Trial of the Moke* (WNET), *In Memory Of* (WMVS).

Missouri Repertory Theatre

Patricia McIlrath
Producing Director

Daniel Baker
Administrative Manager

University of Missouri
Center for the Performing Arts
4949 Cherry St.
Kansas City, MO 64110
(816) 363–4300 (business)
(816) 276–2704 (box office)

Founded 1964
University of Missouri–Kansas City, Patricia McIlrath

Season
July–September
February–March

Schedule
Evenings
Tuesday–Sunday
Matinees
Wednesday, Sunday

Facilities
Helen F. Spencer Theatre
Seating capacity: 733
Stage: flexible
J.C. Nichols Theatre
6903 Oak St.
Seating capacity: 450
Stage: proscenium
Studio Theatre
Seating capacity: 100
Stage: arena

Finances
May 1, 1980–April 30, 1981
$1,214,000 operating expenses
$ 495,000 earned income
$ 754,000 grants/contributions

Audience
Annual attendance: 76,000
Subscribers: 4,995

Milwaukee Repertory Theater. *Julius Caesar.* Photo: Mary Avery.

Missouri Repertory Theatre. Cynthia Dozier, Michael Haney, Robert Lewis Karlin and Walter Atamaniux in *Twelfth Night.*

'ouring contact
)iana Coles

IEA LORT (B) contract

n its 18th year under the same rtistic and administrative eadership, Missouri Repertory 'heatre now performs in a new, ermanent home: the Helen F. pencer Theatre, a part of Kansas 'ity's $11.4 million Center for the 'erforming Arts.

Unusual among resident heatres for its close interaction vith the University of Aissouri-Kansas City professional heatre training program, MRT is professional company playing in otating repertory. The theatre naintains a resident ensemble ompany, while engaging six to ight nationally noted guest irectors, as well as professional esigners and technicians, during s eight-play season.

MRT offers unique outreach ervices throughout Missouri and four-state area. The MRT 'anguard Tour is in its 14th year, ffering two plays in repertory, -school programs for secondary nd elementary school children, nd acting and technical orkshops. The Vanguard nsemble, largely duplicating the esident MRT company, now avels between 8 and 12 weeks through Missouri and the neighboring states following the resident season in Kansas City, affording many artists more than 32 weeks of employment per year.

The 1979 season saw the inauguration of a second stage—MRT II—in a small, 100-seat space at the center. This second space focuses on new or recent American plays, produced by interns and residents from the University's MFA program, for ever-increasing audiences. Staging is simple; the intent is to create a forum for young American playwrights and supplement the mainstage season. In 1980, MRT instituted signed performances for the hearing-impaired.

Missouri Repertory Theatre is sponsored by the MRT Guild of almost 800 members, which hosts director's briefings, opening night receptions and annually makes significant financial contributions to MRT.

Productions 1979–80
Hamlet, William Shakespeare
Resencrantz and Guildenstern Are Dead, Tom Stoppard
The New York Idea, Langdon Mitchell
The Chalk Garden, Enid Bagnold
Oh, Coward! music and lyrics: Noel Coward; adapt: Roderick Cook
The Visit, Friedrich Duerrenmatt
Twelfth Night, William Shakespeare
Look Homeward, Angel, adapt: Ketti Frings, from Thomas Wolfe

Productions 1980–81
Medea, Euripides; adapt: Robinson Jeffers
What Every Woman Knows, James M. Barrie
The Learned Ladies, Moliere; trans: Richard Wilbur
Catsplay, Istvan Orkeny; trans: Clara Gyorgyey
Lady Audley's Secret, adapt: Francis J. Cullinan, from Mary Elizabeth Braddon
The Night of the Iguana, Tennessee Williams
Wings, Arthur Kopit
• *The Perfect Gentleman,* Herbert Appleman

Directors
James Assad, Norman Ayrton, Francis Cullinan, Gerald Gutierrez, George Hamlin, George Keathley, Albert Marre, Patricia McIlrath, Ellis Rabb, John Reich, Eric Vos

Designers
Sets: Franco Colavecchia, John Ezell, James Gohl, Richard Hay, James Leonard Joy, Carolyn Ross. *Costumes:* Michele Bechtold, Judith Dolan, Carolyn Ross, Douglas Russell, Vincent Scassellati, Baker Smith. *Lights:* Joseph Appelt, Arden Fingerhut, Ruth Ludwick, Michael Scott.

Media resources
Video: *Watermelon Boats* (KCPT).

Music-Theatre Group/Lenox Arts Center

Lyn Austin
Margo Lion
Producing Directors

18 East 68th St.
New York, NY 10021
(212) 371–9610 (business)
(212) 582–1978 (box office)

Citizens Hall
Stockbridge, MA 01262
(413) 298–9463

Founded in 1970
Lyn Austin

Season
New York
October–May
Stockbridge
June–August

Schedule
Evenings
Wednesday–Sunday

Facilities
Citizens Hall
Seating capacity: 100
Stage: flexible
Cubiculo Theatre
414 West 51st St.
Seating capacity: 75
Stage: flexible

Finances
July 1, 1980–June 30, 1981
$183,000 operating expenses
$ 23,000 earned income
$160,000 grants/contributions

Audience
Annual attendance: 18,000

Touring contact
Lyn Austin

Booked-in events
Theatre, music, dance

AEA Mini contract

The Music-Theatre Group/Lenox Arts Center, entering its 11th year, is a laboratory for the development of new American music-theatre. Fusing experimental theatre techniques with a wide range of musical forms (contemporary, jazz, opera) and

Music-Theatre Group/Lenox Arts Center. Sam Schacht and Alexandra Borrie in *Was It Good for You?* Photo: Stephanie Saia.

dance, the organization pioneers the development of a music-theatre which has proved itself a dynamic offshoot of the American musical comedy tradition.

The working process begins with extensive rehearsal periods so that the writers, composers, directors and performers may put full focus on the work itself and not on technical trappings. Projects then proceed to full production for performances on, Off and Off-Off Broadway, throughout the country, in Europe and on television. Nine months are spent in preparation and performance in New York, and the three summer months are spent in Stockbridge, Massachusetts.

The company has sought to create fresh, dynamic collaborations by bringing together just the right writer (who up to that point might have been working solely as a poet or novelist), or just the right composer with just the right director (who up to that point might have been solely a choreographer). MTG/LAC's structure focuses on in-depth work with each artist in the hope of developing major writers, composers and directors far more successfully than when using a kind of "sausage factory" approach to artistic enterprise.

Representative productions from a list of more than 50 include: *Doctor Selavy's Magic Theatre, Hotel for Criminals* and *The American Imagination* by Stanley Silverman and Richard Foreman; *Nightclub Cantata* by Elizabeth Swados; *The Club* by Eve Merriam, directed by Tommy Tune; and *The Tennis Game* by George Trow, directed by Timothy Mayer, with music by William Schimmel.

Productions 1980
- *Daisy,* adapt: Victoria Rue, from Joyce Carol Oates; music: Daniel Werts
- *The Ladder,* adapt: Olga Bernal, from Lara Jefferson; music: Amina Claudine Myers
- *Was It Good for You?* adapt: Susan Rice, from Edward Koren; music: Amy Rubin
- *The Brides,* Harry Kondoleon; music: Hal McKusick

Productions 1980–81
- *Elizabeth Dead,* George W.S. Trow; music: Robert Dennis
- *Disrobing the Brides,* Harry Kondoleon; music: Gary S. Fagin
- *The Columbine String Quartet Tonight!,* concept: Tina Howe and Stanley Silverman
- *Hers and His,* Andre Gregory
- *A New Music-Theatre Piece,* music and lyrics: Gary S. Fagin

Directors
Martha Clarke, Andre Gregory, Harry Kondoleon, Larry Pine, Susan Rice, Victoria Rue, Charles Turner

Designers
Sets: Mike Boak, Lawrence Casey, Lenny Cowles, David Mitchell, Loren Sherman. *Costumes:* Whitney Blausen, Mike Boak, Lawrence Casey, Ann Emonts, Rita Ryack. *Lights:* William Armstrong, Lenny Cowles, Cynthia Hawkins, Rick Pettit, Loren Sherman.

Media resources
Recordings: *Dr. Selavy's Magic Theatre* (United Artists).

National Black Theatre

Barbara Ann Teer
Executive Producer

Zuri McKie
Managing Director

9 East 125th St.
New York, NY 10035
(212) 427–5615

Founded 1968
Barbara Ann Teer

Season
Year-round

Schedule
Evenings
Thursday–Saturday
Matinees
Sunday

Facilities
Temple Theatre
Seating capacity: 100
Stage: thrust
Street Side Theatre
Seating capacity: 100
Stage: thrust

Finances
November 1, 1980–October 31, 1981
$131,000 operating expenses
$ 28,000 earned income
$114,000 grants/contributions

Audience
Annual attendance: 10,000

Touring contact
Keibu Faison

The National Black Theatre was founded 13 years ago in the center of Harlem to maintain and perpetuate the beauty inherent in the spiritual form and feeling of the black lifestyle. Rapidly developing into an institution of re-education, NBT's sole mission today is to transform the experience of Western theatre into a celebration of life. Toward this end, NBT has developed a theatrical performance technology that allows people to experience themselves as creative, powerful, healthy, wholesome, alive and loving beings. Theatre is an enormously powerful instrument in the company's hands, giving them an opportunity to transform the lives of hundreds of people each evening a performance takes place.

NBT's art form employs a scientific method through which an environment is created for people to experience and express their interrelatedness, joyously and freely. Adult workshops are offered, as well as a creative Center for Children, and a touring outreach program. The programs offered at the National Black Theatre perpetuate values and images needed to raise the consciousness of its participants. NBT is a place where the potential artist can develop his full potential by learning to restore a relationship with himself and his audience—where each person experiences himself as an integral, rhythmic and interdependent aspect of the whole.

Productions 1979–80
Softly Comes a Whirlwind Whispering in Your Ear, Barbara Ann Teer; music: Nabii Faison
Riding on the Wings of Love, book, music and lyrics: Nabii Faison

Productions 1980–81
Soul Fusion, Nabii Faison and Barbara Ann Teer; music: Nabii Faison
The Boiling Marriage, George McKinley White

Directors
Nabii Faison, Zuri McKie, Lizz Omilami, Barbara Ann Teer

Designers
Sets: Felix Cochren, Nabii Faison, John Harris. *Costumes:* Evelyn Brown Chisolm, Leslie V. Day. *Lights:* John Harris, Lanere Holmes, Tim Phillips.

Media resources
Film: *Rise, a Love Poem for a Love People* (company-produced), *Me and My Heritage* (WCBS, documentary), *Black Theatre in America* (Woodie King, documentary). Video: *Ritual* (WNET), *Revival* (company-produced), *Harlem* (Gary Brewer, documentary).

National Black Theatre. *Softly Comes a Whirlwind Whispering in Your Ear.* Photo: Larry Neilson.

The National Shakespeare Company

Philip Meister
Artistic Director

Albert Schoemann
General Manager

414 West 51st St.
New York, NY 10019
(212) 265–1340

Founded 1963
Philip Meister, Elaine Sulka

Season
October–May

Finances
June 1, 1980–May 31, 1981
$225,000 operating expenses
$269,000 earned income

Audience
Annual attendance: 250,000

Touring contact
Michael Hirsch

The 1982–83 season will mark the National Shakespeare Company's 20th year of bringing classical theatre to colleges and communities across the country. Priding itself on taking Shakespeare to audiences who might not otherwise experience live theatre, the NSC gives American actors a valuable chance to play classical roles. The company consists of 12 actors who tour with complete scenery, lights and costumes, and has played in more than 700 cities in 46 states to a total audience of 1,125,000. Actors are selected each spring from auditions held throughout the country.

NSC has also developed a matinee series geared to high school students, and aimed at enhancing the study of Shakespeare's plays while aiding teachers of English, history and drama. The 1980–81 Student Matinee Series was presented to 21,000 students in New York, Pennsylvania, Illinois, North Carolina, Ohio, Maryland and Arkansas.

After 19 years, NSC has become familiar with the problems of professional actors. As a result, the National Shakespeare Company Conservatory was founded as a professional training program designed to prepare the actors's body, imagination and intellect. The conservatory offers a two-year program in New York City and an eight-week intensive summer program at the company's property in the Catskill Mountains. The conservatory is fully accredited, and recognized by the U.S. Office of Education. The National Shakespeare Company offices and conservatory are located at the Cubiculo Theatre, which offers dance, theatre and music programs throughout the year.

Productions 1979–80
Much Ado About Nothing, William Shakespeare
Julius Caesar, William Shakespeare

Productions 1980–81
The Comedy of Errors, Willia Shakespeare
Romeo and Juliet, William Shakespeare
Richard III, William Shakespeare

Directors
Jerome Guardino, Sue Lawless, Mario Siletti, Kirk Wolfinger

Designers
Sets: Terry Bennett, Bob Phillips. *Costumes:* Terry Bennett, Sharon Hollinger, Amanda Klein. *Lights:* Terry Bennett, Angus Moss.

Nebraska Theatre Caravan

Charles Jones
Executive Director

Carolyn Rutherford
Company Manager

6915 Cass St.
Omaha, NE 68132
(402) 553–4890

Founded 1976
Charles Jones, Nebraska Arts Council, Omaha Playhouse

Season
October–May

Schedule
Monday–Saturday

Facilities
Omaha Playhouse
Seating capacity: 514
Stage: proscenium

Finances
July 1, 1980–June 30, 1981
$325,000 operating expenses
$279,000 earned income
$ 41,000 grants/contributions

Audience
Annual attendance: 180,000

Touring contact
Carolyn Rutherford

Established in 1976 as the professional wing of the Omaha Community Playhouse, the Nebraska Theatre Caravan has provided the thrill and excitement of live professional theatre—as well as valuable educational opportunities—to students, educators, colleges and universities, and communities in 19 states. The primary goal of the Caravan is to provide high calibre professional theatre and creative workshops to communities where distance, financial limitations or lack of resources have previously hindered or prevented such activities.

Each season, the Caravan prepares at least four major productions for its midwestern tour, including one musical, a production for children and a production of Shakespeare. The Caravan has developed a style of performance which allows the company to remain efficiently mobile and flexible, performing in almost any available space when a traditional theatre is not available.The Caravan has found great success in a zesty, energetic approach to Shakespeare for young people, while simultaneously achieving a performance level suited to adult audiences. The company is committed to providing entertainment as well as educational opportunities for all age groups.

Under the direction of professional workshop leaders, the Caravan actors, technicians and managers craft workshops that offer students, teachers and community performers personalized opportunities to explore their creative resources. Each Caravan member is dedicated to the importance of personally sharing his craft with both children and adults. The Caravan offers each community artistic flexibility and complete community ownership of the residency program, and provides educational and publicity materials to aid the sponsor in residency preparation.

The National Shakespeare Company. Peter Powell, Norris Browne, Mykael O'Struitheain and Lary Ohlsen in *Richard III.* Photo: John Brosseau.

Productions 1979–80
Sacramento 50 Miles, Eleanor and Ray Harder
A Midsummer Night's Dream, William Shakespeare; adapt: Bill Kirk
Diamond Studs, book, music and lyrics: Jim Wann and Bland Simpson
The Robber Bridegroom, book and lyrics: Alfred Uhry; music: Robert Waldman
A Christmas Carol, adapt: Charles Jones, from Charles Dickens; music: Robert Waldman

Productions 1980–81
A Hans Christian Andersen Storybook, adapt: Charles Jones
Romeo and Juliet, William Shakespeare; adapt: Charles Jones
Gold Dust, book: Jon Jory; music and lyrics: Jim Wann
A Christmas Carol

Directors
Eleanor Jones, Charles Jones, Bill Kirk

Designers
Sets: Erik Jabloner, James Othuse. *Costumes:* Denise Ervin, Pat Moser, Anne Winsor, Kathryn Wilson. *Lights:* James Othuse.

Media resources
Video: *The Travelin' Theatre* (ITV, documentary).

Nebraska Theatre Caravan. Jim Goggess, Mack Porter and Doug Kolbo in *Diamond Studs.* Photo: John McIntyre.

Negro Ensemble Company

Douglas Turner Ward
Artistic Director

Leon B. Denmark
Managing Director

165 West 46th St.
New York, NY 10036
(212) 575–5860 (business)
(212) 246–8545 (box office)

Founded 1967
Douglas Turner Ward, Robert Hooks, Gerald S. Krone

Season
September–April

Schedule
Evenings
Tuesday–Sunday
Matinees
Saturday, Sunday

Facilities
Theatre Four
424 West 55th St.
Seating capacity: 299
Stage: proscenium

Finances
July 1, 1980–June 30, 1981
$1,132,235 operating expenses
$ 451,913 earned income
$ 691,822 grants/contributions

Audience
Annual attendance: 67,626
Subscribers: 1,800

Touring contact
William D. Edwards

AEA LORT (C) contract

The Negro Ensemble Company remains committed to the presentation of theatrical material inspired by the lives of African-Americans, Afro-Caribbeans and continental Africans.

The 1981–82 season is the NEC's 15th anniversary and is highlighted by the presentation of plays written by some of the company's award-winning alumni: Charles Fuller, Lonnie Elder III, Leslie Lee, Paul Carter Harrison, Dan Owens, Joseph Walker and Samm-Art Williams. And, of course, the NEC plans to maintain its commitment to the discovery and presentation of unproduced authors. During its anniversary year, efforts to market the NEC are being greatly increased. Membership and subscription programs were recently launched, and discount and complimentary tickets are being made available.

The year 1981 also marks the beginning of the company's second season in a larger theatre, as well as the successful, but sometimes rocky, continuation of a long-range plan for revitalization and institutional stabilization. During the past two seasons, the NEC has managed to develop a number of promising new plays, revamp its administrative staff,

Negro Ensemble Company. Carl Gordon and Phylicia Ayers-Allen in *In an Upstate Motel.* Photo: Bert Andrews.

expand its board structure, stabilize its development unit and, most important, extend the scope and length of its production activities.

The NEC completed its second southeastern tour in the spring of 1980 and is planning another for 1982. The organization is now looking into touring possibilities in other areas of the country, as well as continuing its efforts to participate in the joint development of productions with other resident theatres. During the 1980–81 season, the company appeared in a guest residency at the Guthrie Theater in Minneapolis.

The NEC continues to offer on-the-job training and intern programs for developing theatre artists, administrators and technicians. It also continues its commitment to the new playwright through an expanded Playwrights Unit.

Finally, the company continues to pursue special projects such as television presentations, the production of a season of African classical theatre and the revival of earlier works.

Productions 1979–80

- *The Michigan,* Dan Owens
- *Home,* Samm-Art Williams
- *La Grima Del Diablo,* Dan Owens
- *Companiona of the Fire,* Ali Wadud
- *Big City Blues,* Roy R. Kuljian

Productions 1980–81

- *The Sixteenth Round,* Samm-Art Williams
- *Zooman and the Sign,* Charles Fuller
- *Weep Not for Me,* Gus Edwards
- *In an Upstate Motel,* Larry Neal

Home

Directors
Richard Gant, Paul Carter Harrison, Dean Irby, Horacena Taylor, Douglas Turner Ward

Designers
Sets: Edward Burbridge, Felix Cochren, Rodney J. Lucas, Wynn Thomas. *Costumes:* Judy Dearing, Alvin B. Perry, Quay Barnes Truitt. *Lights:* William H. Grant III, Kathy A. Perkins, Shirley Prendergast.

Media resources
Video: *The First Breeze of Summer* (WNET), *Ceremonies in Dark Old Men* (ABC), *The First Breeze of Summer, Ceremonies in Dark Old Men, The Offering, Home* (Lincoln Center Research Collection).

New American Theater

J.R. Sullivan
Artistic Director

Judith Barnard
Director of Development

117 South Wyman St.
Rockford, IL 61101
(815) 963–9454 (business)
(815) 964–8023 (box office)

Founded 1972
J.R. Sullivan

Season
October–June

Schedule
Evenings
Wednesday–Sunday
Matinees
Saturday

Facilities
118 South Main St.
Seating capacity: 270
Stage: thrust

Finances
July 1, 1980–June 30, 1981
$214,000 operating expenses
$126,000 earned income
$ 72,000 grants/contributions

Audience
Annual attendance: 30,000
Subscribers: 2,014

Touring contact
Judith Barnard

Booked-in events
Theatre

AEA Guest Artist contract

Founded to create and support a permanent, professional resident company, New American Theater continues to expand both in the diversity of its programming and the scope of its artistic and administrative staffing. Contemporary American drama is emphasized, but international works and plays from America's heritage are also presented annually.

Under the artistic direction of founder J.R. Sullivan, NAT presents its 10th season in 1981–82, having doubled the subscription audience in less than three seasons. Its production policy emphasizes diversity in presentation by a company of resident artists. Each actor, director and designer faces a wide range of challenges and the fullest opportunity to realize his artistic potential.

New American Theater is committed to community involvement and has made itself a resource to the Illinois/Wisconsin stateline area's academic and community organizations. Internship opportunities exist for students of local colleges, and NAT's Young American Theater serves local high school students. The NAT touring program has expanded, with special attention paid to senior citizen centers and recreation sites.

The NAT Black Theater Collective came to full flower in 1981, producing Ray Aranha's *My Sister, My Sister* and doubling its membership in both workshop classes and productions.

While a relocation and expansion of facilities is contemplated, New American Theater's goal remains the same: the production of professional regional theatre marked by innovative, honest performance that—in variety and vitality—actively includes its audience.

Productions 1979–80

Sizwe Bansi Is Dead, Athol Fugard, John Kani and Winston Ntshona
Same Time, Next Year, Bernard Slade
The Glass Menagerie, Tennessee Williams
The Great White Hope, Howard Sackler
Side by Side by Sondheim, music and lyrics: Stephen Sondheim, et al.; adapt: Ned Sherrin
Sly Fox, Larry Gelbart
The Norman Conquests, Alan Ayckbourn
Table Manners
Living Together
Round and Round the Garden
The Time of Your Life, William Saroyan

Production 1980–81

Ben Hecht—Child of the Century, adapt: J.R. Sullivan, from Ben

Hecht
The Mistress of the Inn, Carlo Goldoni; trans: Clifford Bax
Rosencrantz and Guildenstern Are Dead, Tom Stoppard
• *A Midwinter Night's Dream,* company-developed
Da, Hugh Leonard
My Sister, My Sister, Ray Aranha
Deathtrap, Ira Levin
Getting Out, Marsha Norman
The Philadelphia Story, Philip Barry

Directors
E. Michael Dobbins, Richard Henzel, H. O'Niel Eley, J.R. Sullivan, Matt Swan, James Wolk

Designers
Sets: Michael S. Philippi, James Wolk. *Costumes:* Jon R. Accardo. *Lights:* Michael S. Philippi, James Wolk.

New American Theater. Richard Raether, Mel Schwartz and Joseph Keyes in *Mistress of the Inn.*

New Dramatists

Thomas G. Dunn
Executive Director

David Juaire
Program Director

424 West 44th St.
New York, NY 10036
(212) 757-6960

Founded 1949
Michaela O'Harra, John Golden, Moss Hart, Oscar Hammerstein II, Richard Rodgers, John Wharton, Howard Lindsay

Season
September–July

Facilities
Theatre
Seating capacity: 110
Stage: proscenium
Studio
Seating capacity: 40
Stage: flexible

Finances
June 1, 1980–May 31, 1981
$150,000 operating expenses
$ 3,000 earned income
$147,000 grants/contributions

Audience
Annual attendance: 7,200

New Dramatists was founded in 1949 to encourage and develop playwriting in America. In order to participate in New Dramatists' programs, a playwright applies for membership, submitting two full-length original scripts to be evaluated by an admissions committee of active members. Once admitted, a playwright is a full participating member for a minimum of three and maximum of seven years.

New Dramatists offers a range of programs for members, centered on the idea that playwriting is not only an art, but also a craft, and that knowing the basics of this craft is an essential complement to talent. Most members have already achieved a certain level of achievement before joining New Dramatists, and all have demonstrated professional intent and exceptional promise. In the end, however, education, ambition, talent and dreams are only part of the prerequisite for becoming a successful playwright. New Dramatists can provide the second part, giving writers an opportunity to explore the "how" of their craft.

Programs include readings of works-in-progress, craft discussions, production observerships, a members' bulletin, library, loan fund and script analysis panels. The intangible components are more difficult to list: encouragement, support, membership in a community of writers and perhaps most important—a belief in the process.

New Dramatists alumni in the 32 years of its existence include such playwrights as Robert Anderson, Ed Bullins, Richard Foreman, John Guare and Lanford Wilson. Current and alumni members have contributed more than 200 plays to the American theatre.

While commercial success for any member is gratifying and welcome, it is not the primary goal of New Dramatists. Focused always on producing *playwrights* rather than plays, it is a workshop in the purest sense of the word: a place where work can be done, a climate and opportunity for inspiration, and the means to realize aspiration.

Productions 1979–80
• *Graciela,* Lynne Alvarez
• *The Resurrection of Jackie Cramer,* Frank Gagliano
• *Family Friends,* Harvey Zuckerman
• *Writers Camp,* Peter Dee and Albert Lynch
• *Disappearing Acts,* Philip Bosakowski
• *The Good Ship Columbia,* Philip Bosakowski
• *Memorial to the Honored Dead,* Stephen Levi
• *The Child,* Anthony Giardina
• *Little Bird,* Mary Gallagher
• *Dancers,* Brendan Ward
• *Things Left Standing,* David Risk
• *At the River,* Michael Carton
• *Revolution of the Heavenly Orbs,* John Orlock
• *The Final Voyage of Aphrodite,* Diane Kagan
• *Quartet,* Peter Dee
• *An American Story,* Ernest Abuba
• *Guitarron,* Lynne Alvarez
• *Badgers,* Donald Wollner
• *In the Rockaways,* John Patrick Shanley
• *House of Secrets,* John Patrick Shanley
• *Mummers,* Jack Gilhooley
• *Alcestis,* David J. Hill
• *The Saddest Summer of Val,* Dennis McIntyre
• *A Play About Lovers,* Robert Wallsten

Productions 1980–81
• *Ketchup,* John Patrick Shanley
• *My Sister in This House,* Wendy Kesselman
• *These Days the Watchmen Sleep,* Karl Evans
• *Shirley Basin,* Jack Gilhooley
• *La Visionaria,* Renaldo Eugenio Ferradas
• *Gorilla,* John Patrick Shanley
• *Brigitte Berger,* Stanley Taikeff
• *The War Brides,* Terri Wagener
• *Eve of All Saints,* Syl Jones

- *About Spontaneous Combustion,* Sherry Kramer
- *Snow in the Virgin Islands,* Marisha Chamberlain
- *Quartet,* Peter Dee
- *Love Minus,* Mary Gallagher
- *Red Storm Flower,* John Patrick Shanley
- *Jass,* John Pielmeier
- *Sweet Dreams,* David J. Hill

Directors
Raymond Benson, Joseph Cali, Pat Carmichael, Tisa Chang, Paul Collins, John Henry Davis, Richard Dow, Sabin Epstein, Jason Grant, Susan Gregg, Tom Gruenwald, Richard Harden, David Juaire, Elaine Kanas, Trueman Kelley, Jim Kramer, Inverna Lockpez, Salem Ludwig, Peter Maloney, Stephen Maro, Bill Partlan, Kent Paul, Livia Perez, Kathleen Phelan, Scott Redman, Ellen Sandler, Robert Siegler, Kristofer Tabori, Michael Wright

New Dramatists. Patricia Charbonneau and Sofia Landon in *My Sister in This House.* Photo: Meryl Joseph.

New Federal Theatre

Woodie King, Jr.
Steve Tennen
Producers

Henry Street Settlement
466 Grand St.
New York, NY 10002
(212) 598–0400

Founded 1970
Woodie King, Jr.

Season
October–July

Schedule
Evenings
Thursday–Sunday
Matinees
Saturday, Sunday

Facilities
Playhouse
Seating capacity: 350
Stage: proscenium
Experimental Theatre
Seating capacity: 150
Stage: arena

Finances
July 1, 1980–June 30, 1981
$305,000 operating expenses
$ 60,000 earned income
$175,000 grants/contributions

Audience
Annual attendance: 35,000

Touring contact
Woodie King, Jr.

Booked-in events
Dance, music, poetry

AEA Showcase code

The New Federal Theatre has carved a niche for itself by bringing minority theatre to Manhattan's lower east side as well as the greater metropolitan area. At the same time, it has brought the work of minority playwrights and actors to national attention and has sponsored productions by other ethnic theatres. The Henry Street Settlement's Arts for Living Center includes three theatres, rehearsal studios and modern stage equipment, all of which are made available to the company.

Each year, 10 showcase productions (6 mainstage and 4 Ethnic Heritage productions) are offered, as well as a series of new play readings that allows playwrights to review and improve a work before production. Additionally, NFT sponsors a poetry and film series. Workshops both at Henry Street and in the Bronx have attracted considerable patronage.

Over the past 11 years NFT ha produced more than 80 plays, bringing to public attention such dramatists as J.E. Franklin (whos *Black Girl* was filmed with severa original cast members from NFT) Ron Milner, Ed Pomerantz, Joseph Lizardi and Ntozake Shange. Ed Bullins' *The Taking o Miss Janie* was the first play produced under a trial arrangement between NFT and the New York Shakespeare Festival, whereby plays are showcased first at Henry Street and then produced at the Festival's Public Theater. Shange's *For Colored Girls . . . ,* a second collaborative effort with the Festival, later moved successfully to Broadway and across the country. David Henry Hwang's Obie Award-winning *The Dance and the Railroad* is the latest NFT production to move to the Public Theater.

In addition to the Obie, New Federal productions have received Drama Desk, Drama Critics' Circle and Audelco awards.

Productions 1979–80
- *Suspenders,* Umar Bin Hassan
- *Crazy Horse,* Louis Peterson
- *Friends,* Crispin Larangeira
- *Puerto Rican Obituary,* Pedro Pietri
- *Branches from the Same Tree,* Marge Eliot
- *Take It from the Top,* Ruby Dee

Productions 1980–81
The Connection, Jack Gelber
- *Something Lost,* Anthony Wisdom
- *Grand Street,* Robert Reiser
- *Things of the Heart,* Shauneille Perry

The Trial of Dr. Beck, Hughes Allison

New Federal Theatre. Pamela Poitier, Tina Sattin and Victoria Howard in *Widows.* Photo: Bert Andrews.

- *La Morena,* Beth Turner
- *Widows,* Mfundi Vundula
- *The Dance and the Railroad,* David Henry Hwang
- *No,* Alexis DeVeaux
- *Zora* and *When the Chickens Came Home to Roost,* Laurence Holder
- *Steal Away,* Ramona King

Directors
Ossie Davis, Raul Davila, Glenda Dickerson, Al Freeman, Arthur French, Richard Gant, Denise Hamilton, Elaine Kanas, Carl Lee, Philip Lindsay, John Lone, Charles Maryan, Louis Peterson, Elizabeth Van Dyke, Allie Woods, Vantile Whitfield

Designers
Sets: Robert Edmonds, Llewellyn Harrison, Bil Mikulewicz, Wynn Thomas, Fred Voelpel, Andrea Zakin. *Costumes:* Sydney Brooks, Myrna Colley-Lee, Rise Collins, Judy Dearing, Glenda Dickerson, Carlo Thomas, Edna Watson. *Lights:* Leo Gambacorta, George Greczylo, Larry Johnson, Debra J. Kletter, Allen Lee Hughes, Craig Miller, Grant Orenstein, Shirley Prendergast, Sandra Ross, Marshall Williams.

New Jersey Shakespeare Festival

Paul Barry
Artistic Director

Ellen Barry
Producing Director

Drew University
Madison, NJ 07940
(201) 377-5330 (business)
(201) 377-4487 (box office)

Founded 1963
Paul Barry

Season
June–December

Schedule
Evenings
Tuesday–Sunday
Matinees
Wednesday

Facilities
Bowne Theatre
Seating capacity: 238
Stage: thrust

Finances
January 1, 1980–December 31, 1980
$453,000 operating expenses
$257,000 earned income
$144,000 grants/contributions

Audience
Annual attendance: 40,000
Subscribers: 3,300

Booked-in events
Dance, music, mime, children's theatre, drama

AEA LORT (D) contract

The New Jersey Shakespeare Festival is an actor's theatre dedicated to the preservation of the world's great drama, classic and contemporary, and to the development of artists. The company began in 1963 with a single play, *The Taming of the Shrew,* as part of a 10-week stock season at the Cape May Playhouse. Over the next several summers, the company employed internal subsidy, alternating commercial and noncommercial fare, to work toward a full repertory season with a resident professional group of actors.

By 1970, three fall residencies in Boston and two fall tours of the New Jersey schools had also been mounted. In 1972, having had two theatres demolished and recognizing that Cape May's resort economy could not provide a year-round constituency, the Festival moved north to Drew University in Madison. Now, after nine Madison seasons, the Festival plays 25–27 weeks annually: three classics in nightly rotation are followed by three plays, usually modern, running four weeks each. Twelve Monday Night Specials (guest attractions of dance, drama, mime, music) provide an additional audience lure.

The Festival has staged 133 productions, including 39 mountings of Shakespeare as well as works by some 60 other authors. Recent successes include the repertory pairing of *Hamlet* with *Rosencrantz and Guildenstern Are Dead,* and *Travesties* with *The Importance of Being Earnest;* a production of *The Comedy of Errors* set in 1930s New Orleans during Mardi Gras; and a Roman black mass interpretation of *Titus Andronicus.*

The Festival's intern program attracts hundreds of applicants annually, from which approximately 80 are selected. Increasingly, the professional company includes "graduates" of the intern program: in 1981, for example, Romeo, Juliet and Mercutio had all been Festival interns, as had the stage manager, public relations director, lighting designer and one guest director. Over the past nine years, the number of contributors to the Festival has increased sixfold. Subscribers in 1980 came from 170 communities, and audiences are at near-capacity levels. Seven out of ten Madison seasons have ended "in the black."

Productions 1980
The Comedy of Errors, William Shakespeare
Macbeth, William Shakespeare
Volpone, Ben Jonson
The Caretaker, Harold Pinter
Waltz of the Toreadors, Jean Anouilh
Knock Knock, Jules Feiffer
A Christmas Carol, adapt: Paul Barry, from Charles Dickens

Productions 1981
Romeo and Juliet, William Shakespeare
Cymbeline, William Shakespeare
Tartuffe, Moliere
The Entertainer, John Osborne
Da, Hugh Leonard
Vanities, Jack Heifner

Directors
Paul Barry, Dan Held, Sue Lawless, Ron Martell, Samuel Maupin

Designers
Sets: Peter B. Harrison. *Costumes:* Kathleen Blake, Ann Emonts, Erica Hollmann, Alice S. Hughes. *Lights:* David Bosboom, Richard Dorfman.

New Jersey Shakespeare Festival. David Howard and Victoria Boothby in *Waltz of the Toreadors.* Photo: Jerry Dalia.

New Jersey Theatre Forum. Barbara MacKenzie and Matthew Lewis in *The Importance of Being Earnest.* Photo: Thomas O. Kriegsmann.

New Jersey Theatre Forum

R. Timothy Moses
Artistic Director

Judith C. Laufer
Managing Director

232 East Front St.
Plainfield, NJ 07060
(201) 757–2882 (business)
(201) 757–5888 (box office)

Founded 1977
R. Timothy Moses, Judith C. Laufer, Warren Rorden

Season
September–May

Schedule
Evenings
Wednesday–Saturday
Matinees
Sunday

Facilities
Seating capacity: 120
Stage: proscenium

Finances
July 1, 1980–June 30, 1981
$167,000 operating expenses
$ 51,000 earned income
$122,000 grants/contributions

Audience
Annual Attendance: 10,000
Subscribers: 900

AEA letter of agreement

Founded in 1977, the New Jersey Theatre Forum is committed to producing the best of the classic and contemporary theatre. But more important, the Forum is a "director's theatre." Based on the premise that there is a plethora of excellent American acting talent, the Forum is dedicated to helping new and talented directors, giving them all the tools of the craft to develop their artistic vision.

In four years, the Forum has become a valuable psychological symbol of the rebirth and rejuvenation of its host city—Plainfield, New Jersey. The city, surrounded by affluent upper-middle class communities, was rocked by race riots in the late 1960s, and much of its major industry and private wealth fled. The Forum has been instrumental in bringing thousands of people back into Plainfield at night and has, to some extent, been able to restore civic pride to the community. It has been estimated that the Forum generates over $1 million per year in spin-off monies, and therefore enjoys the support of city, county and state governments.

As a result, the Forum feels committed to both the citizenry of its host city and to the surrounding area it serves. Presenting a broad selection of plays to a diverse community, the Forum has been able to attract a racially mixed audience, and its board is representative of the racial makeup of the area. Through several outreach programs, the theatre has been able to make contact with all segments of the community and, consequently, to encourage them to attend the Forum.

Employing a production and administrative staff of more than 110 people during its six-play season, the staff works together with the board on policy-making, fund-raising and special events. The theatre and its support space are rented from the local YMCA, and the theatre was substantially rebuilt before opening in 1977, adding an open proscenium stage for versatility in production design.

The Forum is currently negotiating with the city administration to purchase and renovate a movie theatre in the heart of the city, which will be the core of a long hoped-for performing arts center in Plainfield.

Productions 1979–80
How the Other Half Loves, Alan Ayckbourn
The Glass Menagerie, Tennessee Williams
See How They Run, Philip King
Pools Paradise, Philip King
A Doll's House, Henrik Ibsen
Oh, Coward!, music and lyrics: Noel Coward; adapt: Roderick Cook

Productions 1980–81
On Golden Pond, Ernest Thompson
The Sty of the Blind Pig, Phillip Hayes Dean
A Life in the Theatre, David Mamet
A Moon for the Misbegotten, Eugene O'Neill
Inner City, music: Helen Miller; lyrics: Eve Merriam

Directors
Dana Coen, Geoffrey Hitch, Bernard Johnson, R. Timothy Moses, James Neissen, John Schwab

Designers
Sets: Jonathan Arkin, William M. Camp, James Chesnutt, Larry Von Werrsowetz. *Costumes:* Steven Birnbaum, Janet Leavee, Molly Maginnis, Kevin Reid, Michelle Reisch, Florence Rutherford. *Lights:* Jonathan Arkin, Gerard Klug, Kenneth Leavee.

New Playwrights' Theatre

Harry M. Bagdasian
Producing Director

1742 Church St., NW
Washington, DC 20036
(202) 232–4527 (business)
(202) 232–1122 (box office)

Founded 1972
Harry M. Bagdasian

Season
July–June

Schedule
Evenings
Wednesday–Sunday
Matinees
Saturday

Facilities
Seating capacity: 125
Stage: flexible

Finances
July 1, 1980–June 30, 1981
$215,000 operating expenses
$ 95,000 earned income
$121,000 grants/contributions

Audience
Annual attendance: 14,421
Subscribers: 848

The purpose of the New Playwrights' Theatre is to foster the growth and development of American playwrights and composers through workshops, readings and productions of new or developing plays and musicals. Its board of trustees, staff and volunteer guild believe that playwrights and composers need a stage—their *own* stage—a safe environment where they can hone their material and skills.

To this end, NPT offers residencies to playwrights and composers from all over the country, ranging from four days to two years, in order to develop works through podium-style readings, staged readings and, possibly, full productions. From 15 to 20 projects and their creators are selected each season. The company selects playwrights and composers by screening unsolicited full-length manuscripts (accepted October 1 through

March 30 only) as well as scouting works-in-progress at other regional theatres. This second means of contacting playwrights and composers allows NPT to offer "second step" productions to artists whose works may have been previously produced, but who can still benefit from more process work.

New Playwrights' also works with authors of shorter works through its annual National One-Act Play Competition and accepts manuscripts (no musicals) from October 1 through December 1. Three winners are presented in a showcase production each spring.

The needs of each playwright and composer vary, and therefore NPT "jobs in" all artists, with auditions held three times a year.

Now entering its 10th season, NPT is pleased that many of the works that have emerged from its process have gone on to be produced at other theatres across the country.

Productions 1979–80
- *Mr. Wilson's Peace of Mind,* Mark Stein
- *Helen, Joan and Half-Crazy Claire,* Terryl Paste
- *Grownups,* Tim Grundmann
- *Practice,* Jack O'Donnell
- *The Freak,* Granville Wyche Burgess
- *An Evening without Liza Minelli,* Tim Grundmann
- *A Former Gotham Gal,* Gloria Gonzalez
- *Holding On,* Ernest Joselovitz
- *Incidental Incidents,* Douglas Setinberg

Productions 1980–81
- *The Amsterdam Avenue Theater Presents Direct from Death Row the Scottsboro Boys,* Mark Stein
- *American Polar,* John Alan Spoler
- *Dear Desperate,* Tim Grundmann
- *The Waiting,* Ken Greenman
- *Our Lady of the Depot,* Tony Stafford
- *Tomorrow's Another Day,* Peter Perhonis
- *Fourplay,* Ross McLean
- *Mash Note to an Old Codger,* Toni Press
- *Tuba Solo,* Michael Lynch
- *The Diviners,* Jim Leonard, Jr.

Directors
Harry M. Bagdasian, Josh Billings, Ron Canada, Doc Dougherty, Tim Grundmann, John Healey, John Noah Hurtzler, John A. Morse, Dorothy Neumann, Jim Nicola, Alan O'Donovan, E. Lloyd Rose, Robert Schulte

Designers
Sets: Mark Bachman, Dan Conway, Douglas A. Cumming, Paul Dempsey, Russell Metheny. *Costumes:* Liz Bass, Theeta Bell, Willie Richardson, Bonnie Ann Stauch, Silk, Peter Zakutansky. *Lights:* Greg Basdavanos, Allen Lee Hughes, Michael Lodick, Robert Marietta, Tomm Tomlinson.

Media resources:
Video: *The Freak, Dear Desperate* (company-produced).

New Playwrights' Theatre. *The Amsterdam Avenue Theater Presents Direct from Death Row the Scottsboro Boys.* Photo: Doc Dougherty.

New York Shakespeare Festival

Joseph Papp
Producer

Robert Kamlot
General Manager

Public Theater
425 Lafayette St.
New York, NY 10003
(212) 598–7100 (business)
(212) 598–7150 (box office)
(212) 535–5630 (Delacorte box office)

Founded 1954
Joseph Papp

Season
Year-round

Schedule
Evenings
Tuesday–Sunday
Matinees
Saturday, Sunday

Facilities
Newman Theater
Seating capacity: 299
Stage: proscenium
Anspacher Theater
Seating capacity: 275
Stage: thrust
Martinson Hall
Seating capacity: 190
Stage: flexible
LuEsther Hall
Seating capacity: 115–150
Stage: flexible
The Other Stage
Seating capacity: 75–100
Stage: flexible
Old Prop Shop
Seating capacity: 55–93
Stage: flexible
Little Theater (Cinema)
Seating capacity: 96
Delacorte Theater, Central Park
Seating capacity: 1,932
Stage: thrust
Mobile Theater
Seating capacity: 1,500
Stage: flexible

Finances
July 1, 1980–June 30, 1981
$6,346,000 operating expenses
$3,819,000 earned income
$2,527,000 grants/contributions

Audience
Annual attendance: 2,800,000
Subscribers: 19,300

Booked-in events
Theatre, dance, special events

AEA Production, LORT (B) and Off Broadway contracts, and Showcase code

Under the leadership of Joseph Papp, the New York Shakespeare Festival is committed to bringing new American plays and musicals, and new approaches to the classics to a wide, popular audience.

Each summer, the Festival presents free Shakespeare at the Delacorte Theater in Central Park, as well as admission-free performances on the Mobile Theater which tours New York City parks and playgrounds. As its headquarters, the Festival operates the Public Theater year-round, a landmark building converted into a seven-theatre complex where more than 20 plays are produced each season. In addition, the Public Theater is a center for all the performing arts with its weekly series "New Jazz at the Public" (an award-winning program of contemporary jazz); "Film at the Public" (new or rarely seen films); and "Poets at the Public" (writers, actors and directors working together).

The multiple stages of the Public Theater also serve as home for a number of theatre companies and guest artists, including Mabou Mines (listed separately in this book); Des McAnuff and the Dodger Theater Company, whose most recent productions at the Public included Wolfgang Hildesheimer's *Mary Stuart* and an adaptation of Michael Baumann's *How It All Began;* Elizabeth Swados and Andrei Serban, veterans of Peter Brook's international company and LaMama ETC; and Joseph Chaikin of the now disbanded Open Theatre, who in collaboration with playwright Sam Shephard created and performed *Tongues* and *Savage/Love* at the Public, and in collaboration with Steven Kent produced an adaptation of Beckett's *Texts.*

In order to make Public Theater and Central Park productions available to a larger audience, the lives of a number of

New York Shakespeare Festival. Meryl Streep, Richard Cox and Rodney Hudson in *Alice in Concert.* Photo: Martha Swope.

productions have been extended on Broadway, Off Broadway, on network television and on national tours. These include *A Chorus Line, I'm Getting My Act Together . . . , For Colored Girls . . . , Sticks and Bones, Runaways, That Championship Season, Much Ado About Nothing* and *The Pirates of Penzance.*

The Festival is also reaching new audiences through productions of its own television specials and national and international tours. Student and senior citizen discounts, its unique Quiktix (day of performance discounts), discounts for employees of corporate contributors and free admision events have helped develop new and vibrant audiences.

Productions 1979–80

A Chorus Line, book: James Kirkwood and Nicholas Dante; music: Marvin Hamlisch; lyrics: Edward Kleban
Coriolanus, William Shakespeare
Othello, William Shakespeare
The Mighty Gents, Richard Wesley
- *Marie and Bruce,* Wallace Shawn
- *Salt Lake City Skyline,* Thomas Babe
- *Tongues* and *Savage/Love,* Sam Shepard and Joseph Chaikin
- *The Art of Dining,* Tina Howe

Happy Days, Samuel Beckett
- *The Sorrows of Stephen,* Peter Parnell
- *The Haggadah,* book, music and lyrics: Elizabeth Swados
- *Mother Courage and Her Children,* Bertolt Brecht; adapt: Ntozake Shange
- *Sunday Runners in the Rain,* Israel Horovitz
- *Hard Sell,* Murray Horwitz, Roger Director and John Lewis
- *Scenes from the Everyday Life,* Ned Jackson
- *FOB,* David Henry Hwang
- *The Music Lessons,* Wakako Yamauchi

Productions 1980–81

A Chorus Line
- *The Pirates of Penzance,* book and lyrics: W.S. Gilbert; music: Arthur Sullivan; musical adapt: William Elliot
- *Under Fire,* book, music and lyrics: Elizabeth Swados
- *you know Al he's a funny guy,* Jerry Mayer
- *The Sea Gull,* Anton Chekhov; trans: Jean Claude van Itallie
- *True West,* Sam Shepard
- *Alice in Concert,* book, music and lyrics: Elizabeth Swados, from Lewis Carroll
- *Penguin Touquet,* Richard Foreman
- *Mary Stuart,* Wolfgang Hildesheimer; trans: Christopher Holmes
- *Texts,* Samuel Beckett; adapt: Joseph Chaikin and Steven Kent

Long Day's Journey into Night, Eugene O'Neill
The Haggadah
- *The Hunchback of Notre Dame,* adapt: Ron Whyte, from Victor Hugo
- *How It All Began,* Michael Baumann; adapt: John Palmer, Des McAnuff and Group 10
- *An Evening of Sholom Aleichem,* adapt: Joseph Singer
- *Girls, Girls, Girls,* Marilyn Suzanne Miller; music: Cheryl Hardwick
- *Presenting All of David Langston Smyrl (Or Is It?),* book, music and lyrics: David Langston Smyrl

Directors

Robert Allan Ackerman, A.J. Antoon, Bob Balaban, Michael Bennett, Edward Cornell, Geraldine Fitzgerald, Richard Foreman, John Pynchon Holms, Murray Horwitz, Steven Kent, Michael Langham, Sheldon Larry, Wilford Leach, Mako, Richard Maltby Jr., Des McAnuff, James Milton, Joseph Papp, Elinor Renfield, Andrei Serban, Ntozake Shange, Elizabeth Swados, Robert Woodruff

Designers

Sets: Gerald Bloom, Edward Burbridge, Jack Chandler, Jim Clayburgh, Richard Foreman, David Gropman, David Jenkins, Marjorie Kellogg, Heidi Landesman, Wilford Leach, James E. Mayo, John Scheffler, Bob Shaw, Paul Steinberg, Julie Taymor, Stuart Wurtzel, Michael Yeargan, Robert Yodice, Akira Yoshimura. *Costumes:* Theoni V. Aldredge, Mary Brecht, Myrna Colley-Lee, Peggy Goodman, Jane Greenwood, John Helgerson, Susan Hum, William Ivey Long, Patricia McGourty, Carol Oditz, Beverly Parks, Hilary Rosenfeld, Karen Roston, Paul Steinberg, Julie Taymor, Grace Williams, Robert Wojewodski. *Lights:* Fred Bucholz, Ian Calderon, Pat Collins, Gail Daht, Arden Fingerhut, Paul Mathiesen, Craig Miller, Roger Morgan, Dennis Parichy, Victor En Yu Tan, Jennifer Tipton, Martin Tudor.

Media resources

Video: *Dispatches, The Umbrellas of Cherbourg, Spell #7, The Woods, Coriolanus, Julius Caesar, I'm Getting My Act Together and Taking It on the Road, Runaways, A Chorus Line, The Mighty Gents, Othello, Tongues, The Sea Gull, Penguin Touquet* (Lincoln Center Research Collection), *Jack MacGowran in the Works of Beckett, King Lear* (PBS), *Much Ado About Nothing, Sticks and Bones* (CBS), *Wedding Band* (ABC), *Happy Days* (WNET), *The Haggadah, The Pirates of Penzance* (company-produced), *Alice in Concert* (NBC), *Kiss Me Petruchio* (company-produced, documentary).

Next Move Theatre. Geraldine Librandi, Joe Muzikar and Martin Anderson in *Saints and Martyrs.*

The Next Move Theatre

Steven Warnick
Producing Director

Harry Wellott
General Manager

One Boylston Place
Boston, MA 02116
(617) 423-7588 (business)
(617) 423-5572 (box office)

Founded 1977
Martin R. Anderson, Bradford Jones, Geraldine Librandi, Helene Zera, Gil Schwartz, Andrew Gaus, Cynthia Caldwell, Karen MacDonald

Season
October–June

Schedule
Evenings
Tuesday–Sunday
Matinees
Saturday, Sunday

Facilities
Seating capacity: 275
Stage: thrust

Finances
June 30, 1980–July 1, 1981
$517,000 operating expenses
$428,000 earned income
$ 89,000 grants/contributions

Audience
Annual attendance: 45,000
Subscribers: 1,000

Touring contact
Harry Wellott

Booked-in events
Theatre, staged readings

AEA LORT (D) contract

Since its inception seven years ago, The Next Move Theatre has been committed to the presentation of new works and works never before produced in Boston. The 1980–81 season marked a major step in the growth of The Next Move, with the acquisition of a new, larger facility in the downtown theatre district.

For the past three years, the theatre's play development program has included Monday evening staged readings, providing local playwrights, directors and actors with a forum for developing new work. Plans include the expansion of this program to include playwrights from throughout the country through a new play competition entitled "Playsearch." The contest will culminate in publication of the two winning scripts.

Throughout its history, The Next Move has been dedicated to the Boston community, sponsoring a large theatre education program, including a collaboration with Boston's Institute of Contemporary Art, on-site programming in six Boston elementary schools and a model program for severely retarded children. The theatre's newest program, Next Move Unlimited, is generating an original full-length theatre piece to be performed at various Boston area locations by an acting company of able-bodied and disabled adults. In addition, The Next Move Conservatory offers beginning, intermediate and advanced acting courses.

Each season for the past five years, The Next Move Theatre has received the Boston Association for the Performing Arts Award for Excellence in Theatre.

Productions 1979–80
- *Cuckolds,* book, music and lyrics: Andrew Gaus
- *Saints and Martyrs,* James Carroll
- *This End Up 1980,* company-developed

Under Milk Wood, Dylan Thomas

Productions 1980–81
- *All That Glitters,* adapt: Earl McCarroll; music and lyrics: Robert Johanson

Loose Ends, Michael Weller
A Christmas Carol, adapt: Robert Johanson, from Charles Dickens
Talley's Folly, Lanford Wilson
- *Take Two,* company-developed

Directors
John Henry Davis, Robert Johanson, Earl McCarroll, Susan McGinley, Stephen Rosenfield, Peter Thompson

Designers
Sets: Michael Anania, Barry Bailey, Roger Mooney. *Costumes:* Barbara Forbes, Mary Thomsine Harkins. *Lights:* Steven Gambino, Steven Friedlander, Glen Heinmiller.

The North Carolina Shakespeare Festival

Malcolm Morrison
Artistic Director

Mark Woods
Managing Director

Box 6066
High Point, NC 27262
(919) 889-1544 (business)
(919) 887-3001 (box office)

Founded 1977
Mark Woods, Stuart Brooks

Season
July–December

Schedule
Evenings
Tuesday–Saturday
Matinees
Sunday

Facilities
High Point Theatre
200 East Commerce St.
Seating capacity: 640
Stage: modified thrust

Finances
April 1, 1980–March 31, 1981
$458,000 operating expenses
$176,000 earned income
$282,000 grants/contributions

Audience
Annual attendance: 39,972

Touring contact
Mark Woods

AEA letter of agreement

As an actor-oriented theatre, the North Carolina Shakespeare Festival is committed to creating an environment in which artists are given every opportunity to develop and express their versatility.

NCSF explores plays of all types that demonstrate breadth of vision, depth of perception and enduring treatment. The belief that the actor is at the heart of all major theatrical experiences is paramount.

Productions are chosen on the basis of the opportunities they afford the artist through stylistic

The North Carolina Shakespeare Festival. Howard Lee Sherman and Laura Gardner in *Macbeth.* Photo: Michael Spanel.

and thematic diversity. The concept of any given production is executed with a profound concern for excellence and definition.

NCSF recognizes the need of theatre artists to develop and establish new modes as well as express the contemporary human experience. Consequently, the firm intention of the company (while mounting the major dramatic works of previous generations and cultures) is to develop as yet unrecognized American works and nurture and challenge the artists who present that work.

NCSF also recognizes its responsibility to engage in activities other than performance. An Actor-in-the-Schools program exists to promote a heightened awareness of the creative process and an excitement about attending live theatre.

Productions 1979
A Midsummer Night's Dream, William Shakespeare
The Rivals, Richard Brinsley Sheridan; music: David Bishop; lyrics: Dan Friedman
Henry IV, Part I, William Shakespeare; music: David Bishop
Sherlock Holmes, adapt: William Gillette, from Arthur Conan Doyle
She Stoops to Conquer, Oliver Goldsmith
Summer and Smoke, Tennessee Williams
A Servant of Two Masters, Carlo Goldoni
A Christmas Carol, adapt from Charles Dickens

Productions 1980
• *The Fleece,* John Orlock
Macbeth, William Shakespeare
Twelfth Night, William Shakespeare
The Imaginary Invalid, Moliere; adapt: Miles Malleson; music: Stephen Joseph
Born Yesterday, Garson Kanin
The Last Meeting of the Knights of the White Magnolia, Preston Jones
The Heiress, Ruth and Augustus Goetz
A Christmas Carol

Productions 1981
Hamlet, William Shakespeare
Hay Fever, Noel Coward
As You Like It, William Shakespeare
Wait Until Dark, Fredrick Knott
The Comedy of Errors, William Shakespeare
• *Just a Song at Twilight,* company-developed
A Christmas Carol

Directors
Peter Bennett, Geoffrey Hitch, Mikel Lambert, Richard Mangan, Malcolm Morrison, Robert Murray, Louis Rackoff, Martin Rader, Pedro Silva

Designers
Sets: Jonathan Arkin, Campbell Baird, Harry Feiner, Deborah Jasien, Judie Juracek, Mark Pirolo, John Sneden. *Costumes:* Ginger Blake, Judie Juracek, Doreen S. Paley, Mark Pirolo, Christine Turbitt. *Lights:* Philip Gibson, Paul Valoris, Michael Orris Watson.

North Light Repertory Company

Eric Steiner
Artistic Director

Jeffrey Bentley
Managing Director

2300 Green Bay Road
Evanston, IL 60201
(312) 869–7732 (business)
(312) 869–7278 (box office)

Founded 1974
Gregory Kandel

Season
September–June

Schedule
Evenings
Tuesday–Sunday
Matinees
Saturday, Sunday

Facilities
Kingsley Theatre
Seating capacity: 298
Stage: proscenium

Finances
July 1, 1980–June 30, 1981
$493,000 operating expenses
$325,000 earned income
$145,000 grants/contributions

Audience
Annual attendance: 52,000
Subscribers: 6,500

Touring contact
Mary F. Monroe

AEA LORT (D) contract

North Light Repertory is a seven-year-old company based in Evanston, Illinois, and serving the metropolitan Chicago area. Founded by Gregory Kandel, the theatre maintains a commitment to contemporary works and outreach programming.

Under the leadership of its new artistic and managing directors, North Light produces plays of an international character, both contemporary and classic, that strongly address the human condition. New works and regional premieres are stressed in both the Main and Satellite seasons. Recent mainstage productions have included Sam Shepard's *Buried Child,* Ernest Thompson's *On Golden Pond* and Amlin Gray's *How I Got That Story.* The Satellite Season presents three new American works concurrent with the mainstage productions, with playwrights in attendance. The theatre supports and encourages the talents of the Chicago arts community and, on occasion, employs guest artists from outside the Chicago area.

North Light's outreach programming is extensive, including the highly successful and innovative Creative Drama for the Elderly; high school and middle school touring companies in the parks; and services for the handicapped.

Productions 1979–80
Catsplay, Istvan Orkeny; trans: Clara Gyorgyey
Buried Child, Sam Shepard
Angel Street, Patrick Hamilton
• *Who They Are and How It Is with Them,* Grace McKeaney
Cold Storage, Ronald Ribman

Productions 1980–81
Light Up the Sky, Moss Hart
Family Business, Dick Goldberg
On Golden Pond, Ernest Thompson
The Incredible Murder of Cardinal Tosca, Alden Nowlan and Walter Learning
How I Got That Story, Amlin Gray

Directors
Montgomery Davis, Gregory Kandel, Michael Maggio, Mark Milliken, Tony Mockus, Sharon Ott, Edward Stern, Joseph Sturniolo

Designers
Sets: Maher Ahmad, Tom Beall, Jeremy P. Conway, Patricia Dunbar, Joseph C. Nieminski. *Costumes:* Kate Bergh, Julie Jackson, Anne Jaros, Marsha Kowal, Colleen Muscha, Kaye Nottbusch, Christa Scholtz. *Lights:* Maher Ahmad, Patricia Dunbar, Mark Mongold, Robert Shook, Rita Pietraszek.

North Light Repertory Company. James Eichling, James Deuter, Ron Parady, Colin Lane and Michael Tezla in *The Incredible Murder of Cardinal Tosca.* Photo: Lisa Ebright.

Odyssey Theatre Ensemble

Ron Sossi
Artistic Director

Beth Hogan
Administrative Director

12111 Ohio Ave.
Los Angeles, CA 90025
(213) 879–5221 (business)
(213) 826–1626 (box office)

Founded 1968
Ron Sossi

Season
January–December

Schedule
Evenings
Wednesday–Monday

Facilities
Odyssey 1
Seating capacity: 99
Stage: flexible
Odyssey 2
Seating capacity: 99
Stage: thrust
Odyssey 3
Seating capacity: 82
Stage: arena

Finances
July 1, 1980–June 30, 1981
$236,000 operating expenses
$198,000 earned income
$ 38,000 grants/contributions

Audience
Annual attendance: 32,000
Subscribers: 2,100

Touring contact
Ron Sossi

Booked-in events
Dance, music, children's and experimental theatre

AEA 99-seat waiver

Founded in 1969 as a maverick in an industry-oriented city, the Odyssey Theatre Ensemble continues to strive for . . .

—Theatre passionately devoted to its differences from other media, rather than its similarities
—Theatre as an art form, not as a social service mechanism
—Theatre that is dangerous
—Theatre that is magical
—Theatre that is an event
—Theatre that is global, rather than nationalistic in both form and content.
—Theater that deals with the farthest frontiers of human experience and consciousness, rather than with the exploitation of everyday melodramas
—Theatre that aggressively updates the forms and techniques necessary to its effectiveness as a contemporary art form
—Theatre that constantly questions the purity or corruption of its motives.

In its complex of three performing spaces, the Odyssey functions year-round, producing an International Season of six productions, a New American Play Season of five productions, two to four laboratory productions, and the presentation of numerous guest companies from elsewhere in America (Mabou Mines, for example) and from abroad (Red Mole Company from New Zealand).

In the past two years, Odyssey tours of California sponsored by the California Arts Council have included Rozewicz's *White Marriage* and *The Great American Playwright Show,* to be followed in 1982 by Elizabeth Swados' *Nightclub Cantata.* Future goals include the creation of an International Experimental Theatre Center on the West Coast, a kind of artistic "think tank" meant to gather the expertise, foster the research and collaboration, and produce the work of artists from all parts of the world.

Productions 1979–80
- *The Chicago Conspiracy Trial,* Ron Sossi and Frank Condon
  Little Mary Sunshine, book, music and lyrics: Rick Besoyan
  The Water Engine, David Mamet
  Caucasian Chalk Circle, Bertolt Brecht
- *Marathon Madness,* adapt: Judy Gabriel and Philip Mishkin, from Horace McCoy
  Nightclub Cantata, Elizabeth Swados
- *Year One of the Empire,* Elinor Fuchs and Joyce Antler

Productions 1980–81
- *The Great American Playwright Show,* various authors
- *Tracers,* company-developed
- *The Man Who Killed the Buddha,* Martin Epstein
  Baal, Bertolt Brecht
- *Cosmic Spunk: A Shock Rock Opera,* book: Paul Vanase and Barbara McCarter; music and lyrics: Paul Vanase
  The Elocution of Benjamin, Steven Spears
- *The Mandrake,* Niccolo Machiavelli; adapt: Igor Dimont and Karl Maurer
  The Fantod: A Victorian Reverie, Amlin Gray
- *Something's Rockin' in Denmark,* Cliff Jones
  Don Juan Comes Back from the War, Odon Von Horvath
  Operetta, Witold Gombrowicz

Directors
Tony Abatemarco, John Allison, G.W. Bailey, Jeremy Blahnik, George Boyd, Bill Castellino, Frank Condon, John Difusco, Igor Dimont, Andrew E. Doe, John Flynn, Danny Goldman, Victoria Hochberg, David Irving, Deborah LeVine, Eve Merriam, Ron Sossi

Designers
Sets: Woody Coleman, Clark Duncan, Leonard Felix, Keith Gonzales, Anatol Krasnyasky, Jerry Pojawa, Russel Pyle, Jim Riddle, Kim Simons, Pierre Vuilleumier, Don Walschlaeger, Jim Youngerman. *Costumes:* Cara Benedetti, Jean Blachette, John Bradford, Vincent Caristi, Martha Ferrara, Susan Nininger, Dwight Richard Odle, Monique Papke, Suzanne Perkins, Kim Simons, Jeannie Traina, Andrew V. Yelusich, ZOE. *Lights:* Doc Ballard, William David Carpenter, Ed Davidson, David Fessendon, Brian Gale, Keith Gonzales, Christine Lomaka, Marcina Motter, Karen Musser, Russel Pyle, Henry Yaeger.

Media resources
Recordings: *The Chicago Conspiracy Trial* (Capitol).

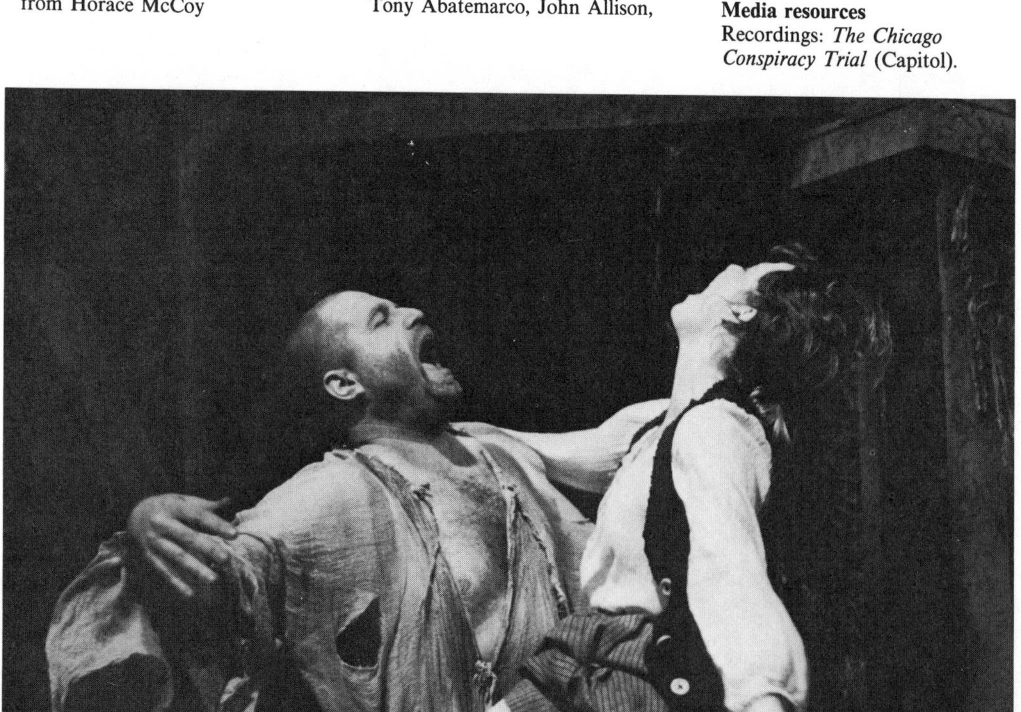

Odyssey Theatre Ensemble. Ron Sossi and Allison Coutts in *Baal.* Photo: Howard Decker.

The Old Creamery Theatre Company

Thomas Peter Johnson
Artistic Director

Jeff Smull
Executive Director

Box 160
Garrison, IA 52229
(319) 477-3925 (business)
(319) 477-3165 (box office)

Founded 1971
Thomas Peter Johnson

Season
May–November

Schedule
Evenings
Thursday–Sunday
Matinees
Sunday

Facilities
Main Stage
Seating capacity: 262
Stage: thrust
Studio Theatre
Seating capacity: 99
Stage: flexible

Finances
January 1, 1981–December 31, 1981
$265,000 operating expenses
$168,000 earned income
$108,000 grants/contributions

Audience
Annual attendance: 100,000
Subscribers: 1,500

Touring contact
Margie Griffin

AEA letter of agreement

In 1971, The Old Creamery Theatre Company began with the dream of taking theatre to as many people in the Midwest as possible. This ideal expanded to include the establishment of a full repertory company now celebrating its 10th anniversary.

During its repertory season, the company performs for an audience of approximately 30,000, while the touring season takes them throughout Iowa and the six surrounding states with original

Old Creamery Theatre Company. Marquetta Senters and Jeff Hartig in *An Italian Straw Hat.* Photo: Chris Young.

"story theatre" productions for school children and adults. The Old Creamery's facilities have recently been expanded to include a Studio Theatre where experimental plays are produced. Says a spokesman from the theatre, "Iowa is far from Broadway, but it is not by any means an uneducated or backward state. Our audience members make the same demands of quality and variety that are found at any theatre, and we are here for them. In a sense, *they* are The Old Creamery Theatre Company."

Basic to The Old Creamery's philosophy are education and community outreach. Workshops are offered both on tour and at the Garrison facilities; artistic, administrative and technical/production internships are available each year; and many post-performance discussions are held for audiences of Old Creamery productions. Negotiations are underway for the adoption of an Equity contract.

In 1980, Iowa Governor Robert D. Ray recognized the theatre for its outstanding contribution to the state with the Governor's Distinguished Service Award.

Productions 1980

Same Time, Next Year, Bernard Slade
A Shot in the Dark, Marcel Achard, adapt: Harry Kurnitz
Showboat Follies, company-developed
An Italian Straw Hat, Eugene Labiche and Marc-Michael; trans: Lynn and Theodore Hoffman
A Bed Full of Foreigners, Dave Freeman
Who's Afraid of Virginia Woolf?, Edward Albee
Loot, Joe Orton
Why Don't They Ever Talk About the First Mrs. Phipps?, Sue Ann Gunn
• *So Far from China,* Howard Blanning
Waiting for Godot, Samuel Beckett
• *Little Things,* company-developed

Productions 1981

California Suite, Neil Simon
13 Rue de l'Amour, Georges Feydeau; adapt: Mawby Green and Ed Feilbert
Where's Charley?, book: George Abbott, from Brandon Thomas; music and lyrics: Frank Loesser
Sleuth, Anthony Shaffer
Jesus Christ, Superstar, lyrics: Tim Rice; music: Andrew Lloyd Webber
• *The Road Show,* company-developed

Directors

Richard Barker, David Berendes, Howard Blanning, Mick Denniston, Breton Frazier, Thomas Peter Johnson, John Logan, Robert Pratt, Sara Stanley

Designers

Sets: Richard Barker, David Berendes, Howard Blanning, Thomas Peter Johnson, Stuart Kadlec, Antonia R. Sheller, Erica Zaffarano. *Costumes:* Richard Barker, Carol Rae Fisher, Judith Johnson, Meg Merckens, Susan Scott, Chris Stokes. *Lights:* Richard Barker, Howard Blanning, Steve Hansen, Thomas Peter Johnson, David Radunsky, Erica Zaffarano.

Old Globe Theatre

Craig Noel
Executive Producer

Jack O'Brien
Artistic Director

Thomas Hall
Managing Director

Box 2171
San Diego, CA 92112
(714) 231–1941 (business)
(714) 239–2255 (box office)

Founded 1937
Community members

Season
January–October

Schedule
Evenings
Tuesday–Sunday
Matinees
Saturday, Sunday

Facilities
Edison Centre for the Performing Arts
El Prado, Balboa Park
Old Globe Theatre
Seating capacity: 570
Stage: proscenium
Festival Stage
Seating capacity: 620
Stage: thrust
Cassius Carter Centre Stage
Seating capacity: 245
Stage: arena

Finances
November 1, 1980–October 31, 1981
$2,211,000 operating expenses
$1,513,000 earned income
$ 900,000 grants/contributions

Audience
Annual attendance: 168,870
Subscribers: 13,472

Touring contact
Tom Corcoran

Booked-in events
Theatre, dance, music, lectures

AEA LORT (B) contract

The Old Globe Theatre is committed to bringing American actors into the fullest expression of classical and contemporary articulation and development. Expanded artistic horizons were announced in 1981, with the appointment of artistic director Jack O'Brien and managing director Thomas Hall joining executive producer Craig Noel. The new creative thrust began with the 32nd San Diego National Shakespeare Festival—with five plays produced in two theatres.

Coinciding with the opening of the new Old Globe Theatre in January 1982, a nine-month professional repertory company is being established. Classical and contemporary theatre will be staged in the $6.5 million Old Globe and the Cassius Carter Centre Stage in Balboa Park from January through May. The summer productions, emphasizing Shakespeare, are performed in the outdoor Festival Stage as well as the two other theatres which collectively comprise the Simon Edison Centre for the Performing Arts in Balboa Park.

Construction of the new Old Globe Theatre began in November 1979, following a 20-month fund-raising campaign after arson destroyed the former landmark theatre. During the past two fall and spring seasons, productions were staged at the leased California Theatre in downtown San Diego and the Cassius Carter Centre Stage. During the summer months, the Festival Stage provided audiences with a beautiful outdoor setting.

The Globe Educational Tour, established in 1974, continues to present classical theatre to students, senior citizens, the handicapped and the incarcerated throughout San Diego and Imperial counties.

The 1981-82 season is one of regrouping for the Old Globe, which plans further to expand and extend its operation to a fuller season with wider audience appeal.

Productions 1979–80

You Can't Take It with You, Moss Hart and George S. Kaufman
The Good Doctor, Neil Simon
Side by Side by Sondheim, music and lyrics: Stephen Sondheim, et al.; adapt: Ned Sherrin
Witness for the Prosecution, Agatha Christie
The Constant Wife, W. Somerset Maugham

Old Globe Theatre. *King Lear.*
Photo: Steve Sealy.

Poor Murderer, Pavel Kohout
The Mound Builders, Lanford Wilson
The Biko Inquest, Norman Fenton and Jon Blair
Romeo and Juliet, William Shakespeare
Two Gentlemen of Verona, William Shakespeare
Love's Labour's Lost, William Shakespeare

Productions 1980–81
On Golden Pond, Ernest Thompson
Night Must Fall, Emlyn Williams
Relatively Speaking, Alan Ayckbourn
Orpheus Descending, Tennessee Williams
Lone Star and *Laundry and Bourbon,* James McLure
A Moon for the Misbegotten, Eugene O'Neill
Who's Happy Now?, Oliver Hailey
Full Circle, Erich Maria Remarque
Dear Liar, Jerome Kilty
King Lear, William Shakespeare
Much Ado About Nothing, William Shakespeare
Measure for Measure, William Shakespeare
The Country Wife, William Wycherley

Directors
Edward Berkeley, William R. Bruce, Gerald Freedman, David Hay, Jerome Kilty, Sandy McCallum, David McClendon, Craig Noel, Jack O'Brien, William Roesch, James Tripp, Jack Tygett, Norman Welsh

Designers
Sets: Mark Donnelly, Kent Dorsey, Sam Kirkpatrick, Steve Lavino, Robert Morgan, Alan Okazaki, Nick Reid, Steve Rubin, Richard Seger, Steph Storer. *Costumes:* Deborah Dryden, Mary Gibson, Dianne Holly, Peggy Kellner, Sam Kirkpatrick, Robert Morgan, Susan Muick, Merrily Murray, Steve Rubin, Steph Storer. *Lights:* Donald Darnutzer, Kent Dorsey, John Forbes, Gilbert V. Hemsley Jr., Raymond E. Mondoux, William Morse, Sean Murphy, Steve Peterson, Steph Storer.

Omaha Magic Theatre

Jo Ann Schmidman
Artistic/Producing Director

2309 Hanscom Blvd.
Omaha, NE 68105
(402) 342–2821 (business)
(402) 346–1227 (box office)

Founded 1969
Jo Ann Schmidman

Season
September–August

Schedule
Evenings
Friday–Monday
Matinees
Sunday

Facilities
1417 Farnam St.
Seating capacity: 100
Stage: flexible

Finances
September 1, 1980–August 31, 1981
$269,000 operating expenses
$ 30,000 earned income
$239,000 grants/contributions

Audience
Annual attendance: 22,400

Touring contact
Eve Felder

Booked-in events
Theatre, film, music

The Omaha Magic Theatre is currently in its 12th year of operation under the artistic direction of Jo Ann Schmidman (a former member of Joseph Chaikin's Open Theatre in New York). The OMT researches, writes and produces six to eight productions per year, all of which are developed with playwright, director, designer and composer in residence. Through this process, more than 50 new American musicals have been created and produced.

The OMT tours extensively throughout the United States. It was one of two American theatres commissioned to perform for athletes and spectators at the 1980 Winter Olympics in Lake Placid, performing *Running Gag,* a musical about Americans' fascination with running and jogging. *Goona Goona,* Megan Terry's musical exploring modern American family "beefs" continues to tour (with postplay discussions) to prisons, training schools, high schools and communities.

The Omaha Magic is dedicated to presenting high quality performances of the newest American works, using innovative, theatrical modes to delight, stimulate and pose new perspectives on the potential of modern theatre. An important objective is to share with audiences the revitalized American musical theatre form integrated with the best performance techniques, dance, docudrama, circus and conceptual art. OMT theatre events strive to present issues of immediate human concern.

Talented designers, visual artists, sculptors and craftspeople create ambitious sets and giant puppet actors; the Midwest's pioneer quilting tradition is echoed through the use of "soft sculpture" sets and props.

In response to demand by theatres, universities and students interested in OMT's works, scripts are published and distributed as complete production packages. The package includes workshop suggestions, a musical score, photos, detailed instructions for "soft sculpture" sets, costumes and props, as well as stage directions, study guides and audience discussion transcripts.

Six pieces are kept in the company's active repertoire. Workshops in ensemble acting and directing, voice and body integration, theatre games and playwriting are open to permanent company members, apprentices and the community. OMT community outreach activities include ticket discounts and free ticket distribution, post–performance discussions, staged readings, a theatre/arts newsletter and guest performers.

Productions 1979–80
- *Goona Goona II,* book and lyrics: Megan Terry; music: Lynn Herrick
- *Running Gag II,* book: Jo Ann Schmidman; music: Lynn Herrick and Marianne de Pury;

lyrics: Megan Terry
- *Comings and Goings: The Musical,* book: Megan Terry; music: John Sheehan
- *Northwestern Bell: Sexual Harassment at the Office,* Megan Terry

Productions 1980–81
- *Blue Tube,* Sora Kim and Jo Ann Schmidman
- *Tix Tox,* Sora Kim
- *Yellow Strappings,* book: Sora Kim and Jo Ann Schmidman; music: Gail Hennig; lyrics: Megan Terry
- *White Out,* Sora Kim and Jo Ann Schmidman
- *Reflected Light,* Sora Kim and Jo Ann Schmidman; adapt: Megan Terry; music: Sora Kim, Jo Ann Schmidman and John Sheehan
- *Objective Love,* Megan Terry; music: John Sheehan

Directors
Jo Ann Schmidman

Designers
Sets: Diane Degan, Sora Kim, Megan Terry. *Costumes:* Jo Ann Schmidman, Megan Terry, Janet Lipsey, Dorothy Oleson, Meg Oleson, Elizabeth Scheuerlein. *Lights:* Colbert McClellan.

Omaha Magic Theatre. Eve Felder, Joe Budenholzer, Jo Ann Schmidman and Cathy Prochazka in *Objective Love.* Photo: Megan Terry.

One Act Theatre Company of San Francisco

Peter Tripp
Artistic Director

Rafaella Del Bourgo
General Manager

430 Mason St.
San Francisco, CA 94102
(415) 421-5355 (business)
(415) 421-6162 (box office)

Founded 1976
Peter Tripp, Jean Schiffman, Laurellee Westaway

Season
October–September

Schedule
Evenings
Thursday–Sunday
Matinees
Wednesday, One Sunday per series

Facilities
One Act Theatre
Seating capacity: 99
Stage: thrust
One Act II
Seating capacity: 80
Stage: thrust

Finances
August 1, 1980–July 31, 1981
$180,000 operating expenses
$ 95,000 earned income
$ 85,000 grants/contributions

Audience
Annual attendance: 18,000
Subscribers: 687

Touring contact
Jean Schiffman

AEA 99-seat waiver

One Act Theatre Company of San Francisco is an ensemble of 60 artists who have been working together for the last five years. Each company member participates by acting, directing, designing—even by selling concessions or running the box office. The work is shared as equitably as possible, and the company has established a cohesive and professional approach to production. In addition, One Act Theatre is the only repertory ensemble company in the country devoted entirely to the development and presentation of the one-act play.

The two theatre spaces are located in the heart of the downtown San Francisco theatre district, offering easy access to public transportation, hotels and restaurants. The mainstage presents a regular subscription season of five or six productions, each containing up to four one-act plays unified by a single theme. The new theatre, One Act II, produces 15 to 20 world premieres annually, with sets of two-to-four plays changing six times per season. Both theatres offer the warmth and intimacy that is One Act's trademark.

Other current programs include Lunchtime Theatre (a few one-acts from the repertoire performed at noon on Wednesdays with programs changing monthly); One Act II/Playwrights' Theatre (all premieres by local writers); free Staged Readings (once a month, from plays written by the Playwrights' Theatre members, or unsolicited manuscripts); One Acts by Women (a national playwriting contest); an educational student matinee program (a double bill of one-acts from the repertoire, followed by discussion among students, teachers, actors and directors); state and local tours; Children's Theatre Tour Wing; the Playwrights' Unit (a group which meets monthly to read and discuss their plays, which are then presented at Staged Readings and/or Playwrights' Theatre); High School Tour Project; One Act Theatre of the Air (a radio program to be developed during the 1981–82 season); and an internship program involving residents of the community as trainees in the theatre.

Productions 1979–80
Birdbath, Leonard Melfi
Lou Gehrig Did Not Die of Cancer, Jason Miller
The Restaurant, Dan Greenburg
Minnesota Moon, John Olive
Comanche Cafe, William Hauptman
Yanks 3, Detroit 0, Top of the Seventh, Jonathan Reynolds
Losers, Brian Friel
Circus Lady, Jason Miller
- *The Painter's Face,* Ira Kamin
- *A Portrait of Katherine Mansfield,* Barbara Oliver
- *Tuba Solo,* Michael Lynch

Home Free, Lanford Wilson
The Gloaming, Oh My Darling, Megan Terry

Here We Are, Dorothy Parker

Productions 1980–81
- *Scream Your Head Off,* Deborah Rogin
- *Questionnaire,* Leslie Brody
American Modern, Joanna Glass
- *Sister Gloria's Penecostal Baby,* Michael Lynch
Split, Michael Weller
The Constituent, Ernest Thompson
A Little Dancing, Robert Kimmel Smith
Memory of Two Mondays, Arthur Miller
The Pushcart Peddlers, Murray Schisgal
- *A Letter from Leo Gorcey,* Michael Lynch
- *Billy Angel,* John Crabtree
- *Suicide Franchise,* John Angell Grant
The Great Nebula in Orion, Lanford Wilson
Bedtime Story, Sean O'Casey
Desert Weather, Michael Lynch
A Good Time, Ernest Thompson
- *A Martyr to Our Times,* Deborah Rogin
Language as Communication, John Angell Grant
Noon, Terrence McNally
- *Sleeping Bag,* Michael Lynch
Johnny and Wilma, Renee Taylor and Joseph Bologna
Ikke Ikke Nye Nye Nye, Lanford Wilson
Save Me a Place at Forest Lawn, Lorees Yerby
- *Eye Exercises,* Martin Russell
- *Dinosaurs, C.D. Arnold*
- *Arizona Highways,* Ronald Meszaros
- *Intelligent Life,* Scott Christopher Wren
- *Mime,* Thomas Fontana
- *The Fight Against Crime,* George Crowe
- *The Burglar,* Ronald Meszaros
- *A Night in Bulgaria,* Deborah Rogin
- *A Sense of Humour,* Lynn Snyder
- *Sunday Morning Services,* Ira Kamin

Directors
Jan Anger, Kasey Arnold-Ince, Simon Levy, William Oliver, Peter Tripp, Neil Stadtmore

Designers
Sets: Bruce Brisson, Stephen Elspas, Joseph Jon Riggs, Cheryl Stewart. *Costumes:* Deborah Capen, Cathleen Edwards, Mary Fullerton. *Lights:* Rhonda Birnbaum.

Media resources
Video: *Theatre Alive!* (KQED, documentary).

O'Neill Theater Center

George C. White
President

Lloyd Richards
Artistic Director
National Playwrights Conference

1860 Broadway
Suite 601
New York, NY 10023
(212) 246–1485

305 Great Neck Road
Waterford, CT 06385
(203) 443–5378 (business)
(203) 443–1238 (box office)
(212) 925–5032 (NY direct line)

Founded 1964
George C. White

Season
July–August

Schedule
Evenings
Monday–Saturday
Matinees
Saturday

Facilities
305 Great Neck Road
Waterford, CT
Barn Theater
Seating capacity: 200
Stage: flexible
Amphitheatre
Seating capacity: 300
Stage: thrust
Instant Theater
Seating capacity: 200
Stage: arena

Finances
July 1, 1980–June 30, 1981
$2,418,000 operating expenses
$1,798,000 earned income
$ 621,000 grants/contributions

Audience
Annual attendance: 4,209

AEA LORT (C) contract

The Eugene O'Neill Theater Center is an umbrella organization supporting and nurturing varied projects in theatre research, development and education. The National Playwrights Conference was the Center's first project and has been under the artistic direction of Lloyd Richards for 12 years.

One Act Theatre Company. Barbara Oliver, Maureen Coyne and Catherine Willis in *The Ex Miss Copper Queen on a Set of Pills.* Photo: Allen Nomura.

O'Neill Theater Center. Rehearsal of *House of Cards.* Photo: A. Vincent Scarano.

NPC was formed at the suggestion of several American writers when George White, the O'Neill's founder and president, asked them "What can the American theatre do for you?" The writers wanted a place where they could work with other theatre professionals on the development of new scripts, where they could have the freedom to fail, far from the reach of criticism and the demands of an audience. Over the years, NPC has attempted to be that place, encouraging experimentation, exploration and the unembellished creative experience as the basis of all work. In 1976, NPC inaugurated the New Drama for Television Project, designed to give playwrights an opportunity to conceive and develop original material specifically for television. In 17 years, NPC has staged 230 new plays by 169 playwrights.

Concurrent with NPC is the National Critics Institute, a professional workshop directed by Ernest Schier, which is designed to help critics explore the performing arts and to expand their interpretive writing skills. In 1978, two more O'Neill Projects began—the Choreographers Conference, and the Composer/Librettist Conference, under the direction of Paulette Haupt-Nolen.

Another program is the National Theater Institute, a professional training program for college students under the direction of Jess Adkins. The O'Neill also sponsors the Creative Arts in Education Program, directed by Joyce Schmidt. The Center houses the Monte Cristo Cottage Museum and Library of which Sally Pavetti is curator, as well as the National and Little Theatres of the Deaf, both under David Hays' artistic direction. In addition, the Center published the *National Playwrights Directory,* edited by Phyllis Johnson Kaye.

Productions 1980

- *Wanna,* Conrad Bishop
- *The Meeting of the Creditors of J. Matthew Spengler,* Michael J. Chepiga
- *The Summer Garden,* Terry Curtis Fox
- *Seconds,* Judy GeBauer
- *Einstein and the Polar Bear,* Tom Griffin
- *Willie,* Leslie Lee
- *Sally and Marsha,* Sybille Pearson
- *The Snow Orchid,* Joseph Pintauro
- *Holy Mary,* John Faro PiRoman
- *Details without a Map,* Barbara Schneider
- *Sundancers,* Craig Volk
- *Ladies in Waiting* (later titled *The War Brides),* Terri Wagener

Productions 1981

- *Sons and Fathers of Sons,* Ray Aranha
- *Hage—The Sexual History,* Robert Auletta
- *Johnny Bull,* Kathleen Betsko
- *Going Over,* Stuart Browne
- *The End of the Teflon-Coated Life,* June Calender
- *Flash Floods,* Dare Clubb
- *C-Section,* William di Canzio
- *Still Life with Cow,* John Gehm
- *Starters,* Jack Gelber
- *Fire at Luna Park,* Theodore Faro Gross
- *Last Looks,* Grace McKeaney
- *Home Remedies,* Paul Minx

Directors
Tony Giordano, Walt Jones, Barnet Kellman, Bill Ludel, Bill Partlan, Dennis Scott, Robert Graham Small, Horacena J. Taylor

Designers
Sets: Hugh Landwehr, Bil Mikulewicz. *Lights:* Frances Aronson, Ian Calderon.

Media resources
Video: *A Thousand Miles to Freedom, Cathexis, Echoes, My Mother, My Father, My Sister and Me, Patterns, Benny, Christchild, Summer Children* (Lincoln Center Research Library).

Oregon Shakespearean Festival

Jerry Turner
Artistic Director

William Patton
Executive Director

Box 158
Ashland, OR 97520
(503) 482–2111 (business)
(503) 482–4331 (box office)

Founded 1935
Angus L. Bowmer

Season
February–October

Schedule
Evenings
Tuesday–Sunday
Matinees
Saturday, Sunday (spring, fall)
Tuesday–Sunday (summer)

Facilities
15 South Pioneer St.
Elizabethan Stage
Seating capacity: 1,173
Stage: thrust
Angus Bowmer Theatre
Seating capacity: 601
Stage: thrust
Black Swan Theatre
Seating capacity: 138–156
Stage: flexible

Finances
November 1, 1979–October 31, 1980
$2,354,000 operating expenses
$2,004,000 earned income
$ 472,000 grants/contributions

Audience
Annual attendance: 330,784

Touring contact
Paul E. Nicholson

Booked-in events
Music, ballet

AEA Guest Artist contract

The Oregon Shakespearean Festival was founded in 1935 to present Shakespeare's works on a stage roughly equivalent to those of Elizabethan playhouses. The large outdoor theatre with its

Oregon Shakespearean Festival. *Wild Oats.* Photo: Hank Kranzler.

neutral, multiple spaces allows for rapid development of the action with minimum technical complexity. Today, the Festival also operates the modern Angus L. Bowmer Theatre, an indoor playhouse with a versatile thrust stage; and the Black Swan, an intimate, flexible space.

The repertory company serving all three stages is composed of actors and technicians who, for the most part, are recent graduates of the best training schools, willing to commit their talents over several years to a rotating repertory of classic and modern plays. The aim of the theatre is to develop a collective of artists dedicated to a wide range of styles and modes, and disciplined enough to function as a unit. Shakespeare is the author most often produced, but by no means the only one.

The Festival is not a museum but a living theatre, relating to a large American and Canadian audience. It strives to be a people's theatre, a classical theatre and even a literary theatre, bringing an immediate contemporary reality to the classics for a heterogeneous population.

The theatre's programs and services include artistic, administrative and technical production internships; student performances; programs-in-schools; study materials; college courses in Renaissance studies; student and senior citizen ticket discounts; post-performance discussions; workshop productions and staged readings; a film series; guest lecturers; a newsletter; souvenir books; script publication; a speakers bureau; a volunteer auxiliary; theatre rentals and touring productions.

Productions 1980

Coriolanus, William Shakespeare
As You Like It, William Shakespeare
The Philadelphia Story, Philip Barry
Ring Round the Moon, Jean Anouilh; adapt: Christopher Fry
Seascape, Edward Albee
Sizwe Bansi Is Dead, Athol Fugard, John Kani and Winston Ntshona
The Merry Wives of Windsor, William Shakespeare
Richard II, William Shakespeare
Love's Labour's Lost, William Shakespeare
Of Mice and Men, John Steinbeck
Lone Star and *Laundry and Bourbon,* James McLure
Juno and the Paycock, Sean O'Casey

Productions 1981

Twelfth Night, William Shakespeare
Wild Oats, John O'Keefe
Death of a Salesman, Arthur Miller
Artichoke, Joanna Glass
The Birthday Party, Harold Pinter
'Tis Pity She's a Whore, John Ford
Henry IV, Part I, William Shakespeare
Two Gentlemen of Verona, William Shakespeare
The Island, Athol Fugard, John Kani and Winston Ntshona
Othello, William Shakespeare

Directors

Dennis Bigelow, Joy Carlin, John Cranney, James Edmondson, Richard Allan Edwards, Luther James, Michael Kevin, Robert Loper, James Moll, David Ostwald, Pat Patton, Sanford Robbins, Audrey Stanley, Andrew J. Traister, Jerry Turner

Designers

Sets: William Bloodgood, Richard L. Hay, Jesse Hollis, Bryan St. Germaine. *Costumes:* Barbara Affonzo, Robert Blackman, Jeannie Davidson, Deborah M. Dryden, Toni M. Lovaglia, Michael Olich, Richard V. Parks, Bryan St. Germaine. *Lights:* Robert Peterson, Richard Riddell, Christopher Sackett.

Palisades Theatre Company.
Wings. Photo: Gale B. Salus.

Palisades Theatre Company

Bobbie Seifer
Artistic Director

Richard Del Greco
Managing Director

Box 10717
St. Petersburg, FL 33733
(813) 823–1600 (business)
(813) 822–8814 (box office)

Founded 1974
Richard Hopkins

Season
November–May (resident)
Year-round (touring)

Schedule
Evenings
Wednesday–Saturday
Matinees
Wednesday, Saturday

Facilities
169 Central Ave.
Seating capacity: 176
Stage: flexible

Finances
July 1, 1980–June 30, 1981
$270,000 operating expenses
$100,000 earned income
$165,000 grants/contributions

Audience
Annual attendance: 188,000
Subscribers: 700

Touring contact
John Berglund

Booked-in events
Music, touring companies, benefits

Palisades Theatre Company began in 1974, dedicated to developing new works for young people and to taking these works to audiences not generally exposed to professional theatre. Through intensive actor/director/playwright improvisations taking place in the Childrens Theatre Lab, Palisades On Tour has created productions that have reached over one-half million young people and their communities stretching from Connecticut to Florida.

These new works utilize a simple theatrical style that combines the artists' unique talents with original music, puppets, mime and "story theatre" techniques. The aim has always been to foster a creative environment in which the actor strives for truth and the sharing of personal visions.

In 1977, Palisades decided to make its permanent home in St. Petersburg, Florida, and two years later—in December 1979—it opened a theatre in downtown St. Petersburg with a six-play resident season. Palisades at St. Pete Central has completed two critically acclaimed seasons combining classics, contemporary productions and original works. The theatre further serves the community through informal "Topical Nights": discussion programs and special events featuring local and visiting artists. Palisades is presently collaborating with the University of South Florida to offer programs leading to the BFA degree in Performance while continuing both resident and tour activities.

Productions 1979–80
Scapino!, adapt: Frank Dunlop and Jim Dale, from Moliere
Brecht on Brecht, adapt: George Tabori
The Effect of Gamma Rays on Man-in-the-Moon Marigolds, Paul Zindel
The Knack, Ann Jellicoe
American Buffalo, David Mamet
Story Theatre, Paul Sills
School for Wives, Moliere; company-adapt; music: A. Paul Johnson
Ama and the White Crane, Maureen O'Toole; music: A. Paul Johnson
The Mime Show, company-developed
The Tinderbox, company-developed; music: Gus Wise
Alice in Wonderland, company-developed, from Lewis Carroll; music and lyrics: A. Paul Johnson

Productions 1980–81
The Water Engine, David Mamet
The Glass Menagerie, Tennessee Williams
Star Child, company-developed, from Oscar Wilde; music and lyrics: Tom Minor and Susan Morgenstern
Wings, Arthur Kopit
The Killing of Sister George, Frank Marcus
Tropical Nights, music and lyrics: Fernando Fonseca
Peter and the Wolf, company-developed; music: Sergei Prokofiev
Snow White, adapt: Richard James and company; music: Gus Wise
Song of Shakespeare; company-adapt, from William Shakespeare

Directors
Lach Adair, James R. Carlson, Henry Fonte, Alfred Gingold, Victoria Holloway, Richard Hopkins, David Johnson, William C. Martin, Gale Salus, Bobbie Seifer, Ron Troutman, Jim Waechter

Designers
Sets: James R. Carlson, Fernando Fonseca, Susan Harlan, Mark Hendren, David Johnson, William Lorenzen, Jennifer Lupton, John McCaughna, Angelyn Page.
Costumes: James R. Carlson, Fernando Fonseca, Victoria Holloway, David Johnson, William Lorenzen, John McCaughna, Angelyn Page.
Lights: Richard Del Greco, Mark Hendren, David Johnson, Charles Medlin, Bruce Rolfsen.

Media resources
Video: *The Killing of Sister George, Tropical Nights* (company-produced). All touring shows of the last five years have also been videotaped by the company.

The Paper Bag Players

Judith Martin
Director

Judith Liss
Administrator

50 Riverside Drive
New York, NY 10024
(212) 362–0431

Founded 1958
Judith Martin, Remy Charlip, Shirley Kaplan, Sudie Bond, Daniel Jahn

Season
Year-round

Facilities
Town Hall
123 West 43rd St.
Seating capacity: 1,400
Stage: proscenium

Finances
May 1, 1979–April 30, 1980
$224,000 operating expenses
$102,000 earned income
$108,000 grants/contributions

Audience
Annual attendance: 120,000

Touring contact
Judith Liss

AEA Guest Artist contract

The Paper Bag Players, founded in 1958, were immediately recognized as outstanding innovators in the field of children's theatre, and continue to receive awards and critical acclaim for their work.

Under the direction of Judith Martin, the company creates and performs original theatre for children which delights adults as well. The themes of Paper Bag's plays are taken from contemporary situations and everyday experiences familiar to every city child. These "modern allegories" draw on reality, rather than fables or fairy tales and are colorful mosaics—part fantasy, part fine art. Full of comedy, dance and catchy rhythms on the electric harpsichord, this unique mix is presented in a rollicking "revue" style and provides an absorbing combination of education and entertainment.

Paper, cardboard, paints and crayons are, of course, basic elements in the Paper Bag Players' theatre. The props and scenery function in several ways—sometimes as a caricature of the image and sometimes as an abstraction. For example, a jagged piece of cardboard gives the impression of an alligator, and a refrigerator box represents a crowded tenement. Costumes or props are drawn and even constructed by the actors on stage as part of the action.

The company has performed in a variety of places, from Lincoln Center and Harlem in New York to rural schools in Kentucky and across the ocean in Israel, Iran, Egypt and London.

Productions 1979–80
Everybody, Everybody
Hot Feet
Dandelion

Productions 1980–81
Everybody, Everybody
Hot Feet
Dandelion

For all productions, Judith Martin authored the book, Donald Ashwander composed the music, and Martin and Ashwander collaborated on the lyrics.

Directors
Judith Martin

Designers
Judith Martin

The Paper Bag Players. Jeanne Michels in *Everybody, Everybody.* Photo: Hugh Grannum.

Pennsylvania Stage Company. Keith Rice and company in *Damon's Song.* Photo: Gregory M. Fota.

Pennsylvania Stage Company

Gregory S. Hurst
Producing Director

Jeff Gordon
Managing Director

837 Linden St.
Allentown, PA 18101
(215) 434–6110 (business)
(215) 433–3394 (box office)

Founded 1977
Anna Rodale

Season
September–May

Schedule
Evenings
Tuesday–Sunday
Matinees
Thursday, Sunday

Facilities
J.I. Rodale Theatre
Seating capacity: 274
Stage: proscenium

Finances
July 1, 1980–June 30, 1981
$585,000 operating expenses
$309,000 earned income
$276,000 grants/contributions

Audience
Annual attendance: 50,000
Subscribers: 4,100

Touring contact
Sally Hanger

Booked-in events
Theatre, concerts, dance

AEA LORT (C) contract

The Pennsylvania Stage Company was founded in 1976 by Anna Rodale, and after two seasons as the Free Hall Theatre Company, PSC took its present name and began a period of dynamic growth. Under the leadership of Gregory Hurst and Jeff Gordon, the audience has grown from 27,300 to 70,000 with earned revenue showing a 116 percent increase and the subscriber family increasing from 800 to 4,100.

Located only 90 miles from New York City and housed in the 274-seat J.I. Rodale Theatre, PSC presents classic and modern plays by major playwrights. Each season features a play by Shakespeare and a world premiere musical. To better understand the American vision, the PSC also emphasizes works that explore the mythic or realistic history and fabric of America.

Committed to development of new plays and musicals, the PSC has presented five world premieres in four years. The impact of discovering a vital new work reaches far beyond the Lehigh Valley, as two of the premieres, *Scenes and Revelations* and the musical *Great Expectations* are scheduled for commercial New York productions during the 1981–82 season, while the other three premieres are receiving regional productions.

The PSC outreach program, begun only two years ago, is testimony to the community's need for the theatre and its willingness to support it. At student/senior citizen Thursday matinees, audience attendance has soared to 12,000. A professional touring company brings original material on student-related issues into schools in Pennsylvania and New Jersey, reaching over 15,000 students. The internship program has provided the transition into professional theatre for over 25 graduates from 20 university theatre programs. Other activities include a range of acting classes offered to the community, a "Live at Five" panel discussion featuring guest professionals, special performance attractions, a volunteer organization, a 10-week summer film series and a newsletter called *Backstage.*

The wide range of community outreach activities reflects the company's commitment to serve as a cultural, educational and recreational resource to the people of the region. The commitment to a diverse repertoire allows the PSC to contribute to the growth of American theatre.

Productions 1979–80
The Philadelphia Story, Philip Barry
Vanities, Jack Heifner
• *Damon's Song,* book: William F. Brown; music and lyrics: George Robertson
Count Dracula, adapt: Ted Tiller
The Glass Menagerie, Tennessee Williams
The Comedy of Errors, William Shakespeare

Productions 1980–81
A Flea in Her Ear, Georges Feydeau; trans: John Mortimer
• *Feathertop,* book: Bruce Peyton; music and lyrics: Skip Kennon
• *Great Expectations,* book: Drew Kalter; music and lyrics: Jeremiah Murray
Private Lives, Noel Coward
That Championship Season, Jason Miller
The Taming of the Shrew, William Shakespeare

Directors
Gregory S. Hurst, Susan Kerner, Ron Lagomarsino, Sue Lawless, Jacques Levy, Louis Rackoff

Designers
Sets: Victor Capecce, Edward Cesaitis, Harry Darrow, Curtis Dretsch, Atkin Pace, Ronald Plazcek, Raymond C. Recht, Quentin Thomas, Kevin Wiley. *Costumes:* Judith Grant Byrnes, Elizabeth Covey, Ann Emonts, Sigrid Insull, Thomas Keller, Andrew Marlay, Lisa Micheels, Elizabeth Palmer, Lewis Rampino. *Lights:* Betsy Adams, Thomas Barrow, Gregory Chabay, Harry Darrow, Curtis Dretsch, Candice Dunn, Todd Lichtenstein, Robby Monk, Quentin Thomas, Andrea Wilson.

The People's Light and Theatre Company. *Treasure Island.* Photo: Eric Schaeffer.

The People's Light and Theatre Company

Danny S. Fruchter
Producing Director

Evelyn V. Andrews
Administrative Director

39 Conestoga Road
Malvern, PA 19355
(215) 647–1900

Founded 1974
Danny S. Fruchter, Margaret E. Fruchter, Richard L. Keeler, Ken Marini

Season
March–January

Schedule
Evenings
Tuesday–Saturday

Facilities
Mainstage
Seating capacity: 300–500
Stage: flexible
Second Stage
Seating capacity: 70–100
Stage: flexible

Finances
January 1, 1981–December 31, 1981
$461,000 operating expenses
$297,000 earned income
$165,000 grants/contributions

Audience
Annual attendance: 65,000
Subscribers: 3,200

Touring contact
Danny S. Fruchter

AEA letter of agreement

According to People's Light and Theatre Company's producing director Danny S. Fruchter, "Americans have few points of cultural or historical reference. This leads them to think that 'now' is all there is. Theatre represents the cultural continuum by which we can see the past, judge the present and plan for the future, if there is to be one."

Since its founding in 1973, The People's Light and Theatre Company has been guided by a dedicated group of actors, directors and designers whose basic aim is to make theatre a vital force in the life of their community. The theatre has developed into a comprehensive producing and teaching arena of high professional standards. Each year, the mainstage program includes eight to ten productions from classical and contemporary literature, including several premieres.

Original children's theatre productions are performed every year in more than 50 elementary schools in the five surrounding counties. In addition, the company tours prisons, juvenile detention homes, therapeutic communities and day care centers with specially designed productions.

From the theatre's inception, thousands of tickets subsidized by the theatre in partnership with corporations and foundations have been distributed to senior citizens; to the socially, physically and emotionally handicapped; and to children in special educational institutions. Readings and workshops of new plays are presented on a second stage throughout the year. Company members conduct professional and avocational acting classes throughout the year.

The unceasing work of bringing outstanding theatre to a diverse but culturally deprived modern society best represents the artistic policy of The People's Light and Theatre Company.

Productions 1979–80
Sleuth, Anthony Shaffer
Hamlet, William Shakespeare
Blithe Spirit, Noel Coward
Holy Ghosts, Romulus Linney
Inca of Perusalem, Augustus Does His Bit and *Dark Lady of the Sonnets,* George Bernard Shaw
The Tempest, William Shakespeare
Toys in the Attic, Lillian Hellman
Treasure Island, company-adapt, from Robert Louis Stevenson

Productions 1980–81
Macbeth, William Shakespeare
Wait Until Dark, Frederick Knott
The Learned Ladies, Moliere; trans: Richard Wilbur
Eden Court, Murphy Guyer
Animal Farm, adapt: Jiri and Blanka Zizka, from George Orwell
Chug, Ken Jenkins
On Being Hit, Clay Goss
Laundry and Bourbon, James McLure
Arms and the Man, George Bernard Shaw
Rear Column, Simon Gray

Directors
Jack Byer, Charles Conwell, Alfred Gingold, Louis Lippa, John Loven, Ken Marini, Tim Moyer, Maryanne McGarry, Michael Nash

Designers
Sets: Norman B. Dodge, Steve Lavino, Jess McFeaters, James F. Pyne Jr., Eric Shaeffer. *Costumes:* Marcia Evers, Margaret E. Fruchter, Lisa Hemphill-Burns, Jane Tschetter, Irene Upchurch, Susan Wilder. *Lights:* Norman B. Dodge, Richard L. Keeler, Steve Lavino, James F. Pyne, Jr.

Media resources
Video: *Animal Farm* (WHYY).

Peoples Theatre

June Judson
Artistic/Administrative Director

1253 Cambridge St.
Cambridge, MA 02139
(617) 354–2915

Founded 1963
Ruth Elder, Tove Gerson

Season
Year-round

Schedule
Evenings
Wednesday–Sunday

Facilities
Mainstage
Seating capacity: 75
Stage: flexible

Finances
June 1, 1980–May 31, 1981
$75,000 operating expenses
$37,000 earned income
$35,000 grants/contributions

Audience
Annual attendance: 20,000
Subscribers: 140

Touring contact
Paul Dedell

Peoples Theatre, now entering its 18th season, is one of the oldest theatres still in operation in the Boston/Cambridge area. It is a professional theatre center dedicated to the exploration of new dramatic concepts, outreach programs involving the greater Boston community, training in the theatre arts, presentation of a broad spectrum of theatrical works by both new and established playwrights, and multiracial casting whenever possible.

Major productions are chosen to reflect a wide range of tastes and aesthetics, from world classics to new works by accomplished local writers.

A series called Theatre In Process introduces new playwrights, directors and actors to the community; Saturday programs for children and senior citizens are held both within the theatre walls and out in the community. Peoples Theatre serves as a professional collective, as well as a showcase for area theatre talent.

Productions 1979–80
- • *Black Dyad,* Evelyn and Mel Moore
- • *Landscape of the Body,* John Guare
- *Ice Wolf,* Joann Krauss
- • *Calm Down Mother,* James Saunders
- • *The T Show,* book and lyrics: Geralyn Horton; music: Ross Dabrusin
- *Death of a Salesman,* Arthur Miller

Productions 1980–81
- *Bus Stop,* William Inge
- *Bits and Pieces,* Corinne Jacker
- *The Love Course,* A.R. Gurney, Jr.
- • *Freedom and Angelina,* June Judson
- • *Behind Enemy Lines,* Rosanna Yamagiwa Alfaro
- *A Streetcar Named Desire,* Tennessee Williams
- • *Clown Alley,* book and lyrics: Martha Moravec; music: Paul Dedell
- *Pins and Needles,* Harold Rome
- *The Rainmaker,* N. Richard Nash

Directors
Jane Armitage, James D'Entremont, Marilyn Duchin, Arthur Feinsod, John Hickok, June Judson, Peggy Mays

Designers
Sets: Paul Dedell, Virginia Land, David Moore. *Costumes:* Cecelia Eller, Betsy Kerr, Carroll Moshier, Jana Rosenblatt. *Lights:* Paul Dedell, Richard Fairbanks.

Peoples Theatre. Donna Lynn Allen and Joshua Perlstein in *The Love Course.* Photo: Richard Fairbanks.

Performance Community

Byron Schaffer, Jr.
Artistic Director/Producer

Ruth E. Higgins
Producer

Theatre Building
1225 West Belmont Ave.
Chicago, IL 60657
(312) 929–7367 (business)
(312) 327–5252 (box office)

Founded 1969
Byron Schaffer, Jr.

Season
July–June

Schedule
Evenings
Wednesday–Sunday
Matinees
Sunday

Facilities
North Theatre
Seating capacity: 138
Stage: flexible

Finances
January 1, 1980–December 31, 1980
$176,000 operating expenses
$119,000 earned income
$ 72,000 grants/contributions

Audience
Annual attendance: 10,580

Booked-in events
Theatre, music, dance

In the 12 years since its inception, Performance Community has been consistent in its dedication to the three main goals set down in its 1969 manifesto: the development of new American plays; the encouragement of young artists; and the provision of services to the profession.

In developing new American plays, PC has been fortunate to have the authors of its 26 premieres present during the production process. In addition, PC has provided second productions for three of its playwrights and has produced a series of readings to aid in its development of each new play.

Performance Community maintains a commitment to affording professional experience to the nascent theatre artist. In addition, the company has given 60 visual artists an opportunity to exhibit their works in the theatre's lobby gallery. PC has also developed an internship program which allows outstanding students to experience intensive individual training in theatre administration.

The best example of PC's service to the profession is the leasing, renovation and management of the Theatre Building, a three-theatre complex used by Performance Community, two other nonprofit companies and numerous groups seeking venues for everything from a day of auditioning to lengthy runs.

Productions 1979–80
- *The Man in 605,* Alan Gross
- *White Horse Black Horse,* Steven Stosny

A Jingle Dingle Festival, company-developed
- *Old Soldiers,* Martin Jones
- *A Sky Full of Blues,* Len Hodera

Productions 1980–81
- *R.S.V.P. Broadway,* book: Barbara D'Amato; music and lyrics: Anthony D'Amato

Pinnacle, Mark Stein
- *The Houseguest,* Alan Gross

Directors
Guy Barile, Susan Boettcher, Ruth Higgins, Dale McFadden, Sheldon Patinkin, Byron Schaffer

Designers
Sets: Alexander Adducci, Jon Gantt, Byron Schaffer. *Costumes:* Kathleen Hart, Patricia Hart, Julie Needleman, Sherry Ravitz, Kevin Seligman, Pat Wallace. *Lights:* Glenn Haines, Byron Schaffer, Robert G. Smith.

Media resources
Radio: *The Man in 605* (Earplay).

Performance Community. Jeff Perry and Byrne Piven in *The Man in 605.* Photo: Byron Schaffer.

Periwinkle Productions

Sunna Rasch
Executive Director/President

Cathy Farris
Business Manager

19 Clinton Ave.
Monticello, NY 12701
(914) 794–1666 (business)
(914) 794–4992 (box office)
(212) 772–0363 (NY direct line)

Founded 1963
Sunna Rasch

Season
Year-round

Finances
August 1, 1980–July 31, 1981
$115,000 operating expenses
$ 81,000 earned income
$ 29,000 grants/contributions

Audience
Annual attendance: 115,000

Touring contact
Kathleen Keeler

AEA Theatre for Young Audiences contract

Periwinkle Productions is an innovative, award-winning touring theatre for young audiences from the primary level through high school. Founded in 1963 by actress/educator Sunna Rasch, Periwinkle is one of the oldest ongoing professional children's theatres in the United States. Recipient of the Jennie Heiden Award from the American Theatre Association and a Special Recognition Citation from the Children's Theatre Association of America, Periwinkle has also been recognized by the educational community for the impact of its programs on youth. For the eighth year in a row, Periwinkle is a featured participant in the New York State Humanities and Arts Conference sponsored by the State Education Department.

All Periwinkle programs, touring primarily during the school day, are based on the concept that good theatre for children has as much educational value as it has entertainment and artistic value.

Periwinkle Productions. Abbe Gail Gross, Anne Temple, William Wesbrooks and Greg Eisenbise in *The Magic Word.*

America, Yes! by Sunna Rasch is a musical that traces the development of the country through its songs. It aims to infuse young people with hope about their country, while providing an understanding of the forces that shaped America, and of the part today's students must play in their country's future.

The Magic Word, known as the "Periwinkle Classic," is a fantasy/adventure for primary schools designed to "turn on" children to the magic of poetry. In 1980–81, *The Magic Word* toured to Michigan, North Carolina, Virginia, Pennsylvania, New Jersey and New York. The 1981–82 season opens with a return engagement in North Carolina, before an eastern seaboard tour.

Periwinkle has a business office in Monticello, New York, and a studio in New York City, and is a founding member of the Producers Association for Children's Theatre (PACT). Its performances have enriched the lives of over two million youths.

Important auxiliary activities of Periwinkle include student workshops in creative dramatics and creative writing, an intern program in arts management with Antioch College and publication

of children's writings inspired by the performances.

Productions 1979–80
The Mad Poet Strikes—Again!, Sunna Rasch
The Magic Word, Sunna Rasch
• *Split Decision,* Scott Laughead
Fabulous Dream of Andrew H. Lupone, Scott Laughead
Hooray for Me!, book: Scott Laughead; music and lyrics: Grenaldo Frazier
• *Edna and the Magic Farumbas,* Dan Diggles
• *This Is My Mythology,* Scott Laughead

Productions 1980–81
• *Elastic,* James Greenberg and Peter Ford
The Magic Word
• *America, Yes!,* Sunna Rasch
Split Decision
• *Mask, Mime and Magic,* Abatar Steier

Directors
Elaine Kanas, Scott Laughead, Sunna Rasch, Audrey Tischler

Designers
Sets: Kathleen Daley, Cathy Farris, Peter Ford, James Greenberg, Brian Hayes, Kathy Ingam, Beth Kunes, Alfred Rasch, Sunna Rasch, Earl Wertheim.
Costumes: Kathy Ingam, Mary Alice Orito, Judy Perry, Sunna Rasch, Susan Scherer.

Philadelphia Drama Guild

Gregory Poggi
Managing Director

220 South 16th St.
Philadelphia, PA 19102
(215) 546-6791 (business)
(215) 243–6791 (box office)

Founded 1956
Sidney S. Bloom

Season
October–May

Schedule
Evenings
Tuesday–Sunday
Matinees
variable

Facilities
Zellerbach Theatre
Annenberg Center, 3680 Walnut St.
Seating capacity: 911
Stage: thrust

Finances
June 1, 1980–May 31, 1981
$1,219,000 operating expenses
$ 659,000 earned income
$ 427,000 grants/contributions

Audience
Annual attendance: 84,000
Subscribers: 14,560

AEA LORT (B) contract

The year 1982 marks the Philadelphia Drama Guild's 11th season as greater Philadelphia's resident professional theatre. Founded in 1956 as an amateur group, the Drama Guild evolved by 1971 into a professional company governed by a volunteer board of directors and incorporated as a nonprofit public charity.

In the past two years, the Drama Guild has undergone substantial change and redirection. The board of directors engaged a new managing director, the management staff and systems were completely retooled, and the company moved to a new performing space: the modern Zellerbach Theatre at University of Pennsylvania's Annenberg Center.

The aim of the Drama Guild is to achieve artistic excellent in a well-rounded program of professional theatre that illuminates the times, that challenges, entertains and excites its audience. To accomplish this, the Drama Guild produces major classic and contemporary works with a professional company of actors, directors, designers and theatre technicians. By providing a flagship standard of theatrical production, the Drama Guild fills an important cultural role in the community.

Managing director Gregory Poggi is continuing the Guild's new artistic direction by seeking variety in programming, both visually and stylistically, and by including more American works and new plays in the repertoire.

An additional objective of the Drama Guild is to create an educated, enthusiastic and supportive audience for theatre. Through its educational and community programs, the theatre makes inexpensive tickets available to students, senior citizens and groups of all ages, and offers its entire audience special materials and activities supplementing the experience of live theatre.

Productions 1979–80
The Last Few Days of Willie Callendar, Val Coleman
You Never Can Tell, George Bernard Shaw
Summer, Hugh Leonard
Twelfth Night, William Shakespeare
Thark, Ben Travers

Philadelphia Drama Guild. Helen Burns and Donald David in *Old World.* Photo: Gerry Goodstein.

Productions 1980–81
Watch on the Rhine, Lillian Hellman
Joe Egg, Peter Nichols
Philadelphia, Here I Come!, Brian Friel
The Front Page, Ben Hecht and Charles MacArthur
Old World, Aleksei Arbuzov; trans: Ariadne Nicolaeff

Directors
Thomas Bullard, Tony Giordano, John Going, Irene Lewis, Michael Montel, Douglas Seale, Tony Van Bridge

Designers
Sets: John Kasarda, Hugh Landwehr, Karen Schulz, Peter Wingate. *Costumes:* Linda Fisher, Jess Goldstein, Dona Granata, David Murin. *Lights:* Pat Collins, Arden Fingerhut, Paul Gallo, Neil Jampolis.

Phoenix Theatre

Steven Robman
Artistic Director

T. Edward Hambleton
Managing Director

1540 Broadway
New York, NY 10036
(212) 730–0787 (business)
(212) 730–0794 (box office)

Founded 1953
T. Edward Hambleton, Norris Houghton

Season
September–June

Schedule
Evenings
Tuesday–Sunday
Matinees
Saturday, Sunday

Facilities
Marymount Manhattan Theatre
221 East 71st St.
Seating capacity: 249
Stage: proscenium

Finances
July 1, 1980–June 30, 1981
$787,000 operating expenses
$282,000 earned income
$400,000 grants/contributions

Audience
Annual attendance: 26,145
Subscribers: 3,000

AEA Off Broadway contract

The Phoenix Theatre is dedicated to the nurturing and development of new plays and their emerging playwrights. This commitment is reflected in a subscription series of five mainstage productions, a series of staged readings, workshop productions and the commissioning of eight new plays.

The Phoenix was founded in 1953 as an alternative to Broadway when few alternatives existed. As theatrical landscapes in New York and the nation have changed, the Phoenix has passed through various incarnations as well, embracing new plays and classics, and even establishing a permanent ensemble performing in rotating repertory.

In 1976, the Phoenix shifted its focus to new plays, balancing new American writing with dynamic European plays. The Phoenix also collaborates with theatres outside of New York to make possible the evolution of such plays as Marsha Norman's *Getting Out* and *Uncommon Women and Others* by Wendy Wasserstein. After a successful engagement at the Phoenix in 1979, Ron Hutchinson's *Says I Says He* was produced at the Mark Taper Forum in Los Angeles in 1981. In the last five years, three Phoenix productions have also been televised over the Public Broadcasting System on the *Theater in America* series.

Now under the artistic leadership of Steven Robman who joined managing director T. Edward Hambleton in June 1980, the Phoenix continues to direct the attention of the press to playwrights and their works, and to provide these writers with the enthusiastic support of a growing subscription audience. The theatre's concern for writers is manifest in its commission program: three plays commissioned by the Phoenix were presented there in a single season during 1980–81.

The company's additional programs and services include artistic and administrative internships, programs-in-schools, free ticket distribution, student and senior citizen ticket discounts, post-performance discussions and publication efforts including a newsletter and a souvenir book.

Productions 1979–80
- *Winter Dancers,* David Lan
- *Shout Across the River,* Steven Poliakoff
- *The Trouble with Europe,* Paul D'Andrea

Phoenix Theatre. Bernie Passeltiner, Alma Cuervo and Jane Hoffman in *Isn't It Romantic.* Photo: Martha Swope.

- *Save Grand Central,* William Hamilton
- *Second Avenue Rag,* Alan Knee

Productions 1980–81
Bonjour, là, Bonjour, Michele Tremblay; trans: John Van Burek and Bill Glassco
- *Beyond Therapy,* Christopher Durang
- *The Captivity of Pixie Shedman,* Romulus Linney
- *Meetings,* Mustapha Matura
- *Isn't It Romantic,* Wendy Wasserstein

Directors
Gerald Freedman, Daniel Freudenberger, Gerald Gutierrez, Keith Hack, John Pasquin, Steven Robman, Gene Saks, Robert Woodruff, Jerry Zaks

Designers
Sets: Robert Blackman, John Kasarda, Marjorie Kellogg, Larry King, Hugh Landwehr, Manuel Lutgenhorst, Karen Schulz. *Costumes:* Jeanne Button, Linda Fisher, Jane Greenwood, Manuel Lutgenhorst, Karen Miller, Dunya Ramicova, Denise Romano, Jennifer von Mayrhauser. *Lights:* Ronald M. Bundt, Paul Gallo, Robby Monk, Spencer Mosse, Richard Nelson, Dennis Parichy, Steven Ross, Jennifer Tipton, Christine Wopat.

Media resources
Video: *Uncommon Women and Others, Secret Service, Rules of the Game* (WNET).

Pilgrim Theater

William Shorr
Producing Director

R. Thomas Ward
Managing Director

Box 9438
Aspen, CO 81612
(303) 925–4752 (business)
(303) 925–6041 (box office)

Founded 1978
William Shorr, Steve and Linda Carmichael

Season
August

Finances
October 1, 1979–September 30, 1980
$93,000 operating expenses
$53,000 earned income
$57,000 grants/contributions

Audience
Annual attendance: 3,500

Booked-in events
Theatre

AEA LORT (D) and Guest Artist contracts

Pilgrim Theater was founded in 1977 to promote the American theatre in the Rocky Mountain region, emphasizing the works of new and established American playwrights.

Pilgrim's annual Aspen Playwrights Conference has presented 12 original American plays since its inception. The conference provides an environment in which actors and directors work with the playwrights to create scripts worthy of commercial production. The late director Harold Clurman and playwright William Gibson have acted as "critics in residence" at the conference, working with the playwrights on the development of their work. The plays are then presented as staged readings before audiences in the Aspen/Snowmass region.

In conjunction with the conference, the Snowmass Festival of American Theater offers a variety of plays, from contemporary comedy to the classics of the American repertoire, in full production. Together with workshops in acting and playwriting—in 1981 taught by William Gibson, Romulus Linney, Paul Blake and Alice Spivak—Pilgrim Theater provides residents and tourists with the opportunity to participate in an exciting and wide range of theatrical experiences.

Productions 1979
The Greatest Day of the Century, Roma Greth
Lot's Wife, Joe Hart
The Screening Room, Alan Brody
Raggedy Dick and Puss, Tim Kelly
The Golden Age, A.R. Gurney, Jr.
Listen to the Lions, John Ford Noonan

Productions 1980
Hero's Home, Mark St. Germain
American Garage, Peter Maloney
New Kid on the Block, Frank X. Hogan
Barefoot in the Park, Neil Simon
The Tavern, George M. Cohan

Directors
Paul Blake, Peter Maloney, William Shorr, Steve Zuckerman

Designers
Sets: Jim Fenhagen. *Costumes:* Christina Weppner. *Lights:* Jackie Manassee.

Pilgrim Theater. Julia Duffy and Shaun Cassidy in *Barefoot in the Park.* Photo: Jeffrey Aaronson.

Pittsburgh Public Theater

Ben Shaktman
Artistic Director

One Allegheny Square
Suite 230
Pittsburgh, PA 15212
(412) 323–3950 (business)
(412) 323–1900 (box office)

Founded 1975
Joan Apt, Margaret Rieck, Ben Shaktman

Season
September–August

Schedule
Evenings
Tuesday–Sunday
Matinees
Thursday, Saturday, Sunday

Facilities
Theodore L. Hazlett, Jr. Theater
Seating capacity: 350
Stage: arena

Finances
July 1, 1980–June 30, 1981
$1,991,000 operating expenses
$1,088,000 earned income
$ 743,000 grants/contributions

Audience
Annual attendance: 105,158
Subscribers: 13,551

Touring contact
Sarah Shelley

Booked-in events
Theatre

AEA LORT (C) contract

The 1980–81 season was the Pittsburgh Public Theater's sixth, as well as being its first year-round season. Included were two significant firsts: the presentation of the Public's first world premiere *(Tangles,* by Robert Litz), and "The Galileo Project," which included the staging of the opening scenes of *The Life of Galileo* at neighboring Buhl Planetarium and Institute of Popular Science. This was the first time that Brecht's classic had been presented in a planetarium, and the production spearheaded a city-wide, year-long Galileo commemoration which included a series of public forums; an educational companion piece called *There's a Message for You from the Man in the Moon,* presented daily at the Buhl Planetarium; and a statewide tour in the fall of 1981.

The sixth season also included the introduction of "Plus 6": a series of six workshop productions and special events such as Geraldine Fitzgerald's *Streetsongs.*

On September 17, 1975, the Pittsburgh Public Theater opened its inaugural season with *The Glass Menagerie.* The City of Pittsburgh offered the Allegheny Theater as a rent-free facility for three months; eventually, this support grew to a year-round allocation of the theatre, now officially called the Theodore L. Hazlitt, Jr. Theater.

The budget has grown from $390,000 to $1,918,919 and the theatre has reached thousands of special constituencies through its resident programs, public and directors forums, and programs for the physically disabled, senior citizens and blind and deaf patrons. During the past six years subscriber ranks have grown to over 13,000; corporate/foundation support to 98; individual contributions to 2,800; and the theatre now receives government support from all major national, state, county and city agencies.

Last year's fifth season marked the Public's first regional tour of *Vanities,* and its production of *Loot* traveled to Philadelphia's Annenberg Center. To close the season, the Public presented a three-week series called "Spring for Great Entertainment," featuring new plays and special events which included Fionnula Flanagan's *James Joyce's Women.* At the end of the season, the Public moved its administrative offices to Allegheny Square, where the theatre itself is located.

Productions 1979–80

Mister Roberts, Thomas Heggen and Joshua Logan
The Seagull, Anton Chekhov; trans: Michael Henry Heim
Loot, Joe Orton
Buried Child, Sam Shepard
Macbeth, William Shakespeare

Productions 1980–81

I'm Getting My Act Together and Taking It on the Road, book and lyrics: Gretchen Cryer; music: Nancy Ford
Death of a Salesman, Arthur Miller
Terra Nova, Ted Tally
• *Tangles,* Robert Litz
Two Gentlemen of Verona, William Shakespeare
Galileo, Bertolt Brecht

Directors

John Going, Stephen Kanee, Bill Ludel, J Ranelli, David Rotenberg, Amy Saltz, Ben Shaktman, Peter Wexler

Designers

Sets: Cletus Anderson, Neil Peter Jampolis, Sandro La Ferla, Steven Rubin, William Schroder, Peter Wexler, Patricia Woodbridge. *Costumes:* Cletus Anderson, Sigrid Insull, Mark Pennywell, William Schroder, David Toser, Fred Voelpel. *Lights:* Bennet Averyt, Bernard J. Brannigan, Bonnie Ann Brown, Pat Collins, Pat Simmons, Ron Wallace.

Pittsburgh Public Theater. John Carpenter in *Loot.* Photo: Adam Weinhold.

Players State Theatre

David Robert Kanter
Artistic/Producing Director

G. David Black
Managing Director

3500 Main Highway
Coconut Grove, FL 33133
(305) 442-2662 (business)
(305) 442-4000 (box office)

Founded 1977
Thomas Spencer, Gerald Pulver

Season
October–April

Schedule
Evenings
Tuesday–Sunday
Matinees
Wednesday, selected Saturdays and Sundays

Facilities
Coconut Grove Playhouse
Seating capacity: 796
Stage: proscenium

Finances
July 1, 1980–June 30, 1981
$1,199,000 operating expenses
$ 615,000 earned income
$ 596,000 grants/contributions

Audience
Annual attendance: 109,463
Subscribers: 6,400

Touring contact
Alan Yaffe

AEA LORT (B) contract

In 1981, Players State Theatre celebrated the beginning of its fifth anniversary season in the historic Coconut Grove Playhouse. Between 1980 and 1981 the theatre watched its audience grow from 66,000 to 90,000 in one of the most active and competitive commercial theatre markets in America.

The fourth season marked a departure into the area of new works rarely seen in this country, including two challenging dramas, *Getting Out* and *Agnes of God;* an Agatha Christie American premiere, *Go Back for Murder,*

Players State Theatre. Barbara Bradshaw, J. Cameron and Anne Gilliam in *Agnes of God.* Photo: Adam Markowitz.

which set a box office record; the recent Broadway play *Gemini;* a new adaptation of Shakespeare's *Hamlet;* and a tremendously successful Christmas bonus—an original adaptation of Dickens' *A Christmas Carol.*

Within five years, Players State has proved to its growing audience that it is not afraid to take a chance, be it with a new play or a forceful contemporary drama. While there will always be a place for dinner theatre and the large, opulent musical, Players believes it provides an entertainment alternative for the entire southeastern Florida audience and produces the very best in dramatic literature, classical or contemporary.

Additionally, Players has maintained its commitment to providing professional productions and related educational and outreach programs including free ticket distribution, post-performance seminars, interpreted performances for the hearing-impaired and other handicapped services. Informational programs include a newsletter and a speakers bureau. The theatre maintains an active volunteer auxiliary and offers professional training in acting, scriptwriting and scene study for nonprofessionals and young adults at Players Conservatory. Student internships are also available. Finally, the touring company, "Culture Caravan," has reached an estimated 60,000 people in three seasons, presenting specially commissioned multicultural, tri-ethnic productions in statewide tours and South Florida appearances.

Productions 1979–80
Ceremonies in Dark Old Men, Lonne Elder III
Three Men on a Horse, John Cecil Holm and George Abbott
The Imaginary Invalid, Moliere
Ashes, David Rudkin
Ten Little Indians, Agatha Christie
The Club, Eve Merriam

Productions 1980–81
Gemini, Albert Innaurato
• *Hamlet,* William Shakespeare; adapt: David Robert Kanter
• *A Christmas Carol,* adapt: David Robert Kanter, from Charles Dickens
Getting Out, Marsha Norman
1959 Pink Thunderbird, James McLure
Agnes of God, John Pielmeier
Go Back for Murder, Agatha Christie

Directors
J. Haskell, David Robert Kanter, Michael Montel, John Chase Soliday, Charles Turner

Designers
Sets: Bob Barnes, Lyle Baskin, Kenneth N. Kurtz, Paul H. Mazer, Robert Soule. *Costumes:* Barbara A. Bell, Joy Breckenridge, Maria Marrero. *Lights:* David Goodman, Kenneth N. Kurtz, Michael Martin, Paul H. Mazer, Jean E. Shorrock, Pat Simmons, Andrea Wilson.

The Play Group

Collective Artistic Leadership

Katharine Pearson
Director

1538 Laurel Ave.
Knoxville, TN 37916
(615) 523–7641

Founded 1973

Season
Year-round

Schedule
Evenings
Friday–Sunday

Facilities
Laurel Theatre
Seating capacity: 100
Stage: flexible

Finances
September 1, 1980–August 31, 1981
\$89,000 operating expenses
\$30,000 earned income
\$56,000 grants/contributions

Audience
Annual attendance: 25,000

Touring contact
Katharine Pearson

Booked-in events
Theatre, dance, music, special events

The Play Group, a professional theatre company whose home is in Knoxville, Tennessee, tours extensively throughout the region to reach diverse audiences. The company's goal is to make theatre a modern ritual in which all can participate. Each play developed attempts to bring more people into the theatre-going community, and to make that community enjoy the communication between actor and audience.

All of the performers in The Play Group's ensemble are from Tennessee. The company is primarily dedicated to the creation of original theatre developed collectively; theatre which springs from the remembrance of play, of individual cultural experiences and

The Play Group. Donna Kelsey, Hugh Sinclair, Mac Pirkle and Katharine Pearson in *If I Live to See Next Fall.* Photo: Turner Hutchison.

of a sense of environment. Early and continuing influences on The Play Group include Grotowski's Polish Laboratory Theatre (with which several members have studied), the Open Theatre, children's games and stories, and a belief in music as a dramatic force.

Since its inception in 1973, subject material for The Play Group's work has come from many sources including the history of its region and children's stories heard first-hand. However diverse the content, the performances seek to allow the audience to feel a part of the experience.

The Play Group has performed in schools, churches, prisons, universities and small theatres throughout the South. It has also appeared at the TNT Festival in Baltimore, at the Performing Garage in New York City, at Washington's Kennedy Center and at the Lincoln Center Out-of-Doors Street Fair.

All of the Play Group's productions are available for touring and the company offers residencies ranging from one day to a month.

Productions 1979–80

If I Live to See Next Fall, book: company-developed; music and lyrics: Si Kahn
The Piper Man, Mark Cantley; music: Mac Pirkle
Tell Me a Story, company-developed
Will the Real Willie Nelson Please Stand Up, Ski Hilenski

Productions 1980–81

If I Live to See Next Fall
Tell Me a Story
More Myths, company-developed

Directors

Tom Cooke, John O'Neal, Katharine Pearson

Designers

Sets: Gary Harris. *Costumes:* Judy Celentano, Donna Kelsey, David Chappell. *Lights:* Jim Houstle, Margo Solod.

Playhouse on the Square

Jackie Nichols
Executive Director

San Stark
Administrative Director

2121 Madison Ave.
Memphis, TN 38104
(901) 725–0776 (business)
(901) 725–4656 (box office)

Founded 1968
Jackie Nichols

Season
Year-round

Schedule
Evenings
Wednesday–Sunday

Facilities
Playhouse on the Square
Seating capacity: 200
Stage: thrust
Circuit Playhouse
1705 Poplar Ave.
Seating capacity: 150
Stage: proscenium

Finances
July 1, 1979–June 30, 1980
$278,000 operating expenses
$176,000 earned income
$111,000 grants/contributions

Audience
Annual attendance: 45,000
Subscribers: 2,000

Playhouse on the Square. Rick Allen and Stephen Foster in *Jesus Christ Superstar.* Photo: Elbert Greer.

Playhouse on the Square is the professional arm of Circuit Playhouse, Inc., consisting of two theatres and housing a deaf theatre company, "A Show of Hands," in addition to its regular company. The Playhouse mainstage is dedicated to presenting classics and contemporary work, while the second stage produces original plays, plays from Off Broadway and productions appealing to a smaller audience.

Several environmental theatre events have also helped the Playhouse make its mark on the community: *The Hot l Baltimore* staged in a local hotel lobby; *The Frogs* in an outdoor swimming pool atop a motel inn; *The Rocky Horror Show* in an old movie house; and *Joseph and the Amazing Technicolor Dreamcoat* in a downtown church.

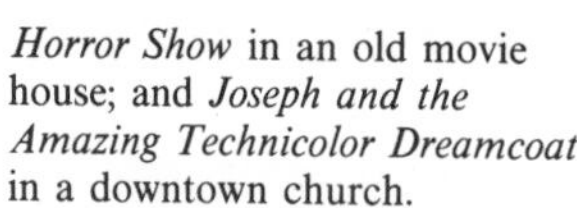

The theatre also maintains an active senior citizen program assisting seniors in producing their own shows and encouraging attendance at Playhouse productions. The mainstage theatre supports an apprentice and actor training program in cooperation with several universities. Primarily, Playhouse on the Square is a theatre which enables students coming out of training programs to gain experience before moving on to larger companies.

Special ticket rates are available for the handicapped, senior citizens and school groups. A new facility has recently been acquired and will greatly aid technical operations of both theatres.

Productions 1979–80

Jesus Christ Superstar, book and lyrics: Tim Rice; music: Andrew Lloyd Webber
Romeo and Juliet, William Shakespeare
Present Laughter, Noel Coward
Hot l Baltimore, Lanford Wilson
Jumpers, Tom Stoppard
Death of a Salesman, Arthur Miller
Company, book: George Furth; music and lyrics: Stephen Sondheim
For Colored Girls who have Considered Suicide/When The Rainbow is Enuf, Ntozake Shange
Joseph and the Amazing Technicolor Dreamcoat, book and lyrics: Tim Rice; music: Andrew Lloyd Webber
• *Into Thy Narrow Bed,* Jack Farris

Productions 1980–81
Pippin, book: Roger O. Hirson; music and lyrics: Stephen Schwartz
Sherlock Holmes, Arthur Conan Doyle and William Gillette
Sly Fox, Larry Gelbart; music: Stephen Keane
A Funny Thing Happened on the Way to the Forum, book: Burt Shevelove and Larry Gelbart; music and lyrics: Stephen Sondheim
Cyrano de Bergerac, Edmond Rostand; trans: Brian Hooker
Cat on a Hot Tin Roof, Tennessee Williams
Grease, Jim Jacobs and Warren Casey
Ernest in Love, book and lyrics: Ann Crosswell; music: Lee Tochriss

Directors
Barry Fuller, Lester Malizzia, John Murphy, Christopher Nunnally, Rich Roberts, Larry Riley, Bill Roudebush, Cathey Sawyer, Gene Wilkins

Designers
Sets: Doug Cook, Regan Cook, J. Robin Modereger, Michael Nemec, Craig Spain, Russ Whaley, Michael Williams. *Costumes:* Maggie Kuypers, Terri Winters-Malolepsy, Rebecca Senske, Craig Spain, Ginger Travis, Becky Wachholtz. *Lights:* Sheila Bam, Chris Barber, Robert Burcham, David Crist, Nancy Creel, John Gregson, John Heizer, John McFadden, Jim Rynning.

Playmakers Repertory Company

David Rotenberg
Artistic Director

Edgar Marston
Managing Director

206 Graham Memorial 052A
University of North Carolina
Chapel Hill, NC 27514
(919) 962–1122 (business)
(919) 962–1121 (box office)

Founded 1976
Arthur L. Housman

Season
September–April

Schedule
Evenings
Tuesday–Sunday
Matinees
Sunday

Facilities
Playmakers Theatre
Seating capacity: 285
Stage: proscenium
Paul Green Theatre
Seating capacity: 505
Stage: thrust

Finances
July 1, 1980–June 30, 1981
$424,000 operating expenses
$152,000 earned income
$273,000 grants/contributions

Audience
Annual attendance: 27,400
Subscribers: 3,553

Touring contact
Edgar Marston

AEA LORT (D) contract

Playmakers Repertory Company is a resident theatre on the campus of the University of North Carolina at Chapel Hill. After five years of growth, PRC enters its sixth season with a new artistic director and a keen eye toward its audiences' needs. The Chapel Hill-Raleigh-Durham triangle is a rapidly developing area attracting young professionals from all over the country. Adding these new arrivals to the highly educated indigenous audience results in a demanding, sophisticated public whose theatrical tastes rival those of any theatre audience in the country. It is to meet this demand that PRC has drawn its season from the best of both the American and British repertoires.

The 1981–82 six-play season culminates in a production of *Twelfth Night* which, like Shakespearean productions in previous seasons, will be a part of the developing outreach program to state secondary schools and colleges. In addition to seeing the plays, students benefit from a speaker's bureau, study guides, post-play discussions and follow-up classroom speakers. Scheduling a Shakespeare play in the same spring production period each year has facilitated long-range planning on the parts of school systems and colleges.

PRC works with the University of North Carolina's graduate training program in dramatic arts in a program in which MFA candidates in acting, directing and design look to the PRC company as their model for professional practices and standards. In the third year of graduate training, selected students are invited to apprentice with the company in their area of discipline.

With strong advances in subscription sales and the use of the theatre as an educational tool, Playmakers Repertory Company has, in its five years, come to be a valuable regional resource.

Productions 1979–80
Of Mice and Men, John Steinbeck
• *Sherman, the Peacemaker,* James Reston, Jr.
Side by Side by Sondheim, music and lyrics: Stephen Sondheim, et al.; adapt: Ned Sherrin
The Gin Game, D.L. Coburn
Othello, William Shakespeare
No Time for Comedy, S.N. Behrman

Productions 1980–81
The Cocktail Party, T.S. Eliot
Mrs. Warren's Profession, George Bernard Shaw
Ghosts, Henrik Ibsen; trans: Kai Jurgensen and Robert Schenkkan

Playmakers Repertory Company. *The Cocktail Party.* Photo: Lydia Bodman.

Agnes of God, John Pielmeier
The Fourposter, Jan de Hartog
A Midsummer Night's Dream,
William Shakespeare

Directors
Peter Bennett, Tom Haas, Arthur L. Housman, David Rotenberg, Amy Saltz, Hal Scott, Errol Selsby, Stephen Willems, Tunc Yalman

Designers
Sets: McKay Coble-Randall, David M. Glenn, Gibbs Murray, Bobbi Owen, Steven Rubin, Patricia Woodbridge. *Costumes:* Holly Jenkins, Bobbi Owen, Michele Piccione, Steven Rubin, Carol Vick, Suzanne Y. Wilkins, Michael Yeuell. *Lights:* Randall J. Bailey, David M. Glenn, Allen Randall, Robert Thurston.

Playwrights' Center

Christopher Kirkland
Artistic Director

Ted Crawford
Managing Director

2301 Franklin Ave. East
Minneapolis, MN 55406
(612) 332-7481

Founded 1971
Erik Brogger, Tom Dunn, Barbara Field, Gregg Almquist

Season
Year-round

Schedule
Evenings
Friday–Sunday

Facilities
Seating capacity: 150
Stage: flexible

Finances
July 1, 1980–June 30, 1981
$262,000 operating expenses
$ 60,000 earned income
$202,000 grants/contributions

Finances
Annual attendance: 80,000

Touring contact
Ted Crawford

AEA letter of agreement

On July 17, 1981, the Playwrights' Center celebrated its 10th year of operation. Formerly known as the Playwrights' Lab, the organization has grown from serving four playwrights with a budget of $2,000 to serving well over sixty playwrights annually with a budget exceeding a quarter of a million dollars. The Center's purpose is to serve playwrights, and it does so through several programs: the Playwrights' Lab, the Midwest Playwrights' Program, the Musical Project and Storytalers.

The Playwrights' Lab awards stipends ranging from $2,800 to $5,000 to 12 playwrights annually and helps to develop scripts through a variety of readings with professional actors and directors. The Lab also offers classes developed to reach a wide range of writers and to emphasize the vital role of the playwright in the theatre. Script referral, script critiques, job and contest listings, and grant information are available, and the Lab has working relationships with theatres across the country—several hundred theatres periodically request script information.

The Midwest Playwrights' Program was established in 1976 by noted playwright Dale Wasserman, and it exists to provide a creative atmosphere and a pragmatic approach to playwriting. Ten playwrights are selected annually to participate in this two-week intensive playwriting workshop.

The Musical Project brings together composers and playwrights to create new musicals. Playwrights and composers receive financial support and access to professional actors, directors and musicians for the development of these works.

The oldest touring company in Minnesota, the Storytalers specializes in audience participation plays, workshops and residencies for children and families. Original works or adaptations are performed by the company.

The Playwrights' Center will continue to grow and expand as necessary, in its attempt to assist new American playwrights in as many ways as possible.

Productions 1979–81
Seasons strictly devoted to staged readings and non-performance workshops.

Playwrights' Center. Marie Mathey, Nancy Gormley and Cosmo White in *Cisterns.* Photo: Kevin Berigan.

Playwrights Horizons. Michael Rupert, James Kushner and Alison Fraser in *March of the Falsettos.* Photo: Susan Cook.

Playwrights Horizons

Andre Bishop
Artistic Director

Paul Daniels
Managing Director

416 West 42nd St.
New York, NY 10036
(212) 564–1235 (business)
(212) 279–4200 (box office)

Founded 1971
Robert Moss

Season
Year-round

Schedule
Evenings
Tuesday–Sunday
Matinees
Sunday

Facilities
Mainstage
Seating capacity: 150
Stage: proscenium
Studio
Seating capacity: 74
Stage: flexible

Finances
September 1, 1980–August 31, 1981
$600,000 operating expenses
$152,000 earned income
$413,000 grants/contributions

Audience
Annual attendance: 35,000
Subscribers: 1,250

Booked-in events
Theatre

AEA Off Broadway and Mini contracts

Now beginning its second decade, Playwrights Horizons continues to be dedicated to producing new American plays and to supporting new American playwrights. Through readings, workshops and full-scale productions, the theatre offers writers a professional facility in which to develop their work and refine their talent.

Playwrights Horizons has produced the work of more than 100 playwrights and its notable successes include *Gemini, Vanities, Kennedy's Children, Passione, Say Goodnight, Gracie, Uncommon Women and Others* and *Coming Attractions.* In 1978 the theatre expanded its commitment to include writers for the musical theatre, producing concerts, revues and musical plays including the premiere of *March of the Falsettos.*

In its two separate performing spaces on West 42nd Street, Playwrights Horizons has been a pioneer in the redevelopment that has transformed a block of "porno parlors" into a thriving string of Off Broadway theatres known as "Theatre Row." In its Studio theatre, the company explores the relationship between the script, the actors and the audience. The emphasis is on finding the combination of director and cast which will best illuminate the author's basic intent. The Mainstage theatre serves those playwrights whose work has developed to a point where a fully mounted production is necessary for further growth. Careful consideration is given to production elements and the play is exposed to critical review.

From 1976 to 1981, Playwrights Horizons produced a subscription season of American and European masterworks at the Queens Theatre-in-the-Park in Flushing. Beginning with the 1981–82 season, the theatre will concentrate all of its activities in Manhattan and will serve as an artistic home for a group of seven playwrights: Christopher Durang, William Finn, Albert Innaurato, James Lapine, Jonathan Reynolds, Ted Tally and Wendy Wasserstein.

Productions 1979–80
- *Justice,* Terry Curtis Fox
- *Passione,* Albert Innaurato

Oh, Coward!, music and lyrics: Noel Coward; adapt: Roderick Cook
- *Two Small Bodies,* Neal Bell
- *Time Steps,* Gus Kaikkonen

Company, book: George Furth; music and lyrics: Stephen Sondheim
Arms and the Man, George Bernard Shaw

Productions 1980–81
- *Coming Attractions,* Ted Tally
- *March of the Falsettos,* William Finn

She Loves Me, book: Joe Masteroff; music: Jerry Bock; lyrics: Sheldon Harnick
The Gentle People, Irwin Shaw
Heat of Re-Entry, Abraham Tetenbaum
Sleuth, Anthony Shaffer

Directors
Thomas Babe, Roderick Cook, Edward Cornell, Harold DeFelice, Andre Ernotte, Gerald Gutierrez, James Lapine, Robert Moss, Harold Scott, Lev Shekhtman

Designers
Sets: William M. Camp, Leo Gambacorta, David Gropman, Andrew Jackness, John Kasarda, Bil Mikulewicz, David Potts, Raymond C. Recht, Dean Reiter, Douglas Stein, Joseph A. Varga. *Costumes:* Nan Cibula, Maureen Connor, Margarita Delgado, Ann Emonts, Roberta Favant, Linda Fisher, William Ivey Long, Molly Maginnis, Karen D. Miller, Jan Morrison, Patricia Paine, Elizabeth P. Palmer, Bob Wojewodski. *Lights:* William D. Anderson, Frances Aronson, David Elliot, Paul Gallo, Robby Monk, David Segal, Jennifer Tipton, David N. Weiss, Annie Wrightson.

Portland Stage Company

Barbara Rosoff
Producing Director

Patricia Egan
Business Manager

Box 4876 DTS
Portland, ME 04112
(207) 774–1043 (business)
(207) 774–0465 (box office)

Founded 1974

Season
October–May

Schedule
Evenings
Tuesday–Sunday
Matinees
Saturday, Sunday

Facilities
15 Temple St.
Seating capacity: 155
Stage: thrust

Finances
June 1, 1980–May 31, 1981
$252,000 operating expenses
$154,000 earned income
$ 90,000 grants/contributions

Audience
Annual attendance: 20,000
Subscribers: 1,600

AEA letter of agreement

At the close of its seventh season in 1981, the Portland Stage Company completed the second phase of a four-year development program. Although institutional strengthening continued (season subscriptions doubled, total attendance grew by 54 percent) a new commitment was made to artistic growth. This part of the development program, called Theatre Alive!, resulted in two seasons of unique achievement for a small company. During the Theatre Alive! period, the PSC established an Equity contract and strengthened its policy of including challenging, probing plays in its season. It is a tribute to Portland's audiences that plays like *Ashes, After the Fall* and *Old Times* have increased their numbers.

The 1980–81 season was scheduled around the living, working playwright. Productions included a world premiere and two regional premieres, and the PSC production of Gardner McKay's *Sea Marks* went on to an Off Broadway run in New York.

In addition to its subscription season, the Portland Stage Company offers a student matinee series of its mainstage productions; both a lecture preview and curtain call discussion series; a student internship program through a local university; and adult acting classes. With a Housing and Community Development grant from the City of Portland, the company is able to offer free tickets to area low income, elderly and handicapped individuals. PSC's resident and guest artists have taken their talents into the classroom through the Maine State Commission on the Arts' Artists in Residence program.

Although its 155-seat thrust theatre exhibits the company's belief in both intimacy and audience involvement in the theatrical process, the limited seating capacity is beginning seriously to hamper the institution's economic growth. Therefore, the PSC is considering the construction or renovation of a new, larger performing space in the near future.

Productions 1979–80
The Guardsman, Ferenc Molnar
Ashes, David Rudkin
Otherwise Engaged, Simon Gray
After the Fall, Arthur Miller
Cold Storage, Ronald Ribman
A Moon for the Misbegotten, Eugene O'Neill
The Man Thoreau, company-developed

Productions 1980–81
Sorrows of Stephen, Peter Parnell
Faith Healer, Brian Friel
A Child's Christmas, company-developed
Old Times, Harold Pinter
Talley's Folly, Lanford Wilson
Island, book: Joe Bravaco and Larry Rosler; concept: Brent Nicholson; music and lyrics: Peter Link
Sea Marks, Gardner McKay

Directors
Jamie Brown, Susan Dunlop, Peter Frisch, Evadne Giannini, David A. Penhale, Patricia Riggin, John Stix, Charles Towers

Designers
Sets: Lisa Devlin, John Doepp, Ken Foy, Matthew Freedman, A. Christina Giannini, Charles Kading, Andria MacLean, G. Robinson Whitten. *Costumes:* A. Christina Giannini, Andria MacLean, Lynda L. Salsbury. *Lights:* John Doepp, Matthew Freedman, Robert Strohmeier, Steven J. Sysko, Jr., Charles Towers.

Portland Stage Company. Jan Granger, Natalie Hurst and David A. Penhale in *Old Times.* Photo: Julie Coxe.

Provisional Theatre. W. Dennis Hunt and Michael E. Dawdy in *Still Time.* Photo: John Paul.

Provisional Theatre

Collective Leadership

Cricket Parmalee
Administrative Director

1816½ North Vermont Ave.
Los Angeles, CA 90027
(213) 664–1450

Founded 1972

Season
Year-round

Finances
January 1, 1980–December 31, 1980
$284,000 operating expenses
$ 52,000 earned income
$228,000 grants/contributions

Audience
Annual attendance: 20,000

Touring contact
Cricket Parmalee

AEA LORT (B) contract

The Provisional Theatre of Los Angeles, long noted for the creation of powerful and exhilarating original theatre pieces, is primarily a touring company. Looking back on a proud 13-year history together, its artistic and administrative core has established a national reputation for warm, accessible works blending humor and music with uncompromising artistic excellence.

As a result of its past six years of extensive local, national and international travel, the theatre has gained a close rapport with a wide range of audiences composed of seasoned theatregoers and non-theatregoers alike. Outreach is central to the group's purpose, and the company strives to present live performances to audiences not traditionally served. Each year, the Provisional takes its plays and workshops into major performing arenas as well as prisons, senior citizen and community centers, churches and other centers of neighborhood activity. The goal is to speak of spirit, hope and potential in a milieu where loneliness, alienation and cynicism are becoming the accustomed routine—and ultimately to share in a popular (re)discovery of an authentic American culture.

In addition to touring, the theatre serves its Los Angeles base with performances, workshops and active community involvement. During the summer of 1980, it hosted a subscription season in downtown Los Angeles which included performances of *Inching through the Everglades*—a funny, compassionate look at ordinary people and their struggle to get by—and *Still Time,* a comical but bittersweet science fiction epic about bizarre spirits and two kidnapped "guest experts" (humans) in a mad chase to save a dying Earth.

The Provisional Theatre's current focus is an important experiment in the bringing together of two worlds: a collaboration, jointly created and performed with the internationally known bilingual Chicano theatre El Teatro de la Esperanza. This new piece, plus the Provisional's other original works, will tour nationally and internationally prior to being featured in the Provisional's 1982 home season.

Productions 1979–80
Inching through the Everglades, book: Candace Laughlin, Michael E. Dawdy and Barry Opper; music and lyrics: Peter Alsop, Steven Kent and Candace Laughlin
• *Still Time,* Candace Laughlin

Productions 1980–81
Inching through the Everglades
• *Who We Are,* company-developed

Directors
Steven Kent, Candace Laughlin

Designers
Sets: John Sefick. *Costumes:* Carlos Larranaga. *Lights:* John Sefick.

Repertorio Español

Rene Buch
Artistic Director

Gilberto Zaldivar
Producer

138 East 27th St.
New York, NY 10016
(212) 889–2850

Founded 1969
Gilberto Zaldivar, Rene Buch, Stella Holt, Frances Drucker, Marian Graham

Season
Year-round

Schedule
Evenings
Tuesday–Thursday, Sunday
Matinees
Sunday, selected weekdays

Facilities
Gramercy Arts Theatre
Seating capacity: 180
Stage: proscenium

Finances
Sept. 1, 1980–August 31, 1981
$380,000 operating expenses
$174,000 earned income
$206,000 grants/contributions

Audience
Annual attendance: 60,000

Touring contact
Gilberto Zaldivar

Booked-in events
Theatre, dance, music

Repertorio Español produces plays in Spanish for a rapidly growing multinational Hispanic community in New York City. The company is pleased to have introduced contemporary Latin American playwrights to American audiences and to have produced rarely seen works of Spanish masters including Calderon, Lorca and de Rojas.

Since its establishment in 1968, Repertorio Español has broadened significantly the scope of its operations to include a year-round cycle of plays at the Gramercy Arts Theatre; puppet theatre for children; and local, national and international tours. Of special interest to the company has been its effort to expose students at every level to Hispanic theatre as a supplement to their classroom studies.

In recent years, the growing recognition of the Repertorio as an artistic force in the Hispanic community has caused a marked increase in its audiences. Through the New York and touring programs, the company's reputation has grown even further in the United States and throughout the Spanish-speaking world. In 1980, Repertorio Español was seen by more than 75,000 people in New York, nationally and on a tour to Latin America under the auspices of the United States International Communication Agency.

The goals of the Repertorio are: to achieve high artistic standards through its work as a resident company dedicated to developing its art; to unify the Hispanic community through the medium of theatre; and to provide opportunities for cultural exchange between English- and Spanish-speaking Americans, as well as between the United States and Spanish-speaking countries.

Productions 1979–80
- *La Celestina,* Fernandos de Rojas
  Tango Para Tres, Diana Raznovich
- *La Casa de Bernarda Alba,* Federico Garcia Lorca
  Te Juro Que Tengo Ganas, Emilio Carballido
- *Mundo de Cristal,* Tennessee Williams; adapt: Rene Buch

Productions 1980–81
- *Los Fantastikos,* book and lyrics: Tom Jones; music: Harvey Schmidt; trans: Rene Buch
  Mundo de Cristal
  La Celestina
  La Casa de Bernarda Alba
- *Toda Desnudez Sera Castigada,* Nelson Rodrigues
- *La Vida es Sueño,* Pedro Calderon de la Barca
- *La Corte de Faraon,* book and lyrics: Guillermo Perrin and Miguel de Palacios; music: Vicente Lleo

Directors
Rene Buch, Delfor Peralta

Designers
Sets: Robert Weber Federico. *Costumes:* Maria Ferreira Contessa, Robert Weber Federico, Boamerses Rubio. *Lights:* Robert Weber Federico.

Media resources
Video: *La Celestina* (El Salvador Educational Television and Peru Educational Television).

Repertorio Español. Juan Troya, Ofelia Gonzales and Vivian Deangelo in *Toda Desnudez Sera Castigada.* Photo: Gerry Goodstein.

Repertory Theatre of St. Louis (formerly Loretto-Hilton Repertory Theatre)

Wallace Chappell
Artistic Director

Box 28030
St. Louis, MO 63119
(314) 968–7340 (business)
(314) 968–4925 (box office)

Founded 1966
Webster College

Season
September–April

Schedule
Evenings
Tuesday–Sunday
Matinees
Wednesday, Saturday, Sunday

Facilities
130 Edgar Road
Mainstage
Seating capacity: 500–900
Stage: thrust
Studio
Seating capacity: 92–145
Stage: flexible

Finances
June 1, 1980–May 31, 1981
$1,700,000 operating expenses
$1,000,000 earned income
$ 700,000 grants/contributions

Audience
Annual attendance: 205,000
Subscribers: 15,500

Touring contact
Kim Bozark

Booked-in events
Theatre

AEA LORT (B) contract

The Repertory Theatre of St. Louis is devoted to the full range of theatrical endeavor: classics of all periods as well as contemporary statements of the nascent author. It is an arena in which new processes, training methods and explorations of the theatrical medium are sought and encouraged. The 700-seat thrust Mainstage and its companion Studio Theatre (150 seats in variable configuration) will often

Repertory Theatre of St. Louis. Jonathan Gillard and Susan Maloy Wall in *American Soap.* Photo: Michael Eastman.

be used "piggyback"—to complement each other or to reinforce the work of the theatre as a whole: for example, *The Threepenny Opera* might play on the Mainstage while *Brecht on Brecht* appears in the Studio.

The theatre also offers a variety of services through its Imaginary Theatre Company, an outreach group that has developed distinctive works through its performances at schools, community centers and for senior citizens groups.

The Repertory Theatre of St. Louis is dedicated to producing outstanding theatre, and to advancing the state of the art.

Productions 1979–80

- • *Crimes of the Heart,* Beth Henley
- • *A Christmas Carol,* adapt: Addie Walsh, from Charles Dickens
- • *Put Them All Together,* Anne Commire
- *A View From the Bridge,* Arthur Miller
- *The Servant of Two Masters,* Carlo Goldoni; trans: Joseph Schraibman
- *Sizwe Bansi Is Dead,* Athol Fugard, John Kani and Winston Ntshona
- • *Father Dreams,* Mary Gallagher

Productions, 1980–81

- • *Eve,* Larry Fineberg
- • *Sweet Prince,* A.E. Hotchner
- *The Island,* Athol Fugard, John Kani and Winston Ntshona
- *A Christmas Carol*
- • *Happy Ending,* Dennis de Brito
- • *American Soap,* Ron Mark
- *Richard III,* William Shakespeare
- *Talley's Folly,* Lanford Wilson
- *A Life in the Theatre,* David Mamet

Directors

Craig Anderson, Wallace Chappell, David Frank, Jim O'Connor, Michael Pitek III, Geoffrey Sherman, Clyde Ventura, R. Stuart White, Steven Woolf

Designers

Sets: Jim Bakkom, Karen Connolly, Christopher Harris, Tim Jozwick, Judie Juracek, John Roslevich, Jr., Carolyn L. Ross, Steven Rubin, John Scheffler. *Costumes:* Judie Juracek, Dorothy L. Marshall, Catherine B. Reich, Carolyn L. Ross, Jeffrey Ross Struckman, John Carver Sullivan, Alison Todd, Bill Walker. *Lights:* Glenn Dunn, Beverly Emmons, Gilbert V. Hemsley, Jr., Jeff Muskovin, Steven G. Rosen, Peter E. Sargent, Max De Volder.

The Ridiculous Theatrical Company

Charles Ludlam
Artistic Director

Christopher Scott
Executive Director

One Sheridan Square
New York, NY 10014
(212) 741–9736, 255–9094 (business)
(212) 260–7137 (box office)

Founded 1967
Charles Ludlam, Black-Eyed Susan, Bill Vehr, Lola Pashalinski, John Brockmeyer, Christopher Scott

Season
Year-round

Schedule
Evenings
Thursday–Sunday

Facilities
Seating capacity: 155
Stage: thrust

Finances
July 1, 1980–June 30, 1981
\$210,000 operating expenses
\$143,000 earned income
\$ 60,000 grants/contributions

Audience
Annual attendance: 18,000

Touring contact
Steven Samuels

The Ridiculous Theatrical Company is a permanent ensemble which, under the artistic direction of Charles Ludlam, has produced and maintained a repertoire of 20 innovative comic dramas over the past 14 years. In addition, the company maintains a children's theatre program which includes *Professor Bedlam's Educational Punch and Judy Show, The Enchanted Pig* and an adaptation of Charles Dickens' *A Christmas Carol.* Company members have received a total of six Obie awards for acting, design, distinguished achievement, and for puppet theatre.

Over the years, the company has been concerned primarily with re-evaluating the theatrical inventions of comic intent. Their plays are modernist works of parody, burlesque, travesty and farce, from the mock-heroic to the wittily paradoxical. Ludlam has created a body of work that gives credibility to the genre known as "theatre of the ridiculous," and "Ludlamization" has become a standard critical term to describe a distinctive comic approach to serious work.

During the 1979–80 and 1980–81 seasons, the company produced four new plays, as well as a new production of Ludlam's 1967 epic, *Conquest of the Universe, or When Queens Collide,* and revivals of *Camille, Bluebeard* and *Stage Blood.* The company is presently raising funds to continue renovation of its theatre in Greenwich Village.

Productions 1979–80

- • *The Enchanted Pig*
- *Conquest of the Universe, or When Queens Collide*
- • *A Christmas Carol,* adapted from Charles Dickens
- *Stage Blood*
- *Bluebeard*
- *Camille*

Productions 1980–81

- • *Reverse Psychology*
- *A Christmas Carol*
- • *Love's Tangled Web*

All productions are created by Charles Ludlam.

Directors
Charles Ludlam

Designers
Sets: Bobjack Callejo, Richard Hennessy, Charles Ludlam. *Costumes:* Gabriel Berry, Arthur Brady, Mary Brecht, Everett Quinton. *Lights:* Richard Currie, Lawrence Eichler.

Media resources
Film: *The Sorrows of Dolores* (company-produced).

The Ridiculous Theatrical Company. Bill Vehr, Black-Eyed Susan, Charlotte Forbes and Charles Ludlam in *Reverse Psychology.* Photo: John Ramsay Thomas.

The Road Company

Robert H. Leonard
Producing Director

R. Raymond Moore
General Manager

Box 5278 EKS
Johnson City, TN 37601
(615) 926–7726

Founded 1975
Robert H. Leonard

Season
November, February–March (resident)
Year-round (touring)

Schedule
Evenings
Friday–Saturday
Matinees
Sunday

Finances
July 1, 1980–June 30, 1981
$165,000 operating expenses
$ 37,000 earned income
$113,000 grants/contributions

Audience
Annual attendance: 9,000

Touring contact
William G. Dunham

The Road Company is a touring theatre performing in northeastern Tennessee and the Southeast. To date, the company has created all of its own works using improvisational techniques and collaboration between the acting company and a resident playwright. The theatre is predicated on the creative potential of an acting ensemble working together as a community, with scripted material added to complement the repertoire of company-developed work. The rigorous discipline that scripted work demands is viewed as a necessary balance to the different talents and skills called for in improvisation.

The 1981–82 season initiates the company's first resident subscription series, with a set of three plays presented in the tri-city area where the theatre is based: Johnson City and Kingsport, Tennessee, and Bristol, Virginia. The southeastern touring season will be maintained, and an in-school workshop series with a strong faculty/artist bond will parallel the performance schedule and assure educators of access to Road Company resources.

Guest directors and/or playwrights are implemented to broaden the actor's exposure to a variety of approaches, as well as to provide the artistic director time to work with other companies in other environments. "Exchange" residencies are sought to provide additional cross-fertilization, and the company welcomes opportunities for its members to create works individually or to work on projects outside the company.

Eventually, The Road Company expects to locate a single "home" playhouse for its subscription season and to serve as a year-round site for visiting artists from across the country. This step would allow the company to

The Road Company. Christine Murdock and Tupper Cullum in *Horsepower—An Electric Fable.* Photo: R. Raymond Moore.

respond to the region's rapidly growing population (over 500,000) and expanding economy by providing the only such facility in a 100-mile radius of Johnson City.

As The Road Company strengthens its ties with other theatres in the Southeast and builds a supporting home audience, it also encourages interchange with groups working in similar disciplines but separated by hundreds—or even thousands—of miles.

Productions 1979–80
- *Mountain Whispers,* company-developed with Sonny Morris and Tommy Bledsoe
- *The Flying Lemon Circus,* company-developed
- *Horsepower—An Electric Fable,* company-developed with Jo Carson

Productions 1980–81
Horsepower—An Electric Fable
- *Little Chicago,* company-developed with Jo Carson; music: Richard Blaustein

The Flying Lemon Circus

Directors
Robert H. Leonard

Designers
Sets: Richard Cannon, Kathie deNobriga, Lucinda Flodin, Kelly R. Hill, Jr. *Costumes:* Sally Carlson, Lucinda Flodin. *Lights:* Robert H. Leonard.

Roadside Theater

Dudley Cocke
Producing Director

Donna Porterfield
Managing Director

Box 743
Whitesburg, KY 41858
(606) 633-9813

Founded 1974
Don Baker

Season
Year-round touring

Finances
January 1, 1980–December 31, 1980
$103,000 operating expenses
$ 26,000 earned income
$155,000 grants/contributions

Audience
Annual attendance: 24,000

Touring contact
Donna Porterfield

Roadside Theater was formed in 1974 as a reorganization of the Appalachian Actors Workshop. Unlike its predecessor, Roadside's purpose was not only to provide a theatre in the mountains, but to determine what *kind* of theatre made sense for the Southern Appalachian area—and then to implement that theatre. Roadside knew that conventional theatre seldom reached the back hollows, farm communities and mining camps which make up so much of the region, and that when it did, it made little impression. Nevertheless, Roadside felt that there was a strong theatrical heritage in the area's church services, music and storytelling—a heritage that was being eroded and forgotten.

Roadside began telling traditional Appalachian tales that its members had heard while growing up; tales that were unique to Southern Appalachia. The actors told them together, batting lines back and forth, speaking some phrases in unison and responding to mutual rhythms, all the while remembering that each

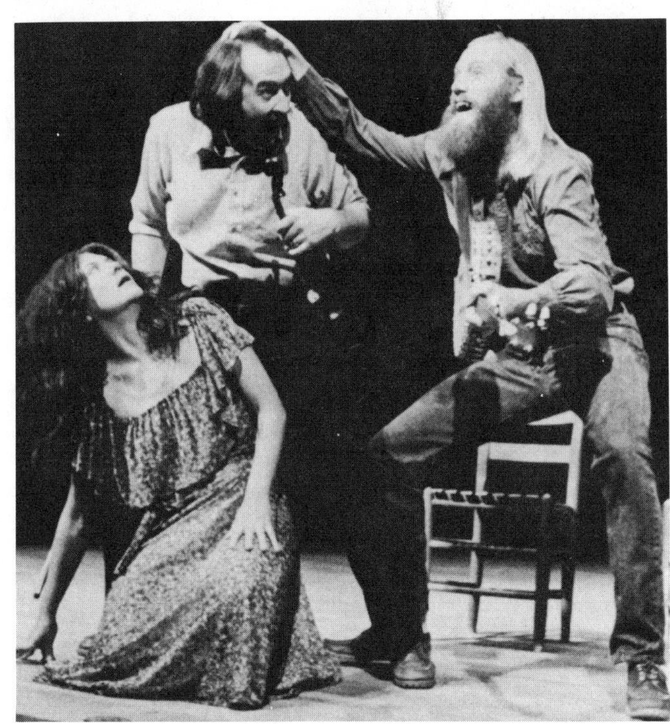

Roadside Theater. Angelyn DeBord, Ron Short and Tom Bledsoe in *Brother Jack.* Photo: Tim Cox.

was an *individual* telling a part of a story. The company was simply taking a language, a subject and a style common to the mountain people, and adapting it for three, four or five tellers, thus increasing the dramatic possibilities without losing the intimacy of storytelling.

Having first developed its style, Roadside has gone on to script and produce all of its own material, train two touring companies, find innovative ways to reach rural audiences, and to tour nationally, including several runs Off Broadway.

Roadside feels that its "homegrown" theatre is important because it teaches children and adults about the culture and history of their region, serves as a medium for exchange and continuing enrichment of the area's traditions, and acts as a lens through which audiences from within and outside the region can focus on human drama. It continually reminds its audiences that the conflicts, the defeats and the yearnings of the Appalachian people are of no less consequence than those of others in other places.

Productions 1979–80
Grandfather Tales, company-developed
Red Fox/Second Hangin', Don Baker and Dudley Cocke

Productions 1980–81
Mountain Tales, company-developed
Brother Jack, Don Baker and Ron Short

Directors
Don Baker, Dudley Cocke, Ron Short

Designers
Lights: Don Baker, Donna Porterfield.

Media resources
Radio: *Mountain Tales, Red Fox/Second Hangin'* (company-produced).

Roundabout Theatre Company. Giulia Pagano, Remak Ramsay and Ralph Clanton in *The Winslow Boy.* Photo: Martha Swope.

Roundabout Theatre Company

Gene Feist
Michael Fried
Producing Directors

333 West 23rd St.
New York, NY 10011
(212) 924–7160 (business)
(212) 242–7800 (box office)

Founded 1965
Gene Feist and Michael Fried

Season
September–August

Schedule
Evenings
Tuesday–Saturday
Matinees
Wednesday, Saturday, Sunday

Facilities
Roundabout Stage One
Seating capacity: 350
Stage: proscenium
Roundabout Stage Two
307 West 26th St.
Seating capacity: 150
Stage: thrust

Finances
July 1, 1980–June 30, 1981
$1,900,000 operating expenses
$1,600,000 earned income
$ 250,000 grants/contributions

Audience
Annual attendance: 265,000
Subscribers: 22,000

AEA LORT (C) and (D) contracts

The Roundabout Theatre Company is deeply committed to the notion that theatre is an important artistic and social force that should be experienced by all people regardless of social, educational or economic background. Theatre, in the Roundabout's view, can be the mirror which reflects our experiences and culture.

Roundabout's repertoire is eclectic, composed of both classical and contemporary works from the living library of world drama. Roundabout considers itself a home for "lost" plays, often rediscovering a neglected or rarely produced masterpiece with a dramatic voice worthy of being heard by a new generation of audiences. While Roundabout does not literally operate as a repertory theatre, a company, or perhaps more accurately a "family" of artists, is developing a sustained body of work. Increasingly, actors, directors and designers return to the Roundabout for play after play, even from one season to the next.

Believing that theatre and the arts should be affordable and accessible to all, Roundabout maintains a wide scope of community service programs, working with 500 senior citizens' institutions in a tristate area and making its programs available for free or at a nominal charge. In addition, the company works with hundreds of community organizations, hospitals, YMCAs and settlement houses. It has created a Union Ticket Program for union members, retirees and their families, and a Corporate Ticket Program for both blue- and white-collar employees. The theatre has also developed a wide range of educational programs, working in city schools, developing internships with high schools and universities, and making it possible for tens of thousands of students to attend performances.

Productions 1979–80

- *Diversions and Delights,* John Gay
- *Letters of Love and Affection,* adapt: Irene Worth

The Dark at the Top of the Stairs, William Inge
A Month in the Country, Ivan Turgenev
The Blood Knot, Athol Fugard
Heartbreak House, George Bernard Shaw
Fallen Angels, Noel Coward
Look Back in Anger, John Osborne

Productions 1980–81

Look Back in Anger
Streetsongs, adapt: Geraldine Fitzgerald
Here Are Ladies, adapt: Siobhan McKenna
The Winslow Boy, Terence Rattigan
Don Juan in Hell, George Bernard Shaw
Inadmissible Evidence, John Osborne
A Taste of Honey, Shelagh Delaney
Hedda Gabler, Henrik Ibsen; trans; Christopher Hampton
Misalliance, George Bernard Shaw

Directors

Ted Craig, Joseph Hardy, Stephen Hollis, Michael Kahn, George Keathley, Siobhan McKenna, Richard Maltby Jr., Anthony Page, Stephen Porter, Douglas Seale, Suzanne Shepherd, John Stix, Tony Tanner

Designers

Sets: Reagan Cook, Philipp Jung, Lawrence King, Roger Mooney, Michael Yeargan. *Costumes:* Shelly Friedman, A. Christina Giannini, Jane Greenwood, Jim Lowe, Andrew B. Marlay, Mimi Maxmen, Noel Taylor, Bill Walker. *Lights:* Norman Coates, Todd Elmer, Arden Fingerhut, Jason Kantrowitz, Robert W. Mogel, Dennis Parichy, Robert F. Strohmeier.

Media resources

Video: *Look Back in Anger* (Showtime).

Round House Theatre

Jeffrey B. Davis
Artistic Director

Eliot Pfanstiehl
Arts Coordinator

12210 Bushey Drive
Silver Spring, MD 20902
(301) 468–4172 (business)
(301) 468–4234 (box office)

Founded 1978
Montgomery County Government

Season
October–May

Schedule
Evenings
Wednesday–Saturday
Matinees
Sunday

Facilities
Seating capacity: 218
Stage: modified thrust

Finances
July 1, 1980–June 30, 1981
$374,000 operating expenses
$192,000 earned income
$182,000 grants/contributions

Audience
Annual attendance: 68,000
Subscribers: 2,380

Touring contact
Vicki Arnold

Booked-in events
Children's theatre

Guest Artist contract

The Round House Theatre is a professional resident company founded and supported by Maryland's Montgomery County Department of Recreation. Located on the outskirts of Washington, DC, the theatre is a pioneer in the modern concept of encouraging actors, directors, designers and staff to live and work in a community setting. Staff members share their talents with citizens through tours and workshops, as well as multidisciplinary classes for all ages; technical support for local arts groups; and coordinated programming with the school system and local municipalities.

The Round House Theatre is committed to the artistic growth of its resident company, with plays chosen to enhance that growth. In this way, the Round House also treats its 2,380 subscribers to a wide spectrum of theatre. Since 1978, it has produced classics, new scripts, original mime compositions, adaptations and dance concerts. The company also operates a children's theatre program of both resident and touring productions.

Round House Theatre. Jerry Whiddon, Betty Clark and Thomas Schall in *The Threepenny Opera.* Photo: Brian Eggleston.

The most significant growth of Round House artists results from their constant interaction with the community. Company members also teach classes for children and adults, finding that their talents flourish in an environment where they can transmit skills as they are acquired—where growth is immediately shared. Students profit not only from their classroom experiences but from the opportunity to observe their teachers in performance during the Round House season.

By bringing artists, community and government together, the Round House Theatre is emerging as a new model for arts development in a contemporary American community.

Productions 1979–80

The Importance of Being Earnest, Oscar Wilde
Angel Street, Patrick Hamilton
• *Goodly Creatures,* William Gibson
The Glass Menagerie, Tennessee Williams
• *Robin Hood,* conceived: Mark Jaster; music: Christopher Patton
Twelfth Night, William Shakespeare
• *Fables,* music: Christopher Patton
• *Pierrot,* conceived: Mark Jaster and Gayle Behrman
• *Mime by Two,* conceived: Mark Jaster and Gayle Behrman

Productions 1980–81

The Birds, Aristophanes; adapt: Walter Kerr; music and lyrics: Alex Rybeck and Christopher Patton
The Belle of Amherst, William Luce
The Lady's Not for Burning, Christopher Fry
Veronica's Room, Ira Levin
Out of Our Fathers' House, Eve Merriam
The Zoo Story, Edward Albee
Krapp's Last Tape, Samuel Beckett
• *Love Song without Words,* conceived: Mark Jaster; music: Christopher Patton
Luv, Murray Schisgal
Slow Dance on the Killing Ground, William Hanley
The Threepenny Opera, book and lyrics: Bertolt Brecht; music: Kurt Weill
• *Canterbury Tales,* adapt: Richard Averbuch and Christopher Patton; music: Christopher Patton
• *Pepperoni,* conceived: Mark Jaster and Gayle Behrman
• *Mime to Mime,* conceived: Mark Jaster and Gayle Behrman

Directors

June Allen, Douglas Cumming, Jeffrey B. Davis, Mark Jaster, John Edwards, William Hanley, John Neville-Andrews, Susan Anthony Proctor

Designers

Sets: Douglas A. Cumming, John Gabbert, Christopher R. Insley, Steven Siegel, Richard A. Young. *Costumes:* Leslie-Marie Cocuzzo, Pamela MacFarlane, Jeffrey Ullman. *Lights:* Douglas A. Cumming, John Gabbert, Barbara Locke, James J. Taylor, Daniel Wagner, Richard Young.

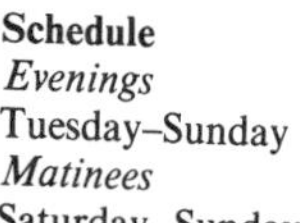

St. Nicholas Theater Company

Cynthia Sherman
Artistic Director

Bill Conner
Managing Director

2851 North Halsted St.
Chicago, IL 60657
(312) 975-2320 (business)
(312) 975-2300 (box office)

Founded 1974
David Mamet, Steven Schacter, William H. Macy, Patricia Cox

Season
September–June

Schedule
Evenings
Tuesday–Sunday
Matinees
Saturday, Sunday

Facilities
Seating capacity: 183
Stage: thrust

Finances
August 1, 1980–July 31, 1981
$626,000 operating expenses
$280,000 earned income
$356,000 grants/contributions

Audience
Annual attendance: 65,000
Subscribers: 4,860

Booked-in events
Music, theatre

AEA letter of agreement

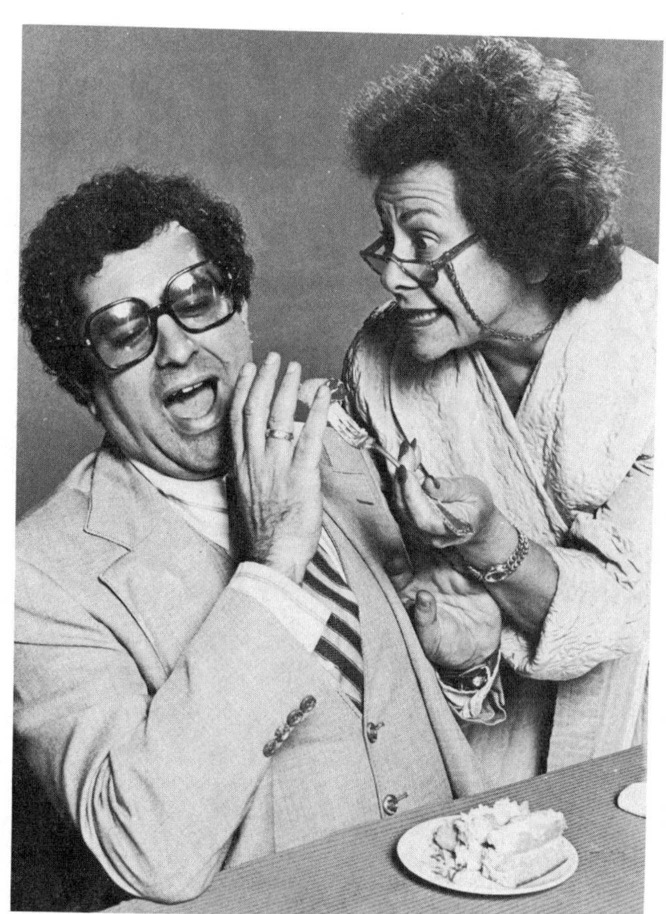

St. Nicholas Theater. Bernard Beck and Patti Wilkus in *Table Settings.* Photo: Dan Rest.

The St. Nicholas Theater Company is dedicated to productions that are innovative, predominantly new and essentially important to the artists who perform and produce them. The theatre focuses on the development and encouragement of a group of artistic associates—individual artists invited to participate as company members on an ongoing but part-time basis. These individuals are selected because of their willingness to participate in activities that will help them grow as artists, as well as for their active commitment to the vision of the St. Nicholas.

The extraordinary excitement and electricity theatre can generate in an audience is a direct result of the participating artists' deep understanding of and connection to the art they present. Immersing actors, directors and designers in the creative and production processes—training and encouraging them to assume direct responsibility for a work's creative life—produces vibrant theatre with motivation and significance. The theatrical form is constantly changing, but the theatre's philosophy remains constant.

By remaining open to artists with varying approaches and to a variety of dramatic literature, the St. Nicholas insures that its seasons will display a wide view of the world and will appeal to a diverse audience, which will remain alert and fluid in its expectations and responses. The St. Nicholas is committed to a theatre that does not depend on the vision and creativity of a single individual and that can continue on the courage and convictions of any and all of its participants.

Productions 1979–80

The Primary English Class, Israel Horovitz
The Diary of Anne Frank, Frances Goodrich and Albert Hackett
• *Enchanted Cottage,* Percy Granger
Character Lines, Larry Ketron
A Shadow of Heroes, Robert Audrey
Celimare, The Good Friend, Eugene Labiche
• *La Gache,* Richard Harris
Another Part of the Forest, Lillian Hellman
Father's Day, Oliver Hailey

Productions 1980–81

Table Settings, James Lapine
Teeth 'n' Smiles, David Hare
• *The Prince, the Dwarf and the Blacksmith's Daughter,* adapt: Tom Mula, from John Gardner; music: Les Stahl
A Sorrow Beyond Dreams, Peter Handke; trans: Ralph Manheim
Nasty Rumors and Final Remarks, Susan Miller
Living at Home, Anthony Giardina
Hooters, Ted Tally

Directors

Bruce Burgun, Betsy Carpenter, Robert Falls, Catherine Goedert, Gerald Gutierrez, Lois Hall, Jan Holby, James Lapine, Tom Mula, Elinor Renfield, Amy Saltz, Steven Schacter, Steve Scott, James Wise

Designers

Sets: Gary Baugh, Jeremy Conway, David Emmons, Joseph Nimenski, David Potts, Barry Robinson. *Costumes:* Kate Berg, Cookie Gluck, Jessica Hahn, Doug Koertge, Juli Nagel, Barry Robinson, Jordan Ross. *Lights:* Robert Christen, Gary Heitz, Dan Kobayashi, Michael Philippi, Rita Pietrazek.

San Diego Repertory Theatre

Sam Woodhouse
Douglas Jacobs
Artistic Directors

Roberta Liszcz Bentz
General Manager

1620 Sixth Ave.
San Diego, CA 92101
(714) 231–3585

Founded 1976
Sam Woodhouse, Douglas Jacobs

Season
January–November

Schedule
Evenings
Tuesday–Sunday
Matinees
Sunday

Facilities
Seating capacity: 212
Stage: modified thrust

Finances
July 1, 1980–June 30, 1981
$251,000 operating expenses
$156,000 earned income
$ 94,000 grants/contributions

Audience
Annual attendance: 40,000
Subscribers: 2,750

Booked-in events
Theatre, dance, music

AEA Guest Artist contract

The San Diego Repertory Theatre is an eclectic and ongoing group of directors, designers, actors and administrators dedicated to bringing to San Diego the best of the contemporary currents in theatre through the production of innovative and often controversial plays not seen previously by local audiences, as well as the revitalization of seldom-seen classics.

Brought into being by a group of artists working in the city's open-air theatres, the San Diego Rep coalesced into a year-round nonprofit repertory company that has since presented over 700 performances of 70 plays and has earned a reputation for outstanding theatre. In the last several years, it has made quantum leaps toward its primary goal of becoming a fully professional Equity theatre.

On June 23, 1977, the Rep became the first local theatre in over a decade to establish its own playhouse. With the help of volunteers, St. Cecelia's Chapel was transformed into an intimate, Spanish-style playhouse complete with stained glass windows. From then on, the company was no

San Diego Repertory Theatre.
Working. Photo: Peter Robinson.

longer a "street theatre."

In its effort to bring innovative theatre to San Diego, the Rep has produced the local premieres of such playwrights as Sam Shepard, David Mamet, Eve Merriam, Marsha Norman and Arthur Kopit. The Rep's revivals of classics have included plays by Moliere, Henry Fielding and George Bernard Shaw, and its original adaptations include an annual production of *A Christmas Carol* adapted by artistic director Douglas Jacobs.

A grant to research San Diego history and create five one-act plays resulted in a play series called "San Diego on Stage," and it was performed free of charge for over 10,000 students, senior citizens, community groups and hospital patients throughout the country. Subsequent company-developed works have been awarded touring grants by the California Arts Council. Such programs have enabled the Rep to extend its work beyond the theatre and even outside the community.

Productions 1979–80
Private Lives, Noel Coward
• *Gold!,* company-developed with Sam Woodhouse and Douglas Jacobs
Curse of the Starving Class, Sam Shepard
Ladyhouse Blues, Kevin O'Morrison
Bleacher Bums, Organic Theater Company
Tartuffe, Moliere
The Club, Eve Merriam
• *A Christmas Carol,* adapt: Douglas Jacobs, from Charles Dickens
Hay Fever, Noel Coward
Getting Out, Marsha Norman
Of Mice and Men, John Steinbeck
Wings, Arthur Kopit

Productions 1980–81
What the Butler Saw, Joe Orton
Androcles and the Lion, George Bernard Shaw
• *The Lady Cries Murder,* John William See
Bonjour, là, Bonjour, Michel Tremblay; trans: John Van Burek and Bill Glassco
A Christmas Carol
Working, book: Stephen Schwartz and Nina Faso, from Studs Terkel; music and lyrics: Stephen Schwartz, et al.
The Petrified Forest, Robert Sherwood
The School for Wives, Moliere; trans: Richard Wilbur
• *Mother Courage and Her Children,* Bertolt Brecht; adapt: Robert Potter
Talley's Folly, Lanford Wilson
Funeral March for a One-Man Band, book: Ron Whyte; music: Mel Marvin; lyrics: Robert Satuloff
The Elephant Man, Bernard Pomerance

Directors
Michael Addison, Douglas Jacobs, Peter Robinson, Tavis Ross, Will E. Simpson, Sam Woodhouse

Designers
Sets: Robert Earl, Robert Green, Charles McCall, Ron Ranson. *Costumes:* Deb Dryden, Tim O'Neil, Margaret Perry, Sally R. Thomas, Terri Tubbs. *Lights:* Lee Sterling Jaffe, Joseph Naftel, Willa Mann Day.

Seattle Repertory Theatre

Daniel Sullivan
Artistic Director

Peter Donnelly
Producing Director

Box B
Queen Anne Station
Seattle, WA 98109
(206) 447–4730 (business)
(206) 447–4764 (box office)

Founded 1963

Season
October–May

Schedule
Evenings
Tuesday–Sunday
Matinees
Wednesday, Saturday, Sunday

Facilities
Seattle Center Playhouse
225 Mercer St.
Seating capacity: 894
Stage: proscenium

Finances
July 1, 1980–June 30, 1981
$2,146,000 operating expenses
$1,640,000 earned income
$ 552,000 grants/contributions

Audience
Annual attendance: 206,230
Subscribers: 21,000

AEA LORT (B) and Theatre for Young Audiences contracts

The Seattle Repertory Theatre was founded in 1963 as an outgrowth of the Seattle World's Fair, which

Seattle Repertory Theatre. Louis Turenne, Roberta Maxwell and John de Lancie in *Saint Joan.* Photo: Greg Gilbert.

provided the city a legacy of performing arts and recreation buildings including the Seattle Center Playhouse, the 890-seat facility which is the theatre's present home.

An integral part of the Northwest cultural scene, the Seattle Rep is the largest theatre in the region, with a mainstage season of six plays blending contemporary and classic works. Most major playwrights have been presented at the Rep, and the mainstage schedule includes premieres of new works as well.

Since the 1979–80 season, the Rep has operated with a shared artistic directorate: consulting artistic director John Hirsch, and resident director Daniel Sullivan. Following Hirsch's departure at the end of the 1980–81 season to head Canada's Stratford Festival, Sullivan assumes command of the theatre's artistic policies, with the support of associate artistic director Robert Egan. Peter Donnelly remains as producing director, a post he has held for 12 years.

During the tenure of Hirsch and Sullivan, the activities of the theatre greatly expanded, encompassing a variety of community outreach programs. A New Plays in Process Project was established, with three new plays presented the first season and five the second. Just one of the activities of the Rep's "Other Season," the New Plays in Process Project includes script-in-hand public performances of plays by new and emerging playwrights. Regional conferences for writers and directors, pre- and post-performance discussions and lectures, signed performances for the hearing impaired, and Sunday afternoon literary cabarets are all part of the theatre's regular programming and have been enthusiastically received by the community.

The Seattle Repertory Theatre also tours the Pacific Northwest, traveling as far east as Montana and as far south as Salt Lake City, offering half-week and week-long residencies to sponsoring communities.

On June 9, 1981, the Rep and the City of Seattle unveiled the model for the new Bagley Wright Theatre, named for its founding president and scheduled for completion during the 1982–83 season. This new home for the Rep, located adjacent to its current building, will bring all of the Rep's shops and offices together under one roof.

Productions 1979–80

Saint Joan, George Bernard Shaw
A History of the American Film, Christopher Durang
An Enemy of the People, Henrik Ibsen; adapt: Arthur Miller
The Taming of the Shrew, William Shakespeare
Spokesong, Stewart Parker
Pal Joey, book: John O'Hara; music: Richard Rodgers; lyrics: Lorenz Hart

Productions 1980–81

Strider: The Story of a Horse, book: Mark Rozovsky; lyrics: Uri Riashentsev and Steve Brown; adapt: Robert Kalfin and Steve Brown; music: Mark Rozovsky, S. Vetkin and Norman L. Berman
The Grand Hunt, Gyula Hernady; adapt: Suzanne Grossman
Ah, Wilderness!, Eugene O'Neill
Born Yesterday, Garson Kanin
The Dance of Death, August Strindberg; adapt: Suzanne Grossman
Tintypes, music and lyrics: various; adapt: Mary Kyte, Mel Marvin and Gary Pearle

Directors

Timothy Bond, Richard Gershman, Judith Haskell, John Hirsch, Daniel Sullivan, M. Burke Walker

Designers

Sets: Richard Belcher, Bob Blackman, Robert Dalstrom, Ralph Funicello, James Leonard Joy, Jim Newton, Cameron Porteous. *Costumes:* Bob Blackman, Laura Crow, Robert Dahlstrom, Andrew R. Marlay, Cameron Porteous, Tom Rasmussen, Carrie F. Robbins. *Lights:* Robert Dahlstrom, Jeffrey Dallas, Richard Devin, F. Dana Mitchell, Robby Monk, David F. Segal, Robert Scales.

Soho Repertory Theatre. *The Cannibals.* Photo: Sally Sherwood.

Soho Repertory Theatre

Jerry Engelbach
Marlene Swartz
Artistic Directors

19 Mercer St.
New York, NY 10013
(212) 925–2588

Founded 1975
Jerry Engelbach, Marlene Swartz

Season
September–June

Schedule
Evenings
Thursday–Sunday
Matinees
Sunday

Facilities
Seating capacity: 90
Stage: thrust

Finances
July 1, 1980–June 30, 1981
$57,000 operating expenses
$37,000 earned income
$21,000 grants/contributions

Audience
Annual attendance: 9,000
Subscribers: 800

AEA Nonprofit Theatre code

Soho Repertory Theatre produces lesser-known plays by established authors and works by promising new writers. Emphasis is placed on distinctive plays tthe public may have heard of but rarely has a chance to see, and on outstanding, unconventional original plays. The theatre is dedicated to work that is intellectually challenging, but that is first and foremost highly theatrical. The lively, three-dimensional aspect of theatre is stressed through the use of a thrust stage close to the audience.

Over the past six seasons, some 80 productions have included many classic and modern revivals, a handful of original plays, and works by unlikely playwrights such as Gertrude Stein, Gunter Grass and Pablo Picasso. About a dozen productions (other than the company's original plays) have been New York premieres, including Aristophanes' 2,000-year-old *The Congresswomen,* Cocteau's *The Knights of the Round Table,* Ghelderode's *Miss Jairus,* J.P. Donleavy's *Fairy Tales of New York* and Rod Serling's *Requiem for a Heavyweight.* In the last two seasons, the theatre has featured a number of mixed media pieces and musicals, an indication of its growing interest in alternative forms of theatre.

A staged reading series called "First Look" was instituted during 1980–81, as a forum for new works and adaptations of, or new approaches to, older works. The first offerings included four plays, two adaptations of novels, a mixed media piece and a musical. Limited initially to an audience of Soho Rep subscribers, the series will be open to the public in future seasons.

Soho Rep has temporarily set aside its goal of building a permanent repertory company. In the current economic climate, the theatre has cut back on full productions and substituted less costly, though aesthetically no less valuable, workshops and readings. Opportunities once available for emerging theatre artists have decreased—over 700 people worked at Soho Rep during its first six seasons—but the theatre remains among the two or three Off-Off Broadway leaders in developing subscription and ticket-voucher audiences. This continuing audience interest, and the artistic success of the 1980–81 season which resulted in five Villager Theatre Awards, may enable Soho Rep eventually to return to its goal of creating a permanent acting company.

Productions 1979–80

The Insect Comedy, Josef and Karel Capek
The Cannibals, George Tabori; music: Lois Britten
The Barber of Seville, Beaumarchais; trans: Albert Bermel; music: Jim Ragland
We Have Always Lived in the Castle, Hugh Wheeler
Twelfth Night, William Shakespeare; music: Gwyl O'Dell
The Second Man, S.N. Behrman
• *Feathertop,* adapt: Trueman Kelley, from Nathaniel Hawthorne
The Ugly Duckling, A.A. Milne
Brewsie and Willie, adapt: Ellen Violett and Lisabeth Blake, from Gertrude Stein
Home Fires, John Guare
The Gamblers, Nikolai Gogol
• *Old Possum's Book of Practical Cats,* adapt: Jonathan Foster, from T.S. Eliot; music: Elyse Goodwin
The Party, Slawomir Mrozek; trans: Nicholas Bethell
The Tricycle, Fernando Arrabal; trans: Barbara Wright
The Life and Death of Tom Thumb the Great, or The Tragedy of Tragedies, Henry Fielding; music: Anthony Bowles
The Caretaker, Harold Pinter
Fairy Tales of New York, J.P. Donleavy

Productions 1980–81

Desire Caught by the Tail, Pablo Picasso; music: Jim Ragland
The Streets of New York, Dion Boucicault; music: Mark Saltzman
The Doctor and the Devils, Dylan Thomas and Donald Taylor; adapt: Carol Corwen
Old Times, Harold Pinter
• *The Idol Makers,* Stephen Davis Parks
• *Love in the Country,* book and lyrics: Michael Alfreds; music: Anthony Bowles

Directors

Michael Bloom, Anthony Bowles, Steven Brant, Carol Corwen, Jerry Engelbach, Jonathan Foster, Penelope Hirsch, Trueman Kelley, Alison MacKenzie, Gene Santarelli, Jude Schanzer, Marlene Swartz

Designers

Sets: Loy Arcenas, Peter Byrne, Duke Durfee, Michael Gallagher, Mark Haack, Rob Hamilton, David Harnish, Peter Harrison, Richard M. Hoover, Valerie Kuehn, Ronald Placzek, Arthur Spero, Joseph A. Varga. *Costumes:* David Bess, Esther M. Bialobroda, Melissa F. Binder. Steven L. Birnbaum, Gail Brassard, Veronica Curcione, K.L. Fredericks, Deborah Friedman, Amanda J. Klein, Sally Lesser, Jim Lowe, Florence L. Rutherford, Kathleen Smith. *Lights:* Faith E. Baum, Steven Brant, Carol Corwen, Mary Jo Dondlinger, Stephen P. Edelstein, Michael Gallagher, Chaim Gitter, Ronald M. Katz, Gail R. Kennison, Scott Pinkney, Karen Singleton, Mark Weingartner.

South Coast Repertory

David Emmes
Producing Artistic Director

Martin Benson
Artistic Director

Box 2197
Costa Mesa, CA 92626
(714) 957–2602 (business)
(714) 957–4033 (box office)

Founded 1964
David Emmes, Martin Benson

Season
September–July

Schedule
Evenings
Tuesday–Sunday
Matinees
Saturday, Sunday

Facilities
655 Town Center Drive
Mainstage
Seating capacity: 507
Stage: modified thrust
Second Stage
Seating capacity: 161
Stage: modified thrust

South Coast Repertory. Megan Cole, Christopher Brown and John de Lancie in *Childe Byron.* Photo: Jay Thompson.

Finances
September 1, 1980–August 31, 1981
$1,950,000 operating expenses
$1,390,000 earned income
$ 560,000 grants/contributions

Audience
Annual attendance: 234,000
Subscribers: 16,795

Touring contact
Kris Hagen

AEA LORT (B) and (D) contracts

Since 1964 South Coast Repertory has mounted more than 150 productions under the leadership of its founders and artistic directors, David Emmes and Martin Benson. SCR remains committed to producing plays which illuminate and celebrate the human condition; works which tend to be overtly theatrical, possess sound dramatic structure and use language imaginatively. Mainstage audiences are offered a challenging and entertaining balance of classical, modern and contemporary plays selected from the finest works in dramatic literature. The Second Stage is home to a full season of contemporary plays, with special emphasis placed upon the production of new work.

SCR has developed a three-faceted approach to its artistic staffing: a core company of resident designers, directors and actors provide SCR with artistic continuity, complemented by artists drawn from the unique Southern California talent pool, who work in other media but remain dedicated to theatre. Finally, artists from across the country are recruited to provide the depth and specific talents needed to fully realize SCR's productions.

A number of playwrights of proven ability who live in Southern California have accepted membership in SCR's Playwrights Unit. These writers use SCR's artistic and technical resources to aid them in the creation of their plays.

Located in Costa Mesa, 35 miles south of Los Angeles, SCR is Orange County's only professional resident theatre. Its growth over the last few years into one of California's major theatres allows it to serve as a model for a number of performing arts facilities now in various stages of development in Orange County.

SCR serves its community with a variety of educational services. Each season an original play commissioned by SCR tours area grammar schools, playing before audiences totaling 50,000. High school students combine classroom study of a play with a visit to SCR to view the play and participate in a post-performance discussion with the artists. SCR's Acting Conservatory offers year-round instruction to approximately 500 children, teenagers and adults annually.

Productions 1979–80
Wild Oats, John O'Keeffe
Wings, Arthur Kopit
Side by Side by Sondheim, music and lyrics: Stephen Sondheim, et al.; adapt: Ned Sherrin
Right of Way, Richard Lees
Much Ado About Nothing, William Shakespeare
Ladyhouse Blues, Kevin O'Morrison
A Life in the Theatre, David Mamet
Forever Yours, Marie-Lou, Michel Tremblay; trans: John Van Burek and Bill Glassco
• *Points in Time,* Elias Davis and David Pollock
No Man's Land, Harold Pinter
• *Time Was,* Shannon Keith Kelley
• *Art, for Pete's Sake,* Robin Frederick

Productions 1980–81
Hotel Paradiso, Georges Feydeau and Maurice Desvallieres; trans: Peter Glenville
The Glass Menagerie, Tennessee Williams
A Christmas Carol, adapt: Jerry Patch, from Charles Dickens
The Elephant Man, Bernard Pomerance
The Merchant of Venice, William Shakespeare
Childe Byron, Romulus Linney
Anything Goes, book: Guy Bolton, P.G. Wodehouse, Howard Lindsay and Russell Crouse; music and lyrics: Cole Porter
American Buffalo, David Mamet
Bosoms and Neglect, John Guare
• *Screwball,* Lawrence Schneiderman
Ashes, David Rudkin
• *Chevaliere,* David Trainer
The Communication Show: Signs, Lines and Waves, book: Doris Baizley; music and lyrics: Robin Frederick

Directors
Martin Benson, Frank Condon, Gordon Duffey, David Emmes, John Going, John-David Keller, David Ostwald, Lee Shallat

Designers
Sets: Michael Devine, Mark Donnelly, Cliff Faulkner, Dwight Richard Odle, Susan Tuohy. *Costumes:* Barbara Cox, Cliff Faulkner, Merrily Ann Murray, Dwight Richard Odle, William Schroder. *Lights:* Dawn Chiang, Brian L. Gale, Cameron Harvey, Mary Martin, Donna Ruzika, Tom Ruzika, Susan Tuohy.

Stage One: Louisville Children's Theatre. Steven McCloskey, Kathy Goodwin and Phillip Cherry in *To Kill a Mockingbird.* Photo: Vickie Masden.

Stage One:
The Louisville Children's Theatre

Moses Goldberg
Artistic Director

Susanne J. Wright
General Manager

2117 Payne St.
Louisville, KY 40206
(502) 895–9486

Founded 1946
Sara Spencer, Ming Dick

Season
September–May

Schedule
Matinees
Monday–Saturday

Facilities
Sara Spencer Campbell Memorial Theatre
Seating capacity: 650
Stage: flexible

Finances
June 1, 1980–May 31, 1981
$188,000 operating expenses
$101,000 earned income
$ 83,000 grants/contributions

Audience
Annual attendance: 52,000
Subscribers: 738

Touring contact
Susanne J. Wright

AEA Theatre for Young Audiences contract

Stage One: The Louisville Children's Theatre entered its 36th season in 1981, and what began as a Junior League project in 1946 has evolved into an expanding operation serving over 50,000 young people annually.

Each production at Stage One is selected to reflect the divergent needs and interests of children of varying ages. The theatre speaks to those needs with plays geared to specific age groups from kindergarten through high school. The youngest children are introduced to theatre through familiar stories presented in intimate productions, often involving audience participation.

StageWest. Douglas Stender, Margaret Winn and Dan Hamelin in *The Night of the Iguana.* Photo: Alan R. Epstein.

As the audience matures, the plays become more complex, often dealing with modern-day problems facing young people. The presentation of period or contemporary classics completes the process which prepares young people to enter the ranks of adult theatregoers. In addition, Stage One's family productions aim to offer something for all ages by presenting the classics of children's literature as well as contemporary plays with wide appeal. Matinees are offered to both schools and the public.

Stage One also provides Saturday and summer classes for young people, workshops relating to productions for teachers and students, and other arts-in-education activities. A regional tour each spring presents three plays from the season in repertory.

The primary objectives of Stage One are to present the highest quality theatre for youngsters, to entertain them and to engage their feelings, and to help them develop psychologically and aesthetically. Progress toward these goals has been recognized: Stage One was recently selected as the outstanding children's theatre in the Southeast by the Southeastern Theatre Conference; the theatre is now operating under its first Equity contract; and construction has begun on a new 620-seat thrust-stage facility in the Kentucky Center for the Arts, scheduled to open in September 1983.

Productions 1979–80

Hansel and Gretel, Moses Goldberg
The Servant of Two Masters, Carlo Goldoni
Just So Stories, Aurand Harris
• *Rip Van Winkle,* company-developed
• *The Analysis of Mineral #4,* Moses Goldberg
The Tingalary Bird, Mary Melwood

Productions 1980–81

• *Jack and the Beanstalk,* company-developed
To Kill a Mockingbird, adapt from Harper Lee
The Snow Queen, Suria Magito and Rudolf Weil
• *Cinderella,* company-developed with Moses Goldberg
• *Something with Jamie in the Title,* Susan Zeder
Reynard the Fox, Arthur Fauquez

Directors

Elizabeth Ball, Moses Goldberg, Bekki Jo Schneider

Designers

Sets: Randall Cochran, Lindsay Davis, Jenan Dorman, Michael F. Hottois, Ken Terrill. *Costumes:* Lindsay Davis, Jenan Dorman, Michael McCallough, Cristine Smith, Ken Terrill, Doug Watts. *Lights:* Randall Cochran, Moses Goldberg, Michael F. Hottois.

Media resources

Video: *Soapbox* (NET, documentary).

StageWest

Stephen E. Hays
Producing Director

Robert A. Rosenbaum
Managing Director

1596 Memorial Ave.
West Springfield, MA 01089
(413) 781–4470 (business)
(413) 781–2340 (box office)

Founded 1967
Stephen E. Hays

Season
October–May

Schedule
Evenings
Tuesday–Sunday
Matinees
Wednesday, Sunday

Facilities
1511 Memorial Ave.
Seating capacity: 384
Stage: thrust

Finances
July 1, 1980–June 30, 1981
$665,000 operating expenses
$448,000 earned income
$217,000 grants/contributions

Audience
Annual attendance: 59,577
Subscribers: 5,407

Booked-in events
Theatre, music

AEA LORT (C) contract

StageWest was founded in 1967 in conjunction with the then newly formed Springfield Theatre Arts Association, and from its inception, the theatre has been dedicated to artistic excellence, education and community enrichment. The intimate 384-seat theatre and thrust stage are located on the Eastern States Exposition Grounds in West Springfield.

Springfield, an industrial city, is a cultural melting pot, a context which consistently adds new dimensions and challenges to the productions at StageWest. Although a wide variety of plays have been produced in the past 14 seasons, in recent years the repertoire has emphasized new American works, particularly those exploring human relationships. StageWest does not maintain a permanent company in residence, but a small group of directors, designers and actors maintain an informal affiliation with the theatre and provide artistic continuity from season to season.

StageWest has also established itself as an educational resource. Among its many programs is its Heritage Matinee Series which has exposed thousands of school students to professional theatre for the first time. Other services include acting classes for adults and children, a theatre arts workshop for teenagers and an internship program employing upper-level university students on the theatre's administrative and production staffs, for concentrated on-the-job training.

StageWest expects to occupy a new facility in time for the 1982–83 season in the new Columbus Center project in downtown Springfield. The new theatre will contain two auditoriums (a 500-seat thrust stage theatre and a 200-seat open space) and a full complement of shops, offices and rehearsal facilities under one roof. After many years in residence at the present improvised facility, the staff anticipates that the move to a permanent home will permit major growth, both in artistic accomplishment and in audience support.

Productions 1979–80

The Night of the Iguana, Tennessee Williams
Sizwe Bansi Is Dead, Athol Fugard, John Kani and Winston Ntshona
Peg o' My Heart, J. Hartley Manners
The Sea Horse, Edward J. Moore
Of Mice and Men, John Steinbeck
Relatively Speaking, Alan Ayckbourn

Productions 1980–81

The Diary of Anne Frank, Frances Goodrich and Albert Hackett
On Golden Pond, Ernest Thompson
Dames at Sea, book and lyrics: George Haimsohn and Robin Miller; music: Jim Wise
Agnes of God, John Pielmeier
A Moon for the Misbegotten, Eugene O'Neill

Othello, William Shakespeare
13 Rue de l'Amour, Georges Feydeau; adapt: Mawby Green and Ed Feilbert

Directors
Robert Brewer, Richard Gershman, Stephen E. Hays, Pamela Hunt, Davey Marlin-Jones, Timothy Near, Harold Scott, Geoffrey Sherman, Russell Treyz, Ted Weiant

Designers
Sets: Bennet Averyt, Frank J. Boros, Joan Brancale, Thomas Cariello, James Guenther, Brian Jackins, Lawrence King, Joseph Long, Arthur Ridley, Tom Schwinn. *Costumes:* Elizabeth Covey, Jan Morrison, Lewis Rampino, Deborah Shaw, Anne Thaxter Watson, Joan Vick, Bill Walker. *Lights:* Barry Arnold, Bennet Averyt, Ned Hallick, Paul J. Horton, Robby Monk, Andrea Wilson.

Starry Night Puppet Theatre

Jan Hacha
Producing Director

Linda Giese
Managing Director

233 Main St.
Vestal, NY 13850
(607) 748–1593
(212) 772–0765 (NY direct line)

Founded 1972
Gary Wurtzel, Sara Wurtzel, Jan Hacha

Season
Year-round touring

Facilities
Cider Mill Playhouse
2 South Nanticoke Ave.
Endicott, NY
Seating capacity: 300
Stage: modified thrust

Finances
September 1, 1980–August 31, 1981
$126,000 operating expenses
$ 86,000 earned income
$ 40,000 grants/contributions

Audience
Annual attendance: 60,000

Touring contact
Gloria Botnick

Booked-in events
Puppet theatre

The Starry Night Puppet Theatre is a professional company for young audiences whose productions are all original and company-developed. The theatre seeks to break new ground outside the traditional literature of children's theatre and, in so doing, introduce new and different forms of puppetry to its audiences.

The current touring repertoire, available on a national basis, features full-size puppets manipulated by masked actors. Current productions are all fully staged, and Starry Night travels with full scenery and sound. Starry Night productions are keyed to different age levels with varying degrees of language and plot sophistication. An extensive in-school residency program offers a wide variety of workshops and educational programs for students and teachers. A Teacher's Study Guide is available for each production.

Starry Night has frequently been the first introduction to live theatre its young audience has ever had, and the company is dedicated to making that experience exciting and worthwhile.

Productions 1979–80
Kitchen Kacciatore, Jan Hacha; music: Susan Peters
The Marsh Mellow Opera, Gary and Sara Wurtzel and Jan Hacha
• *The Griffin and the Minor Canon,* adapt: Christine Crane, from Frank Stockton
The Mysterious Hand, Jan Hacha

Productions 1980–81
The Griffin and the Minor Canon
The Marsh Mellow Opera
• *The Thing in My Closet,* Christine Crane
The Mysterious Hand

Directors
Christine Crane, Jan Hacha, Alan Krulick, William Morris

Designers
Sets: Linda Giese, Jan Hacha. *Costumes and puppets:* Christine Crane, Linda Giese, Jan Hacha. *Lights:* David Becker, Jan Hacha.

Media resources
Video: *The Nooze Report* (Gateway Communications).

Starry Night Puppet Theatre. *The Griffin and the Minor Canon.* Photo: Dennis Dunda.

Steamboat Repertory Theatre. David Ode and Akanda in *Dracula.* Photo: Richard Geer.

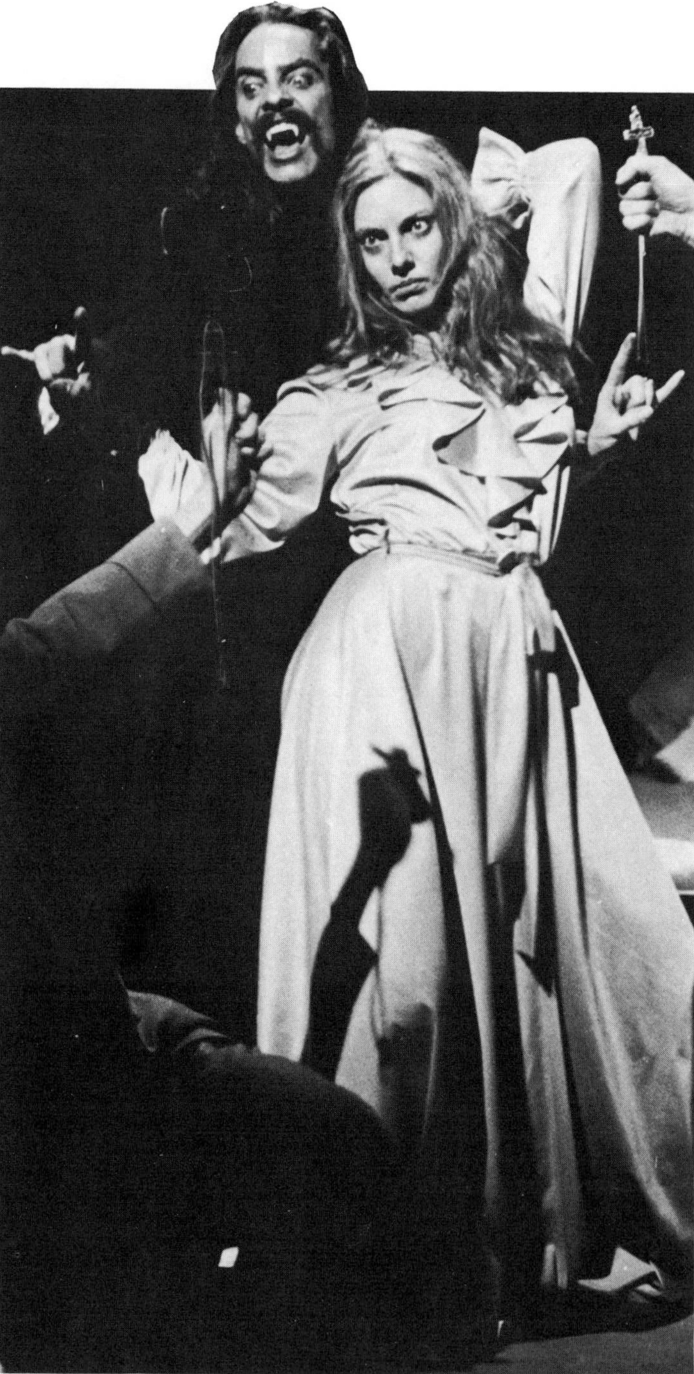

Steamboat Repertory Theatre

Richard Geer
Artistic Director

Andrew T. Eiseman
Managing Director

Box 771589
Steamboat Springs, CO 80477
(303) 879–6900 (business)
(303) 879–9900 (box office)

Founded 1978
Richard Geer

Season
December–April, June–September

Schedule
Evenings
Wednesday–Sunday

Facilities
Mt. Werner and Pine Grove Road
Seating capacity: 200
Stage: thrust

Finances
October 1, 1979–September 30, 1980
$197,000 operating expenses
$ 44,000 earned income
$127,000 grants/contributions

Audience
Annual attendance: 16,000
Subscribers: 500

Touring contact
Curt Olson

Booked-in events
Dance, music, mime

Now in its third season under the guidance of founder and artistic director Richard Geer, Steamboat Repertory Theatre is helping to define a new role for theatre: that of the rural repertory theatre. Based in the tiny and isolated resort community of Steamboat Springs, SRT is Northwest Colorado's only professional performing arts group. It celebrates the ability of a community and its artists to work for cultural and economic goals.

At the core of SRT's philosophy is the belief that artistic growth is potentially unlimited under the right conditions. The size and isolation of Steamboat Springs have forced each member of the theatre company and staff to develop the widest possible variety of talents, and the results are often fresh and original.

SRT recognizes an ever deepening necessity to respond to the needs of its region. The natural splendor of Northwest Colorado covers vast expanses of potential energy; coal, oil and oil shale. The challenge of preserving the wild while extracting the resources demands heroic effort and great vision. SRT dramatizes this challenge in plays that profile the struggle of the individual toward an almost unattainable goal; a goal which becomes attainable only through melding opposing forces in a spirit of cooperation and trust. Theatre can point the way for a region in which a new mythos must preceed a new ethos.

Major funding from the Federal Comprehensive Education and Training Act in 1979 and '80 made possible a touring program that took SRT's work directly into energy-impacted communities. An original musical on career opportunities in the energy industry received regional acclaim and toured to 20 towns.

Steamboat Rep's artistic policy of producing plays that portray the potential of the human spirit has led the company to mount a number of new works as well as significant reworkings of established plays. An original adaptation of *Dracula* toured the region and was the first guest production at the Denver Center Theatre Company's new home. A rapidly growing reputation for quality and an abiding concern for the needs of the region have made year-round theatre possible in a community of only 5,000 people.

Productions 1979–80
The Thwarting of Baron Bolligrew, Robert Bolt
When You Comin' Back Red Ryder, Mark Medoff
Luv, Murray Schisgal
Tartuffe, Moliere
Arms and the Man, George Bernard Shaw
Jesse and the Bandit Queen, David Freeman
The Curate Shakespeare As You Like It, Don Nigro

Productions 1980–81
- *Hans,* Joseph Brockett
- *Dracula,* Richard Sharp
- *Penny Candy and All Star Wrestling,* Timothy Elliott
- *Two-Men,* David Seals

The Rainmaker, N. Richard Nash
Camelot, book and lyrics: Alan J. Lerner; music: Frederick Loewe
The Importance of Being Earnest, Oscar Wilde

Directors
Ned Bobkoff, Joseph Brockett, Mark Cuddy, Timothy Elliott, Richard Geer, David Ode

Designers
Sets: Ziska Childs, Michael Duran, Bruce Jackson Jr., Clayton Grant Peterson, Jon Ring. *Costumes:* Sarah Campbell, Carol Kotsifakis, Karen S. Ohlmann, Margaret Perry. *Lights:* Steve Cobb, Mark Cuddy, Michael Duran, Margie Howard, Ren Hinks.

The Street Theater

Gray Smith
Executive Director

White Plains Armory
35 South Broadway
White Plains, NY 10601
(914) 761–3307

Founded 1970
Gray Smith

Season
Year-round

Finances
June 1, 1980–May 31, 1981
$220,000 operating expenses
$ 5,000 earned income
$206,000 grants/contributions

Audience
Annual attendance: 15,330

Touring contact
Gray Smith

The Street Theater is a developmental company with an equal commitment to process and performance. Throughout its 11-year history, workshops have encouraged the development of original plays and performance pieces in prisons, community centers and schools. Touring companies have performed for street, prison, college and school audiences, and for the last five years all touring productions have featured original work, either commissioned or developed through company collaboration.

After 1976, the company turned its attention from national touring and statewide prison workshops to focus on Westchester County. Currently, workshops are held in school districts throughout the county, at the County Penitentiary and at the theatre's base of operations in White Plains. High school workshops often develop original productions and also serve to recruit members for the theatre's Youth Company. With an age range of 16–26, this company is committed to the development of original plays which speak from and to youth. Two examples are: *Crime Don't Pay No Wages,* which has toured schools and streets throughout Westchester, and *Youth in Crisis,* which has two versions exploring both the inner and outer landscapes of alienation. The Youth Company develops an average of four productions per year, performing for an audience of about 15,000.

The Street Theater's workshop directors also function as actors in the professional company's season. During the past year, this staff conducted workshops for 330 participants, meeting at least twice a week for 16 weeks.

Productions 1979–80
- *This One's for You,* company-developed
- *The Magic Jungle,* company-developed
- *A Play About Us?,* company-developed
- *Generation Rap,* company-developed

Productions 1980–81
- *WannaJob,* C. Lester Franklin
- *Changing Times,* company-developed
- *Crime Don't Pay No Wages,* Martin Henderson, Pat Smith and Lonnie James; music: Lonnie James
- *Youth in Crisis I and II,* company-developed; music: Lonnie James
- *Made in America,* Donald Nathanson

Directors
C. Lester Franklin, Martin Henderson, Patricia Smith, Ray Barry, Donald Nathanson

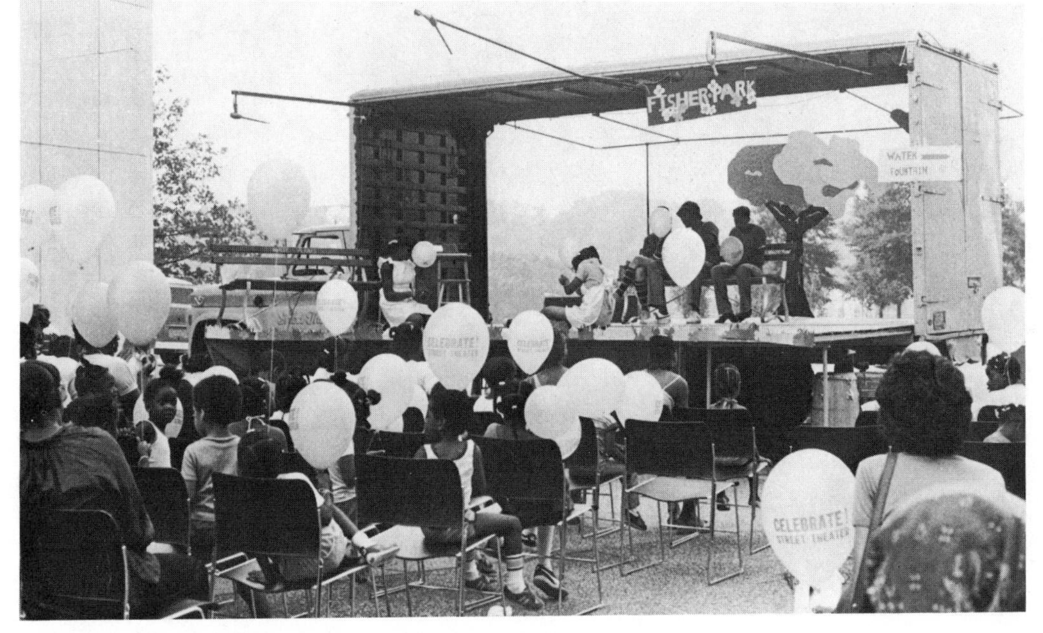

The Street Theater. Photo: Susan Harris.

Studio Arena Theatre

David Frank
Artistic Director

Barry Hoffman
Managing Director

710 Main St.
Buffalo, NY 14202
(716) 856–8025 (business)
(716) 856–5650 (box office)

Founded 1965
Neal Du Brock

Season
September–May

Schedule
Evenings
Tuesday–Sunday
Matinees
Wednesday, Thursday, Sunday

Facilities
Studio Arena Theatre
Seating capacity: 651
Stage: thrust
Shea's Buffalo
646 Main St.
Seating capacity: 3,100
Stage: proscenium

Finances
June 1, 1980–May 31, 1981
$1,846,000 operating expenses
$1,383,000 earned income
$ 445,000 grants/contributions

Audience
Annual attendance: 147,816
Subscribers: 12,070

AEA LORT (B) contract

Since 1965, Buffalo's Studio Arena Theatre has been serving the 1.5 million people of western New York State. It has presented 134 productions in 16 years, 23 of which were world or American premieres. A subscription series of seven plays is offered each season, varied and balanced to generate audience appeal. The proximity of the theatre to New York City additionally gives Studio Arena access to the vast reservoir of New York acting, directing and design talent.

Committed to serving the community, Studio Arena's

Theatre School offers professional training in acting, directing and production. The school has been in operation for 54 years, since long before its affiliation with the theatre. Other educational programs include internships and Career and Education Day programs. The Theatre extends to the public such services as student, military and senior citizen ticket discounts; a voucher program; a speakers bureau; a singles program; a newsletter; post-performance discussions; interpreted performances for the deaf; taped program notes for the blind; and theatre rentals.

Artistically, Studio Arena places an emphasis on contemporary theatre but maintains a commitment to a wide range of stimulating theatrical encounters, which might include selected period pieces, new works and the best productions from the Broadway theatre that might otherwise be unavailable to the community. The theatre strives to sustain the highest possible standards of performance and production in order to serve the community that has nurtured it since its inception. High priority is also placed on forming relationships with outstanding directors, and the eventual development of a small resident or "core" company of actors to aid in the achievement of consistent theatrical quality.

Productions 1979–80
Da, Hugh Leonard
• *My Husband's Wild Desires Almost Drove Me Mad,* John Tobias
The Mousetrap, Agatha Christie
Ashes, David Rudkin
• *I Won't Dance,* Oliver Hailey
The Gin Game, D.L. Coburn
The Letter, W. Somerset Maugham
A Christmas Carol, adapt: Mary Elizabeth Holmes, from Charles Dickens

Productions 1980–81
• *Lady of the Diamond,* Mark Berman
One Flew over the Cuckoo's Nest, Dale Wasserman, from Ken Kesey
Write Me a Murder, Frederick Knott
Curse of the Starving Class, Sam Shepard
Ah, Wilderness!, Eugene O'Neill
Loot, Joe Orton
Talley's Folly, Lanford Wilson
A Christmas Carol, adapt: Geoffrey Sherman, from Charles Dickens

Directors
Neal Du Brock, Warren Enters, David Frank, Davey Marlin-Jones, Lawrence Kornfeld, Jack O'Brien, Tom O'Horgan, Stephen Porter, Geoffrey Sherman

Designers
Sets: John Arnone, John T. Baun, Zack Brown, Robert Morgan, Mischa Petrow, Bob Phillips, Bill Stabile, Christian Thee, Hal Tine, Paul Wonsek. *Costumes:* Randy Barcelo, Zack Brown, Donna Eskew, Robert Morgan, Mischa Petrow, Sayuri N. Pinckard, Lewis D. Rampino, Kristina Watson. *Lights:* Frances Aronson, James H. Gage, Peter Gill, John McLain, Robby Monk, Joe Pacitti, Mischa Petrow, Marc B. Weiss, Paul Wonsek.

Media resources
Video: *H.M.S. Pinafore* (WGR), *Into the Arena* (WKBW, documentary), *Artscene* (WNED, documentary).

Studio Arena Theatre. John G. Kellogg, Stanja Lowe and Steven Sutherland in *Da.* Photo: Phototech Studios.

Syracuse Stage

Arthur Storch
Producing Director

James A. Clark
Managing Director

820 East Genesee St.
Syracuse, NY 13210
(315) 423–4008 (business)
(315) 423–3275 (box office)

Founded 1974
Arthur Storch

Season
October–May

Schedule
Evenings
Tuesday–Sunday
Matinees
Wednesday, Saturday, Sunday

Facilities
John D. Archbold Theatre
Seating capacity: 455–510
Stage: modified proscenium
Experimental Theatre
Seating capacity: 202
Stage: proscenium
Daniel C. Sutton Pavilion
Seating capacity: 100
Stage: flexible

Finances
July 1, 1980–June 30, 1981
$1,106,000 operating expenses
$ 544,000 earned income
$ 562,000 grants/contributions

Audience
Annual attendance: 96,000
Subscribers: 10,500

Touring contact
Barbara Beckos

Booked-in events
Dance, theatre

AEA LORT (C) contract

On November 14, 1980, Syracuse Stage opened the new John D. Archbold Theatre as the culmination of three years of planning, fund-raising, designing and building. For the six seasons prior to 1980, Syracuse Stage performed exclusively in the 202-seat Experimental Theatre in the Regent Theatre Complex. In

Syracuse Stage. *The Comedy of Errors.* Photo: Bob Lorenz.

March 1980, the old movie house adjacent to the Experimental Theatre was gutted and the renovation started.

The new Archbold theatre features a proscenium stage with an expandable thrust; two passageways or vomitories from beneath the audience allowing actors to enter from the house; and a small orchestra pit. The flexibility of the stage allows for a seating capacity varying from 455 to 510. In addition, a space called the Daniel C. Sutton Pavilion adjoins the Archbold, and is used for staged readings, cabaret and children's theatre, and as a bar and reception area for Archbold performances.

In the first season at the new theatre, the audiences increased by 75 percent, and by year two, season ticket holders had increased from 6,300 to 10,500.

The six-play mainstage season is the major activity of the theatre, and a variety of classics, established contemporary works and original plays are chosen each year by producing director Arthur Storch. The fifth play of each season goes on a month-long tour of New York State. Most of the actors and designers who work on Syracuse Stage productions are selected in New York City on a show-by-show basis.

Other programs of the theatre include a cabaret series, staged readings of new scripts, and educational services such as study guides and actor visits to the classroom.

Syracuse Stage receives significant support from Syracuse University which contributes the facilities and a portion of the theatre's staff, as well as some operating funds. An active association with the university's drama department is maintained, and the theatre serves the students as a professional resource: technical staff members teach classes, and students work with staff and actors onstage and behind the scenes.

Productions 1979–80
Naked, Luigi Pirandello
Side by Side by Sondheim, music and lyrics: Stephen Sondheim et al., adapt: Ned Sherrin
• *Damnee Manon,* Sacree Sandra and Michel Tremblay
Man and Superman, George Bernard Shaw
Who's Afraid of Virginia Woolf?, Edward Albee
Old World, Aleksei Arbuzov

Productions 1980–81
The Comedy of Errors, William Shakespeare
Dames at Sea, book and lyrics: George Haimsohn and Robin Miller; music: Jim Wise
• *Paradise is Closing Down,* Pieter-Dirk Uys
Goodnight Grandpa, Walter Landau
For Colored Girls who have Considered Suicide/When The Rainbow is Enuf, Ntozake Shange
A Doll's House, Henrik Ibsen; trans: Christopher Hampton

Directors
Larry Alford, Bill Glassco, Judith Haskell, Lawrence Kornfeld, Peter Maloney, Terry Schreiber, Arthur Storch, John Ulmer

Designers
Sets: John Arnone, John Doepp, Timothy Galvin, Francois LaPlante, Bill Schroder, Hal Tine. *Costumes:* Nanzi Adzima, Carr Garnett, James Berton Harris, Francois LaPlante, Patricia McGourty, Bill Schroder. *Lights:* Frances Aronson, Jonathan K. Duff, Todd Lichtenstein, Paul Mathiesen, Roger Morgan, Michael Newton-Brown, William Thomas Paton, Judy Rasmuson, Robert Thompson.

Tacoma Actors Guild

Rick Tutor
Artistic Director

Marilyn Raichle
Managing Director

1323 South Yakima Ave.
Tacoma, WA 98405
(206) 272-3107 (business)
(206) 272-2145 (box office)

Founded 1978
Rick Tutor, William Becvar

Season
October–March

Schedule
Evenings
Tuesday–Sunday
Matinees
Wednesday, Sunday

Facilities
Seating capacity: 297
Stage: proscenium

Finances
July 1, 1980–June 30, 1981
$458,000 operating expenses
$223,000 earned income
$245,000 grants/contributions

Audience
Annual attendance: 37,351
Subscribers: 4,168

Booked-in events
Theatre, music

AEA LORT (D) contract

The Tacoma Actors Guild is the city's first and only professional resident company, offering a range of theatrical fare designed to reach and develop the widest possible audience.

TAG feels strongly that the essence of theatre is the actor—and it emphasizes the performer as artist as well as the close relationship between actor and audience. In keeping with this philosophy, TAG's major activity is a regular season of plays chosen from the best of contemporary and classic literature—particularly those plays which feature outstanding characters. TAG currently holds open auditions for each season, drawing a major portion of its talent from the West Coast and Pacific Northwest regions.

Since its showcase production of *Guys and Dolls* in August 1978 at Tacoma's Temple Theatre, TAG has produced a summer season of children's theatre at the University of Puget Sound, two full seasons in its currently leased facility, and is looking forward to the acquisition of a new and permanent home for the 1982–83 season.

In addition to its regular programming, TAG has also sponsored local productions of the Young ACT Company and the Seattle Repertory Theatre, produced a staged reading of a play-in-progress by a local playwright, toured an original children's production and provided a local speakers bureau for civic organizations. A detailed five-year plan has been developed by a long-range planning committee and is being rigorously adhered to by TAG's board of directors. As the theatre grows, TAG plans to develop a theatre program for children, increase outreach services to schools and senior citizens, expand regional touring, and initiate productions of experimental works and staged readings of new plays.

The primary goal of the Tacoma Actors Guild is to establish itself as a cultural landmark while providing both a financial and a spiritual spark for the entire community.

Productions 1979–80

One Flew over the Cuckoo's Nest, adapt: Dale Wasserman, from Ken Kesey
Rookery Nook, Ben Travers
Cricket on the Hearth, adapt: Marian Jonson, from Charles Dickens
A Streetcar Named Desire, Tennessee Williams
Ten Little Indians, Agatha Christie
The Amorous Flea, book: Jerry Devine; music and lyrics: Bruce Montgomery

Productions 1980–81

A Man for All Seasons, Robert Bolt
Bus Stop, William Inge
• *Dr. Knowitall and the Magic Bag,* Rick Tutor
The Little Foxes, Lillian Hellman
Light Up the Sky, Moss Hart
South Pacific, book: Oscar Hammerstein II and Joshua Logan; music: Richard Rodgers; lyrics: Oscar Hammerstein II

Directors

Shaun Austin-Olsen, William Becvar, Ted D'Arms, Richard Edwards, Rick Tutor

Designers

Sets: David Butler, Scott DeStefano, Karen Gjelsteen, Frederick Gerard Metzer, Byron Olson, Stephen Packard, J.C. Wills. *Costumes:* Renita Davenport, Ron Erickson, Carol Kotsifakis, Dan McWest, Kenny Olson, Sally Richardson. *Lights:* J. Patrick Elmer, Tom Salkowski, Bill Strock.

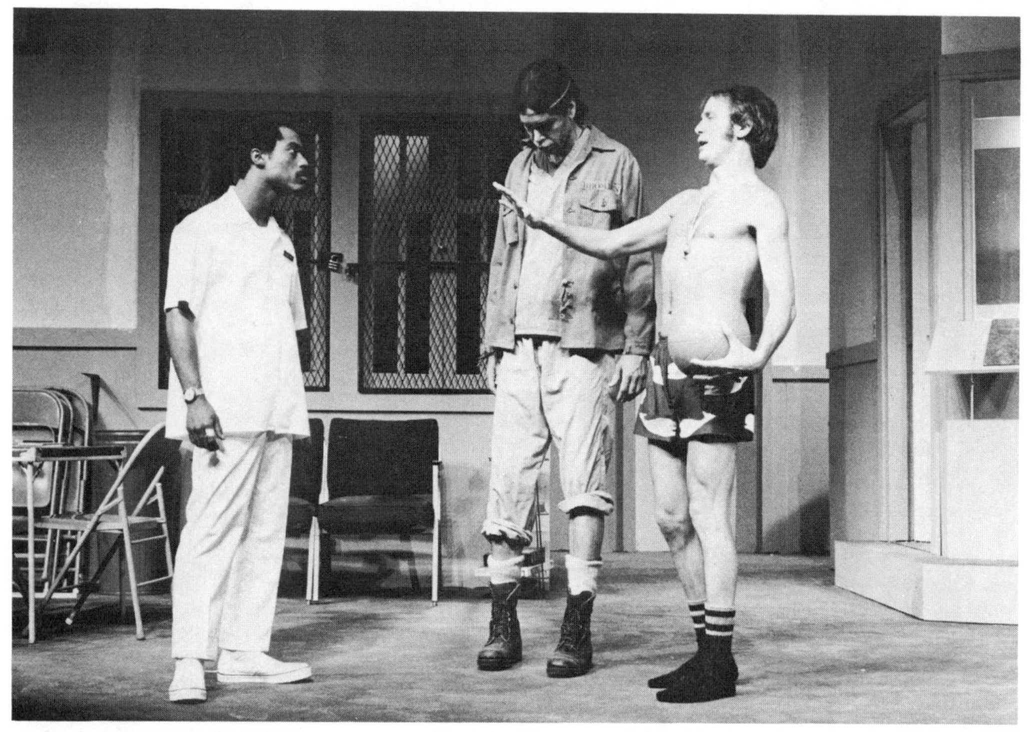

Tacoma Actors Guild. Kenneth Reaves, Jeffrey L. Prather and David Williams in *One Flew over the Cuckoo's Nest.* Photo: Keith Bauer.

Theatre Arts of West Virginia

John S. Benjamin
Artistic Director

Stuart B. Gordon
Business Manager

Box 1205
Beckley, WV 25801
(304) 253–8313 (business)
(304) 763–4185 (box office, summer)

Founded 1961

Season

June–August
Touring
October–May

Schedule

Evenings
Summer:
Tuesday–Sunday

Facilities

Cliffside Amphitheatre
Seating capacity: 1,442
Stage: proscenium

Finances

October 1, 1980–September 30, 1981
$561,000 operating expenses
$273,000 earned income
$257,000 grants/contributions

Audience

Annual attendance: 115,557
Subscribers: 459

Touring contacts

John S. Benjamin
Stuart B. Gordon

Booked-in events

Theatre, dance

AEA Theatre for Young Audiences and Guest Artist contracts

Theatre Arts of West Virginia, the Mountain State's only resident professional theatre, is located in the center of America's coal fields. Conceived in the late 1950s to produce two summer outdoor productions, Theatre Arts expanded in 1972 to a year-round operation with the establishment of its touring wing, Theatre West Virginia.

Theatre Arts of West Virginia. S. Proctor Gray in *Macbeth.* Photo: Betty Benjamin.

TWV's artistic policy is to produce high quality touring productions of fine theatrical literature. Originally founded to bring live professional theatre to area schools, the company has since broadened its scope to include performances for university and public audiences. TWV believes the arts should be available to all and not reserved for the elite.

Theatre West Virginia tours classics and contemporary works 33 weeks a year throughout West Virginia and other states in the Midwest and Atlantic coastal region. The troupe tours full productions with complete sets, lighting, costumes and sound equipment. A separate touring unit of professional puppeteers presents full-scale marionette productions designed for children.

Workshops are offered in all areas, from improvisation and theatre games to audience development. Promotional kits with instruction guides and student-teacher study packages supplement all performances, and techniques for building and sustaining arts-minded audiences are also detailed.

Over the last 10 years, TWV has worked to establish a creative atmosphere in which theatre professionals can bring more theatre to more people.

Productions 1979–80

- *Alias: Mark Twain,* adapt: John S. Benjamin
  Macbeth, William Shakespeare
  The Last Meeting of the Knights of the White Magnolia, Preston Jones
  Same Time, Next Year, Bernard Slade
- *Circus,* Raymond Masters
  Hatfields and McCoys, book and lyrics: Billy Edd Wheeler; music: Ewel Cornett
  Honey in the Rock, book and lyrics: Kermit Hunter; music: Ewel Cornett and Jack Kilpatrick

Productions 1980–81

- *Mossie and the Strippers,* Billy Edd Wheeler
  Alias: Mark Twain
- *The First Men in the Moon,* adapt: Donald C. Watkins, from H.G. Wells
  Hatfields and McCoys
  Honey in the Rock

Directors
John Arnold, John S. Benjamin, Ewel Cornett

Designers
Sets: Vittorio Capecce, James Kelly, Thomas P. Struthers, Donald C. Watkins, Raymond Masters. *Costumes:* Mary Ellen Allison, Thomas Hansen, Caroline Lentz, Raymond Masters, Suzanne Brown, Vittorio Capecce. *Lights:* Dale Harris, James Kelly, Donald C. Watkins, Stephen R. Woodring.

Theatre by the Sea

Jon Kimbell
Producing Director

Karl Gevecker
Managing Director

125 Bow St.
Portsmouth, NH 03801
(603) 431–5846 (business)
(603) 431–6660 (box office)

Founded 1964
Pat and C. Stanley Flower

Season
September–August

Schedule
Evenings
Tuesday–Sunday
Matinees
Wednesday, Saturday, Sunday

Facilities
Bow Street Theatre
Seating capacity: 263
Stage: thrust
Prescott Park Amphitheatre
Seating capacity: 5,000
Stage: arena

Finances
September 1, 1979–August 31, 1980
$685,000 operating expenses
$431,000 earned income
$136,000 grants/contributions

Audience
Annual attendance: 305,027
Subscribers: 4,350

Touring contact
Jon Kimbell

Booked-in events
Music, dance, mime, lectures, community events

AEA LORT (C) contract

Theatre by the Sea's 17-year history is evidence that a theatre dedicated to artistic quality can survive and flourish in a region thought to be unsuitable for professional art because of its small population base. From its founding in 1964 to its current status as an Equity theatre, TBS has produced critically acclaimed theatre, been a vigorous advocate of the arts, and an important educational and economic asset to the area.

The most recent season included a solid repertoire of plays expressing the breadth of human thought and emotion—love, cruelty, secrets of the heart and incredible fantasy—along with a new country and western musical about America's last cowboy: the truck driver.

In recent years, TBS's outreach program of classes, internship and scholarship programs, and presentations to schools and organizations has extended its impact far beyond the stage. Moreover, the summer Prescott Park Arts Festival, produced by TBS and now in its seventh year, drew over 250,000 visitors and tourists to downtown Portsmouth last year (200,000 of them to TBS musicals), while the annual Ceres Street Fair attracted a crowd of 10,000 to view the work of 150 artists and craftspeople.

Theatre by the Sea's insistence on excellence and its commitment to accessibility have won the strong support of its community. This support was, in great part, responsible for the theatre's move to a new and greatly enlarged facility during the 1979–80 season. The move has expanded artistic and economic potential and created challenges at the same time.

Productions 1979–80

Godspell, book: John-Michael Tebelak; music and lyrics: Stephen Schwartz
Scrooge and Marley, adapt: Israel Horovitz
Streamers, David Rabe
How the Other Half Loves, Alan Ayckbourn
Othello, William Shakespeare
The Gin Game, D.L. Coburn
Berlin to Broadway with Kurt Weill, music: Kurt Weill; lyrics: various; adapt: Gene Lerner
A Funny Thing Happened on the Way to the Forum, book: Burt Shevelove and Larry Gelbart; music and lyrics: Stephen Sondheim
South Pacific, book: Oscar Hammerstein II and Joshua Logan; music: Richard Rodgers; lyrics: Oscar Hammerstein II
Annie Get Your Gun, book: Herbert and Dorothy Fields; music and lyrics: Irving Berlin

Directors

Jack Allison, Tom Celli, Richard Harden, Jon Kimbell, Ben Levit, Philip Minor, Kent Paul, Andrew Rohrer, Peter Thompson

Designers

Sets: John Becker, Joan Brancale, Larry Fulton, Kathie Iannicelli, Fred Kolouch, Bob Phillips, John Wright Stevens, Quentin Thomas.
Costumes: Ann Carnaby, Marcia Dixcy, Kathie Iannicelli, Fred Kolouch, Linda Smith, Quentin Thomas, Holly Urion, J.J. Vak.
Lights: Fred Kolouch, Tyrone E. Sanders, Donald Soule, Mal Sturcio, Paul Sullivan, Quentin Thomas.

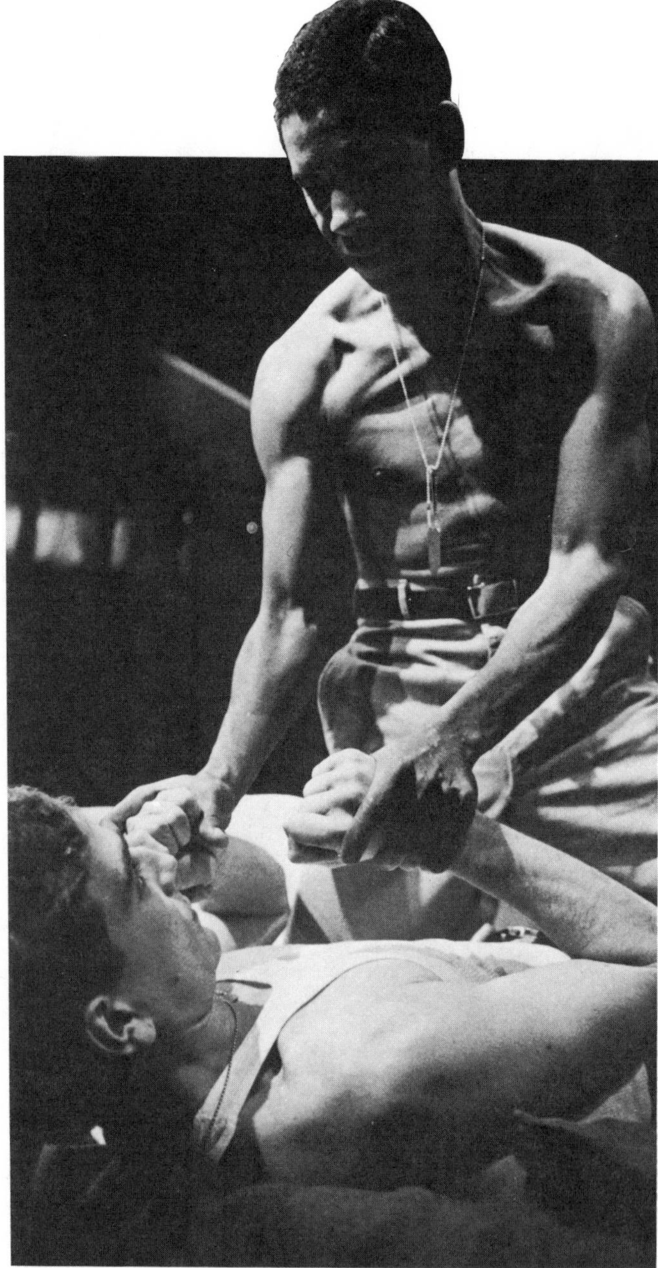

Theatre By the Sea. Max Mayer and James Craven in *Streamers.* Photo: North Light Photo.

Productions 1980–81

A Little Night Music, book: Hugh Wheeler; music and lyrics: Stephen Sondheim
• *On the Marry-Go-Wrong,* Georges Feydeau; adapt: Norman Shapiro
Scrooge and Marley
Emigres, Slawomir Mrozek
Death of a Salesman, Arthur Miller
Talley's Folly, Lanford Wilson
Night Riders, book: Allen Albert; music: Josh Lewis; lyrics: Josh Rubins

Theater for the New City

George Bartenieff
Crystal Field
Artistic Directors

162 Second Ave.
New York, NY 10003
(212) 254–1109

Founded 1970
George Bartenieff, Crystal Field, Lawrence Kornfeld, Theo Barnes

Season
July–June

Schedule
Evenings
Thursday–Sunday
Matinees
Variable

Facilities
James Waring Theater
Seating capacity: 130
Stage: flexible
Joe Cino Theater
Seating capacity: 150
Stage: proscenium
Charles Stanley Chamber Space
Seating capacity: 48
Stage: flexible

Finances
July 1, 1979–June 30, 1980
$180,000 operating expenses
$ 42,000 earned income
$137,000 grants/contributions

Audience
Annual attendance: 53,000

Touring contact
Linda Chapman

Booked-in events
Dance, music, theatre

AEA Showcase code

Theater for the New City is a unique experimental/developmental center with an outreach program to the community. TNC is dedicated to the discovery and development of new American playwrights, as well as the nurturing of new experimental theatre companies. The theatre amalgamates song and dance, live music and poetry into diverse "total theatre" experiences, and annually, the company premieres at least 10 new plays by

Theater for the New City. George Bartenieff and Margo Sherman in *Images of the Coming Dead.*

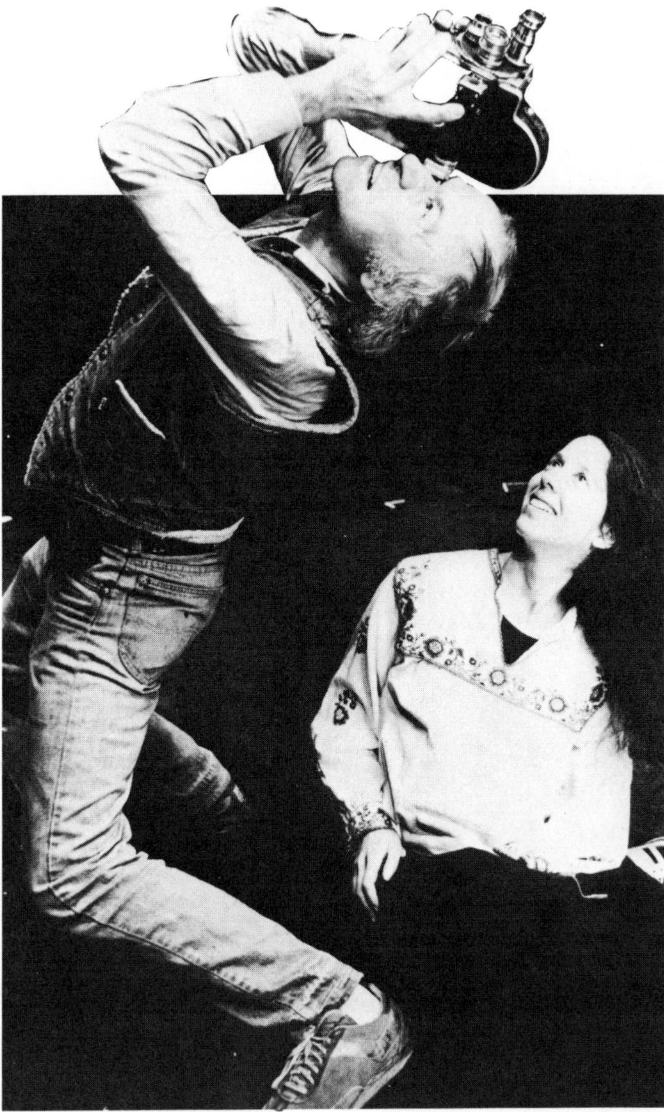

contemporary American playwrights, both established and unknown. These include full-length dramas, musicals, operas (often with original choreography), live music and multimedia presentations. In addition, TNC hosts productions by various performing organizations based in New York and elsewhere, including The Talking Band, Red Mole Theater, Spiderwoman Theater and Bread and Puppet Theater. Great care is taken by the artistic directors to give the writer, director and actors the appropriate conditions to create without undue pressure or interference.

TNC's Free Summer Street Theater involves an interracial cast of forty, including five musicians, and tours the five-borough area to bring spectacle and satire to the streets and parks in the city's poorer neighborhoods. Each year an original script is developed in the Spring Street Theater Workshop, where young apprentices join the regular company and are trained in juggling, tumbling, clowning and other performing skills.

In addition, TNC has performed for such special community events as a Halloween festival, a local library dedication, fund-raising for a neighborhood church and many others.

Productions 1979–80

- *Apoplectic Fit,* Daryl Chin
- *The Dog That Talked Too Much,* Crystal Field
- *Riff Raff Review,* Mike Kellin
- *Politics, Sex, Death, Work and the World,* Walter Corwin
- *Coming from a Great Distance,* Isaac Peretz
  1/3 of a Nation, Arthur Arent
- *Horizontal White,* Barry Marshall
- *Those Darn Kids,* Bob Dahdah and Mary Boylan
- *La Justice,* Ken Bernard
- *Aphrodite,* Eugenia-Macer Storey
- *Bag Lady,* Jean-Claude van Itallie
  Morandi's, Morton Lichter
- *Itchy Britches,* N. Noble Barrett
- *Evelyn Brown—A Diary,* Maria Irene Fornes
- *Graven Image,* Rosalyn Drexler
- *The Pope in Love,* Joseph Renard
- *Dancers on My Ceiling,* Mary Karolly
- *Property,* Lee Schneider
- *The True War Dance of Yankee Reels,* Robert Jacobs
- *Number 14,* Don Rifkin
- *Billy Stars and Kid Jupiter,* William Electric Black

Productions 1980–81

- *Exhausting the Possibilities,* Larry Loonin
- *Cold, Lazy and Elaine,* Stephen Holt
- *Flop—A Hit,* Seth Allen
- *Orpheus and Amerika,* Robert Patrick
- *Butter Faces,* Leonard Melfi
- *Short Timers,* Douglas Anderson
  Farmyard, Franz Xaver Kroetz
- *Sunday Childhood Journeys to Nobody at Home,* Arthur Sainer
- *Norwich News,* Donald Kvares
- *Alias Jimmy Valentine,* Robert Dahdah and Mary Boylan
- *A Wedding Party,* Michael Smith
- *The Yellow Wallpaper,* Charlotte Perkins Gilman and Florence Falk
- *A Day at Harmenz,* Tadeusz Borowski and Steven Reisner
- *Chucky's Hunch,* Rochelle Owens
- *A Midnight Moon at the Greasy Spoon,* Miguel Pinero
- *The Meehans,* Chuck Choset and Sam Pottle
- *Rent,* Walter Corwin
- *Sidekicks,* Barry Marshall
- *The Tardy Bust,* Joseph Renard
- *The Berlin Wall,* Lee Schneider
- *The Housing Show,* Neile Weissman
- *Sword of Glass,* Denice Sherman
- *Zaloominations,* Paul Zaloom
- *The Hampster of Happiness* and *Borders,* Charles Eastman
- *Chapel St. Light* and *Dwelling in Milk,* Barry Marshall
  Men, Stephen Holt

Directors

John Albano, Douglas Anderson, Craig Barish, N. Noble Barrett, Ray Barry, William Electric Black, Lee Breuer, Ken Buckshi, Alice Eve Cohen, Robert Dahdah, Florence Falk, Crystal Field, Maria Irene Fornes, Russell Krum, Susan Lehrer, Larry Loonin, Eugenia Macer-Storey, John Herbert McDowell, Matthew Maguire, Ruth Maleczech, Renato Mambor, Barry Marshall, Muriel Miguel, Peter Napolitano, Lola Pashilinski, Robert Patrick, Gerald J. Quimby, Steve Reed, Steven Reisner, Elinor Renfield, Gordon Rogoff, Lawrence Sacharow, Lee Schneider, Denice Sherman, Chris Silva, Omar Shapli, John Vaccaro, Neile Weissman, Martin Worman, Paul Zaloom

Designers

Sets: Anthony Angel, Donald L. Brooks, Bobjack Callejo, Bill Clark, Reagan Cook, Wes Cronk, Howard Cummings, Donald Eastman, Lise Engel, Geoffrey P. Hall, Jerry Harding, Richard Harmon, Ellen Marie Jervey, Warren L. Jorgenson, Ron Kajiwara, John Kenny, Abe Lubelski, Jun Maeda, Lance Miller, Kerry Minnion, Bill Motyka, Tommy Pace, Uzi Parnes, John Putnam, Molly Renda, Tracy Sherman, John Slavin, Barbara Sonneborn, Elaine Weissman, Susan A. White. *Costumes:* Martha Bard, Deborah Benson, Gariel Berry, Mary Brecht, Maura Clifford, Madeline Cohen, Shay Cunliffe, Sajada Fakar, Lisa Fahrner, Edmund Felix, Diane Fox, Gene Galvin, Max Hager, Bob Horek, Diane Klein, Carla Kramer, Jenna Krempel, Johnetta Lever, Monica Lorca, Ruth Morley, Susan Mosakowski, Natasha, Molly Parkin, Bernard Roth, Wendy Snyder, Angeline Thomas, George Vallo, Alison Yerxa. *Lights:* Betsy Adams, David Adams, Jeff Bartlett, Donald L. Brooks, Pat Collins, Anna Conner, Richard Currie, Marc Daniels, John P. Dodd, Beverly Emmons, Julienne Fisher, Fern Gnesin, Adam Gross, Richard Harmon, Celia Hughes, Scott Hunsberger, Peter Kaczorowski, Marcus Lopez, Barbara Kopit, Terri Lucas, Julie McCallister, Brian MacDevitt, Lance Miller, Melody Percoco, Joe Ray, Amy Richards, Terry Alan Smith, Joanna Snielke, Pat Stern, Neile Weissman, Susan A. White, Joni Wong, Woodstock.

Media resources

Film: *The Red Kimono* (company-produced), *Street Theater/N.Y.C.* (company-produced, documentary).

Theater of the Open Eye. Muna Tseng and Jean Erdman in *The Shining House.* Photo: Redmon Simonsen.

Theater of the Open Eye

Jean Erdman
Artistic Director

316 East 88th St.
New York, NY 10028
(212) 534–6363 (business)
(212) 534–6909 (box office)

Founded 1972
Jean Erdman, Joseph Campbell

Season
September–June

Schedule
Evenings
Tuesday–Sunday
Matinees
Saturday, Sunday

Facilities
Seating capacity: 100
Stage: flexible

Finances
July 1, 1980–June 30, 1981
\$146,000 operating expenses
\$ 62,000 earned income
\$ 58,000 grants/contributions

Audience
Annual attendance: 11,200

Booked-in events
Theatre, dance

AEA Off Broadway contract, Mini contract and Showcase code

The Theater of the Open Eye shares with its parent organization, the Foundation for the Open Eye, an interest in the roots of human thought and feeling as revealed in mythic and poetic images. The theme is evident in its "Total Theater Repertoire" of productions conceived, directed and choreographed by artistic director Jean Erdman. The works are inspired by poets and visual artists, deal with mythic heroes, and are staged in a fusion of performing arts: music, dance and drama. Notable among the Total Theater productions are the award-winning *Coach with Six Insides* and *Moon Mysteries,* and the 1980–81 production of *The Shining House.*

To support its Total Theater approach, the Open Eye provides opportunities for talented directors and choreographers to perfect their craft. The Directors Unit, a group of directors selected from the theatre's New Stagings Lab, searches for new dramatic works or classical adaptations and develops them in collaboration with the playwright, in readings as well as in full-scale productions in the Directors Series.

The Choreographers Unit, a select group of dancer/choreographers from Erdman's dance theatre company, develops new dance works in the Choreographers Series. Then, each season, these two artistic disciplines meet in at least one Total Theater piece—sometimes a new work, sometimes a revival from the ongoing repertoire—sometimes both.

Each season, as a resource to the Open Eye directors and choreographers as well as the community at large, the Foundation for the Open Eye presents the popular seminar series, "Realms of the Creative Spirit," by internationally renowned lecturer and author Joseph Campbell. The series deals with universal philosophical, psychological, artistic and mythical subjects.

Other activities of the Open Eye include touring productions, workshops, dance and acting classes and internships.

Productions 1979–80
Celebration of Michio Ito, Satoru Shimazaki
- *Isle of the Seal,* Leslee Asch; music: Arnold Franchetti
- *Demeter's Daughters,* Nancy Allison, Robert Mahaffay, Bernard Baschet and Michel Deneuve

Moon Mysteries, adapt: Jean Erdman, from William Butler Yeats; music: Teiji Ito
- *The Shining House II,* Jean Erdman; music: Michael Czajkowski; lyrics: Christopher Millis
- *Three Irish Noh Plays,* Ulick O'Connor
- *Details (of the sixteenth frame),* Robert Walter

Productions 1980–81
- *The Shining House III,* Jean Erdman; music: Michael Czajkowski; lyrics: Christopher Millis
- *Damien,* Aldyth Morris
- *Redeye,* Steven Tenney

The Shining House

Directors
Nancy Allison, Leslee Asch, Amie Brockway, Jean Erdman, James Flannery, Nola Hague

Designers
Sets: Campbell Baird, Adrienne J. Brockway, Craig Evans, Rob Hamilton, Scott Johnson, Trueman Kelley, Will Morrison. *Costumes:* Consolata Boyle, Adrienne J. Brockway, Kishiko Coko, Dan Erkkila, Bobbie Hodges, Masayoshi Immamura, Kasaku Ito, Michio Ito, Ralph Lee, Patricia McGourty, Seiji Mano, Polly Smith, Kwok Yee Tai, Kevin Woodworth. *Lights:* Adrienne J. Brockway, Craig Evans, Scott Johnson, Gregg Marriner, Will Morrison, Beth J. Plein, Michael Orris Watson.

Media resources
Video: *The Coach with Six Insides* (WNET), *Moon Mysteries, Haitian Suite, The Shining House* (Lincoln Center Research Library), *Redeye* (company-produced).

Theatre Project Company

Fontaine Syer
Artistic Director

Christine E. Smith
General Manager

711 North Grand St.
St. Louis, MO 63103
(314) 531–1301

Founded 1975
Fontaine Syer, Christine E. Smith

Season
October–May

Schedule
Evenings
Wednesday–Sunday
Matinees
Sunday

Facilities
Mainstage
Seating capacity: 225
Stage: thrust
Childrens Theatre Space
Seating capacity: 300
Stage: flexible

Finances
July 1, 1980–June 30, 1981
$173,000 operating expenses
$122,000 earned income
$ 51,000 grants/contributions

Audience
Annual attendance: 44,285
Subscribers: 1,330

Touring contacts
Courtney Flanagan
Brian Hohlfeld

AEA Chicago Off Loop Theatre contract

The Theatre Project Company is a resident theatre offering the St. Louis area varied theatre experiences in an intimate space. The Project is dedicated to employing St. Louis artists, and its season includes a balance of classic and contemporary works with an "Off Broadway" ambience in regard to play choices and production styles. Committed to a city location, the Project has earned a reputation for quality, energy and creative risk-taking.

With minimal technical elements, the productions are devoted to emotional communication and the maximum interaction between actors and audience. Highlights of previous seasons include *The Taming of the Shrew* set in the American Wild West, *Lenny, Waiting for Godot* and the Missouri premieres of such plays as *Loose Ends, Getting Out* and *Sexual Perversity in Chicago.*

The Muny/Student Theatre Project is a student program designed and operated by the Theatre Project Company for The Muny (an outdoor theatre run by the Municipal Opera Corporation), and is an extensive combination of workshops, residencies and performances for kindergarten through high school. The performance activity includes touring plays, story-telling and one mainstage production each year. With each production tailored to specific grade levels, the Muny/Student Theatre Project is the most comprehensive student program in the state: in 1980–81, over 35,000 students participated in some element of the program.

The Theatre Project Company is currently making plans to move to a new space which will house a 500-seat theatre, a flexible performance space for the student program and extended classroom facilities. In the new theatre, the Project will continue to offer its audiences intimate theatre and an unconventional approach. Priorities will include continued development of St. Louis theatre artists, growth in teaching capabilities and experimentation with new works and non-traditional forms. The Theatre Project Company will also maintain its balance in play selection and its reputation for creativity, imagination and artistic challenges.

Productions 1979–80
Hamlet, William Shakespeare
• *Huck Finn,* adapt: Stoney Breyer, from Mark Twain
The Homecoming, Harold Pinter
The Member of the Wedding, Carson McCullers
Getting Out, Marsha Norman
The Little Foxes, Lillian Hellman
A Child's Christmas in Wales, Dylan Thomas
• *Arabian Nights,* company-developed
• *Monkey Signs,* company-developed
• *American Tall Tales,* company-developed
• *American Indian Tales,* company-developed

Productions 1980–81
Catch-22, Joseph Heller
Treasure Island, adapt: Timothy Mason, from Robert Louis Stevenson
Loose Ends, Michael Weller
Cat on a Hot Tin Roof, Tennessee Williams
A Taste of Honey, Shelagh Delaney
The Tempest, William Shakespeare
A Child's Christmas in Wales
• *And That Is What I Saw,* John Contini
• *The Wrath of Achilles,* David Novak
American Tall Tales
American Indian Tales
• *In the Beginning,* company-developed

Directors
Yvonne Ghareeb, William Grivna, Brian Hohlfeld, David Novak, Wayne Salomon, Fontaine Syer

Designers
Sets: Carol Billings, Hunter Breyer, Mike Hensley, David Novak, Pook Pfaffe, Bill Schmiel, Sue Sessions, Ralph Wilkie. *Costumes:* Linda Bosomworth, Hunter Breyer, Wanda Curth, Deborah Gnadige, Jay Singleton, Jane Alois Stein, Jeffrey Struckman, Kay Webb. *Lights:* Robert Proskow, Christine E. Smith, Deirdre A. Taylor.

Media Resources
Video: *Gypsy Wedding Day* (KETC).

Theatre Project Company. Jim Michael and Bobby Miller in *Cat on a Hot Tin Roof.* Photo: Jerry McAdams.

Theatre Three. Laurence O'Dwyer, Michael Van Dalsem and Megan Eileen Ready in *Strider.* Photo: Andy Hanson.

Theatre Three

Jac Alder
Producer-Director

2800 Routh St.
Dallas, TX 75201
(214) 748–5193 (business)
(214) 748–5191 (box office)

Founded 1961
Norma Young

Season
October–August

Schedule
Evenings
Tuesday–Sunday
Matinees
Sunday

Facilities
Seating capacity: 250
Stage: arena

Finances
September 1, 1980–August 31, 1981
$776,000 operating expenses
$486,000 earned income
$290,000 grants/contributions

Audience
Annual attendance: 97,295
Subscribers: 4,465

Touring contact
Thom Schilling

Booked-in events
Theatre, dance

AEA LORT (D) contract

Theatre Three was named by its founder, Norma Young, for the three elements of theatrical experience: the script, the production and the audience. Young's aim was to create an artistic environment in which each of these elements could make an equal contribution.

At Theatre Three, audiences bring their temperaments and their senses of time and place to bear upon an eclectic play selection. Recognizing the varied constituencies within the audience—and within the arts community—the range includes plays on the black experience, plays with music, works of new playwrights, classics, staples of academic study and a special series of children's plays.

The physical style of Theatre Three's productions reflects the characteristics of the modified arena space designed for the company. Professional actors populate the spectacle, supported by detailed and selective designs. In encouraging the artistic processes, guest directors and designers are frequently employed, while new professionals are developed through an intern program.

Theatre Three also pursues a relationship with sister arts organizations; joint productions have been presented with minority arts companies and musical organizations in Dallas. Other outreach efforts include serving as a sponsor of touring dance companies, mimes and other artists. In addition, Theatre Three is networked to health and welfare organizations and educational institutions, each being served by the theatre's programs and each helping the theatre to refine its focus. Last season Theatre Three toured a production to 14 states, acquiring production experience in a variety of settings.

Productions 1979–80
Chicago, book: Fred Ebb and Bob Fosse; music: John Kander; lyrics: Fred Ebb
The New York Idea, Langdon Mitchell
For Colored Girls who have Considered Suicide/When The Rainbow is Enuf, Ntozake Shange
The Taking Away of Little Willie, Tom Griffin
Drinks Before Dinner, E.L. Doctorow
How I Got That Story, Amlin Gray
The Seagull, Anton Chekhov; trans: Ronald Hingley
Present Laughter, Noel Coward
• *Yip, Yip Hooray!,* lyrics: E.Y. Harburg; adapt: Jac Alder

Productions 1980–81
Strider, book: Mark Rozovsky; lyrics: Uri Riashentsev and Steve Brown; adapt: Robert Kalfin and Steve Brown; music: S. Vetkin and Mark Rozovsky
A Woman of No Importance, Oscar Wilde
Bedroom Farce, Alan Ayckbourn
• *The Miss Firecracker Contest,* Beth Henley
• *Father Dreams,* Mary Gallagher
House of Flowers, book and lyrics: Truman Capote; music: Harold Arlen
The Elephant Man, Bernard Pomerance
• *Say It with Music by Irving Berlin,* music and lyrics: Irving Berlin; adapt: Jac Alder

Directors
Jac Alder, Lynne Gannaway, Michael Gillespie, Charles Howard, Laurence O'Dwyer, Norma Young

Designers
Sets: Jac Alder, Charles Howard, Peter Metz, Linda K. Williamson, Harland Wright. *Costumes:* Patty Greer McGarity. *Lights:* Shari Melde, Peter Metz, Linda K. Williamson.

Theatre X

John D. Schneider
Flora Coker
Associate Artistic Directors

Kathleen A. McCain
Managing Director

Box 92206
Milwaukee, WI 53202
(414) 278–0555

Founded 1969
Conrad Bishop, Linda Bishop, Ron Gural

Season
September–July

Schedule
Evenings
Thursday–Saturday

Facilities
Black Box Theatre
Lincoln Center for the Arts
820 East Knapp St.
Seating capacity: 105
Stage: flexible

Finances
September 1, 1980–August 31, 1981
$121,000 operating expenses
$ 22,000 earned income
$ 78,000 grants/contributions

Audience
Annual attendance: 7,253
Subscribers: 601

Touring contact
Kathleen A. McCain

Booked-in events
Theatre, music, mime, dance, poetry

The "X" in Theatre X has always stood for flexibility of definition; for freedom from a too-closely defined artistic identity. Theatre X exists to facilitate the work of its membership, a core of which has remained consistent for over 10 years. This work represents an ongoing process of theatrical research and experiment, of individual and collective perceptual development and change, of social criticism and cultural analysis, and of political argument. Theatre X provides its audience with a forum for discussion of matters theatrical, perceptual, philosophical and political.

The company divides its year into two parts: a six-month season in Milwaukee during which it presents three to four productions, and a six-month touring season during which its activities include national and international touring, residencies in other American cities or in Europe, and periods of research and development of new material.

On the local and state level, the company's services include an apprentice program, a Milwaukee outreach program, a humanities program, an Open Lab series which includes the public in development of the company's work, and a multiplicity of activities fostering the growth, public awareness and support of the entire Milwaukee arts community. The company also provides workshops as part of its touring program.

While Theatre X is built around the work generated by its membership, it also employs guest directors, performers, composers, designers and playwrights, most of whom have a continuing relationship with the company. A season usually includes both original work and interpretations of extant scripts, classic and contemporary.

Productions 1979–80
The Ride Across Lake Constance, Peter Handke; trans: Michael Roloff
Schmaltz, John Schneider; music: Mark Van Hecke
The Fantod: A Victorian Reverie, Amlin Gray
• *Penelope: Her Limitations,* John Schneider
Dreambelly, Conrad Bishop
Orpheus, Jean Cocteau

Productions 1980–81
• *Lily: or Remind Me Not to Do a Solo Show Again,* John Schneider
An Interest in Strangers, John Schneider; music: Henk van der Mulen
I Used to Like This Place Before They Starting Making All Those Renovations, John Schneider and company; music: Henk van der Mulen
• *Acts of Kindness,* John Schneider and company
Hedda Gabler, Henrik Ibsen

Directors
Conrad Bishop, Flora Coker, June Fortunato, Marcie E. Hoffman, Diane Johnson, John Kishline, Sharon Ott, John Schneider

Designers
Sets: Conrad Bishop, Flora Coker, Kathryn Cornell, Diane Johnson, Stuart Johnson, John Kishline, Sharon Ott, John Schneider, Robert Sieger, Tim Thomas. *Costumes:* Deborah Clifton, Kathryn Cornell, Ellen Kozak, Colleen Scott. *Lights:* Conrad Bishop, John Kishline, Robert Sieger.

Media resources
Video: *Acts of Kindness* (Medusa International, documentary), *I Used to Like This Place Before They Started Making All Those Renovations* (The Mickery Theatre).

Theatre X. *I Used to Like This Place Before They Started Making All Those Renovations.* Photo: Bob Van Dantzig.

Trinity Square Repertory Company. *The Suicide.* Photo: Constance Brown.

Trinity Square Repertory Company

Adrian Hall
Artistic Director

E. Timothy Langan
Managing Director

201 Washington St.
Providence, RI 02903
(401) 521-1100 (business)
(401) 351-4242 (box office)

Founded 1964
Adrian Hall

Season
Year-round

Schedule
Evenings
Tuesday-Sunday
Matinees
Wednesday, Saturday, Sunday

Facilities
Upstairs Theatre
Seating capacity: 485
Stage: flexible
Downstairs Theatre
Seating capacity: 297
Stage: thrust

Finances
July 1, 1980-June 30, 1981
$1,550,000 operating expenses
$1,145,000 earned income
$ 480,000 grants/contributions

Audience
Annual attendance: 175,000
Subscribers: 13,626

Touring contact
E. Timothy Langan

Booked-in events
Dance, music, theatre, cabaret

AEA LORT (C) contract

In 17 stormy years, Trinity Square Repertory Company has established itself as a unique American theatrical ensemble. A permanent company requires a permanent audience as well as a talented group of artists dedicated to learning about themselves through their art. Since 1964 Trinity actors have worked in continuity with founding director Adrian Hall. "Time is the most expensive thing," says Hall. "It usually takes 20 years for an actor to master his craft. The actors at Trinity are much more interested in process than in product. For that, a permanent audience is necessary."

Trinity draws its audience from all over the eastern United States. Project Discovery, which brings high school students to the theatre as part of their curriculum, continues as a major source of new audiences. Originally funded in 1966 by the National Endowment for the Arts and the U.S. Office of Education, the endeavor has become an integral part of area educational systems.

Three programs initiated in 1978 continue successfully: Trinity Rep Conservatory, a full-time training program for actors, directors and playwrights; a Rhode Island Committee for the Humanities-sponsored project offering audiences after-theatre symposia and scholarly essays relating to all main season productions; and a three-play summer season.

The Antoinette Perry ("Tony") Award for distinguished service to the theatre was given to the company in 1981, the same year in which Trinity Rep was chosen by the Arts America Program of the U.S. International Communication Agency to perform two American plays, Steinbeck's *Of Mice and Men* and Sam Shepard's *Buried Child* on a six-week tour of India and Syria.

Productions 1979–80
Born Yesterday, Garson Kanin
A Christmas Carol, adapt: Adrian Hall and Richard Cumming, from Charles Dickens
• *The Suicide,* Nikolai Erdman; trans: George Genereux, Jr. and Jacob Volkov; music: Richard Cumming
The Night of the Iguana, Tennessee Williams
Waiting for Godot, Samuel Beckett
Bosoms and Neglect, John Guare
Sly Fox, Larry Gelbart
Buried Child, Sam Shepard
Sea Marks, Gardner McKay
El Grande de Coca-Cola, Ron House, John Neville-Andrews, Alan Shearman, Diz White and Sally Willis
An Almost Perfect Person, Judith Ross
Deathtrap, Ira Levin

Productions 1980–81
Arsenic and Old Lace, Joseph Kesselring
A Christmas Carol
The Iceman Cometh, Eugene O'Neill
Inherit the Wind, Jerome Lawrence and Robert E. Lee
Whose Life Is It Anyway?, Brian Clark
Betrayal, Harold Pinter
On Golden Pond, Ernest Thompson
• *The Whales of August,* David A. Berry
How I Got That Story, Amlin Gray
The Elephant Man, Bernard Pomerance
Talley's Folly, Lanford Wilson

Directors
Larry Arrick, Peter Gerety, Adrian Hall, Melanie Jones, Jonas Jurasas, Richard Kneeland, James Howard Laurence, George Martin, Philip Minor, William Radka, Henry Velez

Designers
Sets: Eugene Lee, Robert D. Soule. *Costumes:* William Lane. *Lights:* John F. Custer.

Media resources
Film: *Life Among the Lowly* (KCET), *The House of Mirth* (WNET), *Portrait of a Director in Exile* (WGBH, documentary). Video: *Feasting with Panthers, Brother to Dragons* (WNET).

Victory Gardens Theater. *Latino Chicago!* Photo: David Joel.

Victory Gardens Theater

Dennis Zacek
Artistic Director

Marcelle McVay
General Manager

2257 North Lincoln Ave.
Chicago, IL 60614
(312) 871-3000

Founded 1974

Season
September–July

Schedule
Evenings
Tuesday–Sunday
Matinees
Sunday

Facilities
Mainstage
Seating capacity: 200
Stage: thrust
Studio
Seating capacity: 70
Stage: proscenium

Finances
July 1, 1980–June 30, 1981
$338,000 operating expenses
$206,000 earned income
$142,000 grants/contributions

Audience
Annual attendance: 53,000
Subscribers: 1,850

Touring contact
Marcelle McVay

Booked-in events
Theatre

AEA Chicago Off Loop Theatre contract

Victory Gardens Theater was founded to promote and develop Chicago's theatre artists—actors, writers, designers and directors—and to provide locally based professional theatre to Chicago audiences. Under the artistic direction of Dennis Zacek since 1977, the theatre expanded its programming to include five Mainstage productions, five Studio productions, a Readers Theater Series and touring productions.

On the Mainstage, Zacek is committed to producing new works. Approximately three per season are world premieres selected for their appeal to Chicago audiences, and at least one script by a black playwright is produced each year. With funding from CBS Inc., Victory Gardens developed the first professional Latin theatre ensemble in Chicago and, for the past two seasons, this new company has produced one play on the Mainstage. The Latino Chicago Theater Company has also toured extensively to city high schools and community centers. Student matinees for Mainstage productions are heavily attended, and one performance of each play is interpreted for the hearing impaired. In 1981, Victory Gardens welcomed its first playwright in residence, Steve Carter.

In the Studio theatre a five-play season consisting of new plays or plays with a more limited audience appeal are produced. *The Artaud Project,* a stage-video presentation was a unique artistic and commercial success in 1980. Three of the Studio plays feature students from the Theater Center, the educational arm of Victory Gardens. The Theater Center offers classes to over 800 students per year in all aspects of the theatre. Classes are geared both to the novice and the professional, and a minimum of 14 are offered during each eight-week session.

The Readers Theater Series showcases new scripts in free staged readings, with discussion sessions attended by the playwright, director and cast following each performance.

In July of 1981, Victory Gardens, along with the Body Politic Theatre, announced their joint purchase of a facility at 2257–63 North Lincoln Avenue, the building which the Body Politic already occupied on a rental basis. The two theatre companies will maintain distinct identities and produce their own seasons, while collaborating on some programs and services. The Body Politic occupies the upstairs theatre, while Victory Gardens will use the newly renovated Mainstage and Studio theatres on the ground level. Artistic director Dennis Zacek comments, "Our cooperative venture will help to preserve a historical building from which the Chicago Off Loop theatre originated, offering the theatre patron the best of all worlds, as the Body Politic continues to present primarily revivals and classics, while Victory Gardens maintains its tradition of presenting Midwest and Chicago premieres."

Productions 1979–80
- *Hard Feelings,* Jeffrey Sweet
  Hollywood Confidential, Charles Busch
  Nevis Mountain Dew, Steve Carter
  Other Pinter Pauses, Harold Pinter
- *The Artaud Project,* James Rinnert
  The Play's the Thing, Ferenc Molnar; adapt: P.G. Wodehouse
- *Polaroids,* Virginia Smiley
  Porch, Jeffrey Sweet
- *Latino Chicago!,* Latino Chicago Theater Company
  Slow Dance on the Killing Ground, William Hanley
- *The Examen,* Nicholas Patricca
  Cowboy Mouth, Sam Shepard
  Killer's Head, Sam Shepard

Productions 1980–81
- *Solitaire,* Steven Ivcich
  Home, David Storey
  Three Stories High, adapt: Ruth Landis, from Anton Chekhov, O. Henry and Robert Penn Warren
  The Uprooted/Los Dessaraigados, Humberto Robles
- *Ties,* Jeffrey Sweet
- *Minnesota Moon* and *Harvest Sun,* John Olive

- *Dame Lorraine,* Steve Carter
  Ludlow Fair, Lanford Wilson
  The Dumb Waiter, Harold Pinter
- *La Brea Tarpits,* Alan Gross
- *Bo,* Amlin Gray

Directors
Sam Ball, Ramiro Carrillo, Steven Ivcich, Ruth Landis, Michael Maggio, J. Pat Miller, Mary Ellen McGarry, Michael Menedian, Tom Mula, James Rinnert, Sandy Shinner, Richard Shirley, Chuck Smith, Winifred Valentine, Gregory Williams, Dennis Zacek

Designers
Sets: Maher Ahmad, Thomas Beall, Anne Finan, Mary Griswold, Steven Ivcich, Owen Kerwin, Michael Maddux, Rick Paul, Galen Ramsey, John Rodriguez, Alejandro Romero, Robert G. Smith, Dean Tauscher. *Costumes:* Kate Bergh, Rebecca Brown, Marsha Kowal, Julie Nagel, Linda de Flores Quinones, Jordan Ross, Constance Thome. *Lights:* Geoffrey Bushor, Rita Pietraszek, Galen Ramsey, John Rodriguez, Robert Shook, Robert G. Smith, Karl W. Sullivan.

Virginia Museum Theatre

Tom Markus
Artistic director

Ira Schlosser
Managing Director

Boulevard and Grove Aves.
Richmond, VA 23221
(804) 257–0840 (business)
(804) 257–0831 (box office)

Founded 1955
Virginia Museum of Fine Arts

Season
September–April

Schedule
Evenings
Tuesday–Sunday
Matinees
Wednesday, Saturday, Sunday

Facilities
Seating capacity: 500
Stage: proscenium

Finances
July 1, 1980–June 30, 1981
$600,000 operating expenses
$440,000 earned income
$160,000 grants/contributions

Audience
Annual attendance: 92,000
Subscribers: 10,183

Touring contact
Terry Burgler

Booked-in events
Films

AEA LORT (C) contract

The Virginia Museum Theatre's 1981–82 season marks its 27th year as central Virginia's only resident professional theatre, with a burgeoning audience, expanded programming and a growing commitment to new plays. VMT continues its 1980–81 format, a six-play mainstage season and a three-play studio season, that resulted in all-time records in season subscriptions and single-play attendance. While the mainstage programming services the larger, more diverse Richmond community, the studio season is designed to challenge a more select audience of adventurous theatregoers.

Housed in the Virginia Museum of Fine Arts, VMT aspires to offer theatre art equal to the gallery art exhibited in the museum. Expanding VMT's traditional diversity of programming, the 1981–82 season will include three world premieres, one American premiere and a new reader's theatre series of four original scripts. A spring tour of *Macbeth (An Abridged Version)* will conclude a season of traditional and modern classics, musicals, premieres and popular contemporary scripts.

For the third year, VMT will honor a major theatre figure by presenting its Annual Award for Outstanding Contribution to Professional Theatre to Helen Hayes. Previous recipients have been Irene Worth and John Houseman.

VMT places a strong emphasis on educational and community services. In addition to student matinees, there are public lecture series and a Resident Apprentice Program which is accredited by many universities and offers professional training in design, production and administration. The theatre also provides student-ticket discounts, statewide touring, post-performance discussions, a film series, a restaurant, a speakers bureau and a volunteer auxiliary.

VMT believes that theatre is a public celebration and desires to share its vision and enthusiasm with the largest and most diverse audience possible.

Virginia Museum Theatre.
William Denis and Yolande Bavan in *A Midsummer Night's Dream.* Photo: Virginia Museum of Fine Arts.

Productions 1980–81
Side by Side by Sondheim, music and lyrics: Stephen Sondheim, et al.; adapt: Ned Sherrin
- *Mother Courage and Her Children,* Bertolt Brecht; adapt: Robert A. Potter

The Good Doctor, Neil Simon
Waiting for Godot, Samuel Beckett
The Second Man, S.N. Behrman
As You Like It, William Shakespeare

Productions 1980–81
Deathtrap, Ira Levin
Godspell, book: John-Michael

Tebelak; music and lyrics: Stephen Schwartz
Sizwe Bansi Is Dead, Athol Fugard, John Kani and Winston Ntshona
The Fourposter, Jan de Hartog
The Sea Horse, Edward J. Moore
A Midsummer Night's Dream, William Shakespeare
Ghosts, Henrik Ibsen; trans: Rolf Fjelde
Happy Days, Samuel Beckett
Something's Afoot, book, music and lyrics: James McDonald, David Vos and Robert Gerlach; additional music: Ed Linderman

Directors
Terry Burgler, Judith Haskell, Gordon Heath, Darwin Knight, Joseph Leonardo, Tom Markus, Jane Page, Russell Treyz

Designers
Sets: Neil Bierbower, Daniel Bishop, James Bumgardner, Charles Caldwell, Howard Cummings, Joseph A. Varga. *Costumes:* Carol H. Beule, Neil Bierbower, Linda Bradley, Bronwyn Caldwell, Mary L. Hayes, Richard Hieronymus, Andrew B. Marley, Joseph A. Varga, Moppy Vogely. *Lights:* Lynne Hartman, Richard Moore.

Virginia Stage Company

Robert W. Tolan
Producing Director

108–114 East Tazewell St.
Norfolk, VA 23510
(804) 627-6988 (business)
(804) 627-1234 (box office)

Founded 1979
Community members

Season
November–May

Schedule
Evenings
Tuesday–Sunday
Matinees
Wednesday, Saturday, Sunday

Facilities
Wells Theatre
Seating capacity: 700
Stage: modified proscenium

Finances
July 1, 1980–June 30, 1981
$504,000 operating expenses
$246,000 earned income
$234,000 grants/contributions

Audience
Annual attendance: 37,225
Subscribers; 4,150

AEA LORT (C) contract

Surrounded by a population of 1.2 million people and housed in a National Historic Landmark, the magnificent Wells Theatre, Virginia Stage Company is a significant new member of the national resident theatre family.

As a professional theatre serving southeastern Virginia and northeastern North Carolina, VSC is committed to the highest standards of performance. The core of its program is a series of fully mounted productions of distinguished plays offering a broad range of theatrical experience appealing to the widest possible audience. Classics, musicals and new scripts mingled with solid favorites provide the audience with rich and challenging variety.

Productions are cast separately, although artists frequently return, forming a "floating company." VSC's Professional Theatre Intern Program trains aspiring young people who aid the staff and artists in the areas of acting, production and administration as they advance into the professional world. In attempting to present dynamic theatre to the entire region, VSC initiated a children's theatre program in 1980, beginning with the presentation of an original script and a classic fairy tale on Saturday mornings by the intern company.

In its first two seasons, VSC mounted twelve major productions, two children's productions and one intern showcase. The company finished the first phase of renovation on its 1912 home, obtained 4,100 subscribers and 200 volunteers, and published two volumes of its newsletter "OnStage."

Following the second season, in 1981, Robert Tolan succeeded Patrick Tovatt as producing director. In its third season, Virginia Stage Company looks forward to the inclusion of a mini-repertory of three plays in the season, the inception of student matinees, an increase in subscribership and the beginning of a resident company.

Productions 1979–80
Relatively Speaking, Alan Ayckbourn
Count Dracula, adapt: Ted Tiller
The Miracle Worker, William Gibson
Sizwe Banzi Is Dead, Athol Fugard, John Kani and Winston Ntshona
I Do! I Do!, book and lyrics: Tom Jones; music: Harvey Schmidt

Productions 1980–81
On Golden Pond, Ernest Thompson
Mrs. Warren's Profession, George Bernard Shaw
Classic Comics: The Flying Doctor and The Ridiculous Young Ladies, Moliere
Buried Child, Sam Shepard
The Incredible Murder of Cardinal Tosca, Alden Nowlan and Walter Learning
LuAnn Hampton Laverty Oberlander, Preston Jones
Hot Grog!, Jim Wann and Bland Simpson

Directors
Israel Hicks, Jackson Phippin, Patrick Tovatt

Designers
Sets: Peter Gould, Paul Owen, Joe Ragey. *Costumes:* Carrie Curtis, Tiny Ossman. *Lights:* Bonnie Ann Brown, Cameron Dye, Richard Moore, Paul Owen, Joe Ragey.

Virginia Stage Company. *Hot Grog!* Photo: Robert K. Ander, Jr.

Westport Country Playhouse. Timothy Askew and Van Johnson in *Tribute.* Photo: Kellogg Studio.

Westport Country Playhouse

James B. McKenzie
Executive Producer

Todd Haimes
General Manager

Box 629
Westport, CT 06881
(203) 227-5138 (business)
(203) 227-4177 (box office)
(212) 921-8852 (NY direct line)

Founded 1931
Laurence Langner

Season
June-September

Schedule
Evenings
Monday-Saturday
Matinees
Wednesday, Saturday

Facilities
25 Powers Court
Seating Capacity: 800
Stage: proscenium

Finances
November 1, 1980-October 31, 1981
$753,000 operating expenses
$706,000 earned income
$ 65,000 grants/contributions

Audience
Annual attendance: 65,000
Subscribers: 2,200

Touring contact
Jack V. Booch

Booked-in events
Theatre, music

AEA Council on Stock Theatres Resident contract

The Westport Country Playhouse is, by a half-century of tradition, a summer theatre producing 12 plays in the 12 weeks of each summer, with an artistic approach similar to the time-honored methods of Broadway.

Each play is cast separately by the director and producer and productions are usually planned around a recognized leading actor or actress. Its proximity to New York City gives the Playhouse an almost infinite variety of talent to work with.

Rehearsals are held in New York City for two-to-four weeks before a one-week performance run at Westport, and often at several other theatres.

Plays are selected for their mutual interest to the audiences and the actors and directors. New plays, musicals and plays fr^m recent Broadway history are considered for the repertoire, as well as plays of historic or classical interest.

In addition to its regular season, Westport presents a series of nine children's plays and several special Sunday evening concerts or one-person shows.

The theatre maintains a veteran professional support staff of 42 people with an average tenure of more than five years at Westport, creating a distinct continuity of administration. Concurrent with the performing season is an intensive 14-week hands-on intern training program for 12 college seniors. Each department head is responsible for tutorials in his or her discipline.

Of the more than 550 plays produced at Westport, 72 have been world premieres. The theatre plans to continue in its present mode, producing good plays with leading directors and actors under conditions less confining than those found in the commercial theatre.

Productions 1980
The Streets of New York, Dion Boucicault
Chapter Two, Neil Simon
Whose Life Is It Anyway? Brian Clark
• *Children,* A.R. Gurney, Jr.
Horowitz and Mrs. Washington, Henry Denker
Tribute, Bernard Slade

Productions 1981
Tintypes, music and lyrics: various; adapt: Mary Kyte, Mel Marvin and Gary Pearle
Play It Again, Sam, Woody Allen
Battle of Angels, Tennessee Williams
I Ought to Be in Pictures, Neil Simon
Images, David O. Frazier and Joseph J. Garry, Jr.
On Golden Pond, Ernest Thompson

Directors
Clint Atkinson, Jack V. Booch, Wayne Bryan, Warren Crane, John Going, Bill Guske, Martin Herzer, Frank Marino, Robert Morse, Rob Shipp

Designers
Sets: Charles Cosler, Noble Dinse. *Costumes:* Jess Goldstein, Thomas Hansen, Tim Miller, Alvin Perry, Deborah Van Wetering. *Lights:* Charles Cosler, Noble Dinse.

The Whole Theatre

Olympia Dukakis
Artistic Director

Arnold Mittelman
Producing Director

544 Bloomfield Ave.
Montclair, NJ 07042
(201) 744-2996, 2933 (business)
(201) 744-2989 (box office)

Founded 1973

Season
October-April

Schedule
Evenings
Tuesday-Sunday
Matinees
Wednesday, Sunday

Facilities
Seating capacity: 200
Stage: flexible

Finances
July 1, 1980-June 30, 1981
$640,000 operating expenses
$310,000 earned income
$330,000 grants/contributions

Audience
Annual attendance: 40,000
Subscribers: 4,000

Touring contact
Arnold Mittelman

AEA letter of agreement

Now in its ninth year of operation, the Whole Theatre has evolved from a repertory company begun by 16 professional theatre artists holding performances in a church, to a full-fledged producing company in its own award-winning theatre complex with an annual operating budget of close to $650,000.

The Whole Theatre believes that it should be an integral part of its community, and that its artistic riches can be shared in many ways. The theatre's primary commitment is to a 25-week season of five plays beginning in fall and ending in spring. Both traditional and innovative presentations of classics are performed along with new works by both developing and prominent playwrights.

In addition to its main season, the Whole Theatre reaches out to surrounding communities with alternative arts programs coordinated with public schools and social service agencies. The theatre also offers discounts for students and senior citizens, and an internship program for area high schools and colleges, as well as a three-semester professional theatre school offering 30 courses for adults and children.

The Whole Theatre is looking forward to the challenge of its second decade of growth, with those same professional commitments in mind.

Productions 1979–80

The Hostage, Brendan Behan
Spoon River Anthology, adapt: Charles Aidman, from Edgar Lee Masters; music: Naomi C. Hirshhorn
Waiting for Godot, Samuel Beckett
• *Words,* Tony Tanner and Martin Silvestri
• *A Cat in the Ghetto,* Shimon Wincelberg

Productions 1980–81

• *Cole,* music and lyrics: Cole Porter; adapt: Benny Green and Alan Strachen
A Thousand Clowns, Herb Gardner
• *Tartuffe,* Moliere; adapt: Harold De Felice
• *The Death and Resurrection of Mr. Roche,* Thomas Kilroy
• *Daughters,* John Morgan Evans

Directors

Lynne Guerra, Peter Kass, Arnold Mittelman, Philip Polito, David Rotenberg, Amy Saltz, Tony Tanner, Harold De Felice

Designers

Sets: Paul Dorphley, Ronald Placzek, Raymond C. Recht, Patricia Woodbridge. *Costumes:* Sigrid Insull. *Lights:* Marshall Spiller.

Media resources

Video: *Brendan Behan's Ireland, Spoon River U.S.A., Holocaust Fallout, A Godot for the 80s* (company-produced).

The Whole Theatre. Olympia Dukakis, Judith Delgado, Maggie Abeckerly and Apollo Dukakis in *Waiting for Godot.* Photo: Jerry Dalia.

Williamstown Theatre Festival

Nikos Psacharopoulos
Artistic/Executive Director

Gary S. Levine
General Manager

Box 517
Williamstown, MA 01267
(413) 458-8145

Founded 1955
Area residents

Season
July–August

Schedule
Evenings
Tuesday–Saturday
Matinees
Thursday, Saturday

Facilities
Adams Memorial Theatre
Main St.
Seating capacity: 479
Stage: proscenium
Pine Cobble School
Rts. 2/7
Seating capacity: 100
Stage: thrust
Clark Art Institute
South St.
Seating capacity: 300
Stage: proscenium

Finances
December 1, 1980–November 30, 1981
$509,000 operating expenses
$363,000 earned income
$147,000 grants/contributions

Audience
Annual attendance: 49,000

Touring contact
Gary S. Levine

AEA Council on Stock Theatre Resident (Y) contract

Nikos Psacharopoulos helped found the Williamstown Theatre Festival in 1955, and has been its artistic/executive director since 1956. He is advised by a board of trustees, a general manager and a directorate made up of John Conklin, Peter Hunt, Frank Langella, Steve Lawson, Tom Moore, Carrie Nye and Austin Pendleton.

The Festival is divided into four major creative areas. The Main Stage has presented 216 productions of 169 plays in 27 seasons, during which time 2,600 artists have played to over 600,000 people—in recent years, to completely full houses. The focus is on innovative productions of modern masters including Gorky, Brecht, Shaw, Chekhov, Ibsen and Strindberg.

Highlights of the last two seasons include *Cyrano de Bergerac* with Frank Langella and Laurie Kennedy, *Candida* with Blythe Danner and Edward Herrmann, *The Front Page* with Christopher Reeve and Celeste Holm, *The Cherry Orchard* with Colleen Dewhurst and Austin Pendleton, and the American premiere of *The Greeks* with a large cast of renowned actors.

The Second Company has completed its first decade, touring a repertoire of premieres and new plays by David Mamet, Richard Nelson, John Ford Noonan and

Williamstown Theatre Festival. Colleen Dewhurst and Kate Burton in *The Cherry Orchard.* Photo: Joseph Schuyler.

David Rabe, as well as stage adaptations of Kafka, Irving, LeFanu and Machiavelli. The Williamstown Cabaret is a highly popular late-night hotbed of musical revues, and special events at the Clark Art Institute include Sunday afternoons of poetry and song.

WTF also specializes in professional training through its Stage III/General Assistant programs and its nationally known Apprentice Workshop. Graduates of these programs include Laurie Kennedy, Christopher Reeve, Jill Clayburgh and Santo Loquasto. The theatre's aim is to offer a summer home where artists can stretch their talents, far from commercial pressures.

Productions 1980
Cyrano de Bergerac, Edmond Rostand; adapt: Brian Hooker
Candida, George Bernard Shaw
The Front Page, Ben Hecht and Charles MacArthur
Whose Life Is It Anyway?, Brian Clark
The Cherry Orchard, Anton Chekhov
As You Like It, William Shakespeare
Chekhov Creatures, adapt from Anton Chekhov
Pilk's Madhouse, Henry Pilk and Ken Campbell
In the Jungle of Cities, Bertolt Brecht
The Water Engine, David Mamet

Productions 1981
The Greeks, adapt: Kenneth Cavander, from Euripides, Sophocles, Aeschylus and Homer
Arms and the Man, George Bernard Shaw
Summerfolk, Maxim Gorky; adapt: John Tillinger and Edward Gilbert
A Day in the Death of Joe Egg, Peter Nichols
Nude with Violin, Noel Coward
The Winter's Tale, William Shakespeare
Vienna Notes, Richard Nelson
Coming Attractions, Ted Tally
The Inspector General, Nikolai Gogol
• *The Spectre Bridegroom,* adapt: Thomas M. Fontana, from Washington Irving
• *The Haunted Baronet,* adapt: Steve Lawson, from J. Sheridan LeFanu

Directors
Robert Allan Ackerman, John Badham, Gregory Boyd, Arvin Brown, Peter Hunt, John Kazanjian, Steve Lawson, Austin Pendleton, Nikos Psacharopoulous, David Rotenberg, Steven Schachter, David Schweizer, Steve Zuckerman

Designers
Sets: Zack Brown, John Conklin, Andrew Jackness, John Kasarda, Hugh Landwehr, Loren Sherman. *Costumes:* Nan Cibula, John Conklin, Jess Goldstein, Dunya Ramicova, Rita B. Watson. *Lights:* William Armstrong, Pat Collins, Peter Hunt, Roger Meeker, Robby Monk, Dennis Parichy.

Media resources
Video: *The Seagull* (WNET), *Camino Real, The Cherry Orchard* (Lincoln Center Research Library).

Wisdom Bridge Theatre

Robert Falls
Artistic Director

Jeffrey Ortmann
Executive Director

1559 West Howard St.
Chicago, IL 60626
(312) 743-0486 (business)
(312) 743-6442 (box office)

Founded 1974
David Beaird

Season
October–July

Schedule
Evenings
Wednesday–Sunday
Matinees
Sunday

Facilities
Seating capacity: 198
Stage: proscenium

Finances
August 1, 1979–July 31, 1980
$273,000 operating expenses

Wisdom Bridge Theatre. Leland Crooke, Glenne Headly, Sonja Lanzener and Frank Galati in *Mother Courage and Her Children.* Photo: James Goodpasture.

$138,000 earned income
$107,000 grants/contributions

Audience
Annual attendance: 26,000
Subscribers: 650

Booked-in events
Revues, theatre, music

AEA Chicago Off Loop Theatre contract

Wisdom Bridge Theatre, founded in 1974, is a 198-seat theatre located on Chicago's far north side. Under the direction of Robert Falls and Jeffrey Ortmann, the theatre has devoted itself to innovative productions of the classics, new plays by major contemporary playwrights and new adaptations of nondramatic texts.

Wisdom Bridge Theatre considers itself first and foremost a creative environment that encourages its artists to stretch their talents by attempting highly challenging work. By recently renovating and upgrading its performance space, the theatre has encouraged its directors and designers to develop strikingly original physical concepts that greatly amplify and elucidate the texts. Wisdom Bridge strives to produce plays of considerable risk in content, form and the demands they make on the performers. In doing so, the theatre continually stretches its resources and creates large-scale productions that both challenge and amaze its audiences.

Another important aspect of the theatre is the Wisdom Bridge Training Centre. Under the guidance of Edward Kaye-Martin, this professional training program was initiated in March 1981 and is committed to the training and development of both the young actor and the working professional, in a laboratory setting.

Throughout its history, Wisdom Bridge has maintained that its most important element is what happens onstage. This decision has permitted its development as an important producing organization at the forefront of Chicago theatre.

Productions 1979–80
Wings, Arthur Kopit
Travesties, Tom Stoppard
The Importance of Being Earnest, Oscar Wilde
Getting Out, Marsha Norman
Treats, Christopher Hampton

Productions 1980–81
Yentl, Leah Napolin and Isaac Bashevis Singer; music: Mel Marvin
Bent, Martin Sherman
One-Reel Romance, Lenny Kleinfeld; music: Les Stal
Mother Courage and Her Children, Bertolt Brecht; trans: Ralph Mannheim; music: Joseph Reiser
Faith Healer, Brian Friel

Directors
Anne Claus, Robert Falls, Edward Kaye-Martin, Michael Maggio, Jeff Steitzer

Designers
Sets: Gary Baugh, Tom Beall, David Emmons, Don Llewellyn, James Maronek, Michael Merritt. *Costumes:* Ruth Howell, Julie Jackson, Marsha Kowal, Michael Merritt, Kaye Nottbusch, Jordon Ross, Esther K. Smith. *Lights:* Gary Heitz, Dawn Hollingsworth, Michael Merritt, Rita Pietraszek, Robert Shook.

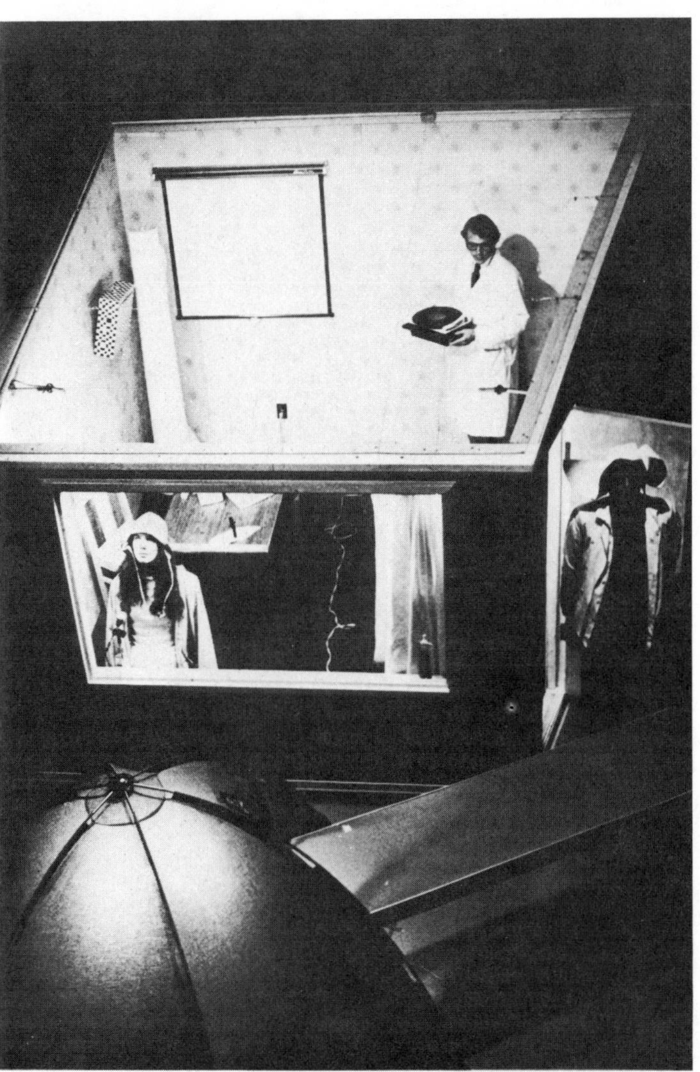

The Wooster Group. Libby Howes, Spalding Gray and Ron Vawter in *Nayatt School.* Photo: Bob Van Dantzig.

The Wooster Group (formerly The Performance Group)

Elizabeth LeCompte
Artistic Director

Jeffrey M. Jones
Administrator

Box 654
Canal Street Station
New York, NY 10013
(212) 966–9796 (business)
(212) 966–3651 (box office)

Founded 1967
Richard Schechner

Season
Year-round

Schedule
Evenings
Monday–Sunday

Facilities
The Performing Garage
33 Wooster St.
Seating: 125
Stage: flexible

Finances
July 1, 1980–June 30, 1981
$129,000 operating expenses
$158,000 earned income
$ 84,000 grants/contributions

Audience
Annual attendance: 40,000

Touring contact
Jeffrey M. Jones

Booked-in events
Experimental theatre, dance, performance art

The Wooster Group is a collaboration of theatre artists: director Elizabeth LeCompte, performers Willem Dafoe, Spalding Gray, Libby Howes, Kate Valk and Ron Vawter, and designer Jim Clayburgh. The Group's most recent works include the trilogy *Three Places in Rhode Island (Sakonnet Point, Rumstick Road* and *Nayatt School), Point Judith* and *The Last Act.* All these works, directed by LeCompte, were composed collaboratively by the Group throughout the rehearsal process.

The Group's pieces are constructed architechtonically;

that is, the structure is defined by space and by language. The pieces employ a dislocated narrative. Compositional elements include film, slide and video imagery, recreations of found material ranging from classic American dramas to family documents, and stagings of original texts. The works focus on themes of breakdown, renewal, authority and autonomy of the individual, family and society. Throughout the Group's 15 years of development, it has been associated with the most significant movements in the theatre of the '60s and '70s: autobiographic theatre, environmental theatre, directors' and performers' theatre, and theatre of images.

The Wooster Group is in residence at The Performing Garage, a performance space which it owns and administers, and which is one of the primary sites of innovative performance work in the country. In addition to producing its own works at the Garage, the Group produces pieces by individual Group members, and presents a season of visiting theatre, dance and performance artists. The Group's other annual activities include foreign and domestic touring, and workshops in performance and composition techniques conducted both on tour and at The Performing Garage.

Productions 1979–80
- • *Point Judith,* company-developed
- • *Three By Gray,* Spalding Gray
  - *Sex and Death to the Age 14*
  - *Booze, Cars and College Girls*
  - *India and After (America)*
- *The Balcony,* Jean Genet

Productions 1980–81
- *Point Judith*
- • *A Personal History of the American Theatre,* Spalding Gray
- • *Standing Room Only,* Libby Howes
- • *The Last Act,* company-developed

Directors
Elizabeth LeCompte, Richard Schechner

Designers
Sets: Jim Clayburgh, Libby Howes, Elizabeth LeCompte, Jerry Rojo, Richard Schechner. *Costumes:* Elizabeth LeCompte, Libby Howes, Karen D. Miller, Kate Valk. *Lights:* Scott Breindel, Jim Clayburgh, Libby Howes, Elizabeth LeCompte, Richard Schechner, Kate Valk.

Media resources
Film: *Dionysus in 69, Tooth of Crime* (company-produced). Radio: *Three by Gray* (company-produced/WBAI). Video: *Rumstick Road* (Lincoln Center Research Library).

Worcester Foothills Theatre Company. Richard Mason and Paul Mayberry in *Chapter Two.* Photo: Lindon E. Rankin.

Worcester Foothills Theatre Company

Marc P. Smith
Executive Producer/Artistic Director

Box 236
Worcester, MA 01602
(617) 754–3314 (business)
(617) 754–4018 (box office)

Founded 1974
Marc P. Smith

Season
September–May

Schedule
Evenings
Wednesday–Sunday
Matinees
Thursday, Saturday, Sunday

Facilities
Foothills Theatre
6 Chatham St.
Seating capacity: 200
Stage: thrust

Finances
June 1, 1980–May 31, 1981
$221,000 operating expenses
$190,000 earned income
$ 19,000 grants/contributions

Audience
Annual attendance: 29,000
Subscribers: 2,150

Touring contact
James D. Moran

The Worcester Foothills Theatre Company is dedicated to maintaining a dialogue with its audience, and to giving artistic expression to that audience's values and beliefs. Plays are selected to please, challenge and sometimes to embroil their viewers in honest debate. For the various generations of Worcester theatregoers, satisfaction is often found in discovering familiar emotions in the worlds of Ibsen, O'Neill, Simon, Moliere, Shakespeare and new authors—worlds which they may never before have entered. Popular plays are often extended or repeated in accordance with the tastes and wishes of the community.

Worcester's professional company is comprised of both resident members and artists working on a one-time basis. The resident company, representing administrative, technical, acting and directing staffs, are encouraged to make themselves active members of the community, and to share the ideas they gather with the rest of the company. Although the ratio of company members to jobbed-in artists is now one-to-three, Worcester hopes eventually to reverse these figures and to base the company upon the European system of resident theatre companies. To that end, the theatre is translating into English the history and rules of the Schauspielhaus in Zurich and adapting that knowledge to its own use.

Within the Worcester Foothills company, each member is assigned to specific duties but participation in active preproduction and production meetings creates an ensemble feeling. The theatre's conservatory offers classes in theatre arts for all ages, and internship, apprentice and volunteer programs are also vital aspects of its service to the community. Company members represent the theatre in local service organizations such as the Rotary and Exchange Clubs, belong to cultural and educational organizations, and actively participate in civic affairs.

Foothills is beginning to expand, sending out tour groups and lecturers, and is now moving into the realms of film and TV, having just completed its first feature-length video production based on an original script.

The sustenance and growth of the Worcester Foothills Theatre Company depend on the success of the dialogue the company maintains with the community it serves.

Productions 1979–80
- *Relatively Speaking,* Alan Ayckbourn
- *Ghosts,* Henrik Ibsen
- *Saint Joan,* George Bernard Shaw
- • *Viva Vaudeville,* adapt: Marc P. Smith
- • *The Hound of the Baskervilles,* adapt: Kricker James, from Arthur Conan Doyle
- *The Glass Menagerie,* Tennessee Williams

Yale Repertory Theatre. James Earl Jones and Dianne Wiest in *Hedda Gabler.* Photo: Gerry Goodstein.

Two Bites of An Irish Apple, Sean O'Casey
A Pound on Demand
The End of the Beginning
• *Memo from a Mad Producer,* book: Marc P. Smith; music and lyrics: Ernest McCarty

Productions 1980–81
How the Other Half Loves, Alan Ayckbourn
Dangerous Corner, J.B. Priestley
• *Sea Marks,* Gardner McKay
• *Bye Bye to Broadway,* adapt: James Kirkland
Dr. Cook's Garden, Ira Levin
Chapter Two, Neil Simon
The Lady's Not for Burning, Christopher Fry
Catch Me If You Can, Jack Weinstock and Willie Gilbert

Directors
Dana Coen, Rose Dresser, Geoffrey Hitch, William E. Hunt, Kricker James, Wyman Kane, William A. Kilmer, James Kirkland, Jack Magune, Paul Mayberry, Marc P. Smith

Designers
Sets: Francis Kiman, Jr. Lindon E. Rankin, Don Ricklin.
Costumes: Wyman Kane, Pamela Kiman, Dianne Lent Holmes.
Lights: Sal Gionesi Jr., Francis Kiman Jr.

Media resources
Video: *Takeover* (Seven Hills Productions).

Yale Repertory Theatre

Lloyd Richards
Artistic Director

Edward A. Martenson
Managing Director

222 York St.
New Haven, CT 06520
(203) 436–1587 (business)
(203) 436–1600 (box office)

Founded 1966
Robert Brustein

Season
October–May

Schedule
Evenings
Monday–Saturday
Matinees
Wednesday, Saturday

Facilities
1120 Chapel St.
Seating capacity: 491
Stage: modified thrust
University Theatre
222 York St.
Seating capacity: 684
Stage: proscenium

Finances
July 1, 1980–June 30, 1981
$1,261,000 operating expenses
$ 320,000 earned income
$ 740,000 grants/contributions

Audience
Annual attendance: 66,500
Subscribers: 5,444

AEA LORT (C) contract

The Yale Repertory Theatre is a professional company affiliated with the Yale School of Drama, under the artistic direction of Lloyd Richards. Since its founding in 1966, the Rep has been devoted to innovative productions of European and American classics, and to fostering the most daring and exciting new plays of emerging playwrights. Of some 107 productions in 15 seasons, 52 have been world premieres, 39 by American playwrights.

During the 1980–81 season, a new element was introduced into the repertoire: the first

"Winterfest" of new American plays, featuring the works of four of this country's most promising writers, in rotating repertory. Winterfest promises to be an integral part of future seasons at the Yale Rep.

The Yale School of Drama (founded in 1924 as the graduate department of drama of the School of Fine Arts, and reorganized as a professional school in 1955) serves as the conservatory wing of the Rep. The two entities exist in close collaboration, with many Rep members teaching at the school and all students training at the Rep. Graduates of the drama school, which is headed by Richards along with associate dean Earle Gister, take their places as distinguished members of many of the country's finest arts institutions. The school offers training in acting, directing, design, technical design and production, administration, playwriting, dramaturgy and literary criticism, as well as technical production internships.

A wealth of student productions and workshops are produced during the course of each year as part of the training program, with plays directed by leading theatre professionals including Lee Breuer, George Roy Hill and Andrei Serban.

The Rep, housed in a former Baptist church since 1971, offers a subscription series of eight plays (including two productions from the Winterfest). Located at the edge of the Yale campus in downtown New Haven, the Rep serves both "town" and "gown" communities, offering student matinees and study guides, discounts for students and senior citizens as well as members of the Yale community, post-performance discussions, workshop productions, staged readings, film series, the Yale Cabaret and a speakers bureau. These elements combine to foster New Haven's status as the "largest little city" in the American theatre world.

Productions 1979–80

Bosoms and Neglect, John Guare
• *They Are Dying Out,* Peter Handke; adapt: Michael Roloff and Carl Weber
Measure for Measure, William Shakespeare
Curse of the Starving Class, Sam Shepard
Ubu Rex, Alfred Jarry; trans: David Copelin; music: Paul Schierhorn
• *A Lesson from Aloes,* Athol Fugard
Timon of Athens, William Shakespeare

Productions 1980–81

Boesman and Lena, Athol Fugard
The Suicide, Nikolai Erdman; trans: Peter Tegel
Twelfth Night, William Shakespeare
A Winterfest
- *Domestic Issues,* Corinne Jacker
- *Rococo,* Harry Kondoleon
- *Sally and Marsha,* Sybille Pearson
- *The Resurrection of Lady Lester,* OyamO

Hedda Gabler, Henrik Ibsen; trans: Rolf Fjelde
The Magnificent Cuckold, Fernand Crommelynck; trans: Marnix Gijsen
• *An Attempt at Flying,* Yordan Radichkov; trans: Bogdan B. Athanassov

Directors

Robert Allan Ackerman, Andrei Belgrader, Athol Fugard, Tony Giordano, Walton Jones, Jonas Jurasas, Barnet Kellman, Mladen Kiselov, Bill Ludel, John Madden, Lloyd Richards, Steven Robman, James A. Simpson, Carl Weber, Dana B. Westberg

Designers

Sets: Lawrence Casey, Randy Drake, Raymond M. Kluga, Charles McCarry, Kevin Rupnik, Steve Saklad, Karen Schultz, Loren Sherman, Michael H. Yeargan. *Costumes:* Nan Cibula, Susan Hilferty, Martha Kelly, Raymond M. Kluga, Judianna Makovsky, Dunya Ramicova, Dean H. Reiter, Rita Ryack, Steve Saklad. *Lights:* William B. Armstrong, Michael H. Baumgarten, Rick Butler, Timothy J. Hunter, David Noling, Loren Sherman, Thomas Skelton, John I. Tissot, William B. Warfel.

Appendices

Theatres That Tour

The following theatres, all of which are listed alphabetically in this book, are available for touring—locally, statewide, regionally, nationally or internationally. For additional information, contact the person listed as the touring contact in each theatre's entry.

A Contemporary Theatre
Academy Theatre
The Acting Company
Actors Theatre of Louisville
Alabama Shakespeare Festival
Alaska Repertory Theatre
AMAS Repertory Theatre
American Conservatory Theatre
The American Place Theatre
American Repertory Theatre
American Stage Festival
American Theatre Company
Arizona Theatre Company
Arkansas Repertory Theatre
Asolo State Theater
Attic Theatre
Barter Theatre
Boston Shakespeare Company
Center Stage
The Children's Theatre Company
The Cincinnati Playhouse in the Park
The Cleveland Play House
Crossroads Theatre Company
Dallas Theater Center
Dell'Arte Players Company
East West Players
El Teatro Campesino
The Empty Space
Fairmount Theatre of the Deaf
The First All Children's Theatre
Florida Studio Theatre
Folger Theatre Group
Goodman Theatre
The Great Lakes Shakespeare Festival
The Guthrie Theater
The Harry Chapin Theatre Center
The Hippodrome Theatre
Honolulu Theatre for Youth
The Independent Eye
Intiman Theatre Company
Invisible Theatre
The Iron Clad Agreement
The Julian Theatre
L.A. Public Theatre
L.A. Theatre Works
The Living Stage Theatre Company
Looking Glass Theatre
Los Angeles Actors' Theatre
Lovelace Theatre
Mabou Mines
Mark Taper Forum
McCarter Theatre Company
Medicine Show Theatre Ensemble
Milwaukee Repertory Theater
Missouri Repertory Theatre
Music-Theatre Group/Lenox Arts Center
National Black Theatre
The National Shakespeare Company
The Nebraska Theatre Caravan
The Negro Ensemble Company
New American Theater
New Federal Theatre
The Next Move Theatre
The North Carolina Shakespeare Festival
North Light Repertory Company
Odyssey Theatre Ensemble
The Old Globe Theatre
Omaha Magic Theatre
One Act Theatre Company of San Francisco
Oregon Shakespearean Festival
Palisades Theatre
The Paper Bag Players
Pennsylvania Stage Company
The People's Light and Theatre Company
Peoples Theatre
Periwinkle Productions
Pittsburgh Public Theater
Players State Theatre
The Play Group
Playmakers Repertory Company
Playwrights' Center
Provisional Theatre
Repertorio Espanol
Repertory Theatre of St. Louis
The Ridiculous Theatrical Company
The Road Company
Roadside Theater
Round House Theatre
South Coast Repertory
Stage One: The Louisville Children's Theatre
Starry Night Puppet Theatre
Steamboat Repertory Theatre
The Street Theater
Syracuse Stage
Theatre Arts of West Virginia
Theatre by the Sea
Theater for the New City
Theatre Project Company
Theatre Three
Theatre X
Trinity Square Repertory Company
Victory Gardens Theater
Virginia Museum Theatre
Westport Country Playhouse
The Whole Theatre
Williamstown Theatre Festival
The Wooster Group
Worcester Foothills Theatre Company

American Repertory Theatre. *As You Like It.* Photo: Richard Feldman.

Theatre Chronology

The following is a chronological list of founding dates for the theatres included in this book, and is intended to chart the growth of the nonprofit professional theatre movement in America. Years refer to dates of the first public performance, or, in a few cases, the company's formal incorporation.

1915
Cleveland Play House

1925
Goodman Theatre

1931
Westport Country Playhouse

1933
Barter Theatre

1935
Oregon Shakespearean Festival

1937
Old Globe Theatre

1946
Stage One: The Louisville Children's Theatre

1947
Alley Theatre

1949
New Dramatists

1950
Arena Stage

1951
Circle in the Square

1953
Phoenix Theatre

1954
Milwaukee Repertory Theater
New York Shakespeare Festival

1955
Honolulu Theatre for Youth
Virginia Museum Theatre
Williamstown Theatre Festival

1956
Academy Theatre
Philadelphia Drama Guild

1958
The Paper Bag Players

1959
Dallas Theater Center

1960
Asolo State Theater
The Cincinnati Playhouse in the Park

1961
The Children's Theatre Company
Theatre Arts of West Virginia
Theatre Three

1962
Great Lakes Shakespeare Festival

1963
Center Stage
The Guthrie Theater
The National Shakespeare Company
New Jersey Shakespeare Festival
Peoples Theatre
Periwinkle Productions
Seattle Repertory Theatre

1964
Actors Theatre of Louisville
The American Place Theatre
Hartford Stage Company
Lovelace Theatre
Missouri Repertory Theatre
O'Neill Theater Center
South Coast Repertory
Theatre by the Sea
Trinity Square Repertory Company

1965
A Contemporary Theatre
American Conservatory Theatre
Detroit Repertory Theatre
East West Players
El Teatro Campesino
Julian Theatre
Long Wharf Theatre
Looking Glass Theatre
Roundabout Theatre Company
Studio Arena Theatre

1966
Arizona Theatre Company
The Harry Chapin Theatre Center
INTAR
The Living Stage Theatre Company
Repertory Theatre of St. Louis
Yale Repertory Theatre

1967
CSC Repertory
Magic Theatre
Mark Taper Forum
The Negro Ensemble Company
The Ridiculous Theatrical Company
StageWest
The Wooster Group

1968
Berkeley Repertory Theatre
The Changing Scene
Hudson Guild Theatre
National Black Theatre
Odyssey Theatre Ensemble
Playhouse on the Square

1969
AMAS Repertory Theatre
Body Politic Theatre
Circle Repertory Company
The First All Children's Theatre Company
Omaha Magic Theatre
Performance Community
Repertorio Espanol
Theatre X

1970
American Theatre Company
BoarsHead Theater
Folger Theatre Group
Interart Theatre
Mabou Mines
Manhattan Theatre Club
Medicine Show Theatre Ensemble
Music-Theatre Group/Lenox Arts Center
New Federal Theatre
The Street Theater
Theater for the New City

1971
The Cricket Theatre
Dell'Arte Players Company
The Empty Space
Ensemble Studio Theatre
The Invisible Theatre

Jean Cocteau Repertory
The Old Creamery Theatre Company
Playwrights' Center
Playwrights Horizons

1972
The Acting Company
Alabama Shakespeare Festival
GeVa Theatre
Indiana Repertory Theatre
Intiman Theatre Company
McCarter Theatre Company
New American Theater
New Playwrights' Theatre
Provisional Theatre
Starry Night Puppet Theatre
Theater of the Open Eye

1973
Florida Studio Theatre
The Hippodrome Theatre
L.A. Public Theatre
The Play Group
The Whole Theatre Company

1974
Berkeley Stage Company
George Street Playhouse
Germinal Stage Denver
Hartman Theatre Company
The Independent Eye
L.A. Theatre Works
North Light Repertory Company
Palisades Theatre
The People's Light and Theatre Company
Portland Stage Company
Roadside Theater
St. Nicholas Theater Company
Syracuse Stage
Victory Gardens Theater
Wisdom Bridge Theatre
Worcester Foothills Theatre Company

1975
American Stage Festival
Boston Shakespeare Company
Fairmount Theatre of the Deaf
Los Angeles Actors' Theatre
Pittsburgh Public Theater
The Road Company
Soho Repertory Theatre
Theatre Project Company

1976
Alaska Repertory Theatre
American Theatre Arts
Arkansas Repertory Theatre
Attic Theatre
BAM Theater Company
The Great-American Children's Theatre Company
The Iron Clad Agreement
Nebraska Theatre Caravan
One Act Theatre Company of San Francisco
Playmakers Repertory Theatre
San Diego Repertory Theatre

1977
Actors Theatre of St. Paul
Horse Cave Theatre
New Jersey Theatre Forum
The Next Move Theatre
North Carolina Shakespeare Festival
Pennsylvania Stage Company
Players State Theatre

1978
Crossroads Theatre Company
Pilgrim Theater
Round House Theatre
Steamboat Repertory Theatre
Tacoma Actors Guild

1979
Merrimack Regional Theatre
Virginia Stage Company

1980
American Repertory Theatre
Denver Center Theatre Company

Regional Index

Yale Repertory Theatre. James Earl Jones, Maria Tucci and Harris Yulin in *A Lesson from Aloes.* Photo: Gerry Goodstein.

The First All Children's Theatre
The Harry Chapin Theatre Center
Hudson Guild Theatre
INTAR
Interart Theatre
Jean Cocteau Repertory
Mabou Mines
Manhattan Theatre Club
Medicine Show Theatre Ensemble
Music-Theatre Group/Lenox Arts Center
National Black Theatre
The National Shakespeare Company
The Negro Ensemble Company
New Dramatists
New Federal Theatre
New York Shakespeare Festival
O'Neill Theater Center
The Paper Bag Players
Phoenix Theatre
Playwrights Horizons
Repertorio Espanol
The Ridiculous Theatrical Company
Roundabout Theatre Company
Soho Repertory Theatre
Theater for the New City
Theater of the Open Eye
The Wooster Group

NEW YORK STATE

GeVa Theatre
Periwinkle Productions
Starry Night Puppet Theatre
The Street Theater
Studio Arena Theatre
Syracuse Stage

NORTH CAROLINA

North Carolina Shakespeare Festival
Playmakers Repertory Company

OHIO

The Cincinnati Playhouse in the Park
The Cleveland Play House
Fairmount Theatre of the Deaf
The Great Lakes Shakespeare Festival

OKLAHOMA

American Theatre Company

OREGON

Oregon Shakespearean Festival

PENNSYLVANIA

The Independent Eye
Lovelace Theatre
Pennsylvania Stage Company
The People's Light and Theatre Company
Philadelphia Drama Guild
Pittsburgh Public Theater

RHODE ISLAND

Looking Glass Theatre
Trinity Square Repertory Company

TENNESSEE

The Play Group
Playhouse on the Square
The Road Company

TEXAS

Alley Theatre
Dallas Theater Center
Theatre Three

VIRGINIA

Barter Theatre
Virginia Museum Theatre
Virginia Stage Company

WASHINGTON

A Contemporary Theatre
The Empty Space
Intiman Theatre Company
Seattle Repertory Theatre
Tacoma Actors Guild

WEST VIRGINIA

Theatre Arts of West Virginia

WISCONSIN

The Great-American Children's Theatre Company
Milwaukee Repertory Theater
Theatre X

Milwaukee Repertory Theater. Daniel Mooney, Ritch Brinkley, James Pickering, Victor Raider-Wexler and Larry Shue in *Dead Souls.* Photo: Mark Avery.

Index of Names

Index of Titles

The Children's Theatre Company. *The 500 Hats of Bartholomew Cubbins.*

Mark Taper Forum. Phyllis Frelich and John Rubinstein in *Children of a Lesser God.*

About TCG

Theatre Communications Group, the national service organization for the nonprofit professional theatre, was founded in 1961 to provide a national forum and communications network for the then-emerging nonprofit theatres, and to respond to the needs of both theatres and theatre artists for centralized services. During the 1960s, TCG sponsored four or five programs for about 20 evolving resident companies, enabling them to benefit from sharing common experiences and helping them to solve common problems.

By 1972, the burgeoning of diverse theatres throughout the country created distinctly different challenges, and TCG set about finding both the common denominators and the differences. Today, TCG is considered a unique national arts organization, managing to straddle creatively the line between service organization and national association, between artistic and management concerns, between artists and institutions, between advocate and provider of services, among diverse aesthetics and across a broad geographical range—always aspiring to help the theatre to achieve excellence.

What has resulted is a structure that allows TCG continually to reassess, improve and expand; to pioneer and respond to change while providing continuity. Today, TCG's almost 200 Constituent and Associate theatres, as well as thousands of individual artists, participate in more than 25 programs and services. Institutions and individual artists, administrators and technicians are served through casting and job referral services, management and research services, publications, literary services, conferences and seminars, and a variety of other programs.

TCG's main goals are to foster cross-fertilization and interaction among different types of organizations and individuals that comprise the profession as a whole; to improve the artistic and administrative capabilities of the field; to improve the visibility and demonstrate the achievement of the field by increasing the public's awareness of theatre's role in society; and generally to encourage and support a nationwide network of nonprofit theatre companies and individuals that collectively represent the "national theatre" of the United States.

New York Shakespeare Festival. Tzi Ma, Calvin Jung and Willy Corpus in *FOB*. Photo: Susan Cook.

TCG Publications

Theatre Communications. The official publication of the American nonprofit professional theatre, this national monthly journal presents feature articles, editorials, in-depth reports and news briefs covering a wide range of artistic, administrative and managerial topics. Regular departments include plays and playwrights, legislative updates, funding news, marketing trends, innovations in technology, theatre book reviews and international events. Every issue also contains comprehensive current production schedules from nearly 200 theatres across the country.

Theatre Directory. TCG's annual guide to 200 theatres nationwide lists telephone numbers, addresses, names of artistic and managing directors, public information officers and performance seasons. Also included is a listing of professional theatre service organizations and descriptions of their programs and resources.

Subscribe Now! Building Arts Audiences Through Dynamic Subscription Promotion. This is the book that has revolutionized audience development in America and around the world. Danny Newman's foolproof promotion techniques have been used successfully by theatres, orchestras, opera companies, dance troupes, museums and sponsoring organizations. The easy-to-read, step-by-step handbook is an indispensable tool for audience development directors, managers and publicists, and a must for students in arts administration.

New Plays USA is the first in a series of annual anthologies devoted to outstanding new plays, translations and adaptations developed in America's nonprofit professional theatres. Showing the full range and richness of these theatres and the artists who work in them, this collection contains Lee Breuer's *A Prelude to Death in Venice, FOB* by David Henry Hwang, *Still Life* by Emily Mann, OyamO's *The Resurrection of Lady Lester,* Adele Edling Shank's *Winterplay* and *Dead Souls,* Tom Cole's translation and adaptation of the Gogol classic. Each script is accompanied by production notes from the author.

Plays in Process. TCG's unique script circulation service distributes promising new play scripts to subscribers. Intended to promote multiple productions of important new plays, the program will circulate at least 12 scripts in 1981–82 to a subscribership of nonprofit professional theatres, educational institutions and other noncommercial organizations.

Computers and the Performing Arts. A one-of-a-kind report on a one-of-a-kind project—the results of the first national survey and landmark conference conducted by TCG's interdisciplinary National Computer Project for the Performing Arts, providing invaluable background material on computer technology and its applications to the worlds of theatre, dance and music.

Dramatists Sourcebook. Formerly entitled *Information for Playwrights,* this timely tool of the trade for working playwrights, translators, adapters, lyricists, librettists and composers is the only resource available that is geared specifically to opportunities for writers in the theatre. The new edition has been completely revised and expanded into a full-sized book listing current data on more than 100 theatres that accept unsolicited scripts—production requirements, reporting time, contact names—plus tips on manuscript preparation, copyright information and valuable listings of national grants, contests, awards, fellowships, media opportunities and artist colonies.

Theatre Facts 81. This vital tool for institutional survival in the 1980s digests the latest financial and statistical information on nonprofit professional theatre nationwide. Production and attendance activity, total expenses, earned income, grants and contributions—all add up to an incisive analytical overview of theatre financing, fund-raising and management in America.

TCG Program Collection. TCG's 20-year collection of 3,000 programs of nonprofit professional theatres is available on microfilm from Greenwood Press, 50 Riverside Ave., Westport, CT 06880 for $1,045. The bound companion index of all plays, authors and directors sells for $39.95.

Graphic Communications for the Performing Arts. This is the new, lavishly illustrated, first-ever interdisciplinary collection of outstanding examples of graphic design—including posters, display advertising, subscription and fund-raising materials, playbills and photography—from the worlds of nonprofit theatre, music and dance.

ArtSEARCH. The national employment service bulletin for the performing arts, *ArtSEARCH* lists the latest job opportunities in theatre, dance, opera and music, including information on internships and educational opportunities, as well as personal availability announcements. Mailed first-class to its subscribers, it is a hotline to the most current developments in the swiftly changing arts personnel arena. *ArtSEARCH* is published every two-to-four weeks year-round and is ideally suited to administrators and production personnel, and to announce the availability of artists. (Please note: *ArtSEARCH* does *not* contain casting information.)

TCG National Conference Report. In June 1980, 300 theatre professionals convened at Princeton University for a landmark conference. They dealt intensively with artistic issues and also tapped the minds of experts from other disciplines—sociology, politics, science and philosophy. Those who weren't there can read about it now in this fascinating document featuring transcriptions of all major speeches and panel discussions, including a two-day "satellite" conference exploring a wide range of management topics. Included are speeches and remarks by Edward Albee, Lanford Wilson, Jane Alexander, Len Cariou, Fritz Weaver, Gordon Davidson and many others.